The Political Economy of Dual Transformations

The Political Economy of Dual Transformations

Market Reform and Democratization in Hungary

David L. Bartlett

Ann Arbor

THE UNIVERSITY OF MICHIGAN PRESS

2000   1999   1998   1997   4   3   2   1

A CIP catalog record for this book is available from the British Library

Library of Congress Cataloging-in-Publication Data

Bartlett, David L., 1956–
    The political economy of dual transformations : market reform and democratization in Hungary / David L. Bartlett.
        p.   cm.
    Includes bibliographical references and index.
    ISBN 0-472-10794-1 (cloth : alk. paper)
    1. Hungary—Economic conditions—1989–   2. Hungary—Economic policy—1989–   3. Post-communism—Hungary. [1. Hungary—Politics and government—1989–]   I. Title.
    HC300.282.B37   1997
    338.9439—dc20   96-36553
                                                                    CIP

To Susan

Contents

Acronyms

CIS	Commonwealth of Independent States
CMEA	Council for Mutual Economic Assistance
CPE	centrally planned economy
FIDESZ	Fiatal Demokraták Szövetsége (Alliance of Young Democrats)
GDP	gross domestic product
GDR	German Democratic Republic
HUF	Hungarian forints
IMF	International Monetary Fund
MDF	Magyar Demokrata Fórum (Hungarian Democratic Forum)
MIER	Ministry of International Economic Relations
MSZDP	Magyar Szocialista Demokrata Párt (Hungarian Social Democratic Party)
MSZP	Magyar Szocialista Párt (Hungarian Socialist Party)
MSZMP	Magyar Szocialista Munkáspárt (Hungarian Socialist Workers' Party)
MSZOSZ	Magyar Szakszervezetek Országos Szövetsége (Hungarian National Federation of Trade Unions)
NEM	New Economic Mechanism
OECD	Organization for Economic Cooperation and Development
OSB	Országos Szanálas Bizottság (National Reorganization Committee)
SAHC	State Asset Holding Company
SPA	State Property Agency
SZDSZ	Szabad Demokraták Szövetsége (Alliance of Free Democrats)
SZOT	Szakszervezetek Országos Tanácsa (National Council of Trade Unions)
TGB	Tervgazdasági Bizottság (Planned Economy Committee)

Tables

Acknowledgments

Many individuals and institutions, both in the United States and Hungary, contributed to the research and writing of this book. I owe a special thanks to my friend and colleague Kurt Weyland, who read multiple drafts of the manuscript and responded with his distinctive combination of thoroughness, scholarly insight, and good humor. Kurt's trenchant critiques and moral support were instrumental in bringing the project to fruition. Deborah Avant, Markus Crepaz, and Hendrik Spruyt read major portions of the book, offering a number of suggestions to sharpen the argument and simplify the presentation. Anna Seleny brought her formidable knowledge of the Hungarian economy to her critique of the manuscript, and I am indebted to her for the encouragement she offered during a low point in the revision process. David Steiner made some useful recommendations for revising the introduction, while Jim Nolt shared with me his extensive knowledge of East Asian political economy to bolster the comparative discussion in chapter 7. My collaborative work with Wendy Hunter advanced my thinking about the role of party and state institutions in democratic transitions. Ben Slay read the entire manuscript with great care, providing many suggestions that helped me resolve several technical issues and elucidate the relationship between privatization, foreign direct investment, and structural adjustment in transitional economies. Paul Hare's detailed comments prompted me to engage more fully the problem of recapitalizing East European industry, which figures prominently in chapters 6 and 7. I would like to thank three anonymous reviewers, whose feedback helped me shorten the book and clarify the institutionalist line of my theoretical arguments. Colin Day and Charles Myers of the University of Michigan Press played a key role in steering the project through its tortuous route from review and revision to publication. I am grateful to the faculty and graduate students of the political science departments of the University of California, San Diego, and Vanderbilt University, who listened to many formal presentations and private discussions over the course of the book's gestation. Finally, I owe a large scholarly debt to Ellen Comisso, Susan Shirk, and Peter Cowhey, who supervised the dissertation from which this book originated.

The book would not have been possible without the cooperation of my interview subjects, whose willingness to share their expertise and knowledge allowed me to piece together the story of Hungary's dual transformation. A comprehensive list of their names and institutional affiliations is in the appendix. However, two people merit special mention. György Surányi first kindled my interest in socialist financial systems back in the mid-1980s, before anyone could even imagine the tumultuous changes that would grip Hungary and the rest of Eastern Europe at decade's end. Over subsequent years, he repeatedly took time out of a busy schedule to keep me abreast of the rapid pace of developments in Hungarian politics and economics. During the late 1980s, Lajos Bokros dedicated many dozens of hours to explaining to me the intricate workings of Hungary's hybrid economy. The information culled from those sessions played a crucial role in the production of my doctoral dissertation. Later, he generously shared his insights on Hungarian policy making in the postcommunist period. I would also like to thank György Szelényi and Mariann Holló, who offered companionship as well as professional assistance throughout my time in Hungary and whose personal warmth has kept our transoceanic family friendship alive and well over the years.

I am grateful for the institutional support I have received for this project. A fellowship from the University of California's Institute on Global Conflict and Cooperation enabled me to undertake extended field research in Hungary in 1986 and 1988. A grant from the Office of Graduate Studies and Research of the University of California, San Diego, financed private tutoring in the Hungarian language. A fellowship from the Joint Committee on Eastern Europe of the American Council of Learned Societies (ACLS) gave me the time and resources to write my dissertation in 1989–90. The latter organization, which is directed by Jason Parker, also sponsored a succession of conferences (Aspen Institute, Maryland, 1989; Munich, Germany, 1991; Arden Homestead, New York, 1992) that gave me the opportunity to present my work before expert audiences. The ACLS and Social Science Research Council cosponsored two summer workshops organized by Herbert Levine and the late Ed Hewett (Washington, D.C., 1987; Berkeley, California, 1989) that deepened my understanding of Soviet-type economies. The International Research and Exchange Board provided short-term field research grants (1993, 1995) that allowed me to return to Hungary to trace the course of the country's reforms in the early 1990s. Travel grants from the Vanderbilt University Research Council (1991, 1993, 1995) also helped me undertake the followup research needed to carry the Hungarian story into the postcommunist period.

On a more personal note, I would like to thank the many friends and family members who showed unwavering support and interest during the years of work that culminated in this book. While I cannot provide a complete inventory of their names, I would like to cite the following people: Steve Anderson, Russell Bartlett, Michael Bess, Yvonne Boyer, Leonard Folgarait, Barbara Goss, Bill and Vickie Holloway, Matt and Sue Holloway, Kevin Keller, Carrie and Doug Leever, Laurie Loughmiller, Lynn Seely, and Gayl Wheeler. I owe a great debt of gratitude to my parents, Jim and Ruth Bartlett, whose dinner-table conversations first inspired my interest in politics and whose support (all varieties) was indispensable in bringing the book to completion. I would like also to acknowledge the contributions of my children, Jordan and Emily. Neither of them were yet born when the research for this book began in the mid-1980s. But in the intervening years, they displayed unflagging enthusiasm for the project, persistent curiosity about the status of the book, and patient understanding during the prolonged absences when I was in Hungary completing the field research. They also played a crucial part in keeping the project in perspective, periodically reminding me that baseball, chess, and newts occupy an equally important place in the broader scheme of things.

Finally, I would like to thank my wife, Susan, to whom the book is dedicated. Her role in this project was so integral and varied that words do not give it full justice. During my graduate school years, Susan gave me the confidence and inspiration to dedicate years of my life to the study of a small East European country and took a hiatus in her career to live in Budapest and care for our infant son while I did my field work. Later, she went the extra mile at home, managing the requirements of two young children and a demanding job while I made a series of return trips to Hungary before hunkering down for the final phase of writing and revision. Throughout, she used her own keen understanding of Hungary and feel for political science to act as a sounding board, tirelessly listening as I formulated and reformulated the arguments that ultimately formed the core of the book. Susan's faith in my work enabled me to see the project to its end, and for that I am forever grateful.

Introduction

Is political liberalization compatible with economic transformation? That question, long a central concern of scholars of Latin America, Southern Europe, and East Asia, has assumed special significance in postcommunist Eastern Europe. The socioeconomic costs of stabilization, adjustment, and reform pose serious challenges to the capitalist South, where market economies and private capital ownership long preceded political democracy. For the fledgling democracies of Eastern Europe, market reforms entail not merely price deregulation, trade liberalization, and similar policies but the thoroughgoing reorganization of entire systems of resource allocation and property ownership. Claus Offe succinctly describes the "vicious circle" of simultaneous marketization and democratization in the region.

> A market economy is set in motion only under predemocratic conditions. In order to promote it, *democratic rights must be held back in order to allow for a healthy dose of original accumulation* [emphasis added]. Only a developed market economy produces the social structural conditions for stable democracy and makes it possible to form compromises within the framework of what is perceived as a positive-sum game. But the introduction of a market economy in the postsocialist societies is a "political" project, which has prospects of success only if it rests on a strong democratic legitimation. And it is possible that the majority of the population finds neither democracy nor a market economy a desirable perspective. If all of those propositions hold true at the same time, then we are faced with a Pandora's box full of paradoxes, in the face of which every "theory"—or, for that matter, rational strategy, of the transition must fail.[1]

Recent developments appear to validate Offe's pessimistic scenario for the postcommunist countries: the rise of the nationalist right in Russia and Ukraine, armed conflict in Georgia and other Soviet successor states, the

---

1. "Capitalism by Democratic Design? Democratic Theory Facing the Triple Transition in East Central Europe," *Social Research* 58, no. 4 (winter 1991): 881.

war in the Balkans, and the return to power of former Communists in Poland, Lithuania, Bulgaria, and Hungary.

In this book, I explore the tension between political and economic transformation in Eastern Europe. How has the transition from communism to democracy affected macroeconomic stabilization, structural adjustment, and systemic reform in the region? I focus on Hungary, whose historical trajectory makes it an ideal vehicle for an intertemporal analysis of the impact of political change on economic reform. In 1968, the ruling Magyar Szocialista Munkáspárt (Hungarian Socialist Workers' Party, or MSZMP) launched the program of reforms known as the New Economic Mechanism (NEM). While beset by periodic backtracking by the Communist Party leadership as well as the systemic constraints of "market socialism," NEM was the most ambitious economic reform program ever undertaken in a Warsaw Pact country. Indeed, many of the policies enacted by the successor government in the early 1990s followed the main lines of the program initiated by the Communist Party. Hungary's long history of market reforms thus allows one to trace the course of economic policy across the pre- and post-1989 periods.[2]

The Hungarian case defies conventional wisdom regarding the perils of dual transformations: far from unleashing popular resistance to market reform, the transition to democracy subdued it. Hungary's ability simultaneously to pursue democratization and marketization stemmed not from the successor government's choice of a "gradualist" strategy aimed at softening the distributional impact of economic transition. In fact, data presented in the book show that the socioeconomic costs of Hungary's market reforms approached, and in some respects surpassed, those of the "shock therapy" programs launched in other former communist countries. I argue that the decisive factor in Eastern Europe's transition is not the sheer magnitude of the social costs of economic transformation but the

---

2. Other former communist countries are not as well suited for an intertemporal study of reform policy. In the 1950s, Yugoslavia began a series of market reforms that went well beyond Hungary's NEM. But the disintegration of the Yugoslav federation and the outbreak of the Balkan War in 1991 make it difficult to assess the impact of domestic political change on reform policy. Poland also launched a reform program of the "market socialist" type before the political transition. But the Polish reforms were initiated later than Hungary's and were never as far reaching or sustained. The market reforms undertaken elsewhere in Eastern Europe were either aborted (as in Czechoslovakia in 1968 and the German Democratic Republic in 1970) or limited in scope (as in Bulgaria in the 1980s). The program announced at the 1987 Party plenum in the Soviet Union, while ambitious in design, never got off the ground—the victim of bureaucratic resistance and Mikhail Gorbachev's tack to the right in 1990. For a survey of the East European reforms, see Tamás Bauer, "Hungarian Economic Reform in East European Perspective," *Eastern European Politics and Societies* 2, no. 3 (fall 1988): 418–32.

institutional environment in which distributional conflicts occur. The opponents of Hungary's economic reforms enjoyed greater influence under the communist regime, whose institutional structure afforded local agents multiple access points to negotiate individual exceptions to market rules. The demise of communism disrupted the political channels through which vulnerable actors secured compensation for the socioeconomic fallout of adjustment. Democratization facilitated marketization by insulating state agencies from particularistic claims and channeling distributional politics into the electoral arena, where the "losers" of reform operated at a disadvantage in the early postcommunist period. Hungary's experience thus demonstrates not only that political liberalization and economic transformation are compatible but that the former promotes the latter.

The findings of the book have important implications for other East European countries undergoing simultaneous transformations and for the East Asian states that delayed political liberalization while pursuing export-led development. I explore the comparative dimensions of the Hungarian case in the final chapter.

The New Institutionalism and Dual Transformations

The argument of the book rests not on the presumption of any functional or instrumental correspondence between democracy and market. Indeed, the unprecedented scale and high social costs of Eastern Europe's economic transformation give ample grounds to surmise that the region's young democracies would prove unable to navigate the transition from plan to market. I focus instead on the institutional dimensions of dual transformations: How did communist institutions cope with the challenges of economic stabilization and adjustment? How did their democratic successors mediate the distributional conflicts arising from market reforms?

The body of work known as the "new institutionalism" encompasses a variety of theoretical traditions and research agendas. Underpinning this diverse literature are several common themes. Neoclassical economic theory and behavioralist theories of politics view social scientific phenomena as the product of individual choices and strategies, relegating institutions to the role of passive instruments of political agents or neutral arenas of economic competition. By contrast, institutional analysis insists on the central role of institutions—broadly defined as formal organizations, informal networks, rules, and procedures—in shaping political and economic action. Institutions impinge on politics in a variety of ways. They are sources of political power by virtue of their longevity, policy jurisdictions, human and technical resources, and control of information. Where actors are situated in a given institutional structure therefore shapes the distribution of capabilities in the polity as a whole. Institutions affect how agents act on their preferences by designating access routes and veto points in the political process. They circumscribe boundaries of policy innovation by delimiting the range of feasible ideas and options. Institutions also play a decisive part in policy implementation. Irrespective of the alignment of societal forces and the preferences of key actors, execution of policy requires tangible administrative capacities that may or may not be available in a particular institutional setting. Finally, institutions powerfully influence economic activities by lowering transaction costs and delivering an assortment of collective goods vital to the operation of markets.

I focus on two problems central in the new institutionalism literature. The first concerns how variations in constitutional design, party structure, and electoral rules shape the incentives and strategies of political agents. How did the institutional features of the communist regime affect the formulation and implementation of economic reform policy? How did Communist Party leaders, state officials, and societal actors pursue their interests during the period preceding the political transition? How did democratization alter the dynamics of interest representation in Eastern Europe? How did it affect the capacity of successor governments to execute stabilization and adjustment policies imposing heavy costs on major elements of postcommunist society?

The second problem concerns the role of state institutions in the development of markets. One of the core assumptions of the new institutionalism is that the evolution of markets is fundamentally a process of institution building. Contrary to neoliberal economists, proponents of the institutional approach assign to the state a pivotal role in market economies. Far from impeding marketization, robust state institutions promote it by supplying a variety of collective goods essential to market development: property rights to protect individuals from arbitrary seizures of private holdings, a legal structure to enable aggrieved parties to seek redress for externalities and other market failures, a system of monetary control to keep prices and exchange rates stable, uniform regulation of financial and accounting practices to foster transparency and sanction abuses, antitrust policies to break up monopolies and discourage price-fixing, broad-based and efficient tax collection mechanisms to elude fiscal crises and obviate confiscatory taxation rates, and social welfare services to lower the risks of market participation and prevent marginalized groups from falling below the poverty line. I place the relationship between state and market in Eastern Europe in this institutional context: to what degree have state institutions in the region worked in a market-protecting or market-distorting direction?

Communism, Democracy, and Market Reform

The institutional approach employed in the book illuminates the distinctive problems of stabilization and adjustment policy in orthodox communist regimes as well as reformed communist states like Hungary. The communist system, which combined the political monopoly of a Marxist-Leninist party with central economic planning, operated under a wholly different institutional logic than authoritarian regimes in developing capitalist countries. In the latter, enterprise associations and trade unions maintained some separation from the political sphere, even when heavily penetrated by the dominant party or the state. The distinguishing feature of Soviet-style communism was the complete interpenetration of polity and economy, as workers and enterprise managers were subsumed within a comprehensive system of state ownership and centrally administered resource allocation.

On the one hand, this meant that communist authorities could more easily impose economic austerity policies, as factory-level agents lacked independent means of resisting them. On the other hand, it meant that Party leaders had to resort to nonmarket means of executing such measures. Since the conventional methods of stabilization used in market economies (price liberalization, exchange-rate devaluation, monetary contraction, etc.) did not work in centrally planned economies, the central authorities relied on administrative mechanisms such as wage freezes, direct cuts in imports and investment, and diversion of production away from consumer goods. While such instruments could be very effective in reducing domestic consumption and restoring external equilibrium—witness the austerity campaign undertaken by the Ceauşescu regime in Romania during the 1980s—they operated at cross-purposes with structural adjustment. Gross reductions in fixed capital investment and Western imports deprived enterprises of the resources needed to modernize plant and equipment and raise productivity. Thus, whereas authoritarian regimes in the capitalist South could pursue both stabilization and adjustment, in Eastern Europe they could achieve one but not the other.

The market reforms introduced in Hungary, Poland, and Yugoslavia transformed the politico-economic dynamics of stabilization and adjustment. These reforms combined quasi-market-type macroeconomic controls with decentralized decision making at the factory level. This created a dilemma. Enterprise managers and workers now enjoyed greater discretion over wages, prices, investment, and imports. However, if Western-type fiscal and monetary instruments proved ineffective, the loosening of controls at the microeconomic level would cause domestic absorption to rise. The authorities would then have to return to the familiar devices of the old central planning system to restore economic equilibrium. But because of the decision-making authority already relinquished to workers and enterprises, centrally administered cuts in wages and investment now encountered resistance from below.

And so, contrary to conventional wisdom about Communist Party systems, I argue that distributional conflicts were pervasive in the East European countries that sought to use market mechanisms as adjustment instruments. The Marxist-Leninist system did constrain local agents from mounting collective action outside of the ruling party. Only in Poland did workers undertake mass mobilization through independent labor organizations. In Hungary, workers did not stage production strikes until the very end of the communist period, and then under the auspices of Party-controlled trade unions. Factory-level agents relied instead on particularistic links to central Party organizations, local Party committees, and state agencies to press their claims. Distributional politics in communist Hungary thus assumed the form of subterranean conflicts over the allocation of bank credits, budget subsidies, tax exemptions, and other economic resources.

The transition to democracy did more than terminate the political monopoly of the Communist Party. It severed the institutional connections between factory-level agents and central planners that previously allowed vulnerable actors to mitigate the impact of economic adjustment. Hungarian workers and enterprise managers, lacking either strong intermediary organizations or close ties to the successor parties, thus found themselves in a weaker position after 1989 than before. Democratization transformed the political logic of market building. Formerly, actors could draw on the support of their patrons in Communist Party institutions and branch ministries to neutralize the effects of reform policies already enacted. Now their influence was concentrated at the initiation phase. In Poland, organized labor used its political influence in the Sejm to shape a privatization program favorable to the interests of workers' councils. Hungarian labor, poorly represented in the Parliament after the first post-communist elections in 1990, brought little influence to bear on the design of reform policy. The result was a policy-making process that afforded the losers of market reform few opportunities for ex post compensation: a privatization program relying on sales of state enterprises to Western investors via closed-tender bids, a bankruptcy law incorporating automatic triggering mechanisms, a foreign trade strategy combining radical import liberalization and real currency appreciation, and other measures that reinforced the exclusion of the economy's most vulnerable agents.

I further argue that the East European experience supports the "orthodox paradox"[3] thesis that state institutions play an integral role in market building. Indeed, the transformation of state structure is as important to Eastern Europe's transition as are the creation of political parties, the rebirth of civil society, and other phenomena emphasized in the current literature. The notion that strong state institutions are vital for protecting markets is particularly apt in postcommunist countries, whose inchoate markets are highly vulnerable to inflationary spirals and rent seeking. I contend that during the pre-1989 period, the Hungarian state was "pervasive" but "weak" insofar as economic policy was liable to arbitrary intervention by Communist Party officials. As the Party's authority unraveled at the end of the 1980s, likewise did the capacity of state agencies to oversee privatization, which accelerated as a result of the MSZMP's decision to liberalize ownership laws. The political vacuum of the late communist years resulted in a surge of "*nomenklatura* buyouts" and other abuses that undermined public confidence in market processes and compelled the successor government to recentralize privatization policy. Other institutional reforms undertaken after 1989 further augmented the market-protecting attributes of the Hungarian state: elimination of the National Planning Office, diminution of the power of the Ministry of Industry and Trade, strengthening of the global regulatory capacity of the National Bank and Ministry of Finance, and creation of new agencies to regulate commercial banking and securities.

In short, Hungary's transition to democracy involved not merely the creation of competitive parties but the reinsertion of the state into the economy in a manner aimed at facilitating the development of markets. State institutions remained vulnerable to political capture insofar as governing parties stacked those organizations with loyalists. But this danger was checked as incumbent governments faced a reelectoral constraint and abuses were revealed by an active parliamentary opposition. In this respect, pluralization of the party system enhanced the autonomy of state institutions and thereby strengthened the market-protecting dimensions of the state's activities in the economy.

Plan of the Book

In part 1 of the book, I develop a theoretical framework for analyzing the role of party and state institutions in stabilization, adjustment, and economic reform in Eastern Europe. I show that while the Marxist-Leninist

---

3. This term originated with Miles Kahler; see his "Orthodoxy and Its Alternatives: Explaining Approaches to Stabilization and Adjustment," in Joan Nelson, ed., *Economic Crisis and Policy Choice: The Politics of Adjustment in the Third World* (Princeton: Princeton University Press, 1990), 55.

system circumscribed collective action outside of the Communist Party, the logic of central planning encouraged local agents to obtain individual exceptions to Party directives. Hungarian-type market reforms deepened the particularistic bias of communist institutions by enlarging space for individualized bargaining between state bureaucrats and factory-level actors—hindering the ruling party's efforts to execute austerity policies. The events of 1989–90 fundamentally altered the institutional underpinnings of market reform. The demise of the Communist Party removed the linchpin of particularistic bargaining, while the negotiated transition to democracy gave political elites the incentives and opportunities to formulate rules designed to deter each other from exploiting state resources for partisan ends. The result was to reorient state institutions toward universalistic market regulation, thereby facilitating implementation of reform policy.

In Part 2, I draw on this theoretical construct to trace the course of Hungary's market reforms between 1979 and 1989. Chapter 2 investigates the problems of Hungarian stabilization policy during the final decade of communist rule, with particular attention to wage liberalization, monetary policy, and fiscal control. Chapter 3 addresses the structural adjustment side of economic reform, focusing on financial liberalization, enterprise restructuring, and foreign trade and exchange.

Part 3 carries the story forward to the postcommunist period, explaining how the dramatic changes in Hungary's political system affected economic reform policy between 1990 and 1994. In chapter 4, I survey the institutional terrain of postcommunist Hungary, focusing on the design of the country's revamped constitution, the structure of its party system and interest associations, and the organization of its state administration. In chapter 5, I trace the evolution of stabilization policy within this new institutional setting. In chapter 6, I look at the problems of structural adjustment under Hungary's first postcommunist government.

In part 4, I return to the central question of the book. The Hungarian communist regime and its democratically elected successor grappled with similar kinds of economic reform problems, but under markedly different institutional constraints. What does the comparison of the two periods suggest about the relationship between democracy and market in Eastern Europe? I discuss the implications of Hungary's experience for the quality of democracy in former communist countries and the significance of the victory of the Magyar Szocialista Párt (Hungarian Socialist Party, or MSZP) in the second national election in 1994. I conclude by placing Hungary in a comparative context. How does the Hungarian experience contrast with other East European countries undergoing dual transformations and with the developing capitalist economies of East Asia, which are pursuing growth-oriented economic strategies with limited or no political liberalization?

Part 1
An Institutional Approach to Eastern Europe's Transition

CHAPTER 1

Party and State Institutions in Dual Transformations

The Dilemmas of Dual Transformations

What are the theoretical grounds for supposing that political liberalization and economic transformation are mutually antagonistic? The main predicament of dual transformations is that the surge of popular participation following democratization clashes with the austerity requisite to stabilization, adjustment, and market reform. It takes years for states to build public confidence in democratic institutions. Lacking reservoirs of "stabilized expectations," new democracies are often unable to sustain economic policies imposing heavy costs on the population.[1]

The experiences of the capitalist South, where democratic governments grappled with the exigencies of market reform throughout the postwar period, illustrate the problems of simultaneous economic and political change. Some scholars contend that the new East European democracies are moving along a similar trajectory as the dual transformers of the South. During the early postcommunist period, successor governments benefited from the disarray of key societal groups opposed to marketization. But organized opposition is mounting, especially among trade unions and public sector workers. Meanwhile, the segments of postcommunist society likely to benefit from market reform—intellectuals, professionals, private entrepreneurs—remain organizationally weak and hampered by widespread suspicion about their activities. Sustaining and deepening economic reforms in the East is thus proving more difficult than initiating them, as in the South.[2]

On the surface, the prospects for resolving this contradiction between economic and political liberalization appear bleak. Among the Third World countries that implemented ambitious adjustment programs, virtually all did so through concentration of authority in politically insulated

---

1. Joan Nelson, "The Politics of Economic Transformation: Is Third World Experience Relevant in Eastern Europe?" *World Politics,* April 1993, 442–47.

2. Nelson, "The Politics of Economic Transformation," 447–54.

executives. But in the highly fluid circumstances attending the disintegration of communist rule, executive authority in Eastern Europe is weak. "Windows of technocratic opportunity" did open up in a few countries, notably Poland, but quickly closed in the aftermath of parliamentary elections. Repressive measures of the sort employed by the East Asian and South American countries in the 1960s and 1970s might improve the chances for economic transformation while endangering democratic consolidation. Delaying economic adjustment, the strategy pursued by post-Francoist Spain in the late 1970s, is hardly feasible in view of the magnitude of the problems facing the East European economies. And democratic corporatist arrangements, which in postwar Western Europe helped to ease distributional conflicts between labor and capital, seem unlikely to emerge in the East.[3] Under these circumstances, postcommunist governments will be strongly tempted to resort to executive decrees and other quasi-authoritarian methods. Eastern Europe is therefore unlikely to escape the recurrent economic crises, political instability, and social inequities of the capitalist South: "The East has become the South."[4]

This book challenges such arguments concerning the dangers of simultaneous transformation in Eastern Europe. Far from hindering marketization in the former communist countries, democratization facilitated it by insulating successor governments from particularistic claims, bolstering the capacity of state institutions to administer global regulations, and channeling distributional conflicts into the electoral arena, where the "losers" of market reform operated at a disadvantage in the early 1990s.

In this chapter, I develop an institutional theory to investigate the relationship between political and economic liberalization in Eastern Europe. I focus on party organizations and state agencies, assessing how the transformation of those institutions altered the distributional politics of stabilization, adjustment, and market reform. I argue the following: While the legal authority of the communist states was vast, their capacity to enforce universal rules of economic conduct was limited. The exigencies of central planning compelled factory-level actors to procure inputs outside the state's formal allocation system, conceal information from ministerial officials, and commit other illicit activities. Communist leaders tolerated these deviations from legal/rational norms because they helped enterprises meet the ruling party's own production goals. The result was to skew the communist states toward institutional particularism. While the

3. Nelson, "The Politics of Economic Transformation," 454–63.

4. Adam Przeworski, *Democracy and the Market: Political and Economic Reforms in Eastern Europe and Latin America* (Cambridge: Cambridge University Press, 1991), 139–46, 180–91.

Marxist-Leninist system deprived local agents of means to advance their interests via collective action outside the Communist Party, it afforded them multiple access points to lobby state agencies for individual exemptions from central directives.

The market socialist reforms introduced in Hungary and other countries deepened the particularistic bias of communist states by expanding institutional channels for societal actors to extract compensation for the distributional effects of adjustment. This created severe problems for reform Communists, who by the 1980s had come to rely on market mechanisms as austerity instruments. Decentralization of control to the plant level enlarged the bargaining power of workers and enterprise managers, who seized on their newly won freedoms to bid up wages and prices. The resultant increase in domestic purchasing power compromised macroeconomic stability and forced Party leaders to reimpose central controls. But because of the decision-making authority already relinquished to local agents, full restoration of the status quo ante was no longer possible. The upshot of this push-pull dynamic was continued economic deterioration and progressive unraveling of Communist Party power.

The transition to democracy had the following repercussions for economic reform policy in the region: The demise of communism weakened the particularistic elements of the East European states by disrupting the institutional connections through which local actors negotiated exceptions to market rules. Democratization strengthened the universalistic dimensions of the successor states by establishing institutional checks on partisan manipulation of the bureaucracy, demarcating the jurisdictional spheres of state agencies, and creating alternative outlets—political parties, electoral systems, legislatures—through which social grievances over market reforms could be mediated. At the same time, democratization undercut antimarket agents in East European society by limiting their possibilities for particularistic bargaining and increasing their dependence on the party system, where the costs of political mobilization were markedly higher after 1989 than before.

An Institutional Approach to Dual Transformations

For many years, scholars of the politics of economic reform used broad regime types—"authoritarianism" and "democracy"—as their primary units of analysis. Prevailing wisdom held that authoritarian regimes are better equipped than democracies to mediate distributional conflicts arising from economic transformation. Macroeconomic stabilization produces declines in real income that antagonize consumers, while structural adjustment creates labor dislocations that impose hardships on major sectors of the workforce. Other measures provoke resistance by key producer groups. Trade liberalization threatens agriculture and import-substituting industries; currency devaluation imperils producers of nontradable goods and enterprises dependent on high-cost capital imports. Import licensing agencies, export subsidy offices, and other state bureaucracies also perceive economic reform as a threat, as market liberalization means reduced staff, smaller budgets, and diminished jurisdictional turf.

These effects give rise to what Mancur Olson calls "distributional coalitions" that seek to maximize particularistic benefits and minimize the short-term costs of adjustment.[5] Such coalitions enjoy important advantages over the putative supporters of market reform. The costs of adjustment programs are immediate, certain, and concentrated; the benefits are long-term, uncertain, and diffuse. Because the losers have a better sense of who they are and what is at stake, they are better organized and more vocal than the winners.[6]

Facing such an alignment of societal forces, democracies are unable to resist pressure to water down or abandon reform programs. Not only do democratic institutions supply a wide range of mechanisms through which distributional coalitions press their opposition. Democratic leaders, facing an electoral constraint and limited tenure in office, have strong incentives to cater to immediate popular demands. New democracies encounter special difficulties sustaining programs carrying high distributional costs. Democratization emboldens labor and other previously repressed groups to advance their claims; newly elected leaders respond with expansionary budgetary policies and generous wage settlements that raise inflationary expectations and make adjustment even more difficult than before the political transition.[7]

By contrast, authoritarian regimes possess the capacity to implement harsh adjustment policies. They can call out the military to suppress street demonstrations and secure the acquiescence of labor and capital by co-opting trade unions and enterprise associations. Even authoritarian rulers who face a formal competitive constraint can lengthen their tenures by rig-

5. *The Rise and Decline of Nations* (New Haven: Yale University Press, 1982).

6. Nelson, "The Politics of Economic Transformation," 434–35.

7. Alberto Alesina, "Political Models of Macroeconomic Policy and Fiscal Reform," *Policy Research Working Papers: Transition and Macro-Adjustment,* Country Economics Department of the World Bank, WPS 970, September 1992, 31; Stephan Haggard and Robert Kaufman, "Economic Adjustment in New Democracies," in Joan Nelson, ed., *Fragile Coalitions: The Politics of Economic Adjustment* (New Brunswick: Transaction Books, 1989), 59–66; Stephan Haggard and Steven Webb, "What Do We Know About the Political Economy of Economic Policy Reform?" *World Bank Research Observer* 8, no. 2 (July 1993): 145, 147.

ging the electoral rules, intimidating opposition parties, manipulating the media, and delivering selective payoffs to mobilize voter support.

This stylized picture of the economic policy consequences of political regime type held sway in scholarly circles through the 1970s and early 1980s.[8] However, by the mid-1980s regime theory had come under attack. The economic crises of the Southern Hemisphere escalated in the aftermath of the second oil-price shock, and most authoritarian regimes were proving little more adept than democratic ones at coping with them. Meanwhile, new empirical research cast serious doubt about causal links between broad regime types and economic transformation.[9] The notion of an affinity between authoritarian rule and orthodox adjustment was chiefly based on the experiences of a handful of Southern Cone countries during the 1960s and 1970s. But those were distinctive kinds of authoritarian regimes, hardly typical of Third World authoritarianism in general. Other countries coded as "authoritarian" have a very mixed record of policy implementation. Likewise, developing "democratic" countries have produced wide variations in policy outcomes.[10] The experiences of the former communist countries further confound the expectations of regime theory, as several of Eastern Europe's new democracies managed to enact austerity programs imposing exceptionally high costs on politically important constituencies.

In sum, regime analysis offers limited explanatory power, as countries possessing broadly similar political systems exhibit large disparities in eco-

---

8. Alejandro Foxley, *Latin American Experiments in Neo-Conservative Economics* (Berkeley: University of California Press, 1983), 18–39; Guillermo O'Donnell, *Modernization and Bureaucratic-Authoritarianism: Studies in South American Politics,* Politics of Modernization Series, no. 9 (Berkeley: Institute of International Studies, University of California, 1973); Thomas Skidmore, "The Politics of Economic Stabilization in Postwar Latin America," in James M. Malloy, ed., *Authoritarianism and Corporatism in Latin America* (Pittsburgh: University of Pittsburgh Press, 1977), 149–90.

9. Marc Lindenberg and Shantayanan Devarajan, "Prescribing Strong Economic Medicine: Revisiting Myths about Structural Adjustment, Democracy, and Economic Performance in Developing Countries," *Comparative Politics* 25, no. 2 (January 1993): 169–82; Karen Remmer, "The Politics of Economic Stabilization: IMF Standby Programs in Latin America, 1954–1984," *Comparative Politics* 19, no. 1 (October 1986): 1–24.

10. Stephan Haggard, "The Politics of Adjustment: Lessons from the IMF's Extended Fund Facility," in Miles Kahler, ed., *The Politics of International Debt* (Ithaca: Cornell University Press, 1986), 162–71; Robert Kaufman, "Democratic and Authoritarian Responses to the Debt Issue: Argentina, Brazil, Mexico," in Kahler, *The Politics of International Debt,* 195–203; Joan Nelson, "Conclusions," in Nelson, ed., *Economic Crisis and Policy Choice: The Politics of Adjustment in the Third World* (Princeton: Princeton University Press, 1990), 331–48; George Philip, "The New Economic Liberalism and Democracy in Latin America: Friends or Enemies?" *Third World Quarterly* 14, no. 3 (1993): 555–71.

nomic policy trajectories.[11] The mixed empirical record underscores the need to disaggregate "authoritarianism" and "democracy" and determine how specific institutional arrangements affect the course of stabilization, adjustment, and market reform.

To this end, I develop a theoretical framework to assess the role of institutions in dual transformations. Until recently, the diverse literature known as the "new institutionalism" dealt exclusively with aspects of Western democracies and developing capitalist countries: political parties and electoral behavior,[12] state structure,[13] macroeconomic policy,[14] capitalist economic development,[15] and international political economy.[16] The collapse of communism inspired scholars to apply institutionalist theory to Eastern Europe, whose politico-economic transition raised critical questions regarding the design of democratic institutions and the role of state agencies in the shift from plan to market.[17]

While the institutional approach devised in this chapter draws on these works, it diverges from the extant literature in two important ways. First, I dismiss the ongoing debate over the relative virtues of neoliberal and dirigiste strategies of marketization that animates much of the schol-

---

11. Robert Bates and Anne Krueger, "Generalizations Arising from the Case Studies," in Bates and Krueger, eds., *Political and Economic Interactions in Economic Reform Policy: Evidence from Eight Countries* (Cambridge: Basil Blackwell, 1993), 459; Barbara Geddes, "Challenging the Conventional Wisdom," *Journal of Democracy* 5, no. 4 (October 1994): 104–18; José María Maravall, "The Myth of the Authoritarian Advance," *Journal of Democracy* 5, no. 4 (October 1994): 17–31.

12. Gary Cox, *The Efficient Secret: The Cabinet and the Development of Political Parties in Victorian England* (Cambridge: Cambridge University Press, 1989); Matthew Shugart and John Carey, *Presidents and Assemblies: Constitutional Design and Electoral Dynamics* (Cambridge: Cambridge University Press, 1992).

13. Peter Evans, Dietrich Rueschemeyer, and Theda Skocpol, eds., *Bringing the State Back In* (Cambridge: Cambridge University Press, 1985); Barbara Geddes, *Politician's Dilemma: Building State Capacity in Latin America* (Berkeley: University of California Press, 1994); Margaret Levi, *Of Rule and Revenue* (Berkeley: University of California Press, 1988).

14. Peter Hall, *Governing the Economy: The Politics of State Intervention in Britain and France* (Oxford: Oxford University Press, 1986); John Woolley, *Monetary Politics: The Federal Reserve and the Politics of Monetary Policy* (Cambridge: Cambridge University Press, 1984).

15. Robert Bates, *Beyond the Miracle of the Market: The Political Economy of Agrarian Development in Rural Kenya* (Cambridge: Cambridge University Press, 1989); Thráinn Eggertsson, *Economic Behavior and Institutions* (Cambridge: Cambridge University Press, 1990); Douglass North, *Institutions, Institutional Change, and Economic Performance* (Cambridge: Cambridge University Press, 1990).

16. Judith Goldstein, *Ideas, Interests, and American Trade Policy* (Ithaca: Cornell University Press, 1993); Robert Keohane, *After Hegemony: Cooperation and Discord in the World Political Economy* (Princeton: Princeton University Press, 1984).

17. Arend Lijphart, "Democratization and Constitutional Choices in Czechoslovakia, Hungary, and Poland," *Journal of Theoretical Politics* 4, no. 2 (April 1992): 207–23.

arly discourse over the role of state institutions in Eastern Europe's economic transition. I maintain that it is the balance between the universalistic and particularistic dimensions of the state's role in the economy, not the sheer extent of state intervention, that determines whether political institutions operate in a market-distorting or market-promoting fashion. I show that while institutional particularism fostered market reforms in China and East Asia, it impeded them in communist Eastern Europe by encouraging local agents to lobby state bureaucrats for individual exceptions to market rules. Democratization strengthened the capacity of successor governments to implement reform policies by disrupting the institutional channels through which factory-level actors secured articularistic favors and by bolstering the authority of state agencies responsible for global regulations. But while the recasting of postcommunist states toward the universalistic model promoted market processes in the region, it hindered successor governments from launching selective industrial policies—defying the hopes of some Western analysts that the East European countries could emulate the rapid growth strategies of the East Asian developmental states.[18]

Second, I eschew the customary distinction between the "rational choice" and "historical institutionalist" variants of the new institutionalism. The two camps do emphasize different explanatory factors. Rational choice theorists typically begin from the premise that actors' preferences are fixed and exogenously determined; historical institutionalists focus on the ways in which institutions mold actors' expectations and strategies. The rational choice variant sees institutional change as the product of purposive intervention by self-interested politicians; historical institutionalism stresses organizational learning and other modes of internal adaptation. But the two schools exhibit greater theoretical convergence than their proponents often care to admit, sharing the following implicit assumptions about institutions and the agents who operate within them:

1. Actors are "rational" in the minimalist sense that they attempt to devise strategies aimed at maximizing their net benefits. But decision making is bounded by imperfect information, restricted time, and limited technical resources.
2. Owing to the free-rider problem, pursuit of individual self-interest does not always yield optimal collective outcomes. Institutions perform the indispensable role of bridging the gap between individual and collective welfare.

18. See, for example, Alice Amsden, Jacek Kochanowicz, and Lance Taylor, *The Market Meets Its Match: Restructuring the Economies of Eastern Europe* (Harvard: Harvard University Press, 1994).

3. Preference formation is the product of a feedback process between individual agents and the institutional environment. Some preferences are formed independently of the institutional setting, while others are conditioned by extant institutions.
4. Politicians seek to mold institutions to advance their particular interests. However, choices over institutional design often have long-lasting and unintended consequences that thwart the initial goals of the actors who made them.[19]

The artificiality of the rational choice/historical institutionalist "debate" becomes especially clear in the East European context. The abrupt demise of communism created unprecedented opportunities for institutional innovation. But bargaining over constitutional structures, party systems, and electoral rules took place amid exceptionally high uncertainty, which impinged on actors' ability to make politically optimal choices. I approach Eastern Europe's democratic transition from the perspective of this tension between institutional choice and political uncertainty. The region's negotiated transitions reflected the clash between (1) interlocutors' efforts to secure institutional arrangements aimed at maximizing their short-term political prospects and (2) their incentives to hedge against the uncertainty arising from weak voter loyalties and high electoral volatility. In Hungary, this negotiating dynamic yielded an institutional configuration—a strong prime ministerial government, an electoral system dominated by a handful of parliamentary parties, and a state administration commanded by agencies of global regulation—that gave postcommunist leaders a high capacity to implement austerity policies carrying heavy distributional costs.

19. For overviews of the theoretical foundations of the new institutionalism, see Karen Schweers Cook and Margaret Levi, *The Limits of Rationality* (Chicago: University of Chicago Press, 1990); Keith Dowding, "The Compatibility of Behavioralism, Rational Choice, and 'New Institutionalism,'" *Journal of Theoretical Politics* 6, no. 1 (January 1994): 105–17; Thomas Koelble, "The New Institutionalism in Political Science and Sociology," in *Comparative Politics* 27, no. 2 (January 1995): 231–43; James March and Johan Olsen, "The New Institutionalism: Organization Factors in Political Life," *American Political Science Review* 78, no. 3 (September 1984): 734–49; Terry Moe, "The New Economics of Organization," *American Journal of Political Science* 28, no. 4 (November 1984): 739–77; Walter Powell and Paul DiMaggio, eds., *The New Institutionalism in Organizational Analysis* (Chicago: University of Chicago Press, 1991); Kenneth Shepsle, "Studying Institutions: Some Lessons from the Rational Choice Approach," *Journal of Theoretical Politics* 1, no. 2 (April 1989): 131–47; Kathleen Thelen and Sven Steinmo, "Historical Institutionalism in Comparative Politics," in Steinmo, Thelen, and Frank Longstreth, eds., *Structuring Politics: Historical Institutionalism in Comparative Analysis* (Cambridge: Cambridge University Press, 1992), 1–32.

State Institutions and Market Reform

I begin by considering the role of state institutions in market reform. While authoritarianism as a generic regime type is a poor predictor of policy outcomes, there is considerable evidence indicating that concentration of authority in powerful state institutions promotes economic transformation. The experiences of several developing capitalist countries well illustrate the "orthodox paradox," the notion that augmentation of state capacity facilitates marketization.[20] For example, institutional reforms undertaken by Park Chung Hee in the 1960s transformed the Korean state, long beset by rent seeking, into an archetype of the "developmental state."[21] Taiwan and Turkey similarly relied on centralized state organizations to spur the transition from import substitution industrialization to export-led development.[22]

There is also ample evidence demonstrating the importance of strong state institutions in stabilization policy. The capacity of states to enforce monetary discipline hinges on the degree to which central banks are insulated from interest group demands, bureaucratic turf battles, and partisan political pressures.[23] Similarly, protection of fiscal policy from distributional claims requires strong ministries of finance and other institutional-

---

20. Stephan Haggard and Robert Kaufman, "Institutions and Economic Adjustment," in *The Politics of Economic Adjustment: International Constraints, Distributive Conflicts, and the State* (Princeton: Princeton University Press, 1992), p. 25; Miles Kahler, "Orthodoxy and Its Alternatives: Explaining Approaches to Stabilization and Adjustment," in Nelson, *Economic Crisis and Policy Choice*, p. 55.

21. Stephan Haggard, *Pathways from the Periphery: The Politics of Growth in the Newly Industrializing Countries* (Ithaca: Cornell University Press, 1990), 54–74; Haggard, Richard Cooper, and Chung-In Moon, "Policy Reform in Korea," in Bates and Krueger, *Political and Economic Interactions*, 296–98, 302–4, 308–24.

22. See Robert Wade's analysis of the institutional structure of Taiwan's developmental state in *Governing the Market: Economic Theory and the Role of Government in East Asian Industrialization* (Princeton: Princeton University Press, 1990), 195–227. For the Turkish case, see Anne Krueger and Ilter Turan, "The Politics and Economics of Turkish Policy Reforms in the 1980s," in Bates and Krueger, *Political and Economic Interactions*, 351–69; John Waterbury, "The Heart of the Matter? Public Enterprise and the Adjustment Process," in Haggard and Kaufman, *The Politics of Economic Adjustment*, 191–92, 206–11.

23. John Goodman, "The Politics of Central Bank Independence," *Comparative Politics* 23, no. 3 (April 1991): 329–49; Goodman, *Monetary Sovereignty: The Politics of Central Banking in Western Europe* (Ithaca: Cornell University Press, 1992), 6–10. The policy effects of central bank independence are more ambiguous in developing countries, where there are wider discrepancies between de jure and de facto autonomy. See Alex Cukierman, Steven Webb, and Bilin Neyapti, "Measuring the Independence of Central Banks and Its Effect on Policy Outcomes," *World Bank Economic Review* 6, no. 3 (1992): 353–98.

ized "guardians of the treasury" capable of checking the efforts of branch ministries and special interest groups to bid up expenditures.[24]

The role of state institutions in structural adjustment policy is more complex and controversial. While neoliberal economists do not contest the importance of strong central banks for orthodox stabilization, they do favor diminution of the state's role in adjustment policy via trade liberalization, divestiture of state-owned enterprises, and reliance on market-determined prices, interest rates, and exchange rates. The so-called Washington consensus holds that the economic problems of Latin America and other developing regions stemmed chiefly from an excess of statism.

Critics of neoliberal adjustment strategies argue that it is not the literal *degree* of state intervention in the market that matters but rather the *kind* of intervention. The crises of the Latin American economies resulted from the exhaustion of a particular type of statism—import substitution industrialization—that encouraged collusion between state officials and microeconomic agents.[25] The industrialization strategy pursued by the East Asian countries—export-led development—shows how state institutions can protect markets from rent seeking while spurring growth and allocative efficiency.

The institutional perspective of this book is sympathetic with these critiques of neoliberalism. The decisive question at hand concerns not whether the state should play an active role in the market but rather what types of state institutions protect markets and what types distort them.

One view holds that state institutions designed to enforce universal regulations are best suited to market development. The sheer extent of state regulation of the market is less important than its universality. Market distortions arise when the regulatory system is liable to individual exceptions and when enforcement is subject to arbitrary modification. The deficiencies of the Latin American import substitution industrialization strategies resulted from state structures that permitted economic agents to elude market forces by securing favors from bureaucrats and politicians. Robust markets emerge when state institutions establish a level playing field. All contestants in the game are subject to the same impersonal rules, which ensure that winning and losing depend purely on competitive prowess, not political connections. The *universalistic model* is most closely associated with early capitalist countries like Great Britain and the United

---

24. James Alt and K. Alec Chrystal, *Political Economics* (Berkeley: University of California Press, 1983), 218–19; Aaron Wildavsky, *The Politics of the Budgetary Process,* 3d ed. (Boston: Little, Brown, 1979), 160–65.

25. Luiz Carlos Bresser Pereira, "Economic Reforms and Economic Growth: Efficiency and Politics in Latin America," in Bresser Pereira, José María Maravall, and Adam Przeworski, *Economic Reforms in New Democracies: A Social-Democratic Approach* (Cambridge: Cambridge University Press, 1993), 18–33.

States, whose capital-based financial systems minimize opportunities for selective credit allocation and whose state agencies function at arm's length from the private sector.[26]

But while the universalistic model reflects the trajectory of the Anglo-American countries, it hardly describes the state's role in the successful developing economies of East Asia or advanced industrialized countries like France and Japan. Here, state activities favor specific industries and sectors, but in ways that advance the broad goal of market development. For example, import controls, which in Latin America became a means of shielding inefficient import substitution industrialization producers from international competition and which were thus a source of patronage for politicians, emerged in East Asia as an instrument of export promotion. In South Korea, the abolition of import quotas reduced opportunities for state bureaucrats and local capitalists to form rent-seeking alliances. But rather than embracing the neoliberal prescription of radical import liberalization, the Park regime opted for an import licensing system that allowed the state to attach export performance criteria to applications for licenses. Other instruments employed by the Korean state—selective credit facilities, preferential tax schedules—further illustrate the efficacy of particularistic intervention as a market-promoting strategy.[27] Similarly, the credit-based systems of France and Japan enabled state authorities to channel financial resources to targeted sectors of local industry.[28] While both the East Asian newly industrialized countries and the dirigiste industrialized countries moved toward nondiscretionary instruments in the 1980s, they retained an array of policy tools that enabled state institutions to shape industrial strategies for particular sectors.[29]

---

26. John Zysman, *Governments, Markets, and Growth: Financial Systems and the Politics of Industrial Change* (Ithaca: Cornell University Press, 1983), 17–18, 55–71.

27. Haggard, Cooper, and Moon, "Policy Reform in Korea," 323–24.

28. Stephen Cohen, James Galbraith, and John Zysman, "Rehabbing the Labyrinth: The Financial System and Industrial Policy in France," in Cohen and Peter Gourevitch, eds., *France in the Troubled World Economy* (London: Butterworth Scientific, 1982), 58–65; Yoshio Suzuki, *Money and Banking in Contemporary Japan* (New Haven: Yale University Press, 1980), 162–87; Kozo Yamamura, "The Cost of Rapid Growth and Capitalist Democracy in Japan," in Leon Lindberg and Charles Maier, eds., *The Politics of Inflation and Economic Stagnation* (Washington: Brookings Institution, 1985), 470–73; Zysman, *Governments, Markets, and Growth*, 71–72.

29. Yoon-je Cho and David Cole, "The Role of the Financial Sector in Korea's Structural Adjustment," in Vittorio Corbo and Sang-mok Suh, eds., *Structural Adjustment in a Newly Industrialized Country: The Korean Experience* (Baltimore: Johns Hopkins University Press, 1992), 122–23; Byung-Sun Choi, "Financial Policy and Big Business in Korea: The Perils of Financial Regulation," in Stephan Haggard, Chung Lee, and Sylvia Maxfield, eds., *The Politics of Finance in Developing Countries* (Ithaca: Cornell University Press, 1993), 40–53; Jeffrey Hart, *Rival Capitalists: International Competitiveness in the United States, Japan, and Western Europe* (Ithaca: Cornell University Press, 1992), 36–138.

The Japanese and East Asian cases demonstrate the utility of the *particularistic model* for countries facing external pressures for rapid economic development. The state as "surrogate entrepreneur" can help bridge the gap with advanced countries by diversifying risk, nurturing local capitalists, and facilitating entry into industries with high start-up costs.[30] The main danger of particularistic intervention is that it may progressively degenerate into rent seeking, undermining the delicate balance between corporate autonomy and social embeddedness characteristic of developmental states. The Marcos regime in the Philippines demonstrated how institutional particularism can breed corruption and cronyism, preventing state agencies from delivering the collective goods essential for development.[31]

I approach the role of state institutions in Eastern Europe from the perspective of the tension between the universalistic and particularistic dimensions of the state's role in the economy. What institutional arrangements favor one or the other? What are the economic policy consequences of various mixes of universalism and particularism? How does democratization alter the balance?

I argue that state institutions in orthodox communist systems exhibited a strong particularistic bias. But unlike in the East Asian newly industrialized countries, institutional particularism in communist Eastern Europe was not part of a deliberate state strategy to promote the development of export industries capable of competing in world markets. Rather, it was the unintentional consequence of a peculiar administrative system, central economic planning, whose main purpose was to fulfill physical production targets for supplies to the domestic and Council for Mutual Economic Assistance (CMEA) markets—which operated under completely different rules than the world capitalist economy. Despite the communist state's vast formal authority, the institutional logic of central planning prevented state agencies from enforcing universal regulations. State authorities tolerated persistent deviations from central directives, without which local enterprises could not meet the Communist Party's production targets. The market socialist reforms introduced in Hungary and other countries deepened the communist state's particularistic bent by enlarging opportunities for factory-level agents to negotiate individual exceptions to economic regulations.

---

30. Peter Evans, "The State as Problem and Solution: Predation, Embedded Autonomy, and Structural Change," in Haggard and Kaufman, *The Politics of Economic Adjustment,* 142–66.

31. Paul Hutchcroft, "Selective Squander: The Politics of Preferential Credit Allocation in the Philippines," in Haggard, Lee, and Maxfield, *The Politics of Finance in Developing Countries,* 165–98.

The Communist Party's role in this system reinforced the particular-istic tendencies of state institutions. By the late 1980s, state agencies in reformed communist countries like Hungary enjoyed substantial de jure power, as Party leaders devolved day-to-day control of economic policy to subordinate units in the political hierarchy. But like their counterparts in orthodox communist regimes, Party elites retained the de facto right to intercede anywhere and at any time—exemplifying the absence of consti-tutional checks on the Party's political authority. Typically, what triggered intercession from the top were claims by local agents that measures pro-posed by state authorities generated unacceptable socioeconomic effects. Thus, the Communist Party's practice of selective intervention broadened opportunities for local agents to mitigate the distributional fallout of adjustment by extracting regulatory concessions from the state.

I also argue that the tumultuous events of 1989 disrupted the founda-tions of Eastern Europe's distinctive variant of institutional particularism. The East Asian countries engineered the shift from import substitution industrialization to export-led development by retooling state institutions that had already developed a high capacity for selective intervention in local industry. This option was not available to the postcommunist states. The demise of the Communist Party unhinged the institutional links that allowed local agents to secure individual favors from state agencies, while the advent of multiparty contestation and a liberalized press erected barri-ers to partisan exploitation of state resources. The result was to skew post-communist institutions toward the universalistic model—a model con-ducive to the promotion of impartial market forces in Eastern Europe, but not to the formation of proactive industrial policies needed to spur Asian-style economic growth.

The Institutional Structure of the Communist State

I focus on two features of the communist state: the penetration of the state by the ruling party and the institutional foundations of central economic planning.

The literature on bureaucratic politics in Soviet-type systems empha-sizes the ways in which communist state institutions departed from Max Weber's legal/rational ideal type.[32] Charismatic authority typified the Soviet state from the time of the Bolshevik Revolution. The political power of the early Bolshevik leaders derived more from informal, person-alized power bases than from occupation of specific positions in the party/state hierarchy. Lenin's death set in motion a process of institution-

---

32. "Bureaucracy," in *From Max Weber: Essays in Sociology,* trans. H. H. Gerth and C. Wright Mills (New York: Oxford University Press, 1946), 196–244.

alization akin to Weber's "routinization of charisma." But charismatic elements survived to form the basis of Josef Stalin's personality cult. During the Stalinist period, the ruling Party completely subsumed the Soviet state. Stalin used the coercive apparatus of the state to defeat his opponents within the Party leadership and terrorize enemy classes. As part of its de-Stalinization campaign, the Khrushchev regime established a system of "socialist legality" that discouraged the use of state organizations for mass terror and created mechanisms of collective control within the Party Central Committee. But de-Stalinization did not eradicate all vestiges of patrimonial rule, as evidenced by the cronyism that persisted throughout the post-Stalinist period.[33]

In addition to advancing the political aims of individual Party elites, the dominance of "substantive" over "formal" rationality in the communist state served the needs of the central planning system. The centrally planned economies (CPEs) operated under a wholly different institutional logic than market economies. Whereas the "goal-function" of market economies is profit maximization defined in terms of the ratio of outputs and inputs, the driving force of CPEs was maximization of the gross volume of production.[34] The preoccupation of central planners and factory-level agents with physical output targets had profound consequences for the communist state. The violations of central directives, black-market activities, and other maladies of Soviet-type systems reflected not merely the inability of authorities to enforce universal rules of economic behavior. The central planning system itself could not have operated without such departures from Weberian legal rationality.

The well-documented dysfunctions of planned economies—queuing, hoarding, forced substitution, exhaustion of fixed capital, investment cycles—were the inevitable result of the volume maximization principle.[35]

---

33. See the works of T. H. Rigby: "Politics in the Mono-Organizational Society," in Andrew Janos, ed., *Authoritarian Politics in Communist Europe* (Berkeley: Institute of International Studies, University of California, 1976), 31–80; "Stalinism and the Monorganizational Society," in Robert Tucker, ed., *Stalinism: Essays in Historical Interpretation* (London: MacMillan, 1977), 53–76; "A Conceptual Approach to Authority, Power, and Policy in the Soviet Union," in Rigby, Archie Brown, and Peter Reddaway, eds., *Authority, Power, and Policy in the USSR* (London: MacMillan, 1980), 9–31.

34. Ferenc Fehér, Agnes Heller, and György Markus, *Dictatorship over Needs* (Oxford: Basil Blackwell, 1983), 65–86.

35. There is a vast literature detailing the systemic defects of Soviet-type economies. Key works include Tamás Bauer, *Tervgazdaság, Beruházás, Ciklusok* (Planned economy, investment, cycles) (Budapest: Közgazdasági és Jogi Könyvkiadó, 1981); Joseph Berliner, *Factory and Manager in the USSR* (Cambridge: Harvard University Press, 1957); David Granick, *Enterprise Guidance in Eastern Europe* (Princeton: Princeton University Press, 1975); Paul Gregory and Robert Stuart, *Soviet Economic Structure and Performance*, 3d ed. (New York: Harper and Row, 1986); Franklyn Holzman, ed., *Readings on the Soviet Econ-*

The combination of soft budget constraints from below and incessant pressure from above to expand production induced enterprise directors to procure as many inputs as they could absorb. Facing insatiable demand, manufacturers of capital goods ramped production up to the limits imposed by available physical resources. As a result, production constantly ran up against the resource constraints of the economy, creating pervasive shortages.[36] Fulfilling the center's production targets amid constant shortage forced producers to engage in illicit practices (*blat*). With the obliteration of horizontal factor markets, plant directors were formally required to obtain specific authorization from branch ministries to procure the capital inputs needed to sustain production. But acute shortages of those goods compelled them to resort to black-market transactions and interenterprise transfers. These secondary supply networks were illegal but tolerated by the political authorities. They compensated for the deficiencies of the central allocation system and enabled factory-level agents to meet the Communist Party's production targets.[37] State bureaucrats and local Party officials not only permitted these activities but actively participated in them, serving the indispensable role of intermediaries to help state enterprises overcome bottlenecks through informal supply channels.[38]

At the same time, the central planning system endowed state institutions with greater decision-making authority than they could manage. Even with the advent of computers and linear programming techniques, central planners lacked the technical capability to make efficient choices concerning the thousands of allocation problems for which they were responsible. Much of the information needed to make these decisions remained concealed within lower levels of the hierarchy. Moreover, the reliability of the economic data available to central planners was suspect owing to the tendency of plant directors to overreport current production to curry favor with their superiors, disguise production shortfalls to avoid sanctions, and understate capacity to avert upward ratcheting of next year's quotas.

Overloading of the communist state had several repercussions. The inability of the state institutions to carry out all the de jure tasks assigned

omy (Chicago: Rand McNally, 1962); and János Kornai, *Overcentralization in Economic Administration: A Critical Analysis Based on Experience in Hungarian Light Industry,* trans. John Knapp (London: Oxford University Press, 1957).

36. The standard work on the shortage phenomenon in socialist economies is János Kornai, *The Economics of Shortage,* vol. B (Amsterdam: North Holland, 1980).

37. Edward Hewett, *Reforming the Soviet Economy: Equality versus Efficiency* (Washington: Brookings Institution, 1988), 153–220.

38. Jerry Hough, *The Soviet Prefects: The Local Party Organs in Industrial Decision-making* (Cambridge: Harvard University Press, 1969), 213–52.

to them spawned an array of de facto mechanisms outside the formal reach of the central planning ministries. For instance, inefficient allocation decisions by the center left huge disequilibria between supply and demand for key products. Plant directors thus found themselves holding chits authorizing them to purchase capital inputs that were not actually available in state distribution networks, forcing them to utilize illicit means to obtain the goods needed to execute their production plans.[39]

These institutional features skewed the communist state toward the particularistic model. Far from subjecting economic agents to universal standards of conduct, state regulation of the economy was rife with rule violations and individual exemptions. The imperative of maximizing production amid pervasive shortages necessitated frequent circumventions of the central allocation system, deviations that were either tacitly condoned or actively abetted by Communist Party officials. While state institutions possessed the legal authority to issue directives and apply sanctions for nonfulfillment, local producers controlled much of the information needed to regulate the enterprise sector. Economic production was thus guided less by formal commands dispensed from the center than by individualized bargaining between state bureaucrats and plant directors over resource allocation, with the latter manipulating information to secure favorable decisions from their superiors.

The Impact of Market Reforms on the Communist State

While the reforms launched in Yugoslavia, Poland, and Hungary were intended to augment the universalistic elements of the socialist economy by freeing state enterprises from legally binding directives and exposing them to the discipline of market forces, their effect was to deepen the particularistic tendencies of the communist state that I have already described. I focus here on the institutional manifestations of NEM, Hungary's variant of market socialism.

The reform program launched by the Hungarian Communist Party in 1968 abolished legally binding directives issued by the central ministries to state enterprises. All that remained of the state's formal legal authority over enterprises was the power to appoint and dismiss plant directors, and even this was removed from most of the enterprise sector in the mid-1980s. Nonbinding financial indicators replaced obligatory output targets. The designers of the reform hoped that central intervention in factory operations would cease and that profitability would supplant plan fulfillment as the chief incentive of enterprise directors, thereby raising allocative efficiency.

39. Hewett, *Reforming the Soviet Economy,* 155.

Petty interference by the Hungarian state did in fact diminish, and profitability did become an important standard by which socialist enterprises organized production. But these achievements were not tantamount to the creation of a real market. The reforms terminated directive planning while spawning an array of institutional links through which state bureaucrats transmitted their expectations to local producers. Foremost among these expectations was what Hungarian economists term the "responsibility for supply."[40] State authorities were chiefly concerned with three objectives: fulfilling interstate CMEA agreements, supplying goods to the domestic market, and expanding exports to the convertible currency area.

Ideally, voluntary observance of central expectations by enterprises obviated interference from above. Indeed, the very anticipation of intervention could serve as an ex ante constraint on plant directors, removing any need for the supervisory bodies to become involved. But voluntary compliance often did not suffice. Nonfulfillment of production goals could result from poor decisions, incompetence on the part of plant directors, or objective resource constraints. But frequently, it was the contradictory nature of the center's expectations themselves that prevented enterprises from fulfilling them. For a country like Hungary, burdened with obligations to the socialist alliance, persistent domestic shortages, and an onerous hard currency debt, there was little mystery as to why the three "supply tasks" came into conflict. Owing to the burgeoning debt and deteriorating balance of payments, production of goods for export to the West became the center's top priority in the 1980s. But in a shortage economy, meeting that objective compromised the goals of executing outstanding CMEA contracts and sustaining supplies to the local market.

The conflicting nature of the center's expectations and the physical inability of state enterprises simultaneously to fulfill them had several important consequences. First, enterprise managers, facing a multiplicity of conflicting expectations, focused on whatever ones they believed were most important to their superiors at the moment.[41] Second, the inability of state enterprises to meet at once all of their supply tasks triggered cyclical intervention by the center. Imbalances in one sphere provoked the authorities to intervene. But whatever corrective actions enterprises took caused

---

40. Tamás Bauer, "The Hungarian Alternative to Soviet Type Planning," *Journal of Comparative Economics* 7 (1983): 304–16; Károly Soós, "The Role of Money and Financial Organs in Financial Downswings" (Institute of Economics, Hungarian Academy of Sciences, Budapest, 1986, photocopy).

41. Károly Soós, *Terv, Kampány, Pénz* (Plan, campaign, money) (Budapest: Közgazdasági és Jogi Könyvkiadó, 1986); Soós, "Informal Pressures, Mobilization, and Campaigns in the Management of Centrally Planned Economies," (Institute of Economics, Hungarian Academy of Sciences, Budapest, 1986, photocopy).

imbalances in another sphere, necessitating further interventions. For example, if the authorities became concerned about the worsening balance of payments, they would pressure plant directors to ramp up production of exportable goods. But this merely diverted resources away from the consumer goods, creating imbalances in the household sector that eventually prompted the center to intervene again and admonish enterprises to devote more attention to the domestic market. The practice of central interventionism thus became self-perpetuating.[42]

But while the persistence of bureaucratic interference in plant-level activities underscored the center's continued authority under market socialism, these conditions did not mean that state enterprises operated under total subservience. On the contrary, bargaining power of enterprise managers was greatest precisely when voluntary compliance failed.

As we have seen, bargaining between the center and the enterprise sector was endemic under orthodox central planning, with negotiations centering on physical balances of inputs and outputs. In post-1968 Hungary, state bureaucrats and plant directors bargained primarily over financial regulations: wages, taxes, subsidies, prices, bank credits, foreign exchange, and import licenses. In principle, these regulations were supposed to be applied uniformly. But what emerged instead was a system in which financial regulations were individualized, tailor-made for specific enterprises. While Hungarian enterprise managers, like their counterparts in traditional CPEs, possessed the vital asset of information, this was not their main bargaining chip. Rather, the very fact that the center attached such high priority to the three supply goals enabled enterprises to extract financial concessions from the center.

Suppose, for example, that the Ministry of Industry determined that the hard currency export revenues of a particular enterprise were falling short of expectations. The Ministry did not enjoy the legal authority to command the enterprise to expand its production of exportable products. Instead, ministerial officials would make anxious telephone calls to the plant director, noting that export production was lower than desired. The director would reply that he sincerely regretted this, that his factory was doing everything possible given available resources, and that he would be able to raise export production if he could only obtain a new line of credit, a tax reduction, a special export subsidy, an exemption from wage and price regulations, or an import license to obtain advanced capital equipment.

42. Teréz Laky, "The Hidden Mechanisms of Recentralization in Hungary," *Acta Oeconomica* 24, nos. 1–2 (1980): 95–109; László Antal, "Conflicts of Financial Planning and Regulation in Hungary," *Acta Oeconomica* 30, nos. 3–4 (1983): 341–68.

This was the essence of Hungary's "plan bargaining" system.[43] State institutions exerted pressure on enterprises to attain critical supply goals; the latter extracted financial concessions on the pretext that fulfillment of the center's expectations was not possible without such allowances. Under this system, Hungarian enterprises were not wholly indifferent to profits. But the profit incentive involved not profit maximization but rather the attainment of a level of earnings sufficient to enable the enterprise to meet its supply obligations. The profit motive thus became less an a priori goal of enterprises than another subject of bargaining: they negotiated for that set of financial regulations which would give them the profits needed to carry out their supply tasks.

Hungary's NEM thus illustrated the self-reproductive logic of the "socialist halfway house." The deviations from legal/rational norms long characteristic of orthodox command economies—bending of rules and regulations, forgiveness of financial indiscretions, reinterventions to correct resultant imbalances—continually reappeared within a substantially altered institutional setting. But while the institutional logic of Hungary's market socialist model reproduced many of the behavioral patterns of the prereform system, the resulting economy differed from traditional CPEs in one decisive respect. The devolution of decision-making authority to the factory level gave workers and enterprise managers a measure of bargaining power well exceeding that of their counterparts in command economies. This had major repercussions for the course of stabilization and adjustment policy during the final years of communist rule.

The Economic Policy Consequences of Institutional Particularism

Economists have long noted the peculiar problems of implementing stabilization and adjustment programs in CPEs. The policy measures commonly prescribed by the Washington lending agencies for full-fledged market economies—price reform, currency devaluation, import liberalization, monetary contraction—often did not produce the desired effects in CPEs

43. László Antal, *Gazdaságirányitási és Pénzügyi Rendszerünk a Reform Utján* (Our economic management and financial system on the reform path) (Budapest: Közgazdasági és Jogi Könyvkiadó, 1985); John Hall, "Plan Bargaining in the Hungarian Economy: An Interview with Dr. László Antal," *Comparative Economic Studies* 27, no. 2 (summer 1986): 49–58; Aladár Sipos and Márton Tardos, "Economic Control and the Structural Interdependence of Organizations in Hungary at the End of the Second Decade of Reform," *Acta Oeconomica* 37, nos. 3–4 (1986): 241–65.

and indeed created effects that worsened economic imbalances.[44] The difficulty stemmed in part from the distorted incentive structure of state enterprises. Price liberalization that was aimed at narrowing the gap between supply and demand had little effect on socialist producers, whose demand schedules were highly inelastic. Exchange rate policy was similarly ineffective as a demand-constraining device. Because of their insensitivity to input costs, enterprises' demand for imports remained unabated in the face of devaluations. Likewise, the soft budget constraints of state enterprises defeated attempts to curtail aggregate demand via fiscal or monetary restraint. Enterprise money was "passive." Because the physical production activities of enterprises did not depend on how much money they possessed, macroeconomic policies aimed at squeezing the supply of liquidity had little or no effect on total demand for capital inputs.[45]

The structure of the state institutions responsible for regulating macroeconomic aggregates further reduced the utility of conventional stabilization measures. The Soviet-type central banks bore no resemblance to Western central banks. The functions of currency issue and credit allocation, which are fully or partially separated in capitalist countries, were merged in the single institution of the monobank. Monetary policy was strictly subordinated to the requirements of central planning. Although formally charged with supervising financial flows in the enterprise sector to ensure compliance with regulations, the socialist monobanks were completely subservient to the central planning ministries, obliged to supply enterprises with whatever credit they needed to execute the physical tasks specified in the plan. As a result, the total supply of liquidity in the economy expanded more or less automatically to meet the needs of the enterprise sector.[46]

---

44. Josef Brada, Edward Hewett, and Thomas Wolf, "Economic Stabilization, Structural Adjustment, and Economic Reform," in Brada, Hewett, and Wolf, eds., *Economic Adjustment and Reform in Eastern Europe and the Soviet Union* (Durham: Duke University Press, 1988), 3–37; Imre Tarafás, "The Possibility and Conditions of Anti-Inflationary Economic Policy in Hungary," *Acta Oeconomica* 34, nos. 3–4 (1985): 287–97; Thomas Wolf, "Exchange Rate Systems and Adjustment in Planned Economies," *IMF Staff Papers* 32, no. 2 (June 1985): 211–47; Wolf, "Devaluation in Modified Planned Economies: A Preliminary Model for Hungary," in Brada, Hewett, and Wolf, *Economic Adjustment and Reform,* 39–61.

45. Kornai, *The Economics of Shortage,* 523–24.

46. Joseph Berliner, "Monetary Planning in the USSR," *American Slavic and East European Review* 9, no. 4 (December 1950): 237–54; George Garvy, *Money, Financial Flows, and Credit in the Soviet Union* (Cambridge: Harvard University Press, 1977); Gregory Grossman, ed., *Money and Plan* (Berkeley: University of California Press, 1968); Katherine Hsiao, *Money and Monetary Policy in Communist China* (New York: Columbia University Press, 1971); T. M. Podolski, *Socialist Banking and Monetary Control: The Experience of Poland* (Cambridge: Harvard University Press, 1973); Adam Zwass, *Money, Banking, and Credit in the Soviet Union and Eastern Europe* (White Plains, N.Y.: M. E. Sharpe, 1979).

The unavailability of market-type instruments of stabilization meant that planners in traditional CPEs relied on centrally administered cuts in wages, investment, and imports to correct external imbalances. Such techniques were crude but effective insofar as they enabled the center to engineer deep reductions of domestic consumption. In the 1980s, the regime of Nicolae Ceauşescu implemented a draconian austerity program that succeeded in generating a trade surplus and retiring Romania's Western debt, at the cost of a degree of economic deprivation unmatched in Europe since World War II. But while such methods were effective means of macroeconomic stabilization, they worked at cross-purposes with structural adjustment. Gross cuts in investment sharply contracted aggregate consumption but also impeded reallocation of fixed capital within the state sector. Promising high technology industries were thus denied access to the Western imports needed to retool plant and equipment and reorganize production.[47]

But while this contradiction between stabilization and adjustment deepened the long-term economic problems of orthodox planned economies, it did not present immediate political difficulties for the Communist Party. The central authorities needed only to draw on their existing repertoire of policy instruments to correct economic imbalances. State enterprises and trade unions, lacking the authority to make their own decisions about wages, prices, and investment, had few resources to resist.

Political leaders in reformed communist states like Hungary faced an altogether different set of problems. Here, the center's ability to contract domestic consumption hinged on two factors: (1) whether the state institutions charged with regulating macroeconomic aggregates, notably the central bank and the Ministry of Finance, performed that function; and (2) how workers and enterprises, now enjoying significant microeconomic decision-making authority, reacted to the "market" signals of the reformed economy. If the revamped monetary and fiscal organizations proved ineffectual and factory-level agents responded to their newly won freedoms by raising consumption, state authorities would face mounting disequilibria that could only be corrected by restoring central controls on market processes.

Therein resided the essential political dilemma of stabilization and adjustment in reformed communist states. The particularistic bias of state institutions and the continued weakness of market incentives at the local level induced the putative losers of economic austerity to press their claims on the center. The institutional setting provided the incentives and opportunities for these agents to bargain for individual exceptions to the state's

---

47. Brada, Hewett, and Wolf, "Economic Stabilization," 12–27.

financial regulations to soften the distributional effects of adjustment. Consequently, domestic consumption would rise and aggravate the external imbalance. Restoration of financial order would then force the center to reimpose administrative controls in areas where it had already devolved a considerable measure of authority to local agents. Such authority, once relinquished, could not be easily recovered, as attempts at recentralization of decision making provoked strong resistance from below.

The use of quasi-market mechanisms as instruments of austerity in Eastern Europe thus generated a peculiar push-pull dynamic. Market reforms simultaneously encouraged microeconomic agents to behave in ways contrary to stabilization and adjustment policy and endowed them with the resources to resist the center's ex post attempts to correct the distortions arising from the initial decentralization. Liberalization of decision making enabled workers and enterprise managers to bid up wages, investment, and credit; the resultant surge in domestic purchasing power compromised macroeconomic equilibrium; state authorities sought to reimpose central controls; local agents resisted such attempts at recentralization, attempting to preserve the gains already achieved. In this respect, the political economy of stabilization and adjustment in market socialist systems differed from both developing capitalist countries and orthodox planned economies.

The economic consequences of institutional particularism in Eastern Europe also distinguished the region from communist China. Susan Shirk describes how failed attempts at comprehensive price liberalization and other universalistic reforms prompted the regime of Deng Xiaoping to shift to a strategy of "particularistic contracting" aimed at building a proreform constituency in the Chinese provinces. She notes that China's vast size and decentralized political structure militated toward such a strategy, prompting the Deng leadership to buy off local agents via individual concessions in order to surmount opposition by party conservatives in the center. But the main explanation of the "power of particularism" in post-1978 China was the fact that market reforms were pursued in the context of economic growth. Rapid growth transformed emergent markets into opportunities for state enterprises to increase their profits by "growing out of the plan."[48]

Hungary and other reformed communist states in Eastern Europe faced entirely different politico-economic circumstances. By the 1980s, the phase of "extensive growth" of the Soviet-type economies was exhausted, and much of the region was burdened by heavy indebtedness, rising

---

48. Shirk, *The Political Logic of Economic Reform* (Berkeley: University of California Press, 1993), 16–17, 280–329, 335, 343–44.

balance-of-payments deficits, and economic stagnation. Whereas institutional particularism in China was embedded in the context of growth, in Eastern Europe it was situated in the milieu of externally imposed economic austerity. In the former, local agents used decentralized political institutions to escape the plan and hook onto nascent markets. In the latter, actors used state institutions to negotiate exceptions to market rules in order to elude the adverse distributional effects of economic adjustment.

This comparison of the Chinese and East European experiences suggests that particularistic institutions are most likely to work in a market-promoting direction when the political economy of reform is positive-sum. When the game is zero- or negative-sum, such institutions are apt to defeat reforms by providing losers with escape routes from market forces.

The Communist Party and Selective Intervention

The behavior of Communist Party leaders reinforced the particularistic bias of the East European states. The Party's de facto monopoly of power enabled communist elites to intervene at will in the activities of state agencies, even when the latter enjoyed substantial de jure independence. State bureaucrats attempting to implement austerity policies were therefore ill positioned to resist appeals for individual compensation by local agents who enjoyed the tacit support of Communist Party officials.

The susceptibility of state institutions to selective intervention from above illustrated the complete interpenetration of party and state in Marxist-Leninist regimes. Research on the relationship between party and state institutions in Soviet-type systems emphasizes the Communist Party's control of the *nomenklatura,* its capacity to issue legally binding directives, and its ability to check policy implementation by state agencies through the parallel departments of the Central Committee Secretariat. Ordinarily, these tools sufficed to ensure state compliance with the objectives of Party leaders. State actors did not possess independent political power, and whatever conflicts occurred in lower levels of the hierarchy were ultimately reflections of tendencies within the Party leadership itself.[49]

By the late 1980s, the empirical reality of countries like Hungary no longer conformed to this picture of Communist Party politics. Hungarian Communist Party leaders had already devolved a substantial measure of formal policy-making authority to the government and state administration. Subordinate organizations now possessed wide discretion to interpret

---

49. Ellen Comisso, "Introduction: State Structures, Political Processes, and Collective Choice," in Comisso and Laura Tyson, eds., *Power, Purpose, and Collective Choice: Economic Strategy in Socialist States* (Ithaca: Cornell University Press, 1986), 19–62.

policy directives issued by the Party Central Committee. The Hungarian Communists also enacted major reductions of the Central Committee bureaucracy. For instance, the crucial Economic Policy Department was left with a professional staff of about 30 people to supervise the activities of all the state institutions involved in reform policy. In the late 1980s, the Party Central Committee relinquished its power of final approval of the national plan prepared by the state. It also slashed its *nomenklatura,* retaining power of appointment only for heads of ministries and state secretaries.[50]

But this retreat from day-to-day involvement in economic policy implied not so much a diminution of the Hungarian Communist Party's political power as a redefinition of it. The subordinate actors did not seize policy-making authority from the Party leadership. On the contrary, the leadership willingly and even happily ceded it. The decentralization of policy-making authority benefited the Party by enabling it to exploit the superior technical resources of the state, relieving the Central Committee of the obligation to fulfill the sorts of functions it never performed very well.

Meanwhile, Party elites retained the authority to intercede at any point on any issue, from the organization of the May Day parade to the most sensitive foreign policy matters. What guaranteed this power of final word was the absence of any countervailing political authority in the Marxist-Leninist system. With no constitutional constraints on Party power and no organized opposition, the Communist Party's political authority was theoretically and practically unlimited: there was nothing to stop Party elites from intervening in the policy-making process whenever they wished to. It was for precisely this reason that subordinate actors continued to respect the Party's authority even as its formal instruments of control unraveled in the late 1980s. The Party's capacity to intervene anywhere and at any time imparted a certain arbitrariness and unpredictability to the behavior of Communist elites, and it was precisely these qualities that made the leadership's selective interventions effective. Subordinate actors could never know for sure whether a particular decision would provoke intercession from above, but they did know that the possibility for such intervention always existed. This served as a continuous ex ante constraint on state bureaucrats, inducing them to abstain from actions that might provoke a costly and futile confrontation with the Party leadership.

Several factors could trigger intervention from the top: the inability of subordinate actors to reach an agreement, the failure of "market forces" in Hungary's mixed economy to determine the allocation of resources, and

---

50. Interviews, MSZMP Central Committee, 7 and 28 July, 30 August, and 8 September 1988.

the leadership's determination that the distributional consequences of stabilization and adjustment created unacceptable risks of a general social crisis that would threaten the Party's position.[51] All three triggering factors imparted a conservative bias to economic reform policy. Subordinate agents dissatisfied with a bureaucratically negotiated outcome had the option of referring the matter to a higher authority. But this was a potentially costly option: Agents who consistently pursued a referral strategy ran the risk of incurring the disfavor of Party leaders and undermining the confidence of other bureaucrats, with whom they would have to negotiate on future issues. State actors therefore had a strong incentive to reach a consensus by formulating lowest-common-denominator policies. The same incentive dissuaded subordinate actors from advancing radical policy proposals that their interlocutors could use against them in appeals to Party elites. The logic of selective intervention also predisposed Communist Party leaders toward conservative policies. When the leadership intervened, it usually did so in ways that defeated the aims of market reform, resolving disputes between state organizations by encouraging adoption of watered-down proposals or reimposing central administrative controls on market processes when radical reforms produced unacceptable distributional effects. The antireform tendencies of this institutional configuration prevailed even when ardent reformers occupied senior posts in the Party Central Committee and key state ministries.

The consequences were ultimately disastrous for the Hungarian Communists, whose post-1956 political strategy hinged on their capacity to manage the economy and improve the population's living standards. The very political hegemony that made the Communist Party's selective interventions effective proved to be its biggest liability: While the Party could delegate policy-making *authority* to subordinate organizations, the nature of the communist system prevented it from eluding final political *responsibility* for the fate of reform policy. By abdicating active leadership of reform policy, the Party left NEM prone to bureaucratic compromises and individual exceptions to market rules. The decisive measures were thus delayed, and by the mid-1980s the Hungarian economy was in a full-blown crisis. The deterioration of the economy, combined with the withdrawal of Soviet cover for the East European communist parties, set the stage for the negotiated transition to democracy at decade's end.

---

51. In the parlance of principal-agent theory, these triggering factors are analogous to what Mathew McCubbins and Thomas Schwartz call the "fire-alarm" control type. In contrast to the "police-patrol" type of oversight systems, where the principal exercises continuous surveillance of the agent, here intervention in the activities of the agent only occurs in matters of political importance to the principal. "Congressional Oversight Overlooked: Police Patrols vs. Fire Alarms," *American Journal of Political Science* 28, no. 1 (February 1984): 165–79.

Societal Actors in the One-Party System

This depiction of party politics in communist Hungary makes clear that while the Marxist-Leninist system deprived societal agents of effective voice via the electoral system, it supplied a number of institutional channels through which local agents vulnerable to economic adjustment could secure particularistic favors from state agencies. The dynamics of selective intervention from the top further enhanced the political position of these actors. What was most likely to sound the "fire alarm" and engage Party leaders' attention were claims by workers and enterprise managers that market reforms were elevating the danger of mass unemployment, inflation, and other maladies likely to create a general social crisis and imperil the Party's political hegemony.

Particularistic bargaining with state agencies and provocation of Party intervention were by no means costless tactics. As I already noted, appeals to higher authorities ran the risk of prompting the disapprobation of Party elites. Moreover, agents who employed these methods incurred organizational costs if they sought out allies. Coalitions of actors could more readily "raise the decibel level" to capture the attention of Party leaders than could single agents working in isolation. Building and sustaining such coalitions demanded expenditures of time and political resources. Referral strategies also entailed certain informational costs. Appeals for central intervention were more apt to elicit sympathetic responses if they were accompanied by credible data and sophisticated economic analysis. But such tactics enjoyed clear advantages over Polish-type mass mobilization and other political methods requiring higher levels of collective action. By generating specific financial concessions and regulatory exemptions, they enabled societal actors to avert free riding and minimize dispersion of benefits.

Societal agents who stood to gain from market reforms, notably high-skill workers and enterprise managers, similarly looked to nonelectoral modes of interest articulation during the final years of communist rule in Hungary. But whereas antireform actors relied on *political* maneuvers aimed at securing individual exceptions from market rules, proreform elements favored *economic* "exit" strategies. For skilled workers, the Communist Party's loosening of controls on informal activities created opportunities for exit to the second economy, where wage rates were less heavily regulated than in the traditional state sector.[52] For entrepreneurial man-

---

52. David Stark, "Bending the Bars of the Iron Cage: Bureaucratization and Informalization in Capitalism and Socialism," *Sociological Forum* 4, no. 4 (1989): 637–64; Stark, "Coexisting Organizational Forms in Hungary's Emerging Mixed Economy," in Victor Nee

agers, the Party's liberalization of ownership laws generated opportunities to form partnerships, joint stock companies, and other variants of what came to be known derisively as "*nomenklatura* capitalism." This process of "socialist embourgeoisement" caused divisions within the ranks of workers and managers in market socialist systems.[53] Local agents with fungible skills could protect themselves from the effects of adjustment by supplementing their regular wages with second economy incomes. Workers and managers burdened with immobile assets remained tied down to the state sector, limiting their possibilities for individualistic economic strategies and heightening their dependence on political means of defending their interests.

The collapse of communism left promarket elements in a *far* stronger position than these latter agents. The private sector, particularly small-scale enterprises, continued to expand after 1989, enlarging the range of exit opportunities for workers and managers possessing fungible assets. Yet the transition left antireform actors in the lurch. Their immobile economic assets kept them tied down to the state sector, which was now undergoing massive contraction as a result of the collapse of the CMEA and the Soviet market. At the same time, the demise of the Communist Party unhinged the institutional links that formed the basis of their political strategy of particularistic bargaining.

Democratic Institutions and Market Reform

I turn now to the impact of political transformation on East European economic policy. How did democratization affect the course of stabilization, adjustment, and reform? In the early postcommunist years, a number of Western scholars predicted that democratization in the region would elevate political barriers to economic reform in Eastern Europe. My institutional analysis indicates that it did precisely the opposite.

I focus on the dynamics of negotiated transitions. Like many countries in Southern Europe and Latin America, Hungary, Poland, and Czechoslovakia became multiparty democracies by way of negotiations between outgoing regime elites and representatives of the political opposition. The speed and magnitude of communism's demise created far greater opportunities for institutional innovation in East Central Europe than had existed in the capitalist South, where the transition from authoritarian rule

---

and David Stark, eds., *Remaking the Economic Institutions of Socialism: China and Eastern Europe* (Stanford: Stanford University Press, 1989), 137–68.

53. The seminal work on the socioeconomic consequences of ownership reform in communist Eastern Europe is Iván Szelényi, *Socialist Entrepreneurs: Embourgeoisement in Rural Hungary* (Madison: University of Wisconsin Press, 1988).

occurred gradually and with substantial organizational continuity. However, this wide latitude for institutional choice in the postcommunist countries was coupled with unusually high political uncertainty. In Hungary, the tension between choice and uncertainty yielded an institutional configuration that *strengthened* successor governments' capacity to implement politically unpopular reforms—notwithstanding the advent of a credible electoral constraint.

I further argue that democratization *weakened* the ability of local agents to defend themselves against the distributional effects of market reforms—contrary to conventional wisdom that the advent of democratic institutions would unleash popular resistance to marketization. While democratization greatly expanded means for citizens to articulate their grievances through the ballot box, it circumscribed opportunities for collective action via *nonelectoral* modes. The communist regimes left in their wake societies bereft of robust, independent civil associations—the "mesolevel" institutions that in mature Western democracies perform the vital functions of buffering social demands and mediating between grassroots agents and national parties. The result was to channel distributional politics into the electoral arena, where the segments of East European society *most* vulnerable to economic adjustment were *least* well represented in the early postcommunist years.

Democracy and the State

As we have seen, the particularistic bias of the communist state emanated from two institutional features of Marxism-Leninism. One was the system of central economic planning, which created rampant shortages and assigned to the state a multitude of functions that it could not fulfill. This system resulted in an array of illicit supply networks aimed at plugging bottlenecks left by the formal allocation system and in individualized negotiations between state bureaucrats and enterprise managers over resource distribution. The second source of institutional particularism was single-party rule. The Communist Party's penetration of the bureaucracy obliterated any meaningful separation between party and state. While use of state institutions as instruments of mass terror ceased in most of the region after Stalin's death, "socialist legality" in the East remained something of a misnomer. The Communist Party's continued claim of a "leading role" in socialist society, the lack of constitutional checks on its power, and the absence of organized opposition meant that the Party's political authority was essentially unlimited. The state enjoyed greater legal independence than before, but there was nothing to stop Party officials from exploiting state resources to advance their own ends.

In short, the communist state was pervasive but weak. The state's formal juridical reach was vast, but the exigencies of central planning and the nature of Communist Party rule rendered it vulnerable to penetration by local agents and Party elites. The theoretical problem at hand is to determine whether and how democratization transformed the particularistic bias of the East European states.

Guillermo O'Donnell succinctly describes the fundamental distinction between the state's position in authoritarian versus democratic systems. In the former, the state becomes a medium for privatized "circuits of power." Such regimes *can* be "representative" in the sense that state agencies serve the needs of local constituencies. But this form of representativeness comes at the expense of the public, national character of the state. In Latin America, the private capture of state institutions enabled capitalists to undertake "anticipatory hedging" and other defensive measures that hampered the ability of authoritarian governments to implement stabilization and adjustment programs.[54] By contrast, the juridical authority of the state in a proper democratic order is universalistic. In principle, the laws enforced by the state apply equally to all citizens and can be invoked by anyone, irrespective of his or her position in society. As O'Donnell puts it, "Against the truncated legality of the authoritarian state, that of the democratic state . . . is complete; it 'closes' its own circuits by the universalistic application of its rules even against other state organizations."[55]

O'Donnell notes that institutional remnants of authoritarian rule have prevented most of the new Latin American democracies from fully realizing the ideal of universal law. Instead, these countries exhibit uneasy mixtures of democratic and authoritarian elements, with formal voting rights intermixed with limited civil liberties. The result is "low-intensity citizenship," polities that fulfill the participatory dimension of polyarchies but lack the "state-as-law" quality of mature liberal democracies. This institutional configuration enables political elites to use state agencies for patronage and thereby to sustain the "system of privatized domination that has elected them."[56]

---

54. O'Donnell, "On the State, Democratization, and Some Conceptual Problems: A Latin American View with Glances at Some Postcommunist Countries," *World Development* 21, no. 8 (1993): 1365.

55. "On the State," 1360.

56. O'Donnell, "On the State," 1359, 1361.

Institutional Choice and Political Uncertainty
in Eastern Europe

The new democracies of Eastern Europe faced an altogether different set
of opportunities and challenges. The encompassing nature of the postcommunist transition created unprecedented possibilities for institutional
innovation. Institutional choices made in the initial phase of the transition
had profound consequences for both the short-term electoral fortunes of
political agents and long-term democratic consolidation. For this reason,
decisions over constitutional design, electoral rules, and political control
of the bureaucracy became a subject of intense bargaining between new
contestants in Eastern Europe's democratic game.

Rational choice theory permits scholars to deduce the institutional
preferences of interlocutors in negotiated transitions. For example, Arend
Lijphart hypothesizes that the exigencies of power sharing in Eastern
Europe would induce both outgoing communist elites and new entrants to
choose presidentialism and proportional representation over parliamentarism and majoritarian electoral systems.[57] Similarly, Barbara Geddes
surmises that Communist Party leaders would look to presidentialism as a
means of sustaining their power in a democratic polity, particularly if they
have nationally visible candidates well-positioned to win popular elections. But she contends that Communists would prefer majoritarian electoral rules, reasoning that individual candidates would be able to win seats
in single-member districts by tapping the Party's preexisting local machinery while downplaying the Communist Party label. Small parties lacking
grassroots organizations and well-known candidates would push for
closed-list proportional representation.[58]

But while rational choice models are useful for sketching out the initial bargaining positions of actors, they do not adequately explain the
actual outcomes of Eastern Europe's negotiated transitions. The only
country that fulfilled Lijphart's hypothesis concerning the allure of presi-
dentialism/proportional representation in new democracies was Poland.
Czechoslovakia chose a moderate proportional representation system but
also embraced a constitutional framework skewed toward parliamentary
power. Hungary meanwhile opted for a highly centralized prime ministerial government and a mixed electoral system with strong majoritarian ele-

---

57. "Democratization and Constitutional Choices in Czechoslovakia, Hungary, and
Poland," *Journal of Theoretical Politics* 4, no. 2 (April 1992): 208–13.

58. Geddes, "Institutional Choice in Post-Communist Eastern Europe" (paper presented at the annual meeting of the American Political Science Association, Washington,
D.C., September 1993), 11–13.

ments. In both of the latter cases, outgoing communist leaders operated from a significantly weaker negotiating position than their Polish counterparts, who parlayed uncertainty over the Soviet Union's response and extracted a deal incommensurate with their actual electoral strength—which was then revealed in the crushing defeat of the Polish United Workers' Party in the June 1989 election.[59] Ignorance, miscalculation, and unintended consequences played a central part in the East European transitions. Hungary's reform Communists, overestimating their actual strength, pushed for majoritarian electoral rules under the assumption they would emerge as the majority party. Representatives of the Hungarian opposition, underestimating their strength, pushed for a proportional representation formula to ensure their representation in the new Parliament. In the end, the interlocutors agreed to split the difference, yielding a numbingly complex electoral system. The actual results of Hungary's founding elections defied the expectations of both sides. The majoritarian bias of the electoral system ended up hurting the Communists—who had argued most aggressively for single-member constituencies—while benefitting the opposition parties that had opposed them.[60] In other cases, notably Bulgaria, negotiators advanced positions that were "irrational" from the standpoint of their objective electoral interests. Factors outside conventional rational choice models shaped institutional choices throughout the region. For example, Hungary and other postcommunist countries adopted high parliamentary thresholds, constructive no-confidence, and other mechanisms that had proven successful in postwar West Germany. In these instances, negotiators were guided less by short-term electoral strategizing than by empirical precedents of stable institutional arrangements.[61]

These results underscore the fact that while East European political elites enjoyed unusual latitude for institutional choice, they operated under exceptionally high uncertainty.[62] Unlike Latin America, where

---

59. Lijphart, "Democratization and Constitutional Choices," 214.

60. Jon Elster, "Bargaining Over the Presidency," *East European Constitutional Review* 2, no. 4 (fall 1993); 3, no. 1 (winter 1994): 95–98.

61. Herbert Kitschelt, "Explaining the Choice of Electoral Laws in New Democracies: The Experience of Southern and Eastern Europe" (paper presented at the Eighth International Conference of Europeanists, Council for European Studies, Chicago, Ill., March 1992), 22, 26–28; Lijphart, "Democratization and Constitutional Choices," 218.

62. Valerie Bunce and Mária Csanádi write that "fluidity and uncertainty are *the* fundamental characteristics of the transitional period. As such, they should be treated not as amendments to data collected, arguments made, and generalizations drawn, but, rather, as *the* point of departure for analyzing post-communism." "Uncertainty in the Transition: Post-Communism in Hungary," *East European Politics and Societies* 7, no. 2 (spring 1993): 273.

opposition parties had functioned (albeit in limited forms) in many countries during the authoritarian period and whose class structures created relatively predictable constituent bases, Eastern Europe's multiparty systems had to be essentially rebuilt from scratch.[63] Burdened with inchoate party organizations, weak voter loyalties, and high electoral volatility, postcommunist political leaders had little confidence that the actual course of events would validate their initial institutional strategies. External contingencies generated additional uncertainty. In contrast to Latin America (whose transition to democracy encountered no external threat) and Southern Europe (whose transition benefited greatly from the support of the European Community), Eastern Europe's democratization faced an array of external constraints: first, anxiety over the credibility of Mikhail Gorbachev's renunciation of the Brezhnev Doctrine; next, the disruptive effects of the disintegration of the USSR and the Balkan War; finally, skepticism over the readiness of the Western countries to support political and economic reform in the region.

In short, while partisan interests obviously shape deliberations over institutional design, negotiated transitions entail more than cui bono: the choices of political elites reflect both assessments of their immediate electoral impact and hedging against unforeseen consequences that may foil those initial calculations. Under conditions of high uncertainty, actors may rationally pursue strategies of *self-binding:* they voluntarily accept institutional constraints on their own power in order to reduce uncertainty.[64] In the following section of this chapter, I examine how these dynamics were played out in the East European countries, which grappled with an exceptional degree of uncertainty during the early postcommunist period.[65]

---

63. Geddes, "Institutional Choice in Post-Communist Eastern Europe," 20–25.

64. For a theoretical analysis of the role of institutions in reducing uncertainty in democratic polities, see North, *Institutions, Institutional Change, and Economic Performance,* 36–45, 85–86, 111. For an application of this line of argument to Western democracies, see Douglass North and Barry Weingast, "Constitutions and Commitment: The Evolution of Institutions Governing Public Choice in Seventeenth-Century England," *Journal of Economic History* 49, no. 4 (December 1989): 803–32.

65. I concur with Jon Elster's dismissal of the unduly cynical view of some rational choice theorists that *all* positions advanced by political actors are motivated purely by self-interest, even when cloaked in the guise of impartial collective welfare. Actors' motives are in reality mixed: some are entirely selfish, others reflect concern over collective interests, others are altruistic, and still others are "irrational"; see Elster, "Constitution-Making in Eastern Europe: Rebuilding the Boat in the Open Sea," *Public Administration* 71 (spring/summer 1993): 191. But the argument I develop here does not rest on the assumption of mixed motives. Rather, I contend that under conditions of high uncertainty, self-interested actors may "rationally" accept constraints on their own exercise of power.

Negotiated Transitions and Democratic Institutions

Constitutions, according to Jon Elster, are "collective acts of self-binding": their essential purpose is to constrain actors from yielding to short-term impulses that may compromise the long-term collective welfare of the body politic.[66] The main dilemma of constitution writing is devising a process that shields institutional choices from political contamination. Several Western countries sought to resolve this problem by creating constitutional assemblies, which were composed of appointed delegates rather than sitting legislators and which were dissolved as soon as their deliberations were completed.[67] The challenges of constitution writing were far more daunting in the East European countries, which not only faced the unique exigencies of the "triple transition"[68] but confronted strong pressures quickly to establish effective governance structures.

These tensions manifested themselves differently in the postcommunist countries. Poland encountered special problems as the first East European country to throw off the communist yoke. Uncertainty over the Soviet Union's response, overestimation of the power of the Polish United Workers' Party, and underestimation of their own electoral potential led Solidarity leaders to accept a deal far more modest than the actual balance of forces dictated. Two of their concessions—the agreement to reserve 65 percent of the seats in the Sejm for the Communists and to elect General Wojciech Jaruzelski as president—were subsequently corrected. But the third—Solidarity's decision to defer key constitutional questions until after the founding elections—had lasting consequences. By the time the Polish authorities got around to framing a new constitution, Solidarity had split apart, Lech Walesa had been elected president, and members of Parliament were embroiled in conflicts over the balance of executive and legislative power and the institutional prerogatives of the two houses of Parliament itself. The failure of the Polish interlocutors to settle these questions during the initial negotiations politicized the constitution-writing process, placing incumbent politicians in a position of writing the rules under which they themselves were playing. Poland's "Little Constitution," approved in 1992, showed the effects of legislative logrolling and institutional turf protection.[69]

66. Elster, "Constitutional Courts and Central Banks: Suicide Prevention or Suicide Pact?" *East European Constitutional Review* 3, nos. 3–4 (summer–fall 1994): 67.

67. Elster, "Constitution-Making in Eastern Europe," 178–86.

68. Claus Offe, "Capitalism by Design? Democratic Theory Facing the Triple Transition in East Central Europe," *Social Research* 58, no. 4 (winter 1991): 865–87.

69. Elster, "Constitution-Making in Eastern Europe," 200–213; Stephen Holmes, "The Postcommunist Presidency," *East European Constitutional Review* 2, no. 4 (fall 1993); 3, no. 1 (winter 1994): 36–39.

While the uncertainty attending Poland's transition compromised its constitutional process, Solidarity's ability to oust the Polish United Workers' Party in 1989 without provoking Soviet intervention cleared the way for the other East European countries to initiate their transitions. Gorbachev's refusal to intervene on behalf of the Polish Communists lowered the perceived risks of challenging the ruling parties, emboldening opposition groups to press for harsher deals. In fall 1989, the Honecker regime in East Germany collapsed under pressure of mass mobilization, and the German Democratic Republic (GDR) was quickly absorbed into the Federal Republic. By that time, Czechoslovakia's neo-Stalinist regime also found itself in a weak negotiating position, allowing the Civic Forum to set the main terms of the country's transition to democracy. The Czech-Slovak split proved the chief obstacle to the formation of a liberal constitution, an issue that was finally resolved in 1992 with the decision of republican authorities to separate into two countries. The Bulgarian Communists emerged from the transition in a much stronger position, even managing to win the first multiparty elections in 1990. Subsequently, conflicts over minority rights hindered Bulgaria's constitutional process. The Romanian Revolution also yielded a constitutional process sorely lacking in liberal elements, as the National Salvation Front unilaterally imposed conditions for the election of a constitutional assembly.[70]

Hungary enjoyed a number of advantages over the other East European countries. Unlike Czechoslovakia, Bulgaria, and Romania, Hungary's constitutional process was not burdened by simmering ethnic-national tensions. And unlike countries where communist power ended as a result of sudden implosion (e.g., Romania, Russia), Hungarian state structure remained basically intact amid the political transition. In the former cases, both state structure and rules governing political control of the bureaucracy were up for grabs. Under these circumstances, the potential for partisan manipulation of state agencies was exceptionally high. With the old state structure in disarray, the key institutions of macroeconomic control were ineffectual and/or vulnerable to capture by political elites. The economic consequences—fiscal crises, hyperinflation, capital flight—fueled social instability and invited restoration of authoritarian rule. At the same time, the process of writing constitutions stood at great risk of degenerating into a political free-for-all between old and new elites preoccupied with advancing their individual positions. As a consequence, the new constitutions reflected little more than the balance of forces among current contestants in the democratic game—an outcome bound to be

---

70. Elster, "Constitution-Making in Eastern Europe," 188–91.

viewed as unfair and illegitimate by major elements of the postcommunist society.

In Hungary and Poland, state structure itself was comparatively stable to the degree that the institutional holdovers from the communist period were capable of performing the basic administrative functions—collecting taxes, controlling the money supply, delivering public services—that were essential for economic and social stability. Moreover, the reforms initiated by the outgoing regimes allowed state agencies to build technically competent staffs and acquire valuable experience in market-type regulation, factors that would enhance successor governments' ability to accelerate market liberalization without prompting a general economic collapse. But while the administrative structures of these states remained essentially intact amid the transition, the political entity that guided their activities—a hegemonic Marxist-Leninist party—had been swept away. Thus, the rules governing political control of the state were subject to negotiation.

Here, the timing and circumstances of Hungary's transition give it a significant edge over Poland. Soviet acceptance of Poland's electoral results encouraged Hungarian opposition radicals to reject the moderates' and reform Communists' compromise decision to hold popular presidential elections, which the Communists expected to win. The radicals staged a national referendum on the presidential question, paving the way for the establishment of a strong prime ministerial government. This and other key institutional questions were basically settled by the time of Hungary's founding elections in spring 1990.

Hungary's distinctive "path of extrication"[71] from communism was crucial insofar as it created incentives and opportunities for negotiators to fashion rules designed to check each other's ability to manipulate political institutions for partisan purposes. After the founding election, which disclosed their actual political standing, Poland's contestants continued to haggle over the constitutional setup and electoral rules. With their true electoral status now revealed, and with a large range of institutional issues still unresolved, actors were strongly inclined to seek arrangements that would either lock in their advantages or compensate for their liabilities. By contrast, Hungarian negotiators operated under a Rawlsian "veil of ignorance." Like any other political agents, the leaders of Hungary's successor parties naturally preferred electoral rules that would maximize their legislative representation. But because the first election had not yet occurred, they could not ascertain with any confidence exactly which set of rules

---

71. This term comes from László Bruszt and David Stark, "Paths of Extrication and Possibilities of Transformation," *Working Papers on Transitions from State Socialism,* Cornell University, #91.5, July 1991.

would in fact optimize their electoral position. This created incentives to devise balanced formulas aimed at hedging against potential losses—hence Hungary's intricate mixture of proportional representation and majoritarianism. It also generated inducements to establish institutional safeguards against penetration of the state by governing parties. This was demonstrated by the decision of the interlocutors to terminate party control of the military, place security agencies under the control of the Council of Ministers, and establish a Constitutional Court endowed with wide powers to void acts of Parliament. The negotiators were not yet sitting legislators, nor did they occupy positions in the state administration—which meant that their choices were not contaminated by the imperatives of defending institutional prerogatives. Obviously, the winners of the elections would be well positioned to dominate legislative deliberation on any remaining institutional questions. But once the elections were completed, constitutional amendments faced a higher hurdle—in Hungary's case a two-thirds majority in the Parliament—which reinforced incentives for agents to use the preelectoral period to lock in rules providing mutual checks. And whatever institutional choices the new governing parties made would enjoy the imprimatur of a popular mandate, subject to qualifications by a parliamentary opposition that had accepted the results of the founding elections as legitimate.

Multiparty Democracy, State Institutions, and Economic Reform

The tension between choice and uncertainty that animated Eastern Europe's negotiated transitions had important consequences for the profile of the region's political institutions and the trajectory of economic reform policy in the early 1990s. As I describe in detail in chapter 4, Hungary's transition yielded an institutional framework that gave successor governments a high capacity to execute market reforms carrying heavy distributional costs. The electoral rules favored a small number of parliamentary parties, facilitating the formation of stable governing coalitions. The constitutional setup concentrated executive authority in the prime minister's office, enhancing party discipline and strengthening the leadership's ability to formulate coherent policy programs. Decisions related to the state administration after the founding elections were held reinforced this institutional configuration, bolstering institutions charged with global economic regulation—notably the Ministry of Finance and the central bank—at the expense of branch ministries and other agencies responsible for particular sectors of local industry.

This institutional setup prompted concerns about the possibility of latent authoritarianism. The exaggerated disproportionality of Hungary's electoral system allowed the winner of the first postcommunist elections, the Magyar Demokrata Fórum (Hungarian Democratic Forum, or MDF), to parlay its 24.7 percent plurality into 42.5 percent of all parliamentary seats. The victor of the second national elections in 1994, the MSZP, transformed a 33 percent vote into a 54 percent legislative majority.[72] But while such features weakened the representative dimension of Hungary's new democracy, they also enhanced governance by giving political leaders the security of tenure needed to implement reform programs whose benefits would take years to materialize.

The institutional outcomes of Hungary's negotiated transition created another, equally serious problem: while the country's centralized prime ministerial system served to insulate successor governments from particularistic demands from below, it also created new opportunities for exploitation of state resources from above. Notwithstanding constitutional guarantees of the bureaucracy's independence, the concentration of executive authority in the prime minister's office threatened to undermine the universalistic elements of the Hungarian state by increasing its vulnerability to capture by the governing parties. The risk of partisan manipulation of the state was particularly high in Eastern Europe, a region burdened by a long authoritarian tradition and a poorly developed "democratic culture." Since 1989, such manipulation was manifested by attempts of leaders of successor governments to purge bureaucrats associated with the communist regimes, stack state agencies with political loyalists, and pressure the organizations overseeing privatization to arrange favorable deals for supporters.

But while democratization did not eliminate such practices, it did alleviate them. The presence of a robust parliamentary opposition and a liberalized press raised the political costs of exploiting state resources by ensuring that abuses would be revealed. Periodic elections provided an additional check on political leaders by enabling opposition parties to hold incumbent governments' behavior up for public scrutiny. In this respect, the position of Eastern Europe's successor governments differed dramatically from that of the communist parties, whose freedom from any kind of electoral constraint allowed them to plunder state resources with impunity.

---

72. Andrew Arato, "Elections, Coalitions, and Constitutionalism in Hungary: Disproportionality and the Danger of Constitutional Dictatorship," *East European Constitutional Review* 3, nos. 3–4 (summer–fall 1994): 26–32.

Interest Representation under Multiparty Democracy

Democratization also fundamentally altered the institutional underpinnings of interest representation in Eastern Europe. Some scholars contend that the transition from communism to democracy intensified distributional conflicts by enlarging grievance articulation opportunities for actors adversely affected by economic change.[73] The institutional theory developed in this chapter suggests otherwise. As my earlier discussion of the communist period indicated, such conflicts were pervasive in reformed communist countries like Hungary but took the form of particularistic claims on state agencies by workers and enterprise managers. The decisive point concerns not the existence of distributional clashes, since they are inevitable in Eastern Europe's economic transition, but where and how they are mediated. I argue that while the transition to democracy greatly expanded possibilities for interest representation through the electoral system, it narrowed opportunities for citizens to articulate their preferences via civil associations. The institutional weakness of East European civil society, not the "authoritarian" tendencies of centralized prime ministerial systems like Hungary, thus emerged as the main obstacle to democratic consolidation in the region.

While participation in the "elections" staged by the communist parties exacted a heavy psychic toll on the citizens of the region,[74] the organizational and informational costs of electoral participation were lower than those of multiparty democracies. On the one hand, the ruling party's extensive and deeply penetrating array of "transmission belts" facilitated mobilization of voters. On the other hand, the lack of a legal opposition reduced the informational demands of electoral politics by precluding the need for voters to make informed decisions. As we have seen, "interest representation," broadly conceived, was not wholly absent in the communist systems, but it assumed the guise of individualized bargaining between local agents and party/state institutions.

As a result of the political transition, East European voters enjoyed a much wider array of electoral choices. But the costs of political action via the party system were markedly higher. These costs included financing campaigns, building grassroots organizations, collecting and disseminat-

---

73. Andrew Arato, "Revolution, Civil Society, and Democracy: Paradoxes in the Recent Transition in Eastern Europe," *Working Papers on Transitions from State Socialism,* Cornell University, #90.5, 1990; Grzegorz Ekiert, "Democratization Processes in East Central Europe: A Theoretical Reconsideration," *British Journal of Political Science* 21, part 3 (July 1991): 285–313.

74. See the essays of Václav Havel in *Living in Truth,* ed. Jan Vladislav (London: Faber and Faber, 1989).

ing the information needed to make discriminating choices, forging party loyalty amid weak voter identities and high cynicism, and mobilizing apathetic voters in an environment where "voluntary exclusion"[75] from electoral politics was now permissible. The specific historical circumstances facing Eastern Europe's new democracies magnified the costs of party politics. In Romania, Bulgaria, and Czechoslovakia, where neo-Stalinist regimes had suppressed all organized opposition, competitive party systems had to be built from scratch. In Poland and Hungary, the new contestants in the electoral arena had to navigate the uneasy passage from opposition movements to credible political parties.

Not only was political mobilization through the party system costlier after 1989 than before. Owing to the institutional legacies of communism, the losers of market reform found themselves more dependent on political parties to represent their interests. Under communism, societal actors did enjoy limited opportunities for collective bargaining via trade unions, enterprise associations, and other intermediary organizations. But with few exceptions (e.g., Poland's Solidarity), these institutions were controlled by the Communist Party. This meant two things. First, to the extent local agents sought to advance their interests through collective action, they could do so only through Party-dominated institutions, on terms approved by Party leaders. Second, the end of communist rule left East European society without a preexisting infrastructure of independent interest associations. Indeed, the weakness of organized civil society throughout the region was the most striking institutional legacy of communism. Interest representation via mesolevel institutions was limited to (1) the legal successors of the old communist-controlled associations, whose ties to the discredited ancien régime restricted their legitimacy and political effectiveness, and (2) the new intermediary associations that emerged after 1989, which were large in number but severely hampered by high organizational fragmentation and weak financing. Thus the domain of representative politics was limited to the party system. In the absence of robust intermediary institutions, social demands were channeled into the national parties, which were already hampered by shallow organizational roots and onerous legislative agendas.

In short, the political power of the societal actors most vulnerable to market reforms—pensioners, blue-collar workers, traditional enterprise managers—was almost wholly derivative of the distinctive institutional structure of the communist system. The demise of that system at the end of

---

75. This term comes from Ellen Comisso, "Property Rights, Liberalism, and the Transition from 'Actually Existing' Socialism," *East European Politics and Societies* 5, no. 1 (winter 1991): 188.

the 1980s left these agents poorly positioned to protect themselves against the distributional fallout of market reforms.

And so, contrary to conventional wisdom, which argues that democratization in Eastern Europe imperiled marketization by *empowering* previously disenfranchised groups threatened by economic reform, my institutional analysis suggests that the transition to democracy *weakened* those actors. The nature of their economic assets foreclosed the option of exiting to the private sector, while the demise of the one-party system disrupted the political channels that insulated them from the socioeconomic effects of marketization. The evolution of postcommunist state institutions along the universalistic lines discussed earlier in this chapter further circumscribed the possibilities for particularistic bargaining. The organizational weakness of civil society curtailed the role of intermediary associations. These circumstances left antireform elements dependent on the party system, where the costs of political mobilization in the early postcommunist years were high.

The victory of former Communists in Hungary, Poland, Lithuania, and Bulgaria showed that an "electoral connection" *was* present in postcommunist Eastern Europe. Voters anxious about their economic future turned out in large numbers to oust governments that had enacted market reforms bearing high social costs. But as I show in chapter 7, these results did not deflect the general trajectory of reform in the East Central European countries—notwithstanding claims of the new socialist governments of their intention to decelerate marketization. Thus, while the advent of multiparty contestation in the East enhanced political *accountability* by subjecting incumbent governments to a credible electoral check, the *representative* dimension was deficient owing to a shortage of the independent civil associations vital for mediating between local agents and national party organizations.

Conclusion

A brief recap of the central arguments of this chapter follows.

First, broad regime types like "democracy" and "authoritarianism" tell us little about the relationship between political change and economic policy. Understanding the political economy of stabilization, adjustment, and reform requires disaggregation of regime types into specific institutional arrangements.

Second, application of new institutionalist theory to Eastern Europe demonstrates that the tension between political liberalization and economic transformation is less acute than commonly supposed. Indeed, institutional analysis suggests that democratization and marketization in the East are not only compatible, but that the former facilitates the latter.

Third, evaluation of institutions in terms of universalistic and particularistic models of the state yields important insights about the politics of market reform in Eastern Europe. Whereas institutional particularism fostered economic growth strategies in East Asia and China, it hindered austerity policy in communist Eastern Europe. Hungarian-type reforms deepened the particularistic bias of communist states by enlarging space for local agents to negotiate individual exceptions to market rules. Notwithstanding the ruling party's monopoly of collective authority in Marxist-Leninist regimes, the push-pull dynamic of market socialism thwarted efforts by reformed communist states to use market instruments for stabilization and adjustment policy.

Fourth, democratization dramatically changed the political dynamics of economic reform in the East, but not because it unleashed popular resistance to marketization. Rather, Eastern Europe's political transition severed the institutional links to state and party organizations that previously allowed vulnerable actors to secure compensation for distributional losses. The particular circumstances of Hungary's negotiated transition, which permitted interlocutors to settle most key institutional questions before the founding elections, strengthened the capacity of successor governments to pursue market reforms by concentrating executive authority in the prime minister's office and shifting the balance of power within the state toward agencies of global regulation.

Fifth, while Eastern Europe's political transition significantly enhanced accountability by confronting successor governments with a real electoral constraint, it weakened representation by deepening local actors' reliance on the party system to articulate their grievances. While multiparty contestation resulted in the ouster of incumbent governments in a number of postcommunist countries in the early 1990s, it did not compensate for the absence of effective intermediary associations. The weakness of organized civil society in Eastern Europe emerged as communism's most damaging institutional legacy.

I develop these themes in the forthcoming chapters on Hungary, whose long history of market reforms predating the political transition provides an ideal vehicle for examining the role of party and state institutions in economic transformations. In part 2, I show how institutional particularism undercut the Hungarian Communist Party's attempts to use market mechanisms as stabilization and adjustment instruments in the 1980s. In part 3, I explore the impact of democratization on economic reform, illustrating how democratic institutions lowered political barriers to austerity policy in the early 1990s. In part 4, I extend the book's institutional framework to generalize from the case study. I assess the implications of Hungary's experience for market and democracy in Eastern Europe, discuss the ramifications of the return to power of former Communists in the country's second democratic election, and compare Hungary's transition strategy with those of other former communist countries and the East Asian developmental states.

Part 2
Economic Reform in Communist Hungary, 1979–89

CHAPTER 2

Macroeconomic Stabilization under Reform Communism

In January 1968, Hungary launched NEM. Like other market socialist reforms, NEM was premised on the assumption that devolving decision-making authority to factory-level agents would heighten allocative efficiency. At the same time, maintaining the dominant position of socialist ownership would promote social equity and preserve the Communist Party's political hegemony.

The original intent of NEM was to spur economic growth and thereby bolster the ruling MSZMP, whose post-1956 strategy of consolidation hinged on improvements in the population's standard of living. For a brief period, the reforms fulfilled this objective, as the Hungarian economy enjoyed robust growth between 1968 and 1972. But subsequent upheavals in the world economy transformed the political economy of Hungary's market reforms. The Party's initial response was to halt NEM and raise large amounts of Western credit to insulate the economy from the external shocks. But this strategy of recentralization did not succeed, and continued deterioration of Hungary's balance of payments compelled the MSZMP to resume economic reform in 1979. The emphasis of this second phase of NEM was export expansion aimed at arresting the decline of Hungary's terms of trade. Communist Party leaders hoped that the new round of reforms would generate a growth of exports sufficient to correct the country's external imbalance without resort to macroeconomic restrictions.

Until early 1980, the reforms appeared to have met that objective. Yet this optimism was short lived, as flaws in the reform program and further setbacks in the international economy halted the surge in Hungarian exports. The country was soon mired in a severe liquidity crunch, and in spring 1982 it came very close to depleting all its hard currency reserves. Meanwhile, developments in Poland and Romania prompted Western banks to cut their credit lines to Eastern Europe. Hungary, despite its reputation for financial probity and commitment to avoid debt rescheduling, was included in the credit embargo.

55

These circumstances made clear that export promotion alone would not enable Hungary to overcome its balance-of-payments problems. In the wake of the 1982 liquidity crisis, the focus of reform policy shifted from economic growth to austerity. That year, Hungary joined the International Monetary Fund (IMF) and World Bank, under whose auspices the MSZMP initiated macroeconomic stabilization and structural adjustment programs. Thus began the third and final phase of NEM, whose key feature was the fusion of stabilization, adjustment, and market reform. The transformation of NEM from an agent of growth into an instrument of austerity had major consequences for the Hungarian economy and the Communist Party.

In this chapter, I examine the political economy of stabilization policy during the final decade of communist power in Hungary. I argue that NEM, while achieving important efficiency gains over the pre-1968 system, proved ineffective as vehicle of economic stabilization. The failure of NEM to stabilize the economy reflected the institutional logic of Hungary's market socialist model. Far from suppressing distributional conflicts, reform communism fostered them by providing local agents with institutional channels to secure compensation for the effects of austerity. Decentralization of microeconomic decision making induced enterprise managers and workers to bid up domestic purchasing power. The resultant deterioration of the balance of payments created pressure on the political leadership to restore central controls in order to meet the conditions of IMF standby agreements. But full restoration of the status quo ante was no longer possible, as the prior devolution of authority gave factory-level agents the means to resist recentralization. Thus, market reforms simultaneously prompted local actors to behave in ways contrary to the aims of stabilization policy and weakened the center's ability to correct those distortions via ex post administrative measures. This distinctive push-pull dynamic played a central role in the demise of Hungarian communism in the late 1980s: the socialist halfway house of NEM deepened Hungary's economic problems while accelerating the progressive unraveling of the MSZMP's political authority.

I focus on the following dimensions of stabilization policy: wage liberalization, monetary control, and fiscal policy. All three cases illustrate how the institutional structure of Hungarian communism defeated the MSZMP's efforts to use market mechanisms as stabilization instruments. Wage liberalization, the sine qua non of a real labor market, induced workers and enterprise managers to bid up wage rates, compromising macroeconomic stability and compelling the Party to recentralize incomes policy in the face of growing resistance from below. Attempts by the National Bank of Hungary to contract liquidity via Western-type monetary tools encountered stiff opposition by state enterprises and commercial banks, whose lobbying prompted Party leaders to intervene and force the monetary authorities to yield. Finally, efforts to reduce domestic absorption through fiscal policy failed, owing to the spending bias of communist state institutions and the political manipulation of the national budget by the ruling party.

Wage Liberalization

Raising allocative efficiency in Hungary's hybrid economy demanded reforms of the MSZMP's cumbersome system of wage controls. By allowing workers and enterprise managers to negotiate their own wage contracts, Communist Party officials hoped to create a more highly differentiated wage scale that would heighten labor mobility and productivity. But enacting wage liberalization within the institutional setting of market socialism generated macroeconomic distortions that jeopardized stabilization policy. With neither workers nor plant directors facing effective inducements to control labor costs, the result of the reforms was growth of the aggregate wage bill and expansion of domestic purchasing power. Reimposition of central controls then became necessary to restore equilibrium. But the decision-making authority already relinquished to the factory level created major obstacles to recentralization.

The wage reforms opened up political space for Hungarian workers, who had endured years of stagnating real income and who seized on the opportunity of the initial decentralization to secure compensatory wage increases. Wage liberalization also enlarged the bargaining power of enterprise managers, who had no compelling incentive to contain labor costs and who utilized their particularistic links to the Hungarian state to obtain exceptions from wage regulations. Thus, the introduction of market mechanisms into Hungary's labor system simultaneously thwarted stabilization policy and empowered local agents to resist the Party's efforts to correct economic distortions via recentralization.

Incomes Policy under NEM

Until the mid-1980s, the Hungarian wage regulation system closely resembled that of orthodox CPEs. This system was based on the separation of the enterprise and household money circuits. Enterprise money was "passive." With minor exceptions, state enterprises were forbidden to hold cash. All of their financial resources were held in accounts controlled by the central bank. By monitoring the flow of funds in and out of those accounts, the bank could determine whether enterprises were fulfilling the requirements of the plan. In this way, financial flows in the enterprise sector became the counterpart of physical processes specified in the plan, with deviations showing up as imbalances in the accounts supervised by the central bank. By contrast, household money was "active." Because possession of cash by the population did translate into purchasing power, control of the household money supply was a vital concern of central planners. But this macroeconomic objective was achieved through microeconomic means. The central bank controlled the flow of cash to the population by carefully monitoring the enterprise wage fund, the primary channel through which currency entered into circulation. Monetary policy in Soviet-type economies thus reduced to incomes policy.[1]

The 1968 reforms abolished administrative restrictions on labor mobility in Hungary; workers in state enterprises no longer required formal permission to switch jobs. Enterprise managers meanwhile acquired greater discretion over wage setting. But wage regulation in the first phase of NEM remained very rigid. The center prescribed upper limits to the average wage level, which meant that plant directors who wished to raise the salaries of outstanding employees or recruit high-wage workers had to compensate by hiring unskilled, low-wage workers. Restricting average wages in this manner not only enabled the center to contain the total emission of household cash through the enterprise wage fund. By forcing directors to pad their payrolls with low-cost labor, the authorities could maintain the Communist Party's full employment guarantee, one of the bulwarks of János Kádár's postrevolutionary "social contract."[2]

At the same time, strict income regulations deprived Hungarian workers of institutional means of collective bargaining over wages. The Party's decision to keep tight reins on organized labor reflected its keen sensitivity to the experience of 1956, when independent workers' councils

---

1. George Garvy, *Money, Financial Flows, and Credit in the Soviet Union* (Cambridge: Harvard University Press, 1977), 13–35, 76–77, 157–58; Paul Gregory and Robert Stuart, *Soviet Economic Structure and Performance* (New York: Harper and Row, 1981), 141; Mieczyslaw Kucharski, "Money in the Socialist Economy," in Zdzislaw Fedorowicz, ed., *Problems of Economic Theory and Practice in Poland: Finances and Banking* (Warsaw: Polish Scientific, 1968), 49–100; T. M. Podolski, *Socialist Banking and Monetary Control: The Experience of Poland* (Cambridge: Harvard University Press, 1973), 335–354; Adam Zwass, *Money, Banking, and Credit in the Soviet Union and Eastern Europe* (White Plains, N.Y.: M. E. Sharpe, 1979), 3–23.

2. Iván Berend, *The Hungarian Economic Reforms, 1953–1988* (Cambridge: Cambridge University Press, 1990), 180–81; Paul Hare, "The Evolution of Wage Regulation in Hungary," in Hare, Hugo Radice, and Nigel Swain, *Hungary: A Decade of Reform* (London: Allen and Unwin, 1981), 55–80; Gábor Révész, *Perestroika in Eastern Europe: Hungary's Economic Transformation, 1945–1988* (Boulder: Westview, 1990), 76–77.

played an integral part in the popular uprising.[3] Workers seeking to counteract the socioeconomic effects of reform had to resort to nonwage strategies, namely seeking freezes of consumer prices. During the conservative backlash against NEM in the early 1970s, trade union organizations lobbied aggressively for recentralization of prices.[4]

While the post-1968 system advanced the center's goal of checking growth of aggregate wage payments, it severely undermined factory-level efficiency. The cap on average earnings kept wage differentials at levels far lower than in market economies. The wage differential between Hungarian white-collar and blue-collar workers was only 5 to 10 percent, compared with 30 to 70 percent in Western countries.[5] The inability of plant managers to recruit and reward highly skilled workers suppressed worker productivity. Economists estimated that labor productivity in Hungary was 40 to 50 percent below that of the advanced industrialized countries.[6] Income leveling also impeded worker mobility, preventing the emergence of a genuine labor market and hindering the structural changes in the workforce that were needed to bring Hungarian industry up to world standards.

In the 1980s, MSZMP leadership initiated a series of wage reforms aimed at rectifying these distortions. The design of these reforms reflected the tension between wage liberalization and macroeconomic control. In the early part of the decade, the authorities replaced caps on average wages with controls on total wage payments, hoping to preserve control of aggregate purchasing power while removing the constraints on income differentials that were impeding structural adjustment within the enterprise sector.[7] In 1987, they created a "wage fund" comprised of enterprises that would be exempted from regulations by meeting certain profitability and hard currency export requirements.[8] The following year, they proposed a radical wage reform that would abolish all rules on wage setting and leave the negotiation of wage contracts entirely to trade unions and enterprise

3. Stephan Noti, "The Shifting Position of Hungarian Trade Unions Amidst Social and Economic Reforms," *Soviet Studies* 39, no. 1 (January 1987): 65.

4. Károly Soós, "Wage Bargaining and the 'Policy of Grievances': A Contribution to the Explanation of the First Halt in the Reform of the Hungarian New Economic Mechanism in 1969," *Soviet Studies* 39, no. 3 (July 1987): 440.

5. "Attempt to Freeze Wages in Response to Worsening Economic Indicators," *Radio Free Europe/Radio Liberty Hungarian Situation Reports* (hereafter cited as *RFE/RL Hungarian Situation Reports*), 23 December 1986, 22.

6. "Full Employment versus Economic Efficiency," *RFE/RL Hungarian Situation Reports,* 25 February 1987, 33.

7. Berend, *The Hungarian Economic Reforms,* 263–64.

8. "Official Comments on Wage Reform Issues," *Foreign Broadcast Information Service/Eastern Europe* (hereafter cited as *FBIS/EEU*), 28 October 1987, 18.

management. To encourage plant directors to contain growth of total labor costs, the authorities introduced an "entrepreneurial tax" whereby all increments to the enterprise wage bill would be added to profits and taxed at 50 percent.[9]

Responses of State Enterprises

The aim of the entrepreneurial tax was to enhance financial discipline and regulatory normativity by subjecting all state enterprises to a simple, universal rule prescribing the consequences of excessive wage disbursements. But plant directors retained a variety of institutional channels through which they could bargain for adjustments of their tax liabilities and for compensation for whatever penalties they incurred as a result of high wage bills. Moreover, with labor costs and profits subject to the same unified tax, managers had every incentive to permit their wage bills to rise without limit. Any increases in wage payments reduced net profits; if wages went up, taxable profits went down. Therefore, the net effect of the entrepreneurial tax on enterprises' tax liability was zero.[10]

The failure of Hungarian managers to exert countervailing pressure on labor's natural affinity for income growth complicated the task of wage reform. Fifteen years after the launching of NEM, enterprise managers remained largely impervious to increases in their wage bills, as soft budget constraints reduced incentives to economize on labor costs. With plant directors in the plan bargaining system still evaluated according to their fulfillment of the center's production goals, enterprises continued the practice, long characteristic of planned economies, of hoarding labor for deployment during rush periods. Consequently, labor demand remained very high under NEM, even in loss-making sectors targeted for downsizing by the MSZMP and the multilateral lending agencies. Efficient enterprises, lacking a well-developed capital market in which they could invest their profits, diverted all of their retained earnings toward the internal wage fund and purchases of new plant and equipment.[11] This generated constant pressure on Hungary's wage and investment bills, contraction of which was vital to the IMF stabilization program.

The institutional structure of the communist state delimited the Party's repertoire of macroeconomic instruments for checking this tendency of enterprises to bid up domestic consumption. Because the National Bank of Hungary lacked the political clout to conduct an inde-

---

9. Interview, Ministry of Finance, 13 July 1988.
10. Interview, National Bank of Hungary, 8 September 1988.
11. Márton Tardos, "The Conditions of Developing a Regulated Market," *Acta Oeconomica* 36, nos. 1–2 (1986): 80–81.

pendent monetary policy, the authorities relied on fiscal devices to regulate wage payments in the state sector. The Ministry of Finance performed annual audits of every state enterprise to determine whether wage disbursements for the year fell within the parameters set by central planners.[12] The ex post nature of this regulatory scheme circumscribed the center's ability to curtail gross domestic consumption. A year or more would pass before the authorities could detect excessive growth of the wage bill, by which time overpayments to workers represented currency already in circulation. Equally important, the individualized nature of the system meant that the prospect of year-end sanctions did not serve as an effective ex ante constraint on enterprises. Plant directors had little hesitation in bidding up their wage bills, confident they could bargain for exemptions from the Finance Ministry's regulations on the pretext that tax penalties would prevent them from meeting the Communist Party's production goals. In short, rather than spurring plant managers to increase productivity by widening the wage scale, the regulatory system induced them to lobby the center for exceptions to the parametric caps on their wage bills. Wage liberalization merely spawned new subjects of bargaining between the communist state and the enterprise sector.

Responses of Organized Labor

As Hungarian enterprise managers continued to exhibit a weak impulse to contain labor costs, workers seized on the Party's reform proposals to obtain wage increases to compensate for rising consumer prices and falling real income. Labor mobilization in Hungary in the late 1980s sharpened the tension between wage reform and stabilization policy. To the degree workers succeeded in bidding up the total wage bill, the authorities could not proceed with wage liberalization without compromising the macroeconomic balance. But their ability to restore wage controls was now limited by the growing power of organized labor.

This convergence of enterprise managers and workers toward wage growth underscored one of the decisive differences between capitalist economies and market socialist systems. Whereas plant directors in capitalist firms usually seek to contain their wage bills in order to maximize profits, Hungarian enterprise managers supported workers' efforts to loosen wage controls, as this strengthened their ability to bid for highly skilled workers in an already tight market. But while managers and workers become de facto allies in distributional conflicts over wage policy in the

---

12. Interviews, National Planning Office, 10 May 1988; National Bank of Hungary, 12 August 1988.

1980s, they employed different political tactics. The former responded to the MSZMP's wage reforms by negotiating individual exemptions from state regulations; the latter resorted to collective action.

In this respect, labor's position was unique in communist Hungary, where distributional politics typically assumed the form of particularistic bargaining between local agents and state agencies. But in contrast to Poland, where worker mobilization occurred through a fully independent trade union movement, in Hungary it took place through the Communist Party's trade union organization. This was politically consequential for two reasons. First, the fact that worker mobilization in the late communist period was spearheaded by the Party's own trade union hastened the disintegration of one of the MSZMP's key instruments of political control. Second, while the collective power of Hungarian workers was directed at the MSZMP, it was also highly *derivative* of that very same ruling party. Ironically, the demise of Hungarian communism, which was expedited by organized labor's challenges to the MSZMP, left workers without an independent organization to defend their interests in the postcommunist period.

The leaders of the Party-controlled trade union, Szakszervezetek Országos Tanacsa (National Council of Trade Unions, or SZOT), had on earlier occasions defended Hungarian workers against the effects of market reforms. In 1969, they allied with local Party secretaries and ideological conservatives on the Central Committee to push for reimposition of price controls, the first in a series of reversals leading to the suspension of NEM in 1972.[13] In late 1983, they pressed for wage indexation and increases in pensions to compensate for the austerity program begun the previous year.[14] SZOT's lobbying was instrumental in securing the Party's assent to a huge increase in industrial wages in December 1985.[15]

But SZOT had not in any sense functioned as an independent trade union. The organization's influence was derivative of the Communist Party itself. In the episodes already cited, the union's efforts to reverse reform policy converged with political currents within the MSZMP leadership. The modest wage reforms undertaken in the early 1980s did not alter SZOT's subordinate position in the single-party system or its role in income regulation. Hungarian workers still lacked independent means of collective bargaining, as wage contracts were negotiated by branch-level

---

13. Soós, "Wage Bargaining," 438–40.

14. Noti, "The Shifting Position of Hungarian Trade Unions," 79–80.

15. "Attempt to Freeze Wages in Response to Worsening Economic Indicators," *RFE/RL Hungarian Situation Reports,* 23 December 1986, 21.

representatives of SZOT, the Ministry of Industry, and the State Office for Wages and Labor.[16]

The IMF standby program launched in the late 1980s by the new Communist Party chief Károly Grósz altered the basic character of organized labor in Hungary. Grósz's stabilization program differed from the one undertaken in 1982–84 in that it explicitly acknowledged the need to reduce the population's standard of living.[17] The shift of the main burden of macroeconomic stabilization onto the population did not provoke Polish-style mass urban protests. However, it did catalyze a previously compliant trade union into open confrontation with the Communist Party. The leaders of SZOT found themselves uncomfortably wedged between two opposing forces: (1) a ruling party forced by economic circumstances to adopt an externally imposed austerity campaign, the centerpiece of which was deep reductions of real household income; and (2) an increasingly agitated working class whose interests the official union supposedly represented. The very trade union that had so long allowed MSZMP leaders to co-opt Hungarian workers had now become a political handicap: the Party could never gain the cooperation of wage earners for stabilization policy as long as they were deprived of effective means of interest representation. These tensions resulted in the transformation of SZOT into an organization willing and able to defy publicly the Communist Party to which it had long been allied.

Facing mounting agitation from rank-and-file members, the SZOT leadership formally proclaimed its independence from the Party in fall 1988, claiming that the MSZMP's subjugation of the union had distorted the goals of the organization and prevented it from effectively representing the interests of Hungarian workers. The SZOT leadership also initiated a set of internal reforms aimed at restoring the confidence of the labor force: elections by secret ballot, limitations of tenure in office for union leaders, and the right of factory-level units to determine the composition of higher bodies within the organization.[18]

The shift in SZOT's position triggered a series of public confrontations between the trade union and the Grósz regime that clearly demonstrated the progressive deterioration of the Party's authority. Armed with

---

16. David Bartlett, "Democracy, Institutional Change, and Stabilisation Policy in Hungary," *Europe-Asia Studies,* 48, no. 1 (January 1996): 54–57; Noti, "The Shifting Position of Hungarian Trade Unions," 68.

17. From *RFE/RL Hungarian Situation Reports:* "HSWP Announces Tough New Stabilization Program," 22 July 1987, 13–16; "The New Program: Where and What is It?" 19 September 1987, 7–11; "Hungary's Prime Minister Means Business," 3 October 1987, 3–7; "The National Assembly Heeds the Call," 3 October 1987, 9–14.

18. "Trade Unions' National Conference," *RFE/RL Hungarian Situation Reports,* 15 December 1988, 37–41.

its revamped policy platform, in December 1988 SZOT negotiated a new agreement with the political leadership. The Party committed itself to containing the 1989 inflation rate to 12 percent. As compensation for the rise in consumer prices, the authorities acceded to SZOT's demand for a 23 percent increase in the minimum wage. They also agreed to proceed with the proposed wage reform. In January 1989, the center formally released large enterprises, representing about 60 percent of the state sector, from all wage regulations.[19]

The main purpose of the latter measure was to heighten labor productivity by encouraging enterprise managers and trade unions to negotiate more highly differentiated wage scales. But because it was undertaken in the face of eroding household income, rising labor mobilization, and cost-insensitive state enterprises, wage reform produced wholly different effects. Far from promoting greater income differentiation, wage liberalization stimulated Hungarian workers to press for across-the-board wage hikes to compensate for the distributional effects of the IMF standby.

During its final year in power, the MSZMP found itself under incessant pressure for ad hoc wage increases from a labor movement spearheaded by the Party's own trade union organization. In spring 1989, the Grósz regime yielded to SZOT's demands to legalize strikes. The new labor code permitted strikes related to grievances within specific enterprises as well as sympathy strikes undertaken to protest broad economic policies, such as consumer price reform. The Party's acceptance of sympathy strikes was important insofar as it solidified the interests of Hungarian workers from different sectors in securing across-the-board increases in wage rates. The extent to which workers mobilized on a cross-sectoral basis impeded wage differentiation (and hence structural adjustment) and stimulated growth in the aggregate wage bill (thereby frustrating stabilization policy). The unions availed themselves of the new strike law to secure wage increases designed to neutralize price increases enacted by the Party. Union leaders insisted that wage liberalization had to accompany price reform, even at the risk of a wage-price spiral that would spur inflation and imperil the IMF stabilization program. SZOT's challenge to the Party visibly weakened Grósz's hand as he entered into formal negotiations with the Hungarian opposition in summer 1989, which culminated with the MSZMP's assent to multiparty elections.[20]

---

19. "Wage Ceilings for 1989 Lifted," *RFE/RL Hungarian Situation Reports,* 12 January 1989, 23–26.

20. "State Secretary Halmos Presents Strike Bill," *FBIS/EEU,* 28 March 1989, 22–24; "A Law to Legalize and Regulate Strikes," *RFE/RL Hungarian Situation Reports,* 9 May 1989, 35–38. From *FBIS/EEU:* "Trade Union Council Considers Economic Policy," 4 October 1989, 33; "Trade Union Council Announces Strategy Shift," 4 October 1989, 33–34;

It is noteworthy that the Hungarian Chamber of Commerce, the enterprise sector's main lobbying organization, remained generally mute throughout the conflict between the unions and the Communist Party. Its role was limited to the issuance of general statements affirming the desirability of holding inflation to planned levels.[21] Predictably, enterprise managers responded to the 1989 wage reform by bidding up their aggregate wage bills.[22] The refusal of Hungarian plant directors to apply offsetting pressure to contain wage costs strengthened the collective bargaining power of labor and complicated the MSZMP's task of restoring macroeconomic equilibrium.

Consequences for the Communist Party

The principal goal of wage reform was to raise labor productivity within the Hungarian state sector by widening income differentiation. Instead, the reform provided workers with the resources to bid up total wages, boosting domestic purchasing power and compromising the macroeconomic balance. Fulfilling the conditions of the IMF standby now required the restoration of central controls on wages. But the Party's opportunities for recentralization were limited once the process of wage liberalization was underway.

The main impediment to recentralization of incomes policy was the growing power of organized labor. The trajectory of the Hungarian labor movement in the late communist period was distinct from that of other East European countries. Labor mobilization did not begin until the end of the 1980s, and it never reached the levels attained by Poland's Solidarity, whose capacity to shut down major portions of industry forced the Polish United Worker's Party to the bargaining table. The power of Hungarian labor was less economic than political, deriving not from its capacity to limit production but rather from its ability to defy publicly the ruling party, whose presumed raison d'être was representation of worker interests. What made the comparatively limited mobilization of the late 1980s politically effective was the fact that it was led by the MSZMP's own trade union. The public confrontations between SZOT and the Grósz regime

---

"Trade Unions Reject Government Economic Program," 21 November 1989, 5. For details of the political battle over wage reform in the final year of communist rule in Hungary, see David Bartlett, "Losing the Political Initiative: The Impact of Financial Liberalization in Hungary," in Andrew Walder, ed., *The Waning of the Communist State: Economic Origins of Political Decline in China and Hungary* (Berkeley: University of California Press, 1995), 126–35.

21. "Chamber of Commerce Comments," *FBIS/EEU,* 14 March 1989, 31.

22. *PlanEcon Report* 5, no. 18 (5 May 1989): 2.

revealed the decomposition of a pivotal mechanism of internal control in the Hungarian Communist Party, whose consolidation of power after 1956 hinged on its co-optation of the Catholic Church, the intelligentsia, and organized labor. In addition to illustrating the Party's deteriorating authority, the decision of the unions to face down the Party on the eve of the 1989 roundtable negotiations strengthened the hand of Hungary's political opposition. Labor's demands for pluralization of the trade union movement paralleled and fortified the opposition's push for broader democratization.

The transformation of the Hungarian labor movement also weakened the Party's external bargaining leverage by impairing its ability to execute stabilization policy and meet the objectives of the IMF standby. The loss of control over its own labor organization prevented the Party from correcting macroeconomic disequilibria via recentralization of incomes policy. Increases in nominal income resulting from wage reform now represented currency in circulation. The center was thus left with the problem of mopping up whatever excess liquidity the initial liberalization had already released into the economy. Having surrendered its authority to manage wage bargaining through a centralized trade union apparatus, the Party was left with two means of absorbing the excess purchasing power in the hands of the population. The first was to neutralize increases in nominal income by permitting inflation to rise.[23] But while a rising inflation rate did indeed erode the real wages of households, it also contradicted a central aim of IMF stabilization programs. The second was to employ ex post measures like currency conversions, compulsory bond sales, and freezing of personal savings accounts. But while such devices were readily available to Party leaders in orthodox CPEs, their efficacy in market socialist systems like Hungary was very limited. Not only would they antagonize a blue-collar working class already pressed to the limit by economic austerity. The expansion of the second economy, decentralization of the financial system, and other reforms the MSZMP had previously undertaken restricted its ability to use income withdrawal measures to contract local purchasing power.

The distinctive character of the Hungarian labor movement in the late 1980s had major implications for workers during the postcommunist period. The fact that labor mobilization was both limited in scope and channeled into the Communist Party's official trade union meant that Hungarian workers lacked a well-institutionalized, politically autonomous base for collective bargaining once the Marxist-Leninist system col-

23. Paul Marer, "Hungary's Balance of Payments Crisis and Response, 1978–84," in Joint Economic Committee of the U.S. Congress, *East European Economies: Slow Growth in the 1980s* (Washington, D.C.: Government Printing Office, 1986), 3:311–17.

lapsed. As I show in part 3, the political power of Hungarian labor appreciably declined after the transition to democracy.

Monetary Control and Stabilization Policy

The wage reform case illustrated the weakness of financial control in Hungary's market socialist system. Plant directors employed particularized bargaining with state institutions to secure exceptions from wage regulations; workers used the Communist Party's own trade union to bid up domestic income. The inability of the National Bank of Hungary to apply countervailing monetary discipline deepened this institutional bias toward financial expansion.

In this section, I examine the political economy of monetary control during the final years of communist rule in Hungary. I show how institutional particularism in the communist state defeated the National Bank's efforts to contract the money supply, notwithstanding a major reform of the banking system intended to enlarge the role of monetary policy as a stabilization instrument.

Monetary Policy under Orthodox Central Planning

Monetary policy in CPEs is best described as the inverse of the "quantity equation" of money: $MV = PQ$, where M is the money supply, V is money velocity, P is the price level, and Q is national output. In Western economies, the equation is read from left to right. V is assumed to be stable, and the central bank adjusts the level of M to produce the desired effects on P and/or Q. In Soviet-type economies the equation was read from right to left. Again, V was regarded as stable. But it was central planners who determined the levels of P and Q, which in turn yielded the value of M. The monetary authorities' responsibility was to issue the amount of money needed to fulfill the planned levels of prices and output. In short, monetary policy in the communist states was a mere residual of the planning process, a by-product of decisions made outside the central bank.[24]

The linchpin of this monetary control system was the separation of the economy into household and enterprise money circuits. As we have seen, central planners were keenly sensitive to excess liquidity in the house-

---

24. Donald Hodgman, "Soviet Monetary Controls through the Banking System," in Franklyn Holzman, ed., *Readings on the Soviet Economy* (Chicago: Rand McNally, 1962), 581–89; Richard Portes, "Central Planning and Monetarism: Fellow Travelers?" in Padma Desai, ed., *Marxism, Central Planning, and the Soviet Economy* (Cambridge: MIT Press, 1983), 152–55; Imre Tarafás, "The Possibility and Conditions of Anti-Inflationary Economic Policy in Hungary," *Acta Oeconomica* 34, nos. 3–4 (1985): 290–92.

hold sector, where money played essentially the same role as in market economies. But monetary growth in the enterprise sector was not a great concern as long as the sphere of "active" money was contained to households. Here, excess enterprise liquidity did not translate into domestic purchasing power, since plant directors could undertake financial transactions only with specific authorization by central planners. Wage payments, fixed capital investments, and all other transactions were recorded as adjustments in the central bank accounts of enterprises. Central bank monitoring of enterprise accounts served no macroeconomic purpose. The bank's regulatory mission was strictly microeconomic: to ensure implementation of the plan by supervising financial flows within the enterprise sector and supplying plant directors with the credit needed to execute their physical production goals.[25]

In theory, monetary control in traditional CPEs was easier than in market economies. The financial structure seemingly afforded producers fewer feedback mechanisms through which imbalances could develop into inflation, while the absence of commercial banks precluded any secondary monetary expansion.[26] But policy practice in the East diverged sharply from theory. Monetary control in Soviet-type economies was always precarious, even during the height of Stalinist centralization. The problem was not so much the specific design of the central bank's regulatory mechanisms as the fact that the institutional logic of central planning militated against the application of any kind of financial discipline. With fulfillment of the production plan their main objective, Communist Party authorities pressured the central bank to furnish state enterprises with whatever credit they needed to attain their output targets. The result was rapid liquidity growth in the CPEs, as the aggregate supply of credit flowing out of the central bank expanded to meet enterprise demand.

Financial control problems in the enterprise sector also spilled over into the household sphere. The fact that there were only two channels through which enterprise money could become cash in circulation (wage payments to workers and state purchases from agricultural cooperatives) presumably simplified the task of achieving equilibria between household income and the supply of consumer goods. But despite its efforts to separate the money circuits, the center could not prevent the transformation of a substantial portion of enterprise liquidity into cash payments to the population. Pervasive shortages, widespread black-market activities, and high

25. Garvy, *Money, Financial Flows, and Credit*, 13–35, 52–77; Gregory and Stuart, *Soviet Economic Structure*, 141, 154; Hodgman, "Soviet Monetary Controls," 113–114; Zwass, *Money, Banking, and Credit*, 3–23, 78–113.

26. Portes, "Central Planning and Monetarism," 152–55.

involuntary savings testified to the failure of central planners to achieve equilibrium in the household sector.[27]

As with lax financial discipline in the enterprise sector, weak control of household liquidity demonstrated the institutional subordination of the central bank in the communist state. Pressure from the Finance Ministry and branch ministries forced the monetary authorities to sustain elastic credit lines to state enterprises, eliminating any crowding out effects that might induce plant directors to economize on wage payments. Meanwhile, loose regulation of financial accounts allowed producers to take credits earmarked for other purposes and divert them to the wage fund. Confronted by central bank officials with evidence of such regulatory infractions, managers appealed to their patrons in the planning agencies, whose political resources enabled them to prevail on the bank to forgive excess wage payments. In this way, "passive" money in the enterprise sector was eventually transformed into "active" household cash.[28]

Monetary Policy under NEM

The reforms launched in Hungary in 1968 did not fundamentally alter the institutional structure of monetary policy under central planning, already described. The reforms did enlarge the National Bank of Hungary's authority to use selective credit policies. They also elevated the political rank of the National Bank president to a level comparable to the heads of other state institutions. But these changes were mostly cosmetic. Financing of the national plan remained the chief responsibility of the National Bank, exemplifying its continued institutional subordination to the Finance Ministry and the National Planning Office. The concept of parametric monetary control was still alien to central bank authorities. Indeed, it was not until 1982 that the National Bank even began to use such standard monetary indices as M1 and M2, and then it only used them because

---

27. Igor Birman, "The Financial Crisis in the USSR," *Soviet Studies* 32, no. 1 (January 1980): 84–105; Birman, "A Reply to Professor Pickersgill," *Soviet Studies* 32, no. 4 (October 1980): 586–91; Birman and Roger Clarke, "Inflation and the Money Supply in the Soviet Economy," *Soviet Studies* 37, no. 4 (October 1985): 494–504.

28. Joseph Berliner, "Monetary Planning in the USSR," *American Slavic and East European Review* 9, no. 4 (December 1950): 237–54; Berliner, *Factory and Manager in the USSR* (Cambridge: Harvard University Press, 1957), 282–87; John Farrell, "Bank Control of the Wage Fund in Poland 1950–1970," *Soviet Studies* 27, no. 2 (April 1975): 265–87; Garvy, *Money, Financial Flows, and Credit,* 52–75, 174–75; Gregory and Stuart, *Soviet Economic Structure,* 146–49; Franklyn Holzman, "Soviet Inflationary Pressures, 1928–1957: Causes and Cures," in Holzman, *Readings on the Soviet Economy,* 617–19; Holzman, *Soviet Taxation* (Cambridge: Harvard University Press, 1962), 22–60; Raymond Powell, "Recent Developments in Soviet Monetary Policy," in Holzman, *Readings on the Soviet Economy,* 573–76.

they were part of its reporting requirements as a new member of the IMF.[29]

Monetary policy in Hungary's monobanking system was a socialist variant of the "flow equilibrium" approach to macroeconomic regulation. Monetary control entailed not the pursuit of a priori targets for growth of the money supply (the "stock equilibrium" approach) but rather manipulation of net income flows in the national economy. Monetary policy was thus treated as a balance-sheet exercise, with central bankers attempting to strike the desired balance of assets and liabilities among the economy's major income groups.[30]

Hungary's version of the flow equilibrium approach worked as follows. The National Planning Office, following negotiations with the Ministry of Finance and the branch ministries, presented the National Bank with an annual financial plan specifying net income targets for the four key sectors of the economy: the Hungarian state, enterprises, households, and the foreign sector. The Bank's duty was to adjust the flows of assets and liabilities of these groups in order to meet the income targets. The Bank financed the liabilities of the income groups: credits to the state budget to finance deficits, loans to the enterprise sector to finance the production plan, credits to the National Savings Bank to finance household loans, and convertible currency borrowed from abroad to finance the economy's foreign exchange requirements. The Bank also held most of the economy's financial assets, including deposits by state institutions and enterprises.

The significance of this institutional arrangement was that any changes in the flow of assets and liabilities of the four income groups had an immediate impact on the financial status of the National Bank itself. The Bank's balance sheet was effectively the mirror image of the balance sheet of the income groups; the latter's liabilities were the former's assets, and vice versa. This meant that the Bank was highly vulnerable to divergences from the net income targets set by the planning authorities.

For example, an unanticipated rise in the state budget deficit obliged the Bank to increase the supply of credit to the treasury. To preserve financial equilibrium, the Bank had to make adjustments of some other items in the balance sheet. How it made those adjustments had a decisive impact on the Bank's ability to the control the total money supply. If the Bank compensated for the expansion of credits to the Hungarian state by reducing flows of credit to one or more of the other income groups, it

29. Tamás Bácskai,"The Reorganization of the Banking System," *New Hungarian Quarterly* 107 (autumn 1987): 130.

30. For a discussion of the differences between the stock equilibrium and flow equilibrium approaches to monetary policy, see David Cobham, *Macroeconomic Analysis: An Intermediate Text* (London: Longman, 1987).

could restore equilibrium without any increase in the total size of the balance sheet. In this case, the net effect on the money supply was zero. To illustrate, consider a scenario in which the Bank remitted 10 billion Hungarian forints (HUF) in fresh credits to the state to finance a budget deficit. It could offset this completely by reducing credit flows to the enterprise sector, as is shown in the following balance sheet.

Balance Sheet of the National Bank of Hungary

Assets		Liabilities	
Credits to the State	+10	Deposits of State Institutions	
Credits to Enterprises	−10	Deposits from Enterprises	
Credits to Households		Notes & Coins in Circulation	
Credits to Foreign Actors		Credits from Foreign Actors	
Net Change	0		0

However, if the Bank was unable to neutralize the increase in credits to the Hungarian state through reductions in credit flows to other sectors, it had to make the adjustment on the liabilities side of the balance sheet. Here the Bank's options were very limited. It lacked effective means of attracting deposits by state institutions and enterprises. Moreover, the huge size of the country's outstanding Western debt constrained its ability to raise new foreign credits. Under these circumstances, the only alternative left to the National Bank was enlarging the stock of notes and coins in circulation, as is shown in the following balance sheet.

Balance Sheet of the National Bank of Hungary

Assets		Liabilities	
Credits to the State	+10	Deposits of State Institutions	
Credits to Enterprises		Deposits from Enterprises	
Credits to Households		Notes & Coins in Circulation	+10
Credits to Foreign Actors		Credits from Foreign Actors	
Net Change	+10		+10

Here, the net result was an increase in the total size of the balance sheet and hence growth of the aggregate money supply. By concentrating the adjustment entirely on the liabilities side of the balance sheet, the Bank eliminated all crowding out effects. And by issuing new currency, it effectively monetized the state budget deficit, magnifying the inflationary consequences of the monetary expansion.[31]

This was precisely the situation facing the National Bank of Hungary in the 1980s. The communist state was running large budget deficits, which the Bank was obliged to finance through a limitless line of credit. The foreign sector was also in a deficit, the consequence of heavy borrowing on hard currency markets. The household sector, traditionally in a surplus, shifted to a net deficit in 1987 as result of expanding mortgages. Its hands tied in the state, household, and foreign sectors, the Bank was left with the option of concentrating the entire burden of adjustment on the remaining income group, Hungarian enterprises. If it were to compensate for those deficits without increasing the money supply, it had to create an offsetting surplus by reducing the flow of credit to the enterprise sector.[32]

But the institutional structure of Hungary's reformed communist state restricted the National Bank's capacity to do so. Liberalization of financial regulation under NEM expanded opportunities for Hungarian enterprises to neutralize contractions of bank credit. By 1985, the Party had basically ended the long-standing practice of organizing enterprise funds into separate accounts supervised by the National Bank. The assorted fixed and working capital accounts were merged into a so-called inter-interestedness fund. Formally, this fund was part of the noncash money circuit. But it effectively functioned as a demand deposit account for enterprises and was nearly as liquid as cash.[33] In the same year, the Party legalized bills of exchange, which proved an important supplement to bank credit. Plant directors facing shortages of funds also resorted to informal trade credits, which were not legal but were beyond the scope of effective state regulation.[34] These alternative liquidity sources gave Hungarian plant directors the flexibility to absorb restrictions of central bank

31. The foregoing analysis of monetary policy procedures in communist Hungary is based on the following interviews: National Planning Office, 21 April 1988; Council of Ministers, 20 May and 6 June 1988; Ministry of Finance, 28 June 1988; Karl Marx University of Economics, 26 May and 4 August 1988; Institute of Economics, Hungarian Academy of Sciences, 7 July 1988; and National Bank of Hungary, 28 June, 12 and 26 August, and 8 September 1988.

32. Dániel Jánossy and László Virágh, "A Pénzmennyiség Alakulása és a Jegybanki Szabályozás 1987-ben" (The tendency of the quantity of money and central bank regulation in 1987), Bankszemle, June 1988, 32–37.

33. Interviews, World Bank, 15 July 1987; Karl Marx University, 4 August 1988.

34. By the mid-1980s, unauthorized trade credit accounted for nearly 20 percent of total outstanding short-term credits in the Hungarian state sector. Interviews, Ministry of Finance, 13 June 1988; Hungarian Chamber of Commerce, 15 July 1988. See also I. Z. Nagy, "Lángreakció: Vállalati Pénzhiány" (Chain reaction: Scarcity of money at enterprises), Figyelő 28, no. 6 (1984): 5.

credit without interrupting their normal production activities. At the same time, a variety of fiscal security devices planted at various points in the pipeline between the state bureaucracy and the enterprise sector filled any remaining liquidity needs. Some of these mechanisms involved direct transfer payments from the national treasury to bridge liquidity gaps. Others were indirect. For instance, plant directors facing shortages of funds could discretely bargain for relaxation of the Finance Ministry's rules governing the use of after-tax profits.[35]

Meanwhile, the National Bank of Hungary still lacked the political autonomy and policy instruments to control primary emission of liquidity to the enterprise sector. During preparations for the transition to a two-tiered banking system in the mid-1980s, the Bank was separated into issuing and crediting divisions. The former was charged with regulating the total money supply. The latter was organized into several directorates organized by branch, operating under global targets set by the issuing division. But this administrative reshuffling did not change the trajectory of money and credit policy. Loan officers in the credit directorates developed identities of interest with the branch sectors under their jurisdictions and continued their previous habit of evaluating loan applications with less attention to performance criteria than to the stated liquidity requirements of the applicants.[36]

In short, market reforms complicated the communist state's task of monetary regulation. They significantly widened the financial discretion of enterprise managers while depriving the central bank of the institutional means of regulating monetary aggregates.

Monetary Policy and Economic Austerity, 1982–86

The course of Hungarian monetary policy during the period preceding the 1987 banking reform well illustrated the problems of financial control under reform communism. As part of the 1982 IMF standby, the National Bank sought to contract the supply of credit in the enterprise sector. The Bank managed to contain nominal growth of working capital credits to about 5 percent per annum in 1982 and 1983, then permitted it to mushroom to 9 percent in 1984, 13.4 percent in 1985, and 18.6 percent in 1986.[37] But the stabilization program did attain most of the other macroeconomic targets specified by the IMF. The liquidity squeeze of the early 1980s had

---

35. Interview, National Planning Office, 21 April 1988.

36. Interviews, National Bank of Hungary, 22 April and 13 May 1988.

37. Központi Statisztikai Hivatal, *Statisztikai Évkönyv 1987* (Statistical yearbook 1987), 342.

an especially pronounced effect on long-term fixed capital credit. Gross fixed capital investment posted negative rates of growth every year between 1982 and 1986.[38] Real household income, total domestic consumption, and convertible currency imports also declined, in line with the terms of the IMF standby.[39]

However, these effects were realized through nonmonetary means. The National Bank's brief success in contracting short-term credit was achieved not through a general monetary contraction but via dissolution of existing credit contracts and accelerated repayment of loans. The reductions of real household income and domestic consumption were accomplished by way of consumer price hikes and restoration of state controls on wage payments. The decline in imports and fixed investment resulted from a sharp increase in the enterprise profits tax, a freeze of enterprise reserves, and recentralization of import licensing. In short, the austerity program of 1982–84 was executed not through monetary policy but rather through restoration of central administrative controls on market processes.[40]

While these techniques restored short-term equilibrium, they failed to rectify the underlying problems of the Hungarian economy. The National Bank's inability to control the base money supply, combined with an undiminished credit demand from state enterprises, set the stage for the resurgence of liquidity growth in 1983–84, when the Kádár leadership shifted from austerity to economic stimulus. The result was rapid growth of the state budget deficit and the external debt between 1984 and 1986, leading to the near collapse of the Hungarian economy in the second half of the decade.

Reliance on administrative-type measures to execute the stabilization program also reinforced those institutional features of the plan bargaining system that favored poorly performing enterprises over strong ones. Reimposition of central controls on wages, investment, enterprise funds, and foreign trade lowered total domestic absorption while enlarging opportunities for inefficient producers to appeal for individual exceptions to the restrictions. Consequently, the economy's weakest performers received special compensation, while the burden of the general liquidity squeeze fell

---

38. *PlanEcon Report* 3, nos. 14–15 (10 April 1987): 8.

39. *PlanEcon Report* 5, no. 18 (5 May 1989): 1–8.

40. László Antal, Lajos Bokros, and István Csillag, eds., "Change and Reform" (Institute for Financial Research, Ministry of Finance, 1987, mimeo); Márton Tardos, "Question Marks in Hungarian Fiscal and Monetary Policy," *Acta Oeconomica* 35, nos. 1–2 (1985): 42–43; Éva Várhegyi, "A Bankhitel Működése Restrikciós Idoszakban" (The operation of bank credits in the period of restrictions), *Gazdaság* 20, no. 2 (1986): 47–61; Várhegyi, "A Monetáris Restrikció Nehézségei" (The difficulties of the monetary restriction), *Bankszemle,* June 1988, 11–17.

on the strongest ones—the very enterprises on which long-term improvements in export performance depended.[41]

Insofar as the flow equilibrium problem was concerned, the National Bank's inability to sustain reductions in enterprise liquidity prevented it from generating a surplus sufficient to offset the deficits in the other three income groups. The Party's decision in 1984 to shift from austerity to economic expansion laid the groundwork for the resumption of the flow of working capital finance, which more than compensated for the contraction of fixed capital credits. By the end of 1986, the net financial deficit of the enterprise sector was 135 percent of the 1981 level.[42] In late 1986, there was an especially large flood of short-term credit into the enterprise sector, as National Bank credit officers hurriedly booked loans with the plant directors who would soon become their clients in the new commercial banks.[43]

Monetary Policy under the Two-Tiered Banking System

The theoretical premise of the Hungarian banking reform was that the monobanking system was incapable of simultaneously performing monetary control and credit allocation. Indeed, in the context of central planning the two functions operated at cross-purposes. As long as the exigencies of plan fulfillment compelled the Bank to furnish state enterprises with an elastic supply of credit, it could not contain expansion of the total money stock. Effective monetary regulation and efficient credit allocation could only come about by separating the two functions. In January 1987, virtually the entire loan portfolio of the National Bank was transferred to five new commercial banks. Organized as profit-seeking joint stock companies and legally protected from central interference in their lending decisions, the banks would disburse credit according to efficiency criteria. The National Bank, freed of the obligation to supply Hungarian enterprises directly with credit, could then operate as a Western-type central bank, regulating the aggregate money supply through reserve requirements, rediscounting and refinancing instruments, and interest rate policies.

---

41. The extent to which loss-making enterprises were shielded from the distributional effects of austerity is illustrated by the fact that of the 52 Hungarian enterprises officially declared insolvent in 1984, half actually managed to *increase* production between 1979 and 1983. During this same period, only five of these enterprises were able to increase their share of exports to the convertible currency area. I. Fenyövári, "Vállalati Gazdálkodás—A Pénzhiany Okai" (Enterprise management—Causes of money shortage), *Figyelő* 28, no. 42 (1984): 4.

42. Központi Statisztikai Hivatal, *Statisztikai Évkönyv 1987,* 342.

43. Márton Tardos, "Can Hungary's Monetary Policy Succeed?" *Acta Oeconomica* 39, nos. 1–2 (1988): 73.

Eventually, the development of a securities market would enable the monetary authorities to undertake open market operations.[44]

During the first phase of the banking reform, the most important policy instruments were refinancing credits issued by the National Bank to the commercial banks. These were controlled through a quota system. Long-term refinancing credits were administered on a case-by-case basis, with the commercial banks submitting individual applications for specific fixed capital investment projects undertaken by client enterprises. The quotas for the short-term refinancing facility, which the banks used to supply working capital credits to the enterprise sector, were calculated as a certain multiple of the base capital of each of the commercial banks.

On the surface, this appeared to be a very effective instrument of monetary control. When the two-tiered system was inaugurated in 1987, the poorly capitalized new banks were extremely dependent on their refinancing lines with the National Bank. Central bank refinancing credits represented over 60 percent of total commercial bank liabilities. With refinancing credit constituting the bulk of liabilities in the commercial banking sector, and with short-term quotas calculated as a simple multiple of capital assets, the National Bank authorities could swiftly and decisively transform the liquidity position of the banks by altering the multiple. Reduction of the refinancing quotas would in turn force the banks to curtail their own credit lines. Relieved of the obligation to supply enterprises directly with credit, and possessing direct control of the commercial banks' most important source of finance, the National Bank now seemed poised to generate the enterprise sector surplus needed to offset the burgeoning deficits in the other income groups.

To this end, during the first two years of the reform the reorganized National Bank used its refinancing facility to reduce liquidity growth in the enterprise sector. But its efforts were not enough to generate a net surplus in that sector. Indeed, Hungarian enterprises continued to run a net deficit, adding to the huge deficits posted by the other three income

---

44. László Antal and György Surányi, "The Prehistory of the Reform of Hungary's Banking System, *Acta Oeconomica* 38, nos. 1–2 (1987): 35–48; L. György Asztalos, Lajos Bokros, and György Surányi, "Reform and Financial Institutional System in Hungary," *Acta Oeconomica* 32, nos. 3–4 (1984): 251–68; Bácskai, "The Reorganization of the Banking System"; Lajos Bokros, "Az Üzleti Viselkedés Kibontakozásának Feltétlei Kétszinten Bankrendszerben" (The conditions of the development of business-like behavior in a two-tiered banking system), *Külgazdaság* 1 (1987); Katalin Bossanyi, "Változó a Bank Rendszerünk" (The changing of our banking system), *Népszabadság,* 10 September 1986; Bossanyi, "Az Üzletfélek Kiadó Hitelek" (Business partners granting credits), *Magyarország,* October 1986; Michael Friedlander, "Hungary's Banking Reform," *Wiener Institut Für Internationale Wirtschaftsvergleiche,* December 1987.

groups. The Bank, following its practice under the monobanking system, ended up monetizing this deficit by printing new money.

Political Conflicts over Refinancing Policy, 1987–88

The continued weakness of monetary control during the initial phase of the banking reform was partly attributable to policy errors committed by the National Bank that revealed its inexperience with Western-type macroeconomic instruments. As I already noted, control of long-term credit remained highly centralized in the two-tiered system, reflecting the high priority assigned to control of fixed capital investment under the IMF stabilization program. But the Bank quickly squandered its control of long-term refinancing, permitting the commercial banks to fill up almost all of their quotas within a few months after the startup of the two-tiered system. Many of the long-term credits had maturities extending to three years and beyond, and the Bank could not amend the terms of the contracts ex post.

With long-term refinancing quotas diminished as a regulatory device, the Bank turned to its short-term facility. Again, National Bank officials committed an early blunder that impaired their ability to contain liquidity growth through short-term refinancing. Attempting to smooth the transition from the monobanking system, the Bank initially set the short-term quotas at an extremely high level, 500 percent of the base capital of the new banks. This was in fact so high that the new banks, eager as they were to book loans with their clients in the enterprise sector, were unable to fill up even half of their quotas.

By spring of 1987, it was apparent that the commercial banks were significantly overlending, prompting the National Bank to begin a series of reductions of short-term refinancing quotas, first to 400 percent of base capital, then to 200 percent, then to 100 percent. But while these measures reduced the amount of refinancing credit outstanding, they had little effect on commercial bank lending. Short-term credits to the enterprise sector at year's end were less than 5 percent lower than their level at the beginning of the reform, while long-term lending actually increased.

The failure of its policies to have the desired bite on commercial bank lending compelled the National Bank authorities to reformulate their strategy. At the end of 1987, they announced plans for a draconian monetary contraction, proposing to reduce refinancing quotas to 60 percent of base capital and establish a schedule of punitive interest rates for above-quota drawings.

This plan provoked vociferous opposition from both commercial banks and state enterprises. The banks launched a public relations campaign aimed at thwarting the proposed monetary contraction. In press reviews and other public statements, commercial bank officials castigated the National Bank, claiming that the refinancing squeeze would not only jeopardize their liquidity positions but impair the day-to-day operations of their clients in the enterprise sector. The commercial banks' lobbying efforts notwithstanding, the National Bank's political position appeared secure. In December 1987, the Communist Party leadership signaled its endorsement of the Bank's program and warned that bank managers who opposed the attempt to curtail monetary growth might be sacked. In January of the new year, the National Bank proceeded with the refinancing squeeze.

The commercial banks responded by raising the degree of political heat on the National Bank. They began by appealing directly to senior officials in the Party to intervene. The managing director of the largest of the banks went so far as to write a letter to Miklós Németh, then MSZMP Central Committee secretary for economic policy, declaring that the Bank's policies threatened to ruin the Hungarian economy. The banks then took steps to provoke other actors to enter into the fray and register their own grievances about the National Bank's policies. In direct contradiction to the approach urged on them by the monetary authorities, the bank managers sustained credit lines to their weakest clients while cutting those to their strongest ones. As a consequence, well-performing enterprises, which might have supported the monetary contraction if the commercial banks had taken the National Bank's suggestion to reallocate credit to more efficient sectors, were moved to join in opposition to the Bank. This strategy was particularly effective in rousing the ire of agricultural cooperatives and food processors, which were highly dependent on short-term working capital credit. Major agricultural producers, literally unable to purchase the materials needed to carry out their production plans, dispatched letters of their own to the Central Committee urging the Party to intervene. The fact that the agricultural sector was one of Hungary's principal sources of hard currency export revenue guaranteed that those appeals would strike a nerve with Communist Party leaders.

With alarms now sounding in the commercial banks, within key industries, and among agricultural producers, the MSZMP leadership was finally provoked to intervene. Under pressure from senior Party officials, the Bank agreed to restore short-term refinancing quotas to the level that obtained before the controversy and to rescind interest rate penalties for above-quota drawings. The episode was a clear political defeat for the National Bank. Indeed, the National Bank president was persuaded to admit publicly before the Hungarian Parliament that the Bank had mismanaged the monetary contraction.[45]

---

45. "'More Restrained' Loan Policy Introduced," *FBIS/EEU,* 11 February 1988, 25.

These setbacks in monetary policy prevented the National Bank from creating an enterprise sector surplus capable of offsetting the deficits of the other income groups. The refinancing squeeze did reduce growth of total enterprise credit in 1987. But virtually the entire contraction fell on the working capital side. Fixed capital credit actually increased following a steady decline dating from the beginning of the decade. This illustrated the Bank's weak control of long-term refinancing during the first few months of the banking reform, which forced the monetary authorities to focus their attention on the short-term facility. The result was a net deficit in the enterprise sector, adding to the burgeoning liabilities of the state, household, and foreign sectors. The National Bank was compelled to finance all of this deficit, amounting to over HUF 200 billion, by expanding notes and coins in circulation. In nominal terms, this exceeded the level of deficit monetization in 1986, the last year of the monobanking system.[46]

Relationship between the Fiscal and Monetary Spheres

The dispute over refinancing policy showed that the National Bank remained a weak institutional actor despite the reorganization of the banking system along Western lines. As we have seen, the monetary authorities committed several policy errors that enhanced the credibility of the particularistic claims of commercial banks and enterprises and increased the likelihood that Communist Party leaders would intervene on the latter's behalf. Such hitches in policy execution were surely inevitable in a country where Western-type monetary procedures were wholly unknown and unpracticed. By while the dysfunctions attending the transition to a new regulatory system played an important role in the clash over monetary policy in 1987–88, the episode underscored a broader problem, namely the domination of the National Bank by the fiscal institutions of the communist state. The Hungarian Ministry of Finance not only failed to come to the National Bank's support but ended up endorsing the Bank's opponents.

Comparison with the experiences of market economies helps illuminate the problem. Western countries have devised a variety of institutional mechanisms to counteract political pressures for fiscal expansion. Switzerland's weak federal state subjects budgetary decisions to popular referenda. Under majority rule, many spending referenda are defeated, as individuals vote against appropriations for programs that do not deliver particularistic benefits for fear of crowding out programs that do.[47] The

---

46. Központi Statisztikai Hivatal, *Statisztikai Évkönyv 1987,* 347.
47. James Alt and K. Alec Chrystal, *Political Economics* (Berkeley: University of California Press, 1983), 218–19.

highly centralized states of France and Japan established powerful ministries of finance possessing broad authority to revise budgets submitted by individual line and branch ministries.[48] Even the federal government of the United States, the paragon of interest group politics, has managed to institute mechanisms that restrain growth of expenditures.[49]

In his seminal work on budgetary politics, Aaron Wildavsky observes that the various actors engaged in U.S. fiscal policy have assumed distinct institutional roles: the federal agencies and the counterpart congressional committees as advocates, the Office of Management and Budget as presidential servant with a cutting bias, the House Appropriations Committee as guardian of the national treasury, and the Senate Appropriations Committee as appeals court. Mutual understanding and respect for the roles played by these organizations create stable expectations, which reduce uncertainty amidst a vastly complex budgetary process. As the "saver" institutions like the Office of Management and Budget and the congressional appropriations committees serve the indispensable role of checking the natural tendency of the "spender" agencies to bid up aggregate expenditures, the "advocates" perform the vital function of easing the burden of calculation on the savers. Absent robust advocacy organizations, the saver institutions would have to determine entirely by themselves which programs to fund, which to cut, and by how much—a task greatly exceeding their time and resources.[50]

In Hungary and other communist states, there was a similar set of expectations regarding the role of the spender institutions. It was widely anticipated that, in the bidding for financial resources, the branch ministries and local Party committees would lobby aggressively on behalf of enterprises under their jurisdictions. However, there were no comparable expectations regarding the institutions charged with national-level financial regulation, no institutionalized "guardians of the treasury" capable of counterbalancing the advocates of financial expansion. Formally, the Ministry of Finance was the agency chiefly responsible for performing that function. Given the high degree of centralization of the communist state,

---

48. G. Lord, *The French Budgetary Process* (Berkeley: University of California Press, 1973), 54–71.

49. Notwithstanding pervasive logrolling, pork barrel, and other, similar practices long familiar to students of the American Congress, the popular image of governmental spending gone amok in the United States is inaccurate. U.S. federal expenditures relative to GDP are actually quite low by international standards. Throughout the postwar period, federal spending has grown in stable proportion to growth of national income. Alt and Chrystal, *Political Economics*, 210–37.

50. Wildavsky, *The Politics of the Budgetary Process* (Boston: Little, Brown, 1979), 160–65.

one might expect that it would discharge this role at least as effectively as its counterparts in dirigiste capitalist states like France and Japan. But far from serving as bastions of financial discipline that would keep the claims of spending advocates in check, the communist finance ministries were in many respects the mainstay of the central planning apparatus, whose primary mission was to finance the production plan.

NEM reinforced the spending bias of the Hungarian Ministry of Finance. By replacing physical output targets with indirect financial regulations, NEM strengthened the Finance Ministry at the expense of the branch ministries. As its policy jurisdiction came to encompass the regulatory areas most vital to enterprises (tax policy, budget subsidies, and wage control), the Ministry became the key institution in the state administration. Hungary's entry into the IMF and World Bank further strengthened the authority of the Finance Ministry, which assumed primary responsibility for conducting negotiations with Western lending agencies and overseeing implementation of standby agreements. But this enhanced political power was not accompanied by a greater institutional bias for financial discipline. Expansion of the Finance Ministry's policy jurisdiction simultaneously elevated the agency's status within the communist state and transformed it into the locus of particularized bargaining by factory-level agents seeking compensation for the distributional fallout of market reform.

The exceptionally high degree of budgetary centralization in Hungary illustrated the Ministry of Finance's spending bias. By the late 1980s, the rate of enterprise profits taxation approached 90 percent. Equally important, over 50 percent of the tax revenue extracted from Hungarian enterprises was reallocated to producers in the form of subsidies.[51] In short, communist Hungary was a budget-driven economy, and this necessarily diluted the impact of money and credit policy. With such a large proportion of enterprise profits confiscated and then reallocated through the Finance Ministry's subsidy system, creditors could not make meaningful distinctions between efficient and inefficient enterprises by examining retained earnings. The exorbitant rate of profits taxation limited the ability of enterprises to assume bank credit, while at the same time the high level of subsidization obviated the need for many of them even to seek it. In fact, at the time of the banking reform barely 50 percent of enterprises had any outstanding bank credits at all. The ready supply of budgetary finance generated pressure on bank officials to lower interest rates and loosen lending terms in order to retain those enterprises that still used

---

51. L. Muraközy, "Hazánk Költségvetéséről—Nemzetközi Összehasonlitásban" (The budget of Hungary in international comparison), *Pénzyügyi Szemle* 29, no. 10 (1985): 745–54.

bank credit. Thus a vicious circle arose: the relaxation of credit conditions weakened financial discipline within the enterprise sector, which in term created the need for more budget subsidies to support weak producers, which in turn further diminished the role of bank credit, and so on.[52]

At the same time, the centrality of budgetary financing in the Hungarian economy neutralized whatever attempts the National Bank made to control liquidity via monetary means. Even if the monetary authorities enacted deep cuts in the flow of bank credits to producers, the enterprise sector's total liquidity supply remained undiminished owing to the continued emission of funds through the reallocative mechanisms of the state budget. A rising budget deficit further circumscribed the utility of monetary policy. The growth of deficit spending obliged the National Bank to issue new credits to the state; the Bank sought to compensate through credit restrictions in the other income groups; but the very flow of budget subsidies to those groups that created the state's deficit in the first place defeated the Bank's attempts to take compensatory action elsewhere.

The procedures for deficit financing under NEM demonstrated the National Bank's institutional subservience to the Finance Ministry. The Bank's obligation to finance the state budget deficit was de facto, not de jure. In 1982, the Communist Party reestablished the legal instruments for bonds and other securities. But despite rapid growth of the securities market, by decade's end the Hungarian state was able to finance only about 5 percent of its deficit through bond sales. The remainder was financed by the National Bank. Central bank financing of the budget deficit did involve real "credits" in the sense that the state paid them back at a specified interest rate and maturation schedule. But effectively, it amounted to a revolving credit line to the state, and thus to monetization of the deficit. Unlike bonds sold to the population or commercial banks, issuing central bank credits to the state did not entail any withdrawal of money from circulation. The state ran up the deficit, the National Bank delivered credits to the Finance Ministry to cover it, and the Finance Ministry paid back the loans and promptly borrowed more to finance new deficits.[53]

For these reasons, deficit spending by the communist state was highly inflationary, more so to the degree the deficits monetized by the National

---

52. István Hagelmayer, "Pénzügyi Politika Magyarországon" (Financial policy in Hungary), *Külpolitika* 12, no. 4 (1985): 59–79

53. Interviews, Council of Ministers, 6 June 1988; National Bank of Hungary, 13 June 1988. By the mid-1980s, outstanding National Bank credits to the Hungarian state amounted to some HUF 480 billion, or approximately $9.4 billion at the official exchange rate. "New Data on Government Debt Revealed at Hungarian Assembly Session," *RFE/RL Hungarian Situation Reports,* 15 December 1988, 31–35.

Bank were used for *nonproductive* purposes, like subsidizing loss-making enterprises. Central bank credits to the state generated a secular increase in domestic purchasing power without a commensurate rise in the supply of marketable goods.[54]

During the preparations for the banking reform, economists proposed to establish a legal limit, equivalent to 2 percent of the gross domestic product (GDP), on the amount of the state deficit subject to direct financing by the National Bank. Any deficit spending above the limit would have to be financed by government securities. But the heads of both the Finance Ministry and the National Bank rejected the proposal. The former argued that the Finance Ministry's hands would be tied if deficit spending exceeded the ceiling and bond sales failed to fill the gap. And the latter declined to accept responsibility for withholding the central bank credits that the Hungarian state needed to finance its bulging deficit.[55]

This open-ended commitment to supply the Finance Ministry with credits underscored the National Bank's ambiguous legal status in the communist state. Formally, the Bank was responsible to the Council of Ministers, the top executive body of the Hungarian government. This meant that the prime minister possessed the power to appoint the president and vice presidents of the National Bank and the authority to approve the annual "credit policy guidelines" stating the Bank's broad macroeconomic policy goals. But the law said nothing about the policy-making jurisdiction of the Bank itself. On a day-to-day basis, National Bank authorities performed a variety of functions vital to the operation of the economy: calculation of refinancing quotas, adjustment of interest rates on refinancing credits, rediscounting of bills of exchange, determination of legal reserve requirements, management of convertible currency assets and liabilities, and modification of the exchange rate. But absent a legal structure codifying the Bank's authority over these matters, there was nothing to stop governmental leaders from intervening at will. The fact that the Council of Ministers itself was subordinate to the MSZMP Central Committee further complicated the National Bank's political position. While the government enjoyed considerable leeway over policy making by the late 1980s, the absence of constitutional checks on the Party's power enabled MSZMP leaders to intercede at any point and at any time. The National Bank therefore operated under a dual subordination. Lacking clearly demarcated authority to carry out its various functions, the Bank was liable to arbitrary intervention by either governmental officials or

---

54. György Surányi, "Lehet-e as Infláció Gazdaságpolitikai Eszköz?" (Inflation as an instrument of economic policy?), *Figyelő* 29, no. 17 (1985): 5.

55. Interview, World Bank, 21 July 1987.

Communist Party leaders.[56] As the dispute over refinancing policy in 1987–88 showed, such intervention was likely to work to the detriment of monetary discipline. What was most apt to trigger intercession from the top were claims by banks and enterprises that the National Bank's policies were preventing them from fulfilling the Party leadership's own production goals.

Fiscal Policy under the Communist State

The institutional structure of Hungarian communism also restricted the utility of fiscal policy as a stabilization instrument. In this section, I focus on the procedures for deficit financing in the communist state, the structure of revenues and expenditures under NEM, and the problems of political control of the budget in the one-party system. I show that the Hungarian state's spending bias generated large budget deficits. The institutional subordination of the National Bank and the absence of an extensive capital market obliged central bank authorities to monetize these deficits through direct credits to the Ministry of Finance, raising inflationary pressures and neutralizing attempts to contract purchasing power via monetary policy. The structure of Hungary's national budget deepened the problems of fiscal control. On the revenue side, the state's reliance on enterprise profits taxation impaired allocative efficiency, broadened opportunities for individualized bargaining over tax rates, and circumscribed the center's ability to stabilize the economy by curtailing household income. On the expenditure side, particularistic claims on budgetary resources combined with the MSZMP's commitment to extensive social welfare services fed rapid growth of state spending. The absence of public accountability in the Marxist-Leninist system enabled the Communist Party to conceal the true magnitude of the fiscal crisis until the very end of its tenure in power. The disclosure of the actual status of Hungary's finances weakened both the MSZMP's external bargaining leverage and its internal authority. During its final years in power, the Party grappled simultaneously with IMF pressure to reduce expenditures and local demands to sustain the flow of social services to a population long inured to "goulash communism."

Financing of the Budget Deficit

Before the appearance of Mikhail Gorbachev, most of the East European communist states reported annual budget surpluses, which central plan-

---

56. Interview, National Bank of Hungary, 12 August 1988.

ners considered useful for reducing local purchasing power. Their guiding assumption was that any surplus in the state budget neutralized an equivalent amount of household cash. Official Soviet data from the preglasnost period supported that proposition. Consumer prices in the USSR declined between 1947 and 1954, then stabilized—an achievement early Western specialists attributed to the sizable budget surpluses the Soviet authorities reported during the postwar years.[57] However, more recent evidence cast serious doubt as to the validity of the Soviets' claims of budget surpluses and indeed suggested that deficit spending was the norm throughout communist Eastern Europe.[58]

Official economic data from communist Hungary, traditionally regarded as the most reliable in the region, revealed budget deficits in virtually every year since the launching of NEM. As table 2.1 shows, deficit spending had become a serious problem in the 1980s.

By international standards, the officially reported Hungarian deficits were not exceptionally large. The peak deficit of 1987, HUF 50.1 billion, represented 5.8 percent of GDP. During the same period, the proportion ranged around 3 percent in Great Britain, France, and West Germany. In other West European countries, deficit spending as a percentage of GDP surpassed that of Hungary, at upwards of 6 percent in Spain, Denmark, and the Netherlands; close to 11 percent in Sweden and Greece; 14 percent in Belgium; and 15 percent in Italy.[59]

But the relative size of a state's budget deficit is less important than the manner in which it is financed. Countries with well-developed capital markets like Great Britain and the United States can easily finance deficits

TABLE 2.1. Hungarian State Budget, 1981–89 (billions of forints)

	1981	1982	1983	1984	1985	1986	1987	1988	1989
Revenues	418.1	438.7	485.5	535.2	539.0	606.8	652.0	789.9	926.6
Expenditures	438.2	453.8	492.3	519.5	549.8	652.4	702.1	792.0	957.8
Balance	−20.1	−15.1	−6.8	15.7	−10.8	−45.6	−50.1	−2.1	−31.2

Sources: IMF, *Government Financial Statistics Yearbook,* vol. 12 (Washington, D.C., 1988); *International Financial Statistics,* September 1994, 280.

57. Powell, "Recent Developments in Soviet Monetary Policy," 575.

58. The first scholar to explore in depth the reliability of Soviet budget statistics was Igor Birman, "The Financial Crisis in the USSR." Subsequently, Mark Harrison examined Soviet budgets of the late Stalinist period, concluding that Party authorities had consistently overstated budgetary revenues *and* understated expenses. "The USSR State Budget under Late Stalinism (1945–55): Capital Formation, Government Borrowing, and Monetary Growth," *Economics of Planning* 20, no. 3 (1986): 179–205.

59. *International Financial Statistics: Supplement on Economic Indicators,* IMF Supplement Series, no. 10 (Washington, D.C.: IMF, 1985).

through public issues of securities. Even capitalist countries lacking extensive capital markets can finance large deficits without resort to monetization. In Japan, the Ministry of Finance and Bank of Japan use their powerful complement of direct controls and indirect modes of persuasion to coax private banks into purchasing bonds to cover state budget deficits.[60] Similarly, the French *encadrement du credit* enables state authorities to prevail on commercial banks to support government bond issues.[61]

Hungary not only lacked a large capital market. Until 1987 it lacked even a commercial banking system. Consequently, all but a small percentage of the state budget deficit was financed via direct credits from the National Bank to the Ministry of Finance. As we have seen, the inability of the National Bank to engineer compensatory cuts in credit flows to the other income groups led to deficit monetization, whose inflationary effects in a shortage economy were particularly acute.

Structure of Revenues and Expenditures

Total budgetary revenues and expenditures relative to national income also rose during the NEM period. In 1968, state expenditures constituted approximately 50 percent of GDP. By 1988, the ratio had risen to nearly 65 percent. Table 2.2 shows how budgetary centralization in communist Hungary compared with Western countries. The data indicate that state revenues and expenditures in Hungary as percentage of GDP well surpassed most of these countries belonging to the Organization for Economic Cooperation and Development (OECD). However, the Hungarian state budget was not dramatically larger than those of Denmark and Sweden, where budgetary turnover approached 60 percent of national income.

But these comparative data do not give a full picture of the magnitude of Hungary's budget problems. The profile of revenues and expenditures of the communist state distinguished Hungary from even Western countries, like the Northern European social democracies, that exhibit high levels of budgetary centralization. What set Hungary apart was the extremely high rates of enterprise profits taxation and redistribution of tax revenues via the Finance Ministry's subsidy system. Table 2.3 shows the composition of tax revenue accruing to the Hungarian state in 1987.

The table shows that direct taxes paid by Hungarian enterprises

---

60. Yoshio Suzuki, *Money and Banking in Contemporary Japan* (New Haven: Yale University Press, 1980), 21–36; and Kozo Yamamura, "The Cost of Rapid Growth and Capitalist Democracy in Japan," in Leon Lindberg and Charles Maier, eds., *The Politics of Inflation and Economic Stagnation* (Washington, D.C.: Brookings Institution, 1985), 499–508.

61. Stephen Cohen, James Galbraith, and John Zysman, "Rehabbing the Labyrinth: The Financial System and Industrial Policy in France," in Cohen and Peter Gourevitch, eds., *France in the Troubled World Economy* (London: Butterworth Scientific, 1982), 51–73.

accounted for 70.1 percent of total tax revenue, those paid by individuals 6.6 percent. Some portion of the turnover tax, which was levied against commodity exchanges at various points in the production chain, was incorporated in the final price paid by end users. The burden of the turnover tax was therefore shared between the enterprise and household sectors. "Other taxes" included import duties and therefore also constituted extraction of enterprise income.

TABLE 2.2.   Budgetary Centralization in Selected Countries (revenue and expenditure as percentage of GDP)

Country	Year	Revenue	Expenditure
Greece	1988	32.7	46.3
United States	1988	34.3	36.5
Spain	1987	35.0	38.6
Canada	1989	40.3	43.9
Portugal	1988	40.7	45.0
West Germany	1989	45.7	45.9
France	1989	46.2	47.8
Austria	1989	46.9	49.7
Netherlands	1989	51.1	56.6
Sweden	1988	59.1	56.9
Denmark	1989	59.6	59.4
Hungary	1989	61.3	63.7

Source: János Kornai, "The Postsocialist Transition and the State: Reflections in the Light of Hungarian Fiscal Problems," *American Economic Review* 82, no. 2 (May 1992): 5.

TABLE 2.3.   Composition of Hungarian State Tax Revenue, 1987 (billions of forints)

Taxes paid by enterprises		409.8
Profits taxes	113.1	
Social security contributions	114.7	
Payroll taxes	28.6	
Property taxes	8.9	
Taxes on goods and services	144.5	
Taxes paid by households		38.7
Income taxes	4.0	
Social security contributions	34.7	
Turnover taxes		60.8
Other taxes		75.0
Total tax revenue		584.3

Source: IMF, *Government Financial Statistics Yearbook,* vol. 12 (1988).

If we include taxes paid directly to the state and indirectly through the turnover tax and import duties, the share of aggregate tax revenue accruing from contributions by Hungarian enterprises surpassed 80 percent. The corresponding proportion was much lower in Western countries, which characteristically allocated higher shares of the tax burden to the household sector through point-of-sales, income, and property taxes.[62] The effective rate of taxation of the enterprise sector was also extraordinarily high. By the mid-1980s, the Hungarian state was extracting nearly 90 percent of enterprise profits.[63]

This revenue structure impaired both allocative efficiency and macroeconomic stability. The earnings of the best-managed enterprises were confiscated and reallocated through the budget to support the economy's weakest performers. Meanwhile, concentration of the tax burden on state enterprises undercut attempts to curtail domestic demand through contraction of household income. The purchasing power of the population remained high while incentives for enhanced productivity within the enterprise sector remained low, exacerbating shortages and inflationary pressures throughout the economy.

Equally important was structure of budgetary expenditures, indicated in table 2.4. The budget was organized into two broad categories. "Current expenditures" encompassed national defense, social security, and other basic services; "capital expenditures" included state spending on infrastructure and international fixed capital investment. Within the current expenditures category, three items consumed the largest shares.

State administrative expenditures (general public services, defense), represented 24 percent of the total spending in Hungary, equivalent to 19.6 percent of GDP. In Western Europe, such expenditures constitute between 4 and 6 percent of national income.[64] The fact that basic services consumed such a large proportion of the Hungarian state budget resulted from four factors: (1) the scope of the central planning bureaucracy; (2) the high costs of internal security; (3) obligations to the Warsaw Pact, whose hegemon was better able than its Western counterpart to impose burden-sharing arrangements on weaker members of the alliance; and (4) state transfer payments to the Communist Party to support a vast network of mass line organizations, local Party committees, and the Hungarian Workers' Militia (Magyar Munkásőrség), the MSZMP's paramilitary arm.

Social expenditures (education, health, social security and welfare,

62. Muraközy, "Hazánk Költségvetéséról."

63. Interview, Ministry of Finance, 13 July 1988.

64. János Kornai, "The Postsocialist Transition and the State: Reflections in Light of Hungarian Fiscal Problems," *American Economic Review* 82 (May 1992): 6.

TABLE 2.4.   Composition of Hungarian State Expenditures, 1987 (billions of forints)

Current expenditures		653.5
General public services	140.2	
Defense	28.4	
Education	13.8	
Health	24.3	
Social security and welfare	170.7	
Housing and community amenities	6.0	
Recreation, culture, and religion	9.2	
Economic affairs and services	238.6	
Other	22.3	
Capital expenditures		48.6
General public services	7.1	
Education	2.4	
Health	1.3	
Housing and community amenities	7.5	
Economic affairs and services	26.0	
Other	4.3	
Total expenditures		702.1

Source: IMF, *Government Financial Statistics Yearbook,* vol. 12 (1988).

housing and community amenities), consumed 30.6 percent of the Hungarian state budget, equivalent to 25 percent of GDP. This exceeded social welfare expenditures in Western countries residing at comparable levels of economic development (Greece, Spain), and approached those of some advanced industrialized countries (Italy, Norway, West Germany, Sweden).[65]

The heavy burden of social welfare services reflected the political rationale of János Kádár's post-1956 social contract, which aimed to secure the population's quiescence in exchange for a range of state services—free education and medical services, mortgage subsidies, generous retirement benefits—incommensurate with Hungary's level of development. By the 1980s, a declining fertility rate, a growing population of pensioners, and other demographic factors were driving up the costs of social welfare services while the exigencies of economic austerity were reducing the economy's capacity to support them. Hungarian budget experts well recognized that this state of affairs was not economically sustainable.[66]

---

65. Kornai, "The Postsocialist Transition," 14–15.
66. István Hagelmayer, "Költségvetési Dilemmák" (Budgetary dilemmas), *Figyelő* 28, no. 29 (1984): 3; Hagelmayer, "Pénzügyi Politika Magyarországon."

But because of popular expectations inculcated over decades of Kádár's brand of goulash communism, cutting social expenditures presented insuperable political problems for the ruling party.

The third, and largest, category in the current expenditures portion of the state budget was the item designated "economic affairs and services," representing 34 percent of total expenditures or 27.7 percent of GDP. These were actually transfer payments to the enterprise sector in the forms of direct producer subsidies and consumer price supports. Within this category, the largest share went to the coal mining, metallurgy, textile, and food processing sectors, wherein resided Hungary's biggest loss makers.

As we have seen, the high rate of subsidization compromised the state's ability to stabilize the economy via parametric macroeconomic regulations. The unremitting flow of budgetary funds neutralized the National Bank's efforts to contract enterprise liquidity through monetary restrictions and enlarged the amount of deficit spending liable to central bank monetization. Moreover, that the lion's share of state subsidies went to the enterprise sector's least productive units undermined export performance and worsened the balance of payments. Heavy subsidization of loss-making enterprises also produced a variety of ill effects at the factory level. Rather than encouraging economic differentiation by rewarding efficient producers, the subsidy system promoted income leveling by confiscating the earnings of profit makers and redistributing them to loss makers. This simultaneously reduced the profit incentive of strong enterprises and weakened inducements for inefficient units to reorganize production and cut costs.[67] By rigidifying production patterns in inefficient sectors, the Hungarian subsidy system also reinforced the economy's high inflationary bias. Direct producer subsidies lowered incentives for weak enterprises to reduce production costs, which were transmitted to final sales prices. At the same time, consumer price subsidies mitigated the reactions of end users by impairing their ability to detect actual increases in social costs.[68]

The second part of the budget, capital expenditures, included state investments financed through the State Development Institute and international investments such as the CMEA oil and gas pipeline and the Gabcikovo-Nagymaros project, the hydroelectric dam on the Danube cofinanced by Hungary, Czechoslovakia, and Austria. Officially reported capital expenditures for 1987, HUF 48.6 billion, represented only 6.9 percent of the consolidated budget. However, a substantial portion of the

67. Muraközy, "Hazánk Költségvetéséról."
68. István Hagelmayer, "The Causes of Inflation in Hungary and the Prospects for Its Reduction," *Acta Oeconomica* 38, nos. 1–2 (1987): 11.

capital budget was classified by the Hungarian state. At that point, neither the Hungarian Parliament nor the IMF were aware of the true size of the capital budget. Adding the unreported capital expenditures, the 1987 budget deficit, reported in table 2.1 as HUF 50.1 billion, was closer to HUF 75 billion.[69]

Neither the separation of state budgets into current and capital expenditures nor the classification of certain elements of those budgets were uncommon international practices. But two factors distinguished Hungary from Western countries that employed such procedures. The first was the magnitude of the unreported expenditures, which were known to only a handful of senior Party and state officials. As I detail later in this chapter, the revelation of the actual size of the budget deficit in 1989 damaged Hungary's carefully cultivated reputation for financial integrity, compromised the political status of an already weak Communist Party, and undercut the Hungarian state's bargaining position vis-à-vis the IMF. Second, in contrast to separated components of the budgets of many Western states (e.g., the U.S. social security fund), Hungary's capital budget had no independent revenue source. Increments to the capital budget could only be financed through central bank credits. In fact, the overwhelming majority of fresh National Bank credits to the Ministry of Finance was earmarked for capital expenditures: of the HUF 40 billion in new central bank credits issued in 1988, HUF 32 billion went to the capital side of the consolidated budget.[70] Accounting for the unreported capital expenditures, the extent of deficit monetization in the late communist period was even higher than indicated in my earlier discussion of the flow equilibrium problem.

Political Control of the Budget under Reform Communism

The ability of the MSZMP leadership to conceal such large amounts of spending from both the Hungarian Parliament and the international lending agencies exemplified the peculiar structure of budgetary control under reform communism. The Hungarian state budget was the product of negotiations between the Ministry of Finance, the National Planning Office, and the branch ministries, operating under vague guidelines issued by the MSZMP Central Committee. The National Assembly, communist Hungary's version of a parliament, played no role in the preparation of the annual budget.[71] While the Parliament possessed the formal legal author-

---

69. Interview, National Bank of Hungary, 13 June 1988.
70. Interview, National Bank of Hungary, 13 June 1988.
71. Hagelmayer, "Költségvetési Dilemmak."

ity to approve the annual budget, the absence of a politically independent legislature rendered budgetary votes essentially meaningless. Since 1985, the MSZMP had staged parliamentary elections that permitted multican-didate contestation, using electoral lists drawn up by local Party commit-tees. But opposition parties were still banned, preventing the formation of an effective opposition within the legislature.[72]

The upshot was a fiscal process that was "representative" in the sense that factory-level agents enjoyed multiple channels through which they could lobby the Hungarian state for individual budgetary favors. Penetra-tion of the fiscal sphere by local actors seeking to soften the distributional impact of austerity fed the expansionary bias of "spender" institutions like the Ministry of Finance and Ministry of Industry. But those organizations were not publicly accountable for their budgetary decisions, reflecting the absence of an organized electoral opposition and the Parliament's inabil-ity to perform a credible oversight function. This peculiar combination of high representativeness and low accountability simultaneously advanced the fiscal interests of large numbers of local agents while depriving society at large of organized means of articulating budget policy preferences.

The Communist Party's role in fiscal policy further weakened the accountability dimension of the budgetary system and augmented the Hungarian state's spending bias. By the mid-1980s, the Central Commit-tee had delegated primary authority over budgetary matters to subordi-nate units in the state administration. But notwithstanding this devolution of policy-making authority, the Party remained free of any constitutional restraints on its capacity to manipulate the budget for political purposes. The Central Committee drew on the national treasury to support Party organizations and acquire new property for the exclusive use of the MSZMP. Individual members of the Central Committee prevailed on state bureaucrats to issue subsidies to politically favored enterprises and funds for local public works. And Communist Party leaders diverted state revenues to costly international projects aimed at currying favor with Hungary's allies in the Warsaw Pact.

The most notorious of those projects, the Gabcikovo-Nagymaros dam, epitomized the political problems of budget control in the commu-nist state. The project originated in the early 1950s, when the ruling parties of Hungary and Czechoslovakia began secret negotiations to build a hydroelectric generator on the Danube. Subsequently released minutes of Central Committee meetings in 1953 showed that senior Hungarian Party officials were already skeptical about the joint venture's economic feasibil-

---

72. Barnabas Racz, "Political Participation and Developed Socialism: The Hungarian Elections of 1985," *Soviet Studies* 39, no. 1 (January 1987): 40–62.

ity. But with its characteristic inattention to the costs of large infrastructural investments, the Party proceeded with the project. In 1977, the Kádár leadership signed an agreement with its Czech counterpart to commence construction. By the late 1970s, Hungarian economists and scientists were openly questioning the project, citing huge cost overruns and environmental damage. However, the Party used its control of the mass media to squelch public dissemination of this information. As late as May 1988, the Party was censoring critical discussion of the issue on Hungarian radio. Meanwhile, the Hungarian Parliament, legally obliged to ratify the national budget, was left completely in the dark about the details of the project. In summer 1988, the Party finally released the text of the 1977 agreement and permitted members of Parliament to visit the construction site.[73]

The Nagymaros episode played an important role in the sequence of developments leading to Hungary's negotiated transition to democracy in 1988–89. It underscored the economic consequences of a budget process bereft of transparency and public accountability, prompting members of Parliament to push for institutional reforms designed to increase the flow of information between the state ministries and Parliament and enlarging the latter body's deliberative role in fiscal policy.[74] It also catalyzed the political opposition: demonstrations organized in 1988 by environmental groups to protest the Danubian project were one of the first manifestations of organized civil opposition in Hungary since the 1956 Revolution, emboldening anti-Party organizations to press for truly momentous political reforms the following year.

During its final years in power, the MSZMP made a number of important initiatives in budgetary policy. In 1988, it launched a major reform of the tax system. The centerpiece of this reform was a new value-added tax and postwar Eastern Europe's first personal income tax, each designed to ease the burden of enterprise profits taxation and reduce the myriad of loopholes and exemptions that encouraged particularistic bargaining. But to soften the distributional effects of the reform, Party leaders accepted several compromises that mitigated attempts to rationalize the tax system.[75] On the expenditure side, the MSZMP began to move on

---

73. "Plans for Danubian Hydroelectric Project May Be Revised," *RFE/RL Hungarian Situation Reports,* 12 August 1988, 31–35.

74. In 1989, the Parliament established the State Audit Office, composed of politically independent budget experts and designed to enhance the quality of the information reaching legislators. "State Audit Office Law Debated," *FBIS/EEU,* 31 October 1989, 31.

75. Otto Gado, "Ervék Pro és Kontra" (Arguments and counterarguments), *Figyelő* 31, no. 16 (1987); István Nagy, "Vállalat Jövedelemszabályozás 1988: Előzetes Elgondolások a Vállati Adórendszer Továbbfejlesztésére" (Enterprise income regulation 1988: Preliminary

the subsidy problem. Yet these measures proved too little, too late. At the end of their tenure, Communist Party leaders found themselves preoccupied with explaining to the local population and Western creditors the existence of long-concealed deficits.

Conflicts over Budget Policy, 1988–89

In December 1988, the National Assembly ratified a budget that proposed to hold the deficit for fiscal 1989 to HUF 19.5 billion, in line with the conditions of the IMF standby approved by the Grósz regime the previous spring. This session was significant in that was first time since 1946 that the Hungarian Parliament played an active role in budget policy. Parliamentary committees proposed amendments of the budget plans submitted by the Finance Ministry, and the members of Parliament engaged in heated floor debate. Live coverage of the event by Hungarian television enhanced the vigor of the proceedings. In the end, the Parliament approved reductions in consumer price supports and producer subsidies. The members of Parliament also enacted cuts in state funds to the Communist Youth League and the Hungarian Workers' Militia. But these expenditure cuts did not suffice by themselves to meet the deficit target, prompting the Parliament to enact a surtax on enterprise profits.[76]

The legislators shied away from cuts in social welfare services and even approved a sizable increase in funds for housing, child support, and pensions. At the same time, they ratified an important institutional reform of the social security system. Beginning in January 1989, the social security fund would be separated from the central budget of the state. This meant, on the one hand, that the social security administration would rely entirely on its own revenue sources: if payroll contributions fell short of expenditures, social security officials would have to cover the gap by issuing bonds. On the other hand, the Finance Ministry could not draw on the social security fund to cover shortfalls in the central budget.[77]

The deficit for the first quarter of 1989 amounted to HUF 42 billion, over twice the target for the entire year. Budget officials estimated that the year-end deficit would exceed HUF 60 billion. This prompted the IMF to

---

concepts regarding the further development of the system of enterprise income regulation," *Figyelő* 31, no. 19 (1987); interview, National Planning Office, 10 May 1988; interviews, Ministry of Finance, 28 June and 13 July 1988.

76. "Small Reduction in the 1989 State Budget," *RFE/RL Hungarian Situation Reports,* 12 January 1989, 17–22.

77. "Social Insurance to Be Apart from State Budget," *FBIS/EEU,* 7 November 1988, 18–19.

suspend the last installment of the standby loan negotiated the previous year, with resumption of credit disbursals contingent on the MSZMP's ability to meet the original deficit target.[78]

The political leadership quickly produced a revised budget, proposing to slash the deficit by HUF 42 billion. The lion's share of the deficit reduction would be achieved through cuts in enterprise subsidies, defense spending, and transfer payments to Party and local governmental organizations. The authorities also announced the termination of Hungarian participation in the Gabcikovo-Nagymaros project. The Party again balked on social security cuts, announcing a new allocation of HUF 4 billion to pensioners and families with children. At the same time, the Minister of Finance announced that the state planned to use HUF 13 billion of the social security fund's surplus to purchase government bonds to finance the current deficit—violating the institutional separation of the budget system implemented just five months earlier.[79]

In late November 1989, the budgetary situation was further complicated by Prime Minister Miklos Németh's public disclosure that the MSZMP had concealed the true size of both the state budget deficit and the convertible currency debt. The accumulated internal deficit was HUF 300 billion higher than previously acknowledged, the external debt $1.5 billion higher. The latter figure placed Hungary's gross hard currency debt at $20 billion, the highest per capita debt in Eastern Europe. The original decision to cook the financial books was taken by senior members of the Communist Party in the late 1970s. The MSZMP inserted a new revenue item in its budget report to the Parliament to narrow the growing internal deficit. As it turned out, this revenue came from private Western credits, whose existence was not acknowledged until Németh's announcement a decade later. The Kádár leadership, fearful that disclosure of Hungary's true financial status would jeopardize its application to join the IMF in 1981, decided to conceal the information from both the IMF and the Parliament. Németh explained that he himself had known about the financial legerdemain and was using the occasion of the impending political transition to effect a general clearing of Hungary's economic accounts. He emphasized that democratic institutions and financial probity went hand in hand; Western support of Hungary's political transition presupposed

---

78. "IMF Forces Economic Changes on Hungary," *RFE/RL Hungarian Situation Reports,* 16 June 1989, 15–17.

79. "Finance Minister Speaks," *FBIS/EEU,* 5 June 1989, 15–16; "MTI Views Package to Reduce Deficit," *FBIS/EEU,* 6 June 1989, 27–28; "Planning Chief on Budget Deficit Package," *FBIS/EEU,* 18 May 1989, 33; "National Assembly Passes Revised Budget for 1989," *RFE/RL Hungarian Situation Reports,* 23 June 1989, 27–31.

restoration of international confidence in the integrity of the information supplied by the state.[80]

Following Németh's announcement, Hungary and the IMF began negotiations for a new stabilization program. The terms of this agreement were tougher than either of the 1982 and 1988 standbys; the new terms included strict macroeconomic control, rapid import liberalization, acceleration of the privatization program initiated by the MSZMP, and other conditions. At this juncture, Hungary's bargaining position was exceptionally weak. The suspension of the earlier standby and the disclosure of the actual size of the twin debts stiffened the IMF's position, and the lame-duck Németh government possessed scant political resources to resist the IMF's demands. While negotiating the agreement, the government sought the tacit approval of the leaders of the new political parties, who were too preoccupied with the forthcoming elections to exhibit much interest in the IMF stabilization program. The agreement went into effect just before the first multiparty elections in March 1990.[81]

Conclusion: The Dilemmas of Stabilization under Reform Communism

The fiscal crisis of the late communist period underscored the unique dilemmas of economic stabilization in market socialist systems. Particularistic claims by state enterprises, the Kádár regime's commitment to comprehensive social welfare, and plundering of budgetary resources by the ruling party pushed state expenditures far above tax receipts. The resultant budget deficits prompted sanctions by the IMF, whose seal of approval was essential to maintain Hungary's access to private credit markets in the West. But meeting the deficit targets specified in the IMF standby placed Party leaders in a severe policy bind. On the one hand, narrowing the budget gap by raising taxes would compromise systemic tax reform, whose central purpose was precisely to reduce an exceptionally high rate of budgetary redistribution of national income. On the other hand, Communist Party leaders could not make the sort of deep spending cuts that were possible in orthodox planned economies. Efforts to reduce expenditures ran into strong resistance by local agents, whose bargaining power was considerable owing to the reforms the Party had already enacted.

---

80. "Németh Addresses Parliamentary Session," *FBIS/EEU*, 30 November 1989, 65–72; "Premier Németh Interviewed on the Economy," *FBIS/EEU*, 6 December 1989, 61–62.

81. Interview, National Bank of Hungary, 21 May 1991.

The deficiencies of fiscal control under reform communism complicated the other two components of stabilization policy discussed in this chapter. Notwithstanding the creation of a two-tiered banking system, the spending bias of the Hungarian state necessarily circumscribed the efficacy of monetary policy as a stabilization instrument. Redistribution of the bulk of national income through the state budget neutralized the reorganized National Bank's efforts to control aggregate liquidity via parametric monetary regulation. The weakness of macroeconomic control in turn exacerbated the dilemmas of wage liberalization: absent effective fiscal and monetary institutions, the communist state could not apply countervailing pressure on efforts by enterprise managers and workers to bid up domestic purchasing power.

Thus, by the late 1980s the Hungarian Communist Party faced the worst possible combination of declining economic performance, eroding political authority, and mounting pressure by international financial institutions. These factors, together with the retreat of the Soviet Union, played a decisive role in the negotiated transition to democracy at decade's end.

CHAPTER 3

Structural Adjustment and Market Socialism

In this chapter, I analyze Hungarian structural adjustment policy in the 1980s, focusing on financial sector reform, industrial restructuring, and foreign trade and exchange. I argue that market reforms undertaken within the institutional setting of reform communism produced contradictory effects that impaired the ruling party's capacity to manage adjustment policy. As with macroeconomic stabilization, the Party's use of market mechanisms for structural adjustment generated distortions that compelled the MSZMP to restore central controls in areas where it had already relinquished a large measure of authority.

The institutional "ratchet effects" of market reform were strongest in the financial sector. In 1987, the Party transferred power of credit allocation from the National Bank of Hungary to commercial banks, whose profit orientation ostensibly gave them incentives to channel funds toward their strongest clients. But far from instigating a redistribution of capital within the enterprise sector, the banking reform reproduced the same patterns of credit allocation that prevailed under the prereform system. The introduction of joint stock ownership into Hungary's financial sector simultaneously broadened the operational authority of commercial bank managers and induced them to sustain credit flows to the economy's weakest performers.

The refusal of the new banks to use market instruments to discipline unprofitable clients increased the MSZMP's reliance on political/administrative mechanisms of adjustment. Under pressure from the Washington lending agencies to accelerate restructuring of Hungary's loss-making sectors, the Party created several new state and government agencies empowered to implement far-reaching industrial restructuring programs. But these institutional reforms merely erected new obstacles to structural adjustment. The Party's delegation of authority to lower-ranking bodies broadened opportunities for branch ministries, local Party organizations, and trade unions to advance their particularistic claims.

The push-pull dynamic of market socialism was less pronounced in foreign trade and exchange. The institutional structure of that issue area enabled Communist Party leaders to reimpose central controls if economic liberalization prompted factory-level actors to behave in ways contrary to adjustment policy. In contrast to other spheres of NEM, where the prior devolution of authority gave local agents the means to resist ex post recentralization, the National Bank's continued monopoly of foreign exchange allowed the MSZMP to proceed with import liberalization without risking an inadvertent loss of control. The main obstacles to marketization of the foreign sector stemmed from other sources. The distorted incentive structures of Hungarian state enterprises, whose demand schedules remained price inelastic under NEM, circumscribed the utility of exchange rate policy as an adjustment tool. Fears of the inflationary consequences of forint devaluation led the Party to pursue a strategy of import liberalization combined with real currency appreciation—a policy mix counter to the standard prescriptions of the Washington lending agencies. I show in part 3 that the successor government of the MDF continued this strategy, illustrating the high degree of continuity in the foreign exchange arena across Hungary's political transition.

Financial Sector Reform and Structural Adjustment

The principal aim of Hungary's banking reform was to transform bank credit from the passive financier of the central plan into an active instrument of structural adjustment. By transferring power of credit allocation from the National Bank to independent commercial banks, Communist Party leaders hoped to force a reallocation of capital within the enterprise sector. The new banks, organized as joint stock companies and driven by the profit motive, would adopt Western-type credit evaluation procedures. The economy's strongest enterprises would thus receive bank credit on favorable terms, while loss makers would be compelled to undertake restructuring programs as condition for restoration of credit lines. For heavily indebted enterprises unable to take the measures needed to become profitable, the banks would avail themselves of Hungary's bankruptcy law and seek liquidation of their clients' assets.

   In this section, I show how the institutional logic of reform communism defeated these objectives. The banks, unwilling to use commercial credit as a restructuring tool, turned the problem of structural adjustment back to the center. Communist Party leaders, having already relinquished the credit function, could not intervene and compel the banks to redirect credit flows in a manner consistent with the aims of adjustment policy. The ineffectiveness of commercial credit as a restructuring instrument forced the political authorities to turn to administrative methods of adjustment. The result was to shift the locus of distributional conflict over structural adjustment away from the banks and toward the center, entangling Party and state officials in a series of disputes over capacity reductions and labor dislocations in targeted sectors.

In short, the ironic result of the introduction of *market* instruments into Hungary's financial sector was to deepen the center's reliance on *nonmarket* mechanisms of adjustment, whose use drew political leaders into conflicts over the pace and extent of industrial restructuring.

Credit Control under Orthodox Central Planning

The primary function of bank credit in orthodox CPEs was to facilitate execution of the physical production processes detailed in the national plan. Credit control was based on the separation of working and fixed capital finance. The Ministry of Finance supplied enterprises with seed capital, representing the minimum amount of funds needed to carry out day-to-day operations. The central bank then advanced working capital credits to cover seasonal fluctuations in liquidity requirements, unanticipated hitches in plan execution, and other expenses exceeding the base capital. By attaching these credits to specific components of producers' working capital assets and requiring quick repayment, the central authorities sought to minimize the temporarily free transaction balances of enterprises and verify that recipients of bank credits used them for the intended purposes. While the central bank operated under global credit targets, the annual credit plan did not exert any functional limits on growth of working capital. The supply of short-term credit adjusted passively to the above-norm inventories of state enterprises.

In theory, the elastic adjustment of short-term credit to the working capital requirements of state enterprises did not present a problem if the central bank ensured that producers actually used the credit for the specified purposes. But the logic of central planning militated against use of bank credit as a financial control device. Attempts by the central bank to penalize enterprises for financial infractions ran up against the goal of plan fulfillment. Restrictions on working capital credits not only disrupted the physical operations of the guilty enterprises. The effects of such sanctions were collateralized across the entire producer sphere. Enterprises subjected to sanctions would withhold payments to their suppliers. The latter, lacking the means to pursue legal action against buyers in arrears, would then face liquidity problems of their own. Central bank sanctions thus drew producers innocent of mismanagement into a chain of mutual indebtedness that prevented the enterprise sector from meeting the Communist Party's production goals. These circumstances compelled the Ministry of Finance, the branch ministries, and Party organizations to prevail on the central bank to forgive the infractions and release the working capital needed to allow production to proceed. The liquidity position of socialist producers thus ceased to be an important determinant of their access to working capital credit. Loss-making enterprises did not view central bank threats to withhold credit as credible, since they could count on intervention by their patrons in the "spender" institutions of the communist state. The result was rapid expansion of the aggregate stock of short-term credit, the bulk of which was channeled toward the enterprise sector's weakest performers.[1]

Mechanisms of fixed capital control similarly reinforced the systemic deficiencies of orthodox CPEs. During the Stalinist period, fixed capital investments were financed entirely through nonrepayable budgetary grants. By divorcing bank credit from the fixed capital sphere, Communist Party leaders sought to avoid the cyclical movements in investment that were endemic to capitalist economies and to pursue a steady expansion of the socialist economy's capital stock. But the actual course of events in the East dashed these expectations, as investment cycles plagued central planners throughout the region. Wavelike fluctuations in fixed capital investment emanated from two factors. First, soft budget constraints fed the expansion drive of state enterprises. Plant directors, facing unceasing pressure for plan fulfillment but no effective liquidity restraints, procured as much investment finance as possible to expand productive capacity. Second, the institutional structure of the central planning system prevented state authorities from controlling investment. The absence of a pricing mechanism deprived investment planners of objective criteria for selecting among competing claims for fixed capital finance and removed incentives for enterprise managers to utilize the funds efficiently once the center allocated them.[2]

---

1. Andrew Feltenstein and Ziba Farhadian, "Fiscal Policy, Monetary Targets, and the Price Level in a Centrally Planned Economy: An Application to the Case of China," *Journal of Money, Credit, and Banking* 19, no. 2 (May 1987): 137–56; George Garvy, *Money, Financial Flows, and Credit in the Soviet Union* (Cambridge: Harvard University Press, 1977), 117, 125–26; Donald Hodgman, "Soviet Monetary Controls through the Banking System," in Franklyn Holzman, ed., *Readings on the Soviet Economy* (Chicago: Rand McNally, 1962), 593–98; Katherine Hsiao, *Money and Monetary Policy in Communist China* (New York: Columbia University Press, 1971), 65–135, 225–53; T. M. Podolski, *Socialist Banking and Monetary Control: The Experience of Poland* (Cambridge: Harvard University Press, 1973), 105–35, 179–240; Adam Zwass, Money, *Banking, and Credit in the Soviet Union and Eastern Europe* (White Plains, N.Y.: M. E. Sharpe, 1979), 3–23, 65, 108–9, 119–20.

2. There is an extensive literature on the investment-cycle phenomenon in planned economies. Key works include Tamás Bauer, "Investment Cycles in Planned Economies," *Acta Oeconomica* 21, no. 3 (1978): 243–60; Bauer, *Tervgazdaság, Beruházás, Ciklusok* (Planned economy, investment, cycles) (Budapest: Közgazdasági és Jogi Könykiadó, 1981); A. Bródy, "About Investment Cycles and Their Attenuation," *Acta Oeconomica* 31, nos. 1–2 (1983): 37–51; Andrea Deák, "On the Possibility of Enterprise Decisions on Investment,"

Hungary's NEM did not change the basic profile of the credit control system I have described, despite the increased authority of the National Bank to apply efficiency criteria to loan applications, the creation of semi-independent specialized financial institutions designed to channel credit into promising areas outside of the state sector, and other measures aimed at enlarging the role of bank credit. Inefficient capital flows persisted even when the first IMF standby agreement forced MSZMP leaders to contract long-term investment credit in the early 1980s. Measured in terms of its impact on total fixed capital investment, the austerity program was successful: by 1984, aggregate investment was 30 percent below the level of 1978. However, within this diminished pool of investment finance, the distribution of long-term credits remained as inefficient as ever. The largest and least profitable state enterprises continued to receive the lion's share of fixed capital and to undertake the bulk of investment projects.[3]

Credit Allocation under the Two-Tiered Banking System

The designers of the two-tiered banking system sought to transform this state of affairs. By moving the crediting function from the National Bank to joint stock commercial banks, they hoped to replace political factors with efficiency standards as the main determinants of credit flows. The incentive structure guiding the lending decisions of the new banks would differ fundamentally from that of the National Bank. The shareholders, interested above all in maximizing returns on their investments, would require bank managers to anchor their credit policies to profitability criteria. Since the most profitable enterprises presumably represented the best credit risks, the banks would redirect the flow of capital from weak to strong producers.

Közgazdasági Szemle, no. 1 (1975): 14–24; Károly Soós, "Some General Problems of the Hungarian Investment System," *Acta Oeconomica* 21, no. 3 (1978): 223–42; Laura Tyson, "Investment Allocation: A Comparison of the Reform Experiences of Hungary and Yugoslavia," *Journal of Comparative Economics* 7 (1983): 288–303; J. Winiecki, "Investment Cycles and an Excess of Demand Inflation in Planned Economies: Sources and Processes," *Acta Oeconomica* 28, nos. 1–2 (1982): 147–60.

3. L. György Asztalos, Lajos Bokros, and György Surányi, "Reform and Financial Institutional System in Hungary," *Acta Oeconomica* 32, nos. 3–4 (1984): 251–68; I. Fenyővári, "On the Hungarian Financial System," *Acta Oeconomica* 25, nos. 3–4 (1980): 277–90; János Kornai, *The Economics of Shortage,* vol. B (Amsterdam: North Holland, 1980), 513–32; Paul Marer, "Hungary's Balance of Payments Crisis and Response, 1978–84," in Joint Economic Committee of the U.S. Congress, *East European Economies: Slow Growth in the 1980s* (Washington, D.C.: Government Printing Office, 1986), 3:311–17; Éva Várhegyi, "Sources of the Growth of Enterprises in Hungary," *Acta Oeconomica* 37, nos. 3–4 (1986): 267–84.

How did the banking reform affect credit flows in the Hungarian economy? Table 3.1 shows the percentile shares of bank credit allocated to the eight principal branches of Hungarian industry in 1986, the last year of the monobanking system, and 1987, the first year of the two-tiered system.

The data show that the reform had a minuscule effect on intersectoral credit flows in the late communist period. Hungary's two biggest loss-making industries, mining and metallurgy, incurred only slight losses in credit shares despite the transfer of their loan portfolios to putatively profit-seeking commercial banks. It was not until the early 1990s, when loan officers operated under wholly different institutional and economic constraints, that the banks withdrew from those sectors.[4]

Equally important, credit flows *within* specific sectors indicated that distortions long associated with the monobanking system persisted after the transition to the two-tiered system. These problems were particularly apparent in the coal mining industry, one of the "crisis sectors" targeted for restructuring in Hungary's adjustment program. Table 3.2 shows the financial indices of Hungary's eight coal mines for 1987.

Not only did the new banks fail significantly to reduce their exposure in the mining sector as a whole. Intrasectoral capital flows in 1987 were precisely the *reverse* of what one would expect of a commercial bank intent on applying exacting standards of credit analysis. The two mining companies that received increases in credit during the year were not only the least profitable enterprises in the sector but the only ones that incurred absolute losses during the year. Both of those enterprises also had exceptionally low liquidity ratios. "X2" in fact lacked sufficient liquid assets even to cover its

TABLE 3.1.   Allocation of Bank Credit in the Hungarian State Sector, 1986–87 (millions of forints)

Sector	1986		1987	
	Credits Issued	Share of Total (%)	Credits Issued	Share of Total (%)
Mining	18,550	16.1	17,859	15.7
Electronics	8,208	7.1	8,298	7.3
Metallurgy	12,374	10.8	10,720	9.4
Machinery	25,505	22.2	24,246	21.3
Construction	216	0.2	182	0.2
Chemicals	34,101	29.6	36,774	32.3
Light industry	16,069	14.0	15,782	13.9
Other	53	0.05	69	0.06
Total	115,076	100.0	113,930	100.0

Source: Hungarian Ministry of Industry.

4. See table 6.1.

TABLE 3.2. Financial Indices of Hungarian Mining Enterprises, 1987

Enterprise	Change in Debt[a]	Rate of Return[b]	Leverage[c]	Liquidity[d]
x1	34.9	5.0	18.5	1.0
x2	28.9	−14.7	78.8	0.8
x3	1.4	3.9	4.5	1.1
x4	−3.6	8.7	11.8	2.8
x5	−5.4	10.5	33.8	2.1
x6	−13.5	16.1	9.6	2.5
x7	−13.9	28.4	24.3	3.9
x8	−18.9	23.6	30.4	5.5

Source: Hungarian Ministry of Industry.
[a]Calculated as the percentage change in total debt outstanding from year-end 1986 to year-end 1987.
[b]Calculated as net income divided by book value of capital.
[c]Calculated as total debt oustanding divided by book value of capital.
[d]Calculated as the ratio of liquid assets to current liabilities.

current liabilities. Moreover, these credit increases came at the expense of the six mining companies that managed to generate positive rates of return.

These distortions were partly a consequence of the new banks' inexperience with sophisticated credit-evaluation procedures. As condition for Hungary's admission to the Washington lending agencies in 1982, the National Bank formally adopted the World Bank's standard loan-analysis criteria: return on capital, debt-service ratio, liquidity, and leverage. However, loan officers in the central bank's credit division paid little heed, continuing their traditional practice of allocating credit on the simple basis of enterprise demand. The problem continued with the transition to the two-tiered system, despite the fact that loan officers in the new banks were now operating under an incentive structure that presumably demanded careful attention to the World Bank criteria. A high percentage of the staff of the banks came directly from the National Bank, bringing with them the habits and organization ethos of the monobanking system.

Even when the banks attempted to apply the standards of the international financial institutions, the dubious reliability of the financial information supplied by Hungarian enterprises complicated the task of evaluating loan applications. The problem was not so much that state enterprises deliberately falsified or concealed data, although this was hardly an unknown phenomenon in the socialist economies. Rather, the main difficulty was Hungary's antiquated accounting system. Before 1987, Hungarian enterprises did not even use double-sided balance sheets. The basic purpose of the accounting system was not to reveal the underlying financial situation of enterprises but to enable the Ministry of Finance to determine enterprise profits taxes, check adherence to yearly targets for enterprise wage payments, and set levels of managerial compensation. In 1987, Hungary formally adopted German-style double accounting. But the objectives of the accounting system remained the same during the final years of communist rule. Balance sheets were prepared by Finance Ministry auditors, not enterprises themselves. Plant directors still lacked any concept of cash flow, any sense of the relationship between assets and liabilities. Moreover, the financial indices of state enterprises only accounted for nominal values. This prevented the new commercial banks from accurately calculating rates of return and leverage, both of which used book value of enterprise capital as the base denominator. High levels of state subsidies further distorted the income statements of enterprises, frustrating the banks' attempts to discriminate between weak and strong performers.[5]

But while Hungary's lack of experience with Western-type banking practices and backward accounting system created obstacles to its adoption of the World Bank's lending criteria, they did not fully explain credit flows within the country's loss-making industries. The problems of those sectors were of long standing, and it did not require sophisticated credit evaluation procedures to determine that loans issued to certain enterprises were highly risky. Yet the new banks continued to channel credit to producers well-known to be running losses. The persistence of seemingly irrational intrasectoral credit flows under the two-tiered system was chiefly attributable to the institutional structure of Hungary's market socialist model, which expanded the decision-making authority of banks and enterprises while foreclosing the Party's options to correct distortions via financial recentralization.

State Regulation of the Commercial Banks

Under the two-tiered system, the Hungarian state possessed an impressive array of instruments for regulating the commercial banking sector. But while these regulatory mechanisms could powerfully influence the overall financial position of the new banks, they did not enable the central authorities to reshape credit allocation patterns to support structural adjustment policy.

The National Bank used three types of financial regulations: legal reserve requirements applied to commercial bank liabilities, rediscounting of bills of exchange, and refinancing credits issued directly to the banks. None of these devices proved able to curb the penchant of the banks to channel funds toward the economy's least creditworthy enterprises.

---

5. Interviews, Hungarian Credit Bank, 8 July 1988; Price Waterhouse Budapest, 27 May 1991.

National Bank authorities quickly found that a legal reserve requirement was an ineffective means of controlling commercial bank liquidity. The monetary authorities could not modify it frequently without disrupting commercial banking operations. And once the reserve requirement was set, the banks sought ways of reducing their liabilities. One trick they used was reclassifying savings deposits as securities, which were not initially subject to the reserve requirement. The banks also discovered means of circumventing legal barriers between the enterprise and household money circuits. The banks, denied licenses to accept deposits by Hungarian citizens, used institutional investors to gain access to household liquidity and thereby enlarge their lendable reserves.[6]

Rediscounting policy likewise proved of limited utility. Commercial bills of exchange were legalized in 1985, enlarging the range of alternatives to commercial bank credit and making it technically possible for monetary authorities to use rediscounting as a regulatory instrument. In market economies, bills of exchange and other types of nonbank credit enhance allocative efficiency by enabling the strongest producers to weather general liquidity contractions. But they created precisely the opposite effect in socialist economies, allowing the weakest performers in the enterprise sector to escape the consequences of their own inefficiencies. Profitable enterprises rarely hesitated to sell intermediate products to illiquid companies on credit, confident that the state authorities would eventually supply the latter with the funds needed to service outstanding payments to suppliers.[7]

The same tendencies appeared in Hungary after the banking reform. Illiquid enterprises responded to the National Bank's monetary squeeze not by increasing productivity through internal adjustments but by expanding their use of nonbank credit. State enterprises still showed little inclination to discipline each other. The high level of concentration of Hungarian industry reinforced this tendency, as the largest and least productive enterprises, many of which enjoyed near monopolies in their sectors, continued to blackmail suppliers into delivering capital goods without payment. The legalization of bills of exchange did not improve this situation. Indeed, the legal enforceability of commercial bills often prompted enterprise managers to turn to informal trade credit, to which

---

6. Interviews, National Planning Office, 21 April 1988; National Bank of Hungary, 12 August 1988.

7. The main theme of the "post-Keynesian" critique of monetarism is that the demand for money creates its own supply. Thus, factory-level agents may easily defeat attempts by central bankers to contract the money supply by expanding nonbank credit. Shirley Gedeon, "The Post Keynesian Theory of Money: A Summary and an East European Example," *Journal of Post Keynesian Economics* 8, no. 2 (winter 1986): 208–21; Gedeon, "Monetary Disequilibrium and Bank Reform Proposals in Yugoslavia: Paternalism and the Economy," *Soviet Studies* 39, no. 2 (April 1987): 281–91.

no legal conditions were attached. Thus, much of the expansion of non-bank credit in the early phase of the banking reform remained completely out of the National Bank's control and was statistically tracked only with great difficulty and significant time delay.[8]

This left refinancing credit as the National Bank's main regulatory instrument. As shown in chapter 2, the Bank encountered a number of problems with refinancing policy during the first year of the reform. The Bank possessed the authority to dispose of individual applications for long-term refinancing credits for fixed capital investments. But this facility proved of limited usefulness, as the National Bank allowed the commercial banks to fill up their long-term credit quotas within a few months after the startup of the two-tiered system.[9] Consequently, the National Bank's regulatory activities were largely confined to short-term refinancing. In theory, the monetary authorities could decisively transform the liquidity positions of the banks by altering the multiples of their registered capital that determined the size of the short-term credit quotas. However, their attempts to do so in late 1987 provoked strong opposition by banks, enterprises, and Finance Ministry officials that quickly forced the National Bank to back down.

The Communist State as Equity Owner

In theory, the Hungarian state's position as majority shareholder in the new banks also gave the center broad legal authority over commercial credit policy. But two factors circumscribed the utility of joint stock ownership as a medium of state influence within the commercial banking sector: (1) the separation of ownership and control characteristic of the joint stock form and (2) the contradictory position of the communist state as equity owner.

The case of the Hungarian Credit Bank, the largest of the new commercial banks, illustrated the problems confronting the state as shareholder. When the Credit Bank began operations in January 1987, the Hungarian state owned 76 percent of its registered capital, with the remaining shares distributed among state enterprises, cooperatives, and local governmental organizations. The composition of the Credit Bank's board of directors testified to the Hungarian state's highly visible role in the Bank. Of the nineteen seats on the board, thirteen were allocated to senior Party and state officials and four to the managing directors of large state enter-

---

8. Interview, Ministry of Finance, 13 June 1988.
9. Interview, National Bank of Hungary, 28 April 1988.

prises.[10] Obviously, the managers of the Credit Bank could not be wholly indifferent to the preferences of political authorities who figured so prominently on the board. But irrespective of the size of the state's ownership share, the high separation of ownership and control in the joint stock company did not readily permit central intervention in individual lending decisions. The board met only infrequently, and on those occasions its formal sphere of authority extended only to appointment of the management, determination of the annual dividend, and approval of the Bank's general business plan.[11]

Beyond the constraints imposed by the joint stock form, the contradictory incentives of the Hungarian state as equity owner diminished the Party's capacity to shape commercial credit policy. Economic theories of property rights ascribe several liabilities to state ownership. Foremost among them is limited asset transferability. In privately owned corporations, high asset transferability helps shareholders to reduce the agency costs stemming from separation of ownership and control. The possibility of shareholder liquidation disciplines managers by confronting them with the threat of hostile takeovers that might result in their dismissal. Trading of shares on the equity market reveals current opinion about the value of the corporation's assets, supplementing profit-and-loss statements as indices of managerial performance.[12]

These effects are missing or attenuated under state ownership. Because asset turnover in an equity market dominated by the state is restricted, enterprise managers do not face any credible threat of a hostile takeover. Moreover, even if the state engages in active trading of its shares, its own incentive structure militates against augmentation of the long-term value of those assets. Private shareholders have a compelling interest in preserving the resale value of their equity, as the losses accruing from a

---

10. Hungarian Credit Bank, *Annual Report, 1987.*

11. David Bartlett, "Banking and Financial Reform in a Mixed Economy: The Case of Hungary," in Perry Patterson, ed., *Capitalist Goals, Socialist Past: The Rise of the Private Sector in Command Economies* (Boulder: Westview, 1993), 179–81. For theoretical analyses of the agency problems arising from joint stock ownership, see Harold Demsetz, "The Structure of Ownership and the Theory of the Firm," *Journal of Law and Economics* 26 (June 1983): 375–96; Eugene Fama and Michael Jensen "Separation of Ownership," *Journal of Law and Economics* 26 (June 1983): 301–25; Fama and Jensen, "Agency Problems and Residual Claims," *Journal of Law and Economics* 26 (June 1983): 327–49; Terry Moe, "The New Economics of Organization," *American Journal of Political Science* 28, no. 4 (November 1984): 739–77; Oliver Williamson, "Organizational Form, Residual Claimants, and Corporate Control," *Journal of Law and Economics* 26 (June 1983): 351–66.

12. Richard Zeckhauser and Murray Horn, "The Control and Performance of State-Owned Enterprises," in Paul McAvoy, W. T. Stanbury, George Yarrow, and Zeckhauser, eds., *Privatization and State-Owned Enterprises: Lessons from the United States, Great Britain, and Canada* (Boston: Kluwer, 1989), 35–44.

decline in the value of any single item in their portfolios are considerable. However, for the state such risks are negligible: its portfolio is so large and diversified that diminution of the long-term value of any particular asset will have only a minimal effect on its overall financial position.[13] The state is apt to have a stronger interest in maximizing short-term returns such as dividends, as these constitute direct and immediate infusions of cash into the national treasury.

The behavior of the Hungarian state as shareholder of the commercial banks well demonstrated these incentive problems. In spring 1988, the shareholders of the Hungarian Credit Bank assembled for their annual meeting, at which they took up the question of the size of the annual dividend. The Ministry of Finance, acting as representative of the state, dispatched three officials to the meeting: the head of the Office of Banking Supervision, the chief of the Ministry's budget division, and the director of the Országos Szanálás Bizottság (National Reorganization Committee, or OSB), a small agency charged with overseeing the restructuring of Hungary's loss-making sectors. These officials held different views regarding the Credit Bank's dividend policy. The head of the Office of Banking Supervision preferred a low dividend, arguing that a high dividend would endanger the long-term financial stability of the new banks whose portfolios included a large number of bad loans taken over from the National Bank. The director of the OSB also preferred a low dividend, reasoning that this would leave the Credit Bank with larger reserves to write off nonperforming loans. But the Finance Ministry's budget chief opted for a high dividend. Consistent with the predictions of property rights theory, his main interest was maximizing short-term returns to produce a quick infusion of cash into the treasury and reduce the state's bulging budget deficit. In fact, this official was sufficiently enthused about the prospect of using the state's equity portfolio as a revenue source that he proposed enacting a special regulation that would enable the Finance Ministry to receive its bank dividend *before* the annual shareholders' meeting. In the end, the Credit Bank shareholders voted themselves a 17 percent dividend, which many economists considered outrageously high for a bank in its first year of operation and saddled with a huge backlog of dubious assets.[14]

In short, the introduction of joint stock ownership into Hungary's financial sector did not augment the power of the communist state as shareholder. Instead, it reduced the state's regulatory capacity by widening the separation of ownership and control and sharpening the tension

13. Ellen Comisso, "Market Failures and Market Socialism: Economic Problems of the Transition," *East European Politics and Societies* 2, no. 3 (fall 1988): 459.

14. Interviews, Budapest Bank, 26 April 1988; Hungarian Credit Bank, 27 May 1988; National Bank of Hungary, 26 August 1988.

between the state's role as executor of adjustment policy and its proprietary interests as equity owner. At the same time, the joint stock form enlarged the operational control of commercial bank managers, enhancing their ability to extract favorable regulatory arrangements from the center.

Conflicts over the Loan Portfolio Problem

The mixed incentives of the Hungarian state as shareholder had important ramifications for the disposition of the large stock of bad loans inherited from the monobanking system. The loan portfolio problem became the key source of contention between the state and the banks, and the chief obstacle to the use of commercial credit for structural adjustment.

At the launching of the two-tiered system, virtually all of the National Bank's loan portfolio was transferred to the new commercial banks. Most of this portfolio consisted of loans issued to Hungary's loss-making sectors over several decades during the pre-1987 period. It was widely understood that many of these loans, amounting to tens of billions of forints, stood little chance of ever being paid back. The issue at hand was who would take the financial hit for writing off nonperforming assets.

The commercial bank managers contended that they could not ask their shareholders to bear the costs of the injudicious lending policies of the National Bank in years past. The political authorities were pressuring them to write down their loan portfolios, while at the same time the Hungarian state was sustaining the flow of subsidies to the very same enterprises that had fallen in arrears on their debts. Until the Party terminated budgetary support of those producers and initiated a coherent restructuring program, the problems of the loss-making sectors would not go away. Weak enterprises would continue to generate losses, more loans would go into default, and the banks would face repeated loan write-offs.[15]

State authorities insisted that the banks should bear final responsibility. The fact that the banks were saddled with a large stock of dubious assets was a regrettable but unavoidable consequence of the transition to the two-tiered system. Budgetary constraints prevented the state from absorbing the losses. Moreover, the unnaturally high profits of the banking sector, which were less a result of the business acumen of management than of the willingness of cost-insensitive enterprises to pay exorbitant rates on commercial loans, would enable the banks to build up loss reserves and write down their portfolios. To this end, the Office of Banking Supervision implemented a regulation requiring the banks to set aside

---

15. Interview, Hungarian Credit Bank, 8 July 1988.

20 percent of their pretax profits to create a special reserve fund covering loan write-offs.[16]

But while the communist state enjoyed the legal power to force the banks to set up these reserve funds, it had no authority to direct them to write off loans that they could still classify as performing assets. And so a standoff emerged: the state pressured the commercial banks to write down their portfolios; the banks maintained they would not do so until the state provided guarantees of partial compensation for the loan losses and launched a restructuring program with the backing of the Communist Party. Until then, the banks would keep the bad loans on their books as performing assets, supplying debtor enterprises with enough fresh credit to permit them to sustain a trickle of payments.

The banks held to this strategy even as the National Bank was squeezing the total supply of liquidity in the commercial banking sector. Indeed, their most generous credit allocations to loss-making enterprises came at a time, winter of 1987–88, when the monetary authorities were enacting draconian cuts in short-term refinancing credit. While the National Bank's intention was to create a liquidity shortage and force the banks to reallocate credit from weak to strong enterprises, the banks did just the opposite: they *cut* credit lines to their most profitable clients and *increased* them to loss makers in the mining industry and other vulnerable sectors, reasoning that it was precisely the latter which were least able to tolerate the liquidity crunch and whose debt-servicing capability was in greatest need of support through the issuance of fresh loans.[17] Notwithstanding protestations by state authorities, the joint stock form gave commercial bank managers the legal authority to pursue this strategy.

Therein resides the main explanation of the persistence of inefficient credit flows in Hungary's commercial banking system. While the loan policies of the new banks were "irrational" in an economic sense, they were "prudent" from the standpoint of management's responsibility to the shareholders of the banks. Until the political leadership initiated a restructuring program for the economy's loss-making sectors, the bank managers could best protect the assets of the shareholders by providing just enough credit to allow weak clients to continue payments on old loans, which would permit the banks to report those loans as performing assets. In this way, the banks could avert large loan write-offs that would both reduce short-term profits and imperil the long-term value of the banks' equity.

---

16. Interview, Ministry of Finance, 28 June 1988.

17. Interviews, Hungarian Credit Bank, 3 August 1988; Budapest Bank, 26 April, 9 May, and 24 August 1988.

The irony, of course, was that the Hungarian state itself was the majority shareholder in the banks and hence the investor most liable to a diminution of the value of commercial bank equity. This underscored the peculiar duality of the communist state's role as shareholder. As executors of adjustment policy, state institutions had a strong interest in (1) exhorting the banks to write off their nonperforming assets and thus relieve pressure on the state budget to cover the losses and (2) persuading the banks to use the commercial credit instrument now at their disposal to discipline illiquid enterprises and promote industrial restructuring. But as majority shareholders in the banks, state authorities had an equally strong interest in *opposing* those very same measures. For the banks themselves to shoulder the entire burden of disposing of the bad loans would reduce current profits and thus deprive the state, as shareholder, of justification for voting itself high dividends for the national treasury. It would also undermine the long-term financial stability of the banks and thus endanger the security of the state's equity holdings.

Thus, the paradoxical result of the introduction of joint stock ownership into Hungary's financial system was to heighten the bargaining power of commercial bank managers while reducing that of the state, which held the majority of shares. Bank managers could present a united front on the loan portfolio question, their resistance to political pressure based on the quite justifiable grounds of defending shareholder interests. By contrast, the contradictory position of the communist state left it deeply divided. As shareholder, it could not unequivocally support loan write-offs, poorly coordinated restructuring programs, and other measures that threatened the value of its equity shares in the banks. As policymaker, the state sought to coerce the banks to take precisely these measures so it might divest itself of the economic and political costs of disposing of the loan stock and restructuring the economy. But here the structure of joint stock ownership limited the range of coercive devices available to state institutions. As we have seen, the Office of Banking Supervision used its regulatory power to compel the banks to set aside a specified portion of their retained earnings to establish reserve funds for loan write-offs. The state could also revise the rules governing loan classification to make it more difficult for bank managers to continue to report dubious loans as performing assets. But there the state's legal jurisdiction stopped: it had no authority to force the banks involuntarily to declare specific loans in default or to sign off on restructuring programs that bank managers deemed unacceptable, as the joint stock form gave the banks the legal independence and operational control to resist the state's efforts to compel them to take those steps.

The Political Economy of Industrial Restructuring

The banking reform, intended to place credit flows under the discipline of market forces, instead created a group of actors unwilling to serve as agents of economic adjustment. The portfolios of the new banks, burdened by a large number of bad assets accumulated during the prereform period, gave loan officers strong incentives to sustain credit lines to loss-making enterprises. At the same time, joint stock ownership gave bank managers the resources to resist the state's efforts to force a reallocation of credit to support structural adjustment policy. Facing a recalcitrant commercial banking sector, continued deterioration of the balance of payments, and mounting pressure from the Western lending agencies to launch a restructuring program, the MSZMP leadership turned to non-market mechanisms of structural adjustment.

Foremost among these instruments was the Tervgazdasági Bizottság (Planned Economy Committee, or TGB), a new intragovernmental body attached to the Council of Ministers and charged with coordinating overall restructuring policy. Responsibility for individual cases fell to the aforementioned OSB, a quasi-independent office affiliated with the Ministry of Finance. The main intent of these institutional innovations was to accelerate industrial restructuring by detaching primary decision-making authority from the Ministry of Industry, whose organizational interests were too closely tied to the targeted enterprises, and investing it with national-level bodies capable of transcending narrow sectoral interests.

In this section, I show that these expectations were dashed. The Communist Party's attempts to recast the institutional setting of structural adjustment merely broadened opportunities for the opponents of industrial restructuring to advance their particularistic claims. Thus, the ultimate result of the commercial banks' disengagement was to draw enterprises, trade unions, and state and Party officials into politically damaging conflicts over adjustment policy.

Industrial Policy under NEM

Since the start of the second phase of NEM in 1979, Communist Party leaders repeatedly asserted their determination to restructure Hungary's loss-making sectors. The main problems were associated with the textile, coal mining, metallurgy, and food processing sectors and with specific enterprises within the heavy machinery industry.

The inefficiencies of those sectors produced a range of ill effects. As shown in chapter 2, state subsidies to loss-making enterprises represented the largest item of the national budget. The high level of subsidization necessitated exorbitant rates of taxation: before the 1988 tax reform, enterprise profits taxation approached 90 percent. Thus, the profits of Hungary's best-managed companies were confiscated and reallocated through the state budget to sustain the economy's weakest performers. Loss makers also consumed a disproportionate share of energy and raw materials, aggravating shortages, raising the import bill, and encouraging investment in ill-conceived energy supply projects like the Gabcikovo-Nagymaros hydroelectric dam.

The distinctive structure of Hungarian industry exacerbated these problems. As a result of a merger movement in the late 1950s and early 1960s, Hungary possessed one of the world's most highly concentrated industries.[18] The level of concentration increased after the launching of NEM in 1968, reflecting the initial belief of reform economists that enterprise mergers would facilitate indicative planning by strengthening the center's ability to coordinate overall industrial policy. But the merger movement impaired allocative efficiency by discouraging horizontal competition between enterprises and enabling the largest and least efficient producers to bid for subsidies, credits, and capital inputs.[19]

In the early 1980s, the MSZMP undertook a series of measures aimed at reducing industrial concentration. It broke up a number of large enterprises and trusts into smaller units, liberalized rules governing the formation of small state enterprises and cooperatives, and eased restrictions on the private sector.[20] In an effort to expand managerial flexibility in state enterprises, it legalized Vállalati Gazdagsági Munkaközösségek (Enterprise Economic Work Associations), infrafirm associations of workers

18. Iván Berend, *The Hungarian Economic Reforms, 1953–1988* (Cambridge: Cambridge University Press, 1990), 85–86. By the mid-1960s, less than 20 percent of the Hungarian labor force was employed in enterprises with fewer than 1,000 workers. Employment in small-scale industry ranges between 40 and 70 percent in advanced capitalist economies. Large state enterprises in Hungary had an average of 4–5 factories each, compared to 1.1–1.4 in the West. Gábor Révész, *Perestroika in Eastern Europe: Hungary's Economic Transformation, 1945–1988* (Boulder: Westview, 1990), 44.

19. Paul Marer, "Economic Reform in Hungary: From Central Planning to Regulated Market," in Joint Economic Committee of the U.S. Congress, *East European Economies,* 3:238–244.

20. Berend, *The Hungarian Economic Reforms,* 266–68; Paul Hare, "The Beginnings of Institutional Reform in Hungary," *Soviet Studies* 35, no. 3 (July 1983): 322–26; János Kornai, "Comments on the Present State and the Prospects of the Hungarian Economic Reform," *Journal of Comparative Economics* 7 (1983): 234–36; Paul Marer, "Economic Reform in Hungary," 247–58; Resző Nyers, "National Economic Objectives and the Reform Process in Hungary in the 1980s," *Acta Oeconomica* 35, nos. 1–2 (1985): 10–12; Révész, *Perestroika,* 113–18; Márton Tardos, "The Increasing Role and Ambivalent Reception of Small Enterprises in Hungary," *Journal of Comparative Economics* 7 (1983): 283–87.

who used plant and equipment after hours on contract with management.[21]

These measures did reverse the trend toward increasing concentration under earlier phases of NEM. By 1985, there were 37 percent more state enterprises than in 1980. The demonopolization program succeeded in breaking up several of the trusts that controlled a disproportionate percentage of industrial assets, notably the giant Csepel Iron and Steel Works.[22] However, these steps did not measurably improve allocative efficiency within the enterprise sector. The largest and least profitable producers continued to receive the lion's share of budget subsidies and bank credits. Within that group, enterprises heavily engaged in convertible currency export attracted the largest share of state largesse. But the financial resources committed by the state to these producers did not yield any increase in their underlying export capacity. Despite changes in the competitive structure of Hungarian industry, the institutional structure of the communist state enabled the economy's weakest performers to extract the most generous allotments of financial support.[23]

The behavior of Hungary's new commercial banks, now the principal creditors of state enterprises, reinforced the inefficiencies of local enterprises. The designers of the two-tiered system had expected that the banks would use the market instruments at their disposal to promote industrial restructuring. But as described earlier, they responded to the National Bank's refinancing squeeze by enlarging credit lines to their weakest clients. Hungary's new bankruptcy law was also available to the banks as a mechanism for disciplining loss makers.[24] However, between the National Assembly's approval of the bankruptcy law in 1985 and the multiparty elections in 1990, there was only *one* full-fledged liquidation of a major state enterprise.[25]

---

21. Stephan Noti, "The Shifting Position of Hungarian Trade Unions amidst Social and Economic Reforms," *Soviet Studies* 39, no. 1 (January 1987): 71–78; David Stark, "Coexisting Organizational Forms in Hungary's Emerging Mixed Economy," in Victor Nee and Stark, eds., *Remaking the Economic Institutions of Socialism: China and Eastern Europe* (Stanford: Stanford University Press, 1989), 140–48.

22. Berend, *The Hungarian Economic Reforms,* 267.

23. Josef Brada and John Michael Montias, "Industrial Policy in Eastern Europe: A Three-Country Comparison," *Journal of Comparative Economics* 8 (1984): 394–99, 409–11; Várhegyi, "Sources of the Growth of Enterprises," 283.

24. "The New Bankruptcy Law," *RFE/RL Hungarian Situation Reports,* 30 September 1986, 3–6.

25. "Bankruptcy: The First Company Goes Under," *RFE/RL Hungarian Situation Reports,* 18 May 1987, 19–22; interview, Hungarian Council of Ministers, 14 April 1988; interview, National Bank of Hungary, 12 April 1988; interviews, Hungarian Credit Bank, 27 May and 8 July 1988; interview, Ministry of Finance, 23 May 1988.

Industrial Restructuring via Nonmarket Means

The banks' refusal to use market instruments to restructure local enterprises effectively placed the ball back in the center's court, forcing Communist Party leaders to turn to administrative mechanisms of structural adjustment. In the early 1980s, primary responsibility for restructuring policy fell to the Ministry of Industry. MSZMP officials expected that the 1980 reorganization of the branch ministries into a single unified ministry would overcome the particularistic lobbying that had impeded earlier restructuring efforts. But like its predecessors, the reorganized Ministry of Industry quickly adopted the role of advocate of narrow industrial interests, and by middecade it had yet to undertake any significant measures in the loss-making sectors. As late as 1988, the Minister of Industry was declaring to the press that as far as he was concerned, there was no "crisis" in Hungarian industry.[26]

With the subsidy bill bulging and the Ministry of Industry dragging its heels, the Party introduced several important changes in the institutional framework guiding restructuring policy. Legal authority to supervise adjustment policy was transferred from that ministry to the TGB.[27] Responsibility for sector- and enterprise-specific cases fell to the OSB, which was authorized to administer the various legal procedures connected with bankruptcy, liquidation of assets, and company reorganizations.[28]

The intent of these institutional innovations was twofold. First, the national visibility and broad legal authority of the TGB and OSB would allow those organizations to transcend the narrow standpoints of the branch ministries and local Party organizations and expedite implementation of the World Bank structural adjustment program. Second, the institutional reforms would widen the array of legal remedies available to the commercial banks, whose portfolios included the bulk of the debts of the crisis sectors and whose appearance on the scene in 1987 had presumably altered the complexion of structural adjustment.

But the actual results of the restructuring campaign undertaken in 1988–89 did not bear out these expectations. The branch ministries, trade unions, and local Party organizations continued aggressively to assert their particularistic claims within the new institutional setting. And the commercial banks, far from supporting the Hungarian state's efforts to

---

26. "Industry Minister Berecz on Major Goals," *FBIS/EEU,* 23 February 1988, 33–37.

27. "Medgyessy on Work of New Planned Economy Group," *FBIS/EEU,* 9 March 1988, 37.

28. "Enterprise Rehabilitation Agency Formed," *FBIS/EEU,* 5 December 1986, 3; interview, Ministry of Finance, 6 September 1988.

restructure loss-making sectors, proved reluctant to apply legal sanctions against their loss-making clients.

Structural Adjustment in the Steel Industry

The dilemmas of restructuring via nonmarket means were particularly evident in Hungary's steel industry. The costs of supporting a large steel industry in a landlocked, resource-poor country like Hungary were considerable. Hungary's huge steel plants relied heavily on imports of raw materials and semifinished rolled products from the CMEA. Under favorable terms of trade, steel producers could obtain cheap supplies from the Soviet Union and other socialist countries and then export a large percentage of their own finished products to the convertible currency area—an arrangement that brought political favor to the metallurgical sector as a whole as well as handsome financial rewards for individual plant directors. But when terms of trade in steel shifted against Hungarian producers in the late 1970s, this arrangement could only be sustained through massive state subsidies. Under pressure of a deteriorating balance of payments, the Kádár leadership assigned higher priority to hard currency export than to reduction of the subsidy bill. This forced the Hungarian state to supply steel enterprises with large subsidies to bridge the growing gap between import and export prices.

Meanwhile, the internal deficiencies of Hungarian steel manufacturers themselves became a tremendous drain on the national economy. Much of the industry operated with open-hearth blast furnaces and other turn-of-the-century technology. This resulted in steel products of substandard quality, rising labor costs, and extravagant levels of energy consumption that required the state to remit large amounts of direct subsidies just to keep the enterprises afloat. In 1988, subsidies to the industry's two biggest loss makers, Ózdi Kohászati Müvek and Lenin Kohászati Müvek, consumed nearly 15 percent of the state's total subsidy bill. A Swedish consulting firm contracted to evaluate the situation estimated that it would be necessary to displace upwards of 20,000 steel workers to eliminate excess capacity and bring the industry up to international competitiveness.[29]

Against this background, in April 1988 the TGB issued a resolution stating the following general goals: reduction and eventual termination of metallurgical subsidies, elimination of excess capacity, and regearing of

---

29. Miklós Bányai, "Hungarian Steel Sector: The Restructuring Syndrome" (Ministry of Industry, 1989, mimeo), 9–10.

the product mix to follow prevailing trends in world steel markets. The TGB appointed a special commissioner, Miklós Bányai, to devise a steel restructuring program. It also established an interministerial committee, chaired by Bányai and designed to subordinate the narrow standpoints of the branch ministries and facilitate achievement of the TGB's sectorwide goals.

Despite his ostensible political independence, the plan Bányai ultimately formulated exhibited a certain sensitivity to the distributional effects of adjustment. The program called for a 20 percent reduction in total steel capacity, to be carried out over a four-year period. This would leave sufficient capacity to cover domestic demand while allowing for a profitable level of exports. All subsidies to the industry would cease by the end of 1991. Within the reduction of aggregate capacity, the plan would reorganize intrasectoral production flows to eliminate redundancy and modernize the product mix. Total projected labor displacement would amount to 10,000 workers, half of what the Swedish consultants had recommended. This seemed a fairly small figure in comparison with the total number of workers employed in the industry. And in view of the fact that implementation would be spread over a four-year period, with a concurrent expansion of unemployment benefits and worker retraining, the plan appeared to have a reasonable chance of gaining broad acceptance. In fall 1988, the Minister of Industry signed off on the program, and implementation began.[30]

But despite Bányai's efforts to scale down the restructuring program to politically manageable proportions, his plan immediately provoked strong resistance by workers and managers at the affected plants, who were abetted by their allies in the trade unions, local Party committees, and Ministry of Industry. The steel lobby's tactics were illuminating. In November 1988, the management of Ózdi Kohászati Müvek, encouraged by union leaders and local Party officials and with the tacit approval of senior officials from the Ministry of Industry, submitted an application to the Ministry of Finance to set up a joint venture with the West German firm Korf KG. Korf proposed to upgrade Ózd's fixed capital and transform it into an inexpensive supplier of primary steel for its own manufacturing facilities in the Federal Republic. This arrangement would advance the commercial interests of both Korf and Ózd: the former would gain access to cheap labor, the latter modernization of its plant and equipment. But while the joint venture would benefit the two companies, it contra-

---

30. Interview, Ministry of Industry, 24 August 1988; Bányai, "Hungarian Steel Sector," 9.

vened the interests of the Hungarian national economy. Bányai's plan envisaged the outright elimination of primary steel production at Ōzd. The special commissioner's office had concluded that one primary steel producer for Hungary was enough, and that Lenin Kohászati Müvek was the company best suited for this task. The joint venture would mean continued Hungarian participation and hence further drain on the state budget.

The Ōzd and Korf managers concluded the deal without the steel commissioner's knowledge. Finance Ministry officials, influenced by appeals from the Ministry of Industry, approved the application. Auditors dispatched to Ōzd to evaluate the progress of the program got wind of the scheme and reported it to Bányai, who prevailed on the Minister of Industry to initiate disciplinary action against the Ōzd management. The minister acceded, but not before privately assuring Ōzd managers of his intention to support their venture with Korf.[31]

It is notable that the Hungarian Credit Bank, the main commercial creditor of the steel companies, remained disengaged from the restructuring effort. The restructuring program included provisions for disposition of the industry's bank debt as well as resumption of credit lines to the targeted enterprises, conditional on their attainment of specific adjustment goals. The Credit Bank's stake in the matter was considerable, as it supplied more than 90 percent of total commercial credit to the steel industry, which represented over 10 percent of its assets. The future of the Bank was therefore closely tied to the success of the restructuring program. But despite the Bank's manifest interest in the case, the management was determined to minimize its involvement and shift the onus of structural adjustment back to the center. Privately, senior managers acknowledged that the Credit Bank would eventually have to write off a significant number of the old steel loans inherited from the National Bank. But they were willing to do so only after a coherent restructuring program was underway, and then only in one fell swoop. To proceed with the writing down of the steel portfolio before the state cut off the flow of subsidies to loss-making plants would simply prolong the process and force the Bank to make repeated loan write-offs. In the meantime, the Credit Bank managers would keep the bad loans on the books as performing assets, rescheduling and refinancing them as necessary to allow the debtors to continue payments.[32]

---

31. Bányai, "Hungarian Steel Sector," 13–20; David Bartlett, "Losing the Political Initiative: The Impact of Financial Liberalization in Hungary," in Andrew Walder, ed., *The Waning of the Communist State: Economic Origins of Political Decline in China and Hungary* (Berkeley: University of California Press, 1995), 125.

32. Interview, Hungarian Credit Bank, 8 July 1988.

Implications of the Steel Case

The steel episode illustrated three key points. First, the creation of the TGB, the OSB, and the special commissioner's office constituted a clear organizational change from the situation in the early 1980s, when the Ministry of Industry dominated restructuring policy. But the practical effect of these institutional reforms was merely to reshuffle authority over adjustment policy within the government and state administration. By delegating primary authority over industrial restructuring to subordinate agencies in the political hierarchy, the Party enlarged the access points through which opponents could press their individual grievances.

Second, the steel case demonstrated the political repercussions of attempts to use Western-type financial mechanisms as vehicles of structural adjustment in market socialist systems. Bank credit was the chief "market" instrument available in Hungary during the late communist period. But the loan portfolio problem induced the new commercial banks to sustain credit lines to their weakest clients, precisely contrary to the aims of structural adjustment policy. The prior devolution of the credit function to the banks limited the possibilities for financial recentralization, as the nature of the regulatory system and the structure of joint stock ownership frustrated the center's efforts to intervene in the banking sector for the purpose of redirecting credit flows. The banks' refusal to use the credit instrument as a restructuring tool left the central authorities with few alternatives but administrative devices whose use unavoidably enmeshed political leaders in local distributional conflicts.[33]

Finally, the specific tactic used by the Ózd managers in their struggle with the steel commissioner's office, the negotiation of a joint venture with a foreign partner, demonstrated the attractiveness of foreign capital as a restructuring tool. As we have seen, the particular form of foreign direct investment in that case did not represent an optimal *economic* solution for Hungary. However, it was *politically* beneficial to the degree that blame

---

33. Bartlett, "Losing the Political Initiative," 125–26. The disengagement of the Hungarian commercial banks contrasted with the experiences of some Western countries confronted with the challenge of structural adjustment in loss-making sectors. For example, in the Federal Republic of Germany, major commercial banks played an instrumental role in guiding the restructuring of the steel industry in the 1970s and 1980s. Whereas in Hungary joint stock ownership created perverse incentives in the financial sector, in Germany the structure of corporate ownership gave the big "universal" banks the means and motivation to force local managers to rationalize production and restore their plants to profitability. See Josef Esser and Wolfgang Fach, "Crisis Management 'Made in Germany': The Steel Industry," in Peter Katzenstein, ed., *Industry and Politics in West Germany: Towards the Third Republic* (Ithaca: Cornell University Press, 1989), 221–48.

for the adverse employment effects of the joint venture could be shifted away from state and Party officials and toward the Korf management.

Property Reform and Structural Adjustment

The Őzd-Korf deal was one of a number of highly publicized Western investments in Hungary during the late communist period. Other notable cases included the purchase of the locomotive division of Ganz Mavag by the British company Telfos, General Electric's acquisition of a controlling share of the lightbulb manufacturer Tungsram, and the sale of a minority share of the tourist company Ibusz to a group of Austrian investors. These deals were the result of the MSZMP's liberalization of foreign investment that culminated in 1989 with the landmark Law on Economic Association. In addition to legalizing private capital ownership by Hungarian citizens for the first time since the communist takeover in 1948, the law entitled foreign investors to acquire up to 100 percent equity shares of state enterprises. It also granted foreign investors generous tax holidays, legal guarantees regarding nationalization, and full right of conversion and repatriation of after-tax profits.[34] The Party's decision to remove legal barriers to foreign capital opened the floodgates to Western investors, who would end up spearheading the privatization campaign initiated by the outgoing socialist government of Miklós Németh.

But while the property reforms undertaken by the Hungarian Communist Party spurred the rapid penetration of Western capital, they did little to advance structural adjustment policy. As we have seen, some foreign direct investment did flow toward loss-making enterprises in dire need of restructuring, like Őzdi Kohászati Müvek and Ganz-Mavag. Western capital also served to accelerate adjustment processes in comparatively robust enterprises like Tungsram. While that company was one of the few Hungarian enterprises capable of producing finished goods competitive on world markets, it had a bloated payroll and other internal problems demanding the attention of its new American owner.[35]

However, the main effect of the property reforms on foreign investment was not to pull Western capital into Hungary's loss-making industries. Foreign investors largely bypassed those sectors, focusing instead on

---

34. David Bartlett, "The Political Economy of Privatization: Property Reform and Democracy in Hungary," *East European Politics and Societies* 6, no. 1 (winter 1992): 102–3; "Foreign Investment Protection Bill Promulgated," *FBIS/EEU,* 15 December 1988, 34–35.

35. General Electric officials estimated that as much as half of Tungsram's 18,000 employees would have to be terminated in order to raise the Hungarian-based operations to a requisite level of cost efficiency. Jane Perlez, "G.E. Finds Tough Going in Hungary," *New York Times,* 25 July 1994, p. C1, 3.

acquiring equity shares in the enterprise sector's strongest performers and expanding "greenfield" investments in new companies and joint ventures. This pattern of foreign direct investment had important political repercussions during the late communist period, feeding public perceptions that the MSZMP's liberal investment laws were allowing Western capitalists to acquire the country's crown jewels on the cheap.[36]

Nor did the MSZMP's property reforms have a salutary effect on domestic capital formation in sectors targeted by the World Bank adjustment program. The Law on Economic Association and subsequent Law on Transformation were important insofar as they established limited liability companies and joint stock companies as legal entities and codified the mechanisms for transforming state-owned enterprises into those ownership forms. This, combined with the deregulation of foreign investment, placed Hungary at a comparative advantage vis-à-vis other East European countries by creating the legal infrastructure for the transition to a market economy. But the immediate consequence of the reforms was to invite "*nomenklatura* buyouts" and other abuses that undermined public confidence in the reform process and compelled the successor government to recentralize privatization policy.

Hungarian plant directors seized on the opportunities presented by the new ownership laws to reap private rents during the final years of communist power. Managers established subsidiaries organized as limited liability companies, transferring the fixed capital assets of the parent enterprises to the new companies in exchange for the latter's shares. In some instances, the managers then sold off the assets of the subsidiaries to foreign or domestic buyers, pocketing the proceeds. In other cases, they engineered salary increases or bonuses from the subsidiaries to repurchase the shares now held by the parent companies. The parents were thus left as shell companies, stripped of their assets but still carrying large debts. As the regulatory capacity of the communist state unraveled in 1989–90, hundreds of such schemes were executed. This created serious complications for the State Property Agency (SPA), created by the lame-duck socialist government in spring 1990 in an attempt to reassert central control of privatization policy. The SPA would have to find buyers of state enterprises burdened with heavy liabilities but deprived of their assets. Tracking down and recovering these assets was no simple matter, since the new subsidiary companies had already liquidated many of them.[37]

---

36. Bartlett, "The Political Economy of Privatization," 103–4.

37. Bartlett, "The Political Economy of Privatization," 104–5; David Stark, "Privatization in Hungary: From Plan to Market or From Plan to Clan?" *East European Politics and Societies* 4, no. 3 (fall 1990): 364–65; interview, SPA, 17 May 1991; interview, National Bank of Hungary, 30 May 1991.

In short, the unintended consequence of the Communist Party's own-ership reforms was to encourage local agents, eager to transform their political resources into private gains amid the demise of the Marxist-Leninist system, to indulge in rent seeking that undermined structural adjustment. Rather than undergoing reorganization and recapitalization, many loss-making enterprises were simply split up into subsidiaries designed to channel private rents to well-connected members of the old *nomenklatura*. Redirecting privatization processes toward the goals of adjustment policy would require the MSZMP's democratically elected successor to strengthen the state institutions charged with overseeing the transformation of ownership relations.

Foreign Trade and Exchange

The banking reform demonstrated the limited utility of commercial credit as an adjustment tool in Hungary's market socialist system. The industrial restructuring case illustrated the political problems confronting a commu-nist state that relied on administrative methods of structural adjustment. The third key element of Hungarian adjustment policy, foreign trade and exchange, exhibited a different politico-economic dynamic.

In this section, I focus on the MSZMP's use of exchange rates to alter relative import/export prices and on its liberalization of rules gov-erning allocation of convertible currency to local enterprises, banks, and households. As in other spheres of NEM, efforts to marketize the for-eign sector created economic distortions that pressured Party leaders to restore central controls. However, the institutional structure of foreign economic policy gave Hungarian policymakers greater leverage than they enjoyed in other issue areas. Local agents, enjoying broader decision-making authority but still operating under the perverse incen-tive structure of market socialism, responded to liberalization of foreign exchange by bidding up Western imports and drawing down the state's hard currency reserves. The consequent deterioration of the external balance forced the central authorities to intervene and slow the pace of the reforms. But while the prior devolution of authority to the factory level prevented full restoration of the status quo ante, the institutional ratchet effects of marketization were less salient in the foreign sector than in other spheres of NEM. The National Bank's continued monop-oly of foreign exchange allowed the center to reimpose controls with comparative ease, at the cost of impeding the transition from plan to market.

The Institutional Structure of the Foreign Sector

Until the late 1980s, formal decision-making authority over foreign trade remained highly centralized. Ruble-denominated trade was managed through interstate contracts negotiated by bureaucrats from the Hungarian Ministry of Trade and their counterparts in other CMEA countries, while the bulk of trade with the convertible currency area was conducted through state-controlled foreign trade companies. The small number of Hungarian enterprises authorized to engage in direct trade abroad were required to obtain import licenses from the Trade Ministry to purchase goods from the West and to remit all of their hard currency export earnings to the National Bank of Hungary. In these respects, the institutional structure of Hungarian foreign trade did not differ markedly from those of orthodox CPEs. What *did* distinguish Hungary from traditional planned economies was the fact that enterprises enjoyed wide discretion over production and marketing decisions—an attribute that gave local producers considerable influence over trade policy despite their limited de jure power in that sphere.

Under NEM, enterprise directors were freed from legally binding directives to fulfill the center's production goals. Deprived of the formal authority to command enterprises to execute CMEA contracts or boost exports to the West, trade officials resorted to financial favors and regulatory exceptions to coax plant directors to reorient production toward those ends. In the CMEA area, these inducements typically assumed the form of indirect subsidies designed to make trade with the socialist countries profitable. In some cases, representatives from enterprises were invited to participate in interstate negotiations, allowing them to extract favorable agreements regarding price, quantity, and terms of delivery.[38]

Inducing enterprises to meet hard currency export targets was more problematic, as central authorities had to overcome the strong preference of Hungarian enterprise managers to gear production toward the softer domestic and Eastern markets. The deterioration of the balance of payments in the mid-1980s enlarged the bargaining leverage of local producers, who exploited the center's keen interest in hard currency export to extract even more generous concessions from the communist state.[39] As we have seen, a sizable portion of the state's subsidy bill was consumed by enterprises (like the steel plants of northeastern Hungary) that were highly

---

38. Révész, *Perestroika,* 63–66.
39. Interview, National Bank of Hungary, 10 November 1986.

inefficient but whose contributions to foreign exchange gave them considerable clout in the bidding for financial resources.

The Hungarian state enjoyed greater authority over foreign exchange than over trade policy. Management of Hungary's hard currency assets and liabilities fell to the National Bank, which retained a monopoly of foreign exchange even after the transition to the two-tiered system in 1987. Enterprises seeking Western currency to procure imports had to purchase it directly from the Bank and were obliged to remit all of their hard currency revenues in exchange for forints. The new commercial banks were licensed to provide export financing, letters of credit, and other intermediary services, but they were not authorized to raise Western credits or maintain hard currency accounts. Hungarian households were entitled to hold personal accounts in convertible currency, but they were also subjected to strict limitations on the amount of local currency they could convert into hard currency for travel to the West. The decision to preserve the National Bank's foreign exchange monopoly reflected policymakers' fear that premature liberalization of foreign exchange was too risky, especially in view of the precarious state of Hungary's current account and its large debt burden. The designers of the two-tiered system were anxious to avert Yugoslavia's disastrous experience in the 1960s and 1970s, when the granting of full foreign exchange licenses to communally based commercial banks led to a rapid buildup of that country's hard currency debt.[40]

Against this institutional backdrop, the Communist Party undertook a series of reforms of the foreign sector. It broadened the use of exchange rate policy as a balance-of-payments tool, following the dictates of the IMF. And it moved cautiously toward expanding the foreign exchange opportunities of state enterprises, commercial banks, and households.

Devaluation and the Systemic Constraints of Market Socialism

Exchange rate policy posed major challenges for the MSZMP. Communist Party leaders had to navigate between two conflicting forces: (1) the Washington lending agencies that pushed aggressively for devaluation of the forint and (2) Hungarian state technocrats and academic economists who were deeply skeptical about the utility of exchange rate policy as an adjustment instrument in socialist economies.

The theoretical assumptions underpinning the "Washington consensus" on exchange rate policy are well known. With rare exceptions, IMF

---

40. Interviews, Karl Marx University, 25 November 1986; National Bank of Hungary, 10 November 1986 and 13 June and 31 August 1988; MSZMP Central Committee, 28 July 1988; Hungarian Foreign Trade Bank, 15 July 1988.

and World Bank officials insist on currency devaluation as part of standby agreements, holding to the neoclassical view that correction of relative prices is essential to raise export competitiveness and reduce import demand. Devaluation is especially appropriate for high inflation economies, where large differentials between domestic and world price levels fuel import demand and exacerbate balance-of-payments deficits. Absent modification of the exchange rate, the gap between internal and external price levels damages the competitiveness of exportable products and import-substituting goods, leading to a redistribution of income from competitive to noncompetitive sectors.

Hungarian economists argued that the international financial institutions' preoccupation with devaluation revealed a misguided faith in the usefulness of techniques devised for full-fledged market economies. For devaluation to work as an adjustment tool in socialist economies, changes in relative prices had to elicit "market"-type responses by local agents. But when domestic enterprises operated under inelastic demand schedules, devaluation could yield precisely the opposite of the intended result. Local producers, undeterred by rising import prices and still favoring the less demanding Eastern markets, might respond by sustaining the same volume mix of imports and exports as before. This would produce the worst possible outcome: a growing import bill, declining export revenues, a widening external deficit, and mounting domestic inflation. The risks of devaluation were particularly acute in reformed communist states like Hungary, where plant directors enjoyed broad decision-making authority while still operating under soft budget constraints. Rising import prices would encourage enterprises to engineer commensurate increases in domestic prices, heightening inflation and placing additional pressure on the exchange rate. The structure of Hungary's foreign trade further increased the dangers of currency devaluation. Imports from the West consisted overwhelmingly of commodities that could not be substituted through domestic production. Thus, devaluation would merely increase the costs of capital inputs and raise the country's aggregate import bill, without creating effective incentives for local enterprises to lower production costs through import substitution.[41]

In short, devaluations in market socialist systems would not produce

---

41. W. Riecke, "Arfolyam és Aralakulás" (Exchange rates and price trends), *Figyelő* 29, no. 26 (1985): 3; István Szalkai, "A Valutaértékelés Szerepe a Fizetési Mérlegek Kiegyensúlyozásában" (The role of currency devaluation in counterbalancing the balance of payments), *Külgazdaság* 24, no. 7 (1980): 39–49; Imre Tarafás, "Arfolyampolitikánk és Indokai" (Exchange rate policy and its motives), *Figyelő* 24, no. 27 (1980): 3; Tarafás, "A Gazdaságpolitikai Koncepció és az Arfolyam Politika" (The economic policy concept and the exchange rate policy), *Közgazdasági Szemle* 28, nos. 7–8 (1981): 913–26.

the same effects as in market economies and would indeed spur local agents to behave in ways that *worsened* the balance-of-payments deficit and elevated domestic inflation. The principle that exchange rate policy could serve as an effective tool of economic adjustment presupposed a thoroughgoing transformation of the enterprise sector, which Hungary was far from achieving.

This dispute over exchange rate policy became a major source of contention between Hungary and the international financial institutions during the 1980s. As part of the 1982 IMF standby, Hungarian negotiators agreed to enact a series of forint devaluations. But these exchange rate adjustments were not enough to offset the growing gap between external and internal price levels. Between 1980 and 1984, real domestic price increases exceeded the average of Hungary's main Western trading partners by 16 percent.[42]

The issue of currency devaluation arose again in 1988, when Hungary and the IMF negotiated a second standby agreement. The terms proposed by the IMF were considerably tougher than the conditions of the 1982 standby; the new terms included deep subsidy cuts, contraction of the money supply, increase in interest rates, import liberalization, acceleration of wage and price reform, and devaluation of the forint. Hungarian negotiators accepted the basic terms of the agreement but resisted the IMF's demand for a large currency devaluation, contending that such a step would prevent the political leadership from holding the yearly inflation rate to the targeted level of 15 percent. Absent a fundamental restructuring of the economy, forint devaluation would cause more harm than good.[43]

But the MSZMP's reluctance to devalue threatened its ability to fulfill other terms of the IMF standby, notably import liberalization. State officials and IMF economists were considering a number of reforms aimed at streamlining Hungary's cumbersome import licensing system: a quota scheme whereby local producers would be permitted to import freely in convertible currency up to a specified limit, an auctioning system under

---

42. Gábor Oblath, "Az Arfolyampolitika és az Infláció" (Exchange rate policy and inflation), *Figyelő* 30, no. 12 (1986): 12–13. The composition of Hungary's currency basket, which was heavily weighted toward the then-rising dollar, augmented the forint's tendency toward real appreciation during the early 1980s. J. Szabó, "További Kérdések a Valutakosárral Kapcsolatban" (Further questions connected with the currency basket), *Külgazdaság* 30, no. 7 (1986): 37–46.

43. Interviews, National Bank of Hungary, 18 May, 2 June, and 22 July 1988; interview, Hungarian Council of Ministers, 20 May 1988; "Hungary: While Access to the $350 Million IMF Stand-By Loan has Been Secured the Country Will be Kept on a Short Lease," *PlanEcon Trade and Finance Review,* July 1988, 1; "Outlook for Hungary," *PlanEcon Review and Outlook,* fall 1987, 82.

which the National Bank of Hungary would sell foreign exchange to bidding enterprises, and a classification regime whereby the Ministry of Trade would draw up lists specifying products subject to licensing. The ultimate goal of these measures was to allow Hungarian enterprises automatically to exchange their surplus forints for hard currency in order to procure the Western capital inputs needed to modernize their plant and equipment. In this way, import liberalization would promote structural adjustment: With profitability, not political criteria, determining access to hard currency, the most efficient enterprises possessing the largest forint surpluses would be best positioned to import products from the West. Loss-making enterprises, which were least likely to make good use of expensive Western imports, would not have access to the foreign exchange needed to carry out the transactions.[44]

Successful reform of the import licensing system presupposed two things. First, the National Bank had to contract domestic purchasing power. If plant directors were to enjoy the right freely to exchange their forint reserves for hard currency, the monetary authorities had to manufacture a shortage of liquidity in the enterprise sector. Failing this, conversions of forints into hard currency would go through the roof, forcing the Bank to draw down on the country's already modest foreign reserves. Second, the Bank had to undertake a substantial devaluation to reduce import demand. Broadening enterprises' access to Western goods without raising the prices of those products would merely drive up Hungary's aggregate import bill. If the central authorities wished to make it easier for local producers to buy hard currency imports, they had to make those goods more expensive in order to prevent further deterioration of the external balance. Specialists in the National Bank estimated that the envisaged import liberalization required an accompanying devaluation of at least 25 percent.[45]

The danger was that in the market socialist context, even a sizable devaluation would not curtail the import demand of cost-insensitive state enterprises. Import liberalization coupled with devaluation would then produce the worst possible scenario. The aggregate volume of Western imports would increase while the prices of those goods rose, generating a rapid drain of hard currency reserves, dramatic deterioration of the balance of payments, and a steep increase in domestic inflation. On the export side, the immediate effect of a big devaluation would be a reduction of the dollar value of Hungarian products sold abroad. Long-term growth of Hungarian exports to the West depended on a range of factors not directly

---

44. Interviews, Karl Marx University, 26 May 1988; National Bank of Hungary, 22 July 1988.

45. Interview, National Bank of Hungary, 15 July 1988.

connected with exchange rates: product quality and reliability, provision of services, expansion of distribution outlets, and reduction of trade barriers in the West.

The MSZMP's Foreign Exchange Policy, 1988–89

During its final years in power, the Hungarian Communist Party responded to the tension between import liberalization and currency devaluation by moving aggressively on the former while proceeding cautiously on the latter. This strategy reflected the high priority Party leaders assigned to containing inflation and to retaining the institutional structure of foreign exchange policy, which gave the MSZMP the means to restore central controls if import liberalization produced unacceptable effects.

The issue of forint devaluation came to a head in summer 1988. In the aftermath of the fall of the Kádár leadership at the special Party conference in May of that year, the MSZMP Central Committee convened to consider two alternative plans for the next phase of NEM. "Plan A" proposed to accelerate the restructuring of loss-making industries, liberalize import controls, and take other measures aimed at effecting a swift transition to a market economy. "Plan B" recommended a less draconian set of measures to soften the distributional effects of reform. The Central Committee, now dominated by the Party's proreform faction, approved Plan A. It was widely understood, if not explicitly acknowledged, that Plan A implied a sizable currency devaluation.[46]

Reform economists in the National Bank also favored the first option, arguing that the rapid economic transformation envisaged in Plan A required a quick and decisive devaluation. They calculated that a 25 percent devaluation would make most manufacturing exporters profitable, even with the elimination of producer subsidies. Marginal exporters with high convertible currency import content would probably fold. But it was not in Hungary's interest to make all export activities profitable. Real structural adjustment required the termination of marginal trading activities. The central bankers conceded that a devaluation of this magnitude meant abandoning the 15 percent inflation target approved by the Party at the beginning of the year. But this was consistent with the spirit of Plan A. The new Grósz regime's endorsement of the radical reform program suggested its willingness to absorb a higher inflation rate in the short-term as the price of long-term economic vitality.[47]

---

46. From *FBIS/EEU:* "Last Day of MSZMP Central Committee Session: Economic Alternatives Debated," 15 July 1988, 26–27; "Further Reportage on MSZMP CC July Session: Economic Issues Discussed," 19 July 1988, 33–34.

47. Interviews, National Bank of Hungary, 15 July and 22 July 1988.

In fact, big devaluation received little support within the Party leadership, even among officials sympathetic with Plan A's goal of hastening the transition to a market economy. Senior officials in the Central Committee Secretariat expressed irritation at the National Bank economists and IMF technocrats who were urging a large devaluation. The IMF was pushing its standard recipe for adjustment as if Hungary were already a market economy.[48]

In July, the National Bank president communicated the following message to his staff: the Grósz leadership stuck to its commitment to hold the yearly inflation rate to 15 percent; the Hungarian currency would be devalued, but only in gradual steps.[49] That month, the Bank devalued the forint by 6 percent. In spring 1989, it followed with two devaluations totaling 11 percent, which was less than the inflation rate for that year. As in the early 1980s, the forint actually appreciated in real terms at the end of the MSZMP's tenure.[50]

The small size of the exchange rate adjustments did not deter the Party from proceeding with liberalization of the import licensing system. In 1988, it authorized all enterprises to engage in direct trade with the convertible currency area in products not on the state's list of restricted items. The following year, it removed licensing requirements for products representing 40 percent of Western imports, including machinery, food products, and major categories of consumer durables. In January 1990, it lifted licensing requirements on an additional 30 percent of hard currency imports.[51]

Fortunately, the MSZMP's decision to proceed with import liberalization under real currency appreciation did not validate the worst expectations of the National Bank economists. During the first eight months of 1989, imports in the liberalized branches rose by 30 percent in nominal terms. But total hard currency imports rose by only 8 percent during the same period, owing to reductions in sectors still subject to central restrictions.[52]

---

48. Interviews, MSZMP Central Committee, 30 August and 8 September 1988.

49. "Bank Official on Devaluation of Forint," *FBIS/EEU,* 20 July 1988, 34.

50. From *FBIS/EEU:* "National Bank Devalues Forint to Boost Exports," 21 March 1989, 35; "National Bank Chairman on Forint's Devaluation," 23 March 1989, 32–33; "Government Devalues Forint by 6 Percent," 14 April 1989, 16.

51. Bart Édes, "Import Liberalization and Industry Protection: International Precedents and Possible Options for Hungary," *Russian and East European Finance and Trade,* winter 1992–93, 31–32.

52. Wim Swaan, "Prices and Market Behavior in Hungary in the Early Stages of the Transition to a Market Economy," *Soviet Studies* 43, no. 3 (1991): 521.

Hungary's current account deficit in convertible currency did increase sharply in 1989, well surpassing the yearly target specified in the 1988 IMF standby agreement. This, together with the violation of budget deficit targets, prompted the IMF to suspend the standby and forced the Hungarian authorities to negotiate a new agreement with harsher terms. However, the main factor causing deterioration of the current account at decade's end was not Hungary's trade in manufactured goods but the outflow of hard currency stemming from the MSZMP's ill-considered decision to liberalize foreign exchange controls on Hungarian citizens traveling abroad. The Party's response to that crisis underscored the communist state's capacity to restore quickly central controls of foreign exchange. The relative weakness of institutional ratchet effects in the foreign exchange sphere distinguished that issue area from other dimensions of NEM and lowered the risks of import liberalization.

Reimposition of Foreign Exchange Controls

In January 1988, the communist state eased regulation of foreign travel. For the first time since 1948, Hungarian citizens holding a valid passport and the required amount of hard currency were allowed to travel to the West without restriction. At that point, Hungarians were permitted to exchange $400 worth of forints per person over a three-year period.[53] The world passport prompted Hungarian citizens, long denied direct access to Western consumer markets, to surge across the border in search of goods unavailable locally. During the first three quarters of 1988, Hungarians made more than 1.4 million visits to Austria alone, nearly a 400 percent increase over the same period the previous year.[54] But the drainage of hard currency had severe repercussions for Hungary's balance of payments. By summer 1989, the current account in hard currency was more than double the target set at the beginning of the year.

The deterioration of the internal and external deficits, together with the Németh government's disclosure of the true status of Hungary's financial books, left state authorities in a very weak bargaining position when they resumed negotiations with the IMF over a new standby in December 1989. The Hungarian authorities agreed to impose a temporary freeze on

---

53. "Restrictions on Foreign Travel to be Eased," *RFE/RL Hungarian Situation Reports,* 28 November 1987, 47–51.

54. "Hungarians 'Celebrate' the October Revolution in Capitalist Austria," *RFE/RL Hungarian Situation Reports,* 17 November 1988, 23–24.

hard currency disbursements to the population. Subsequently, they reduced the amount of Western currency citizens could purchase to $50 dollar allotments for the next two years.[55]

The state's ability swiftly to recentralize foreign exchange controls in the household sector illustrated the National Bank's continued de facto monopoly of that sphere under NEM. The Party's foreign exchange policies in the enterprise and commercial banking sectors similarly illustrated the comparatively high degree of state centralization in that issue area. In summer 1988, National Bank officials announced plans to grant limited foreign exchange licenses to the commercial banks. Whereas previously their foreign exchange operations were limited to providing letters of credit and other intermediary services, the Hungarian banks were now entitled to hold hard currency accounts and open such accounts abroad. However, they were not permitted to raise their own hard currency loans from the West. The fact that this remained the exclusive prerogative of the National Bank of Hungary reflected the prevailing view, shared even by radical reformist economists, that any convertible currency debts procured by nonofficial actors would remain the sovereign debt of the Hungarian state. The heavy burden of the gross debt already outstanding, which at $20 billion was the largest in per capita terms in Eastern Europe, ruled out granting local banks the right to raise additional loans á la Yugoslavia in the 1970s.[56]

Hungarian state enterprises were kept on an even shorter leash in the foreign exchange sphere. As part of the import liberalization program, local enterprises were entitled to exchange surplus forints for hard currency to purchase Western products freed from licensing requirements. But the state retained an array of controls that contained the enterprise sector's foreign exchange operations to short-term transactions on their current accounts. Producers seeking to purchase hard currency were obliged to deposit the required amount of forints with the National Bank several months in advance, at zero interest. And they were still subjected to

---

55. Bartlett, "Losing the Political Initiative"; Károly Okolicsányi, "Growing Shortage of Convertible Currency," *Radio Free Europe/Radio Liberty Background Report* 233 (29 December 1989): 1–2; "Foreign Minister on Convertible Currency Supply," *FBIS/EEU,* 3 November 1989, 55; "Békesi Explains Foreign Currency Restrictions," *FBIS/EEU,* 6 November 1989, 56–57; "*Népszabadság* on Hard Currency Measures," *FBIS/EEU,* 16 November 1989, 56–57; interview, National Bank of Hungary, 21 May 1991.

56. Interview, National Bank of Hungary, 13 June 1988; interview, Magyar Külkereskedelmi Bank, 15 July 1988; "National Bank Head on Plans for 1989," *FBIS/EEU,* 6 October 1988, 24–25.

the old requirement to reconvert all of their convertible currency earnings back into local currency.[57]

The upshot of these measures was a limited form of currency convertibility. Hungarian households were allowed to keep personal accounts in hard currency accumulated through private entrepreneurial activities and remissions of earnings by friends and relatives residing abroad. But following the foreign exchange crisis of 1988–89, the state permitted them to convert only a minuscule amount of forints for tourist purposes. Meanwhile, banks and enterprises were given access to hard currency to cover current account obligations. But the former were forbidden to raise their own Western credits, while the latter were prevented from holding hard currency for any length of time. In short, the MSZMP's initiatives in the foreign exchange arena, while representing a significant departure from orthodox central planning, stopped well short of full currency convertibility.

The absence of strong ratchet effects in the foreign exchange area gave Hungarian state authorities greater latitude for ex post adjustments than they enjoyed in other dimensions of NEM. In contrast to the reforms of wages and commercial credit, where the prior devolution of authority gave local agents the resources to resist recentralization, the National Bank retained the capacity to restore foreign exchange controls quickly if the initial liberalization caused unacceptable effects. The institutional structure of Hungarian foreign exchange thus made it possible for the Communist Party leadership to accept the risks of import liberalization without extensive devaluation. If factory-level actors responded to deregulation of the import licensing system by ramping up hard currency imports and imperiling the external balance, MSZMP leaders could with relative ease prevail on the National Bank to reimpose controls.

Foreign Exchange Controls and Public Accountability

But while the National Bank's foreign exchange monopoly did indeed facilitate political control of that issue area during the late communist period, it also relieved central bankers of public accountability for their decisions. The lack of a legally codified, well-institutionalized system of foreign exchange management led to a number of imprudent decisions that severely compromised Hungary's international financial position. As

---

57. Swaan, "Prices and Market Behavior in Hungary," 521. After 1988, private exporters were permitted to buy back a small percentage—10 percent—of their hard currency revenues to cover expenses related to public relations, advertising, travel abroad, and other export promotion activities. However, state enterprises were still liable to the existing rules regarding reconversion of export earnings denominated in Western currencies. "Private Exporters Can Buy Back Hard Currency," *FBIS/EEU*, 20 July 1988, 35.

described in chapter 2, in the late 1970s the Kádár leadership and senior National Bank officials concealed the magnitude of Hungary's external debt from both the Parliament and the Washington lending agencies. Subsequently, the chief of the Bank's foreign exchange division, János Fekete, colluded with MSZMP leaders to launch a new program of aggressive borrowing on Western credit markets to bolster Hungary's reserves. As a result, the gross convertible currency debt doubled between 1984 and 1987.[58]

In sum, the Hungarian Communist Party left a very mixed legacy in the foreign exchange arena. On the one hand, its decision to preserve the National Bank's monopoly enabled the successor government to continue a strategy of gradual, controlled liberalization of foreign exchange that reduced the risks of depleting Hungary's hard currency reserves. On the other hand, the absence of transparency and accountability in the Marxist-Leninist system allowed political elites not only to run up a huge external debt but to disguise its actual size until the very end of the communist period—leaving the new government with the dual task of servicing an onerous convertible currency debt and restoring domestic and international confidence in the Hungarian state's financial integrity.

Conclusion: Market Reforms and Communist Institutions

Part 2 has examined the consequences of market reforms during the final decade of communist rule in Hungary. My central argument is that the introduction of market mechanisms as austerity instruments generated a distinctive push-pull dynamic that undermined both economic performance and Communist Party power. Wage liberalization enabled factory-

---

58. *PlanEcon Report* 4, nos. 24–25 (17 June 1988): 17–20. During the same period, Hungary's net debt rose by nearly 300 percent—the consequence of Fekete's decision to move Hungary's liabilities into yen, deutschmarks, and swiss francs while shifting its assets into dollars. His strategy was based on the assumption that taking out new loans in strong currencies would allow the Bank to reap the benefits of lower interest rates, while appreciation of the dollar would raise the value of Hungary's hard currency assets. As it turned out, the dollar depreciated vis-à-vis the yen and deutschmark in the aftermath of the 1985 Park Plaza Agreement. *PlanEcon Report* 3, nos. 14–15 (10 April 1987): 4–5; "Hungary: $1 Billion Hard-Currency Current Account Deficit in 1986 and Lack of Radical Policy Response Suggest a Hard Landing for the Country's Economy by Mid-1987," *PlanEcon Trade and Finance Review,* December 1986, 1–2; "Hungary: With $1.2 Billion Hard-Currency Current Account Deficit and the Prospect of $18 Billion Gross Debt by Year-End, The Country's Financial Managers are Now Walking a Precarious Tightrope," *PlanEcon Trade and Finance Review,* September 1987, 1–2; interviews, National Bank of Hungary, 18 May, 31 August, and 9 September 1988; interview, Karl Marx University, 8 July 1988; interview, Hungarian Council of Ministers, 5 September 1988.

level actors to extract compensation for the distributional effects of stabilization while impairing the center's capacity to correct distortions via ex
post measures. At the same time, the spending bias of the communist state
prevented the authorities from curtailing domestic purchasing power
through fiscal and monetary policy. In the sphere of structural adjustment,
the prior devolution of decision-making authority prevented the center
from forcing a reallocation of resources when enterprises and commercial
banks behaved in ways contrary to restructuring policy. Foreign exchange
was a partial exception in that the National Bank retained the capability to
restore controls if economic liberalization elicited undesirable responses
by local agents.

The contradictory effects of market reforms illustrated the particularistic bias of state and party institutions. Far from enlarging the communist
state's capacity for universalistic regulation, NEM broadened the scope of
individualized bargaining between state agencies and microeconomic
actors. Wage liberalization, meant to raise labor productivity by increasing income differentiation, instead induced factory-level agents to bid up
aggregate purchasing power by negotiating exceptions to parametric wage
caps. Banking reform, designed to spur a reallocation of credit from weak
to strong producers, instead created a group of actors unwilling to use
commercial credit as a restructuring instrument.

Like their counterparts in orthodox CPEs, local agents in Hungary
operated under perverse incentive structures that produced effects that
defeated the aims of stabilization and adjustment. The soft budget constraints endemic to socialist economies relieved enterprise managers of the
need to economize on wages, imports, investment, and bank credit. Hungary's market reforms further weakened discipline at the factory level by
widening the institutional channels through which managers could obtain
financial favors and regulatory exemptions. Paradoxically, the absence of
effective liquidity constraints on the enterprise sector transformed
inefficient producers into "creditworthy" clients for the new commercial
banks. Bank managers had little hesitation sustaining credit lines to loss-
making clients, knowing that it was precisely those enterprises which were
the biggest recipients of budgetary support from the state.

But the dilemmas of austerity policy in Hungary's market socialist
system went well beyond perverse microeconomic incentives. Unlike their
counterparts in traditional planned economies, Hungarian state authorities had few tools at their disposal to correct distortions by reimposing
controls. The communist state's decision-making authority, once relinquished to local actors, could not be fully recovered short of a thoroughgoing recentralization of power—an option that was essentially foreclosed
in Hungary by the mid-1980s. This left state institutions in a singularly

weak position: Hungarian policymakers had neither the means to impose economic order in the fashion of orthodox CPEs nor the resources to administer global regulations in the manner of full-fledged market economies.

The structure of Communist Party institutions aggravated the political quandaries of economic austerity under NEM. During the 1980s, Party leaders delegated substantial policy-making authority to state agencies, whose technical resources left them better equipped than the MSZMP Central Committee to carry out adjustment programs. By decade's end, the Party was largely disengaged from day-to-day management of economic reform policy. But notwithstanding decentralization of the policy-making process, the lack of constitutional checks on Communist Party power and the absence of opposition parties allowed MSZMP leaders to intervene at will. This had two important consequences for stabilization and adjustment. First, it rendered state agencies liable to capture by Party officials seeking to exploit national resources for their own political ends. This phenomena was manifested most dramatically in the budgetary and foreign exchange spheres, where penetration of state institutions by MSZMP leaders resulted in massive increases in Hungary's internal and external debts. Second, it increased the state's vulnerability to particularistic bargaining by societal actors seeking compensation for economic austerity. As demonstrated in the controversy over monetary policy in 1987–88, what was most apt to trigger selective intervention by Communist Party elites were claims by local agents that measures proposed by state officials created unacceptable distributional effects. Thus, while Party intervention could in theory assume the form of either exhortations to accelerate market reforms or admonitions to slow them down, it typically worked in the latter direction. Owing to the institutional logic of reform communism, the "losers" of stabilization and adjustment policy were *politically* best positioned to sound the alarm and appeal for Party intercession. Meanwhile, the "winners" of market reforms relied on individualistic *economic* strategies of exit to the second economy, whose expansion in the 1980s stemmed largely from property reforms initiated by the Communist Party itself.

Thus, contrary to conventional wisdom about one-party systems, distributional conflicts were pervasive in communist Hungary, but they assumed the form of subterranean clashes over the allocation of financial resources. For a ruling party like the MSZMP, the consequences of this variant of distributional politics were particularly insidious. It impaired the state administration's ability to execute reform policy and undermined domestic and international confidence in the Party's capacity to manage the economy, the linchpin of János Kádár's post-1956 social contract. The devolution of formal authority to subordinate agencies hastened the progressive unhinging of Communist Party power. It simultaneously enlarged access points to the state for opponents of market reform and increased the Party's political liabilities for the stagnating economy. While the MSZMP could delegate policy-making *authority,* the nature of the one-party system prevented it from eluding ultimate *responsibility* for the general state of the economy. The sole exception to the prevalence of particularistic bargaining in communist Hungary—the labor strikes of 1988 and 1989—proved no less deleterious to the Party's collective authority. What was significant about those exhibitions of mass mobilization was not their physical scope but the fact that they were spearheaded by the MSZMP's own trade union organization.

I show in part 3 that the transition to democracy undercut the political bases of opposition to market reform in Hungary. The demise of communist rule disrupted the institutional channels for particularistic bargaining, sapped the bargaining power of trade unions and other intermediary associations, and increased societal actors' reliance on the incipient multiparty system, where the costs of collective action were exceptionally high during the early postcommunist years.

Part 3
Economic Reform in Democratic Hungary, 1990–94

CHAPTER 4

Political Institutions and Hungary's Negotiated Transition

In this chapter, I survey the institutional terrain of postcommunist Hungary. I begin by assessing how the institutional legacies of the communist period shaped the strategies of the successor government. I then examine the institutional outcomes of Hungary's negotiated transition to democracy, focusing on the problems of constitutional design, the formation of the party system and rules of electoral competition, and the role of intermediary institutions. I conclude by analyzing the structure of state institutions in Hungary's new democracy.

I argue that, contrary to conventional wisdom about the impact of democratization on market reforms, Hungary's political transformation produced an institutional structure that *facilitated* marketization. The country's negotiated transition yielded a strong prime ministerial government, an electoral arena commanded by a handful of elitist parties, an ineffectual system of intermediary interest representation, and a state administration dominated by agencies of global economic regulation. These themes underpin my detailed studies of stabilization and adjustment policy in chapters 5 and 6.

Institutional Legacies of Communism

Hungary's experiment with market socialism had profound consequences for both the Communist Party and its democratically elected successor. Market reforms, originally intended to bolster the MSZMP's political position by raising economic growth and allocative efficiency, ended up hastening the Party's demise. The MSZMP's efforts to use market mechanisms as instruments of austerity stimulated local agents to behave in ways contrary to the aims of stabilization and adjustment policy while reducing the Party's capacity to correct those distortions via ex post recentralization. For the Hungarian Communists, the result was the worst possible combination of declining political authority, deteriorating economic performance, and mounting pressure by the Washington lending agencies. By spring 1989, these factors compelled Party leaders to enter into negotiations with the political opposition over the terms of Hungary's transition to democracy. In fall of that year, the MSZMP itself broke apart.

Ironically, the very same market reforms that led to the unraveling of communist power in Hungary eased the political burden of economic transformation confronting the successor government headed by the MDF. Price liberalization was essentially completed by the time of the political transition, lessening macroeconomic disequilibria and relieving the new government of the need to implement Polish-type shock therapy. The MSZMP's loosening of wage controls and foreign trade and exchange regulations similarly lightened the new government's policy agenda. Its lifting of restrictions on nonstate activities fed the gradual expansion of the second economy, creating alternative supply networks that alleviated domestic shortages and promoting the formation of entrepreneurial and managerial skills vital to market development. Finally, the NEM beget an array of market-type institutions: legal procedures to govern the founding of new private enterprises, the privatization of existing state-owned enterprises, and the management of enterprises still under state ownership; a two-tiered banking system; an incipient capital market; Western-type systems of taxation and financial regulation; and Eastern Europe's most attractive foreign investment laws. As shown in part 2, the problem with these measures was not so much their technical design as the fact that they failed to produce the desired effects in Hungary's communist system, whose particularistic networks allowed local agents to negotiate exceptions to market rules. But because they established many of the institutional foundations of a full-fledged market economy, the reforms initiated by the MSZMP placed postcommunist Hungary at a comparative advantage vis-à-vis the rest of Eastern Europe.

The institutional remnants of reform communism abetted the successor government in another way. While NEM did broaden opportunities for particularistic bargaining, it did not significantly expand means of collective political action. Indeed, in certain respects market reforms worked to *demobilize* Hungarian society—particularly insofar as the Communist Party's legalization of the second economy in the early 1980s induced many citizens to direct their attention away from politics and toward the entrepreneurial sphere. While Polish workers spent much of the decade organizing mass resistance to the ruling party, their Hungarian counterparts devoted their energies to activities generating personal income.

Collective action did escalate during the final years of communist power in Hungary, as evidenced by the coal mining strikes in summer 1988, public demonstrations against the Nagymaros dam project in fall of that year, anticommunist protests in March 1989, and the mass demonstrations attending the reburial of Imre Nagy in June 1989. But while these episodes served to expose the MSZMP's eroding authority and to catalyze the political opposition, they were quite limited compared with what was happening in the rest of Eastern Europe. More so than any other country in the region, Hungary's transition was driven by *political elites*. The MSZMP split apart in the aftermath of the fall of János Kádár in May 1988. By early 1989, proreform leaders had wrested control of the Party from the hard-line faction headed by Károly Grósz, who soon conceded to negotiations with the political opposition over Hungary's future. The so-called Opposition Roundtable was composed of a small number of elite organizations, whose grassroots links were poorly developed and whose very existence stemmed in part from the collaboration of key reformers within the Communist Party. The end of communist rule in Hungary occurred through formalized, orderly, and highly legalistic negotiations between representatives of the ruling party and the Opposition Roundtable.[1] Hungary's distinctive "path of extrication" from state socialism thus differed from that of Poland, whose negotiated transition in 1989 took place against the backdrop of a more militant workers' movement, as well as from those of the neo-Stalinist states in 1989, which collapsed in the face of sudden mass mobilization (the GDR and Czechoslovakia) and armed revolt (Romania).

In short, while the MSZMP's market reforms widened space for individualistic strategies that undermined the Communist Party's control of the economy and sapped its political authority, they left in their wake a civil society that was "weak" to the degree it lacked well-institutionalized modes of collective action. This allowed the new MDF government to proceed with socioeconomically costly reforms without provoking strong resistance from below.

In this chapter, I show how the institutional outcomes of Hungary's negotiated transition to democracy reinforced the political liabilities of the losers of marketization. On the one hand, the elite negotiations of summer 1989 yielded a constitutional structure organized around a strong prime ministerial government and a set of electoral rules favoring a small group of parliamentary parties. On the other hand, the demise of communism removed the political cornerstone of the plan bargaining system. This

---

1. András Bozóki, "Post-Communist Transition: Political Tendencies in Hungary," *East European Politics and Societies* 4, no. 2 (spring 1990): 211–31; Bozóki, "Hungary's Road to Systemic Change: The Opposition Roundtable," *East European Politics and Societies* 7, no. 2 (spring 1993): 276–308; László Bruszt, "1989: The Negotiated Revolution in Hungary," *Social Research* 57, no. 2 (summer 1990): 365–87; László Keri, "The Collapse of Regime—and After: Two Studies on Peaceful Transition in Hungary" (Budapest School of Politics, 1990, mimeo); László Urban, "Hungary in Transition: The Emergence of the Opposition Parties" (Budapest School of Politics, 1990, mimeo).

allowed Hungarian state institutions, now freed of the burden of particularistic bargaining, to build on the technical competence and experience accumulated under NEM and shift toward universalistic regulation of the market.

Negotiating the Rules of Democracy

While Hungary's economic crisis played a decisive role in forcing the Communist Party to the bargaining table, it received little attention in the tripartite negotiations that began in June 1989.[2] The Opposition Roundtable, unwilling to share responsibility for the MSZMP's economic failures, resisted the latter's attempts to include economic reform policy on the agenda. The talks thus focused almost exclusively on constitutional questions, legislation on political parties, and rules governing the electoral system. The negotiating strategies of the interlocutors clearly reflected their own political interests in the run-up to the 1990 parliamentary elections. But the institutional choices taken in summer and fall of 1989 had important consequences for Hungarian democracy that transcended short-term electoral strategizing.

Constitutional Design: Presidential or Prime Ministerial Government?

The central constitutional issue confronting the negotiators concerned the basic form of Hungary's embryonic democracy. The Communist Party pushed for early and direct election of the president of the republic. MSZMP representatives couched this proposal in terms of the overarching needs of the nation. Because it had been elected under the now-defunct 1985 electoral law, the current parliament lacked political legitimacy. An orderly transition to democracy therefore necessitated the election of a president enjoying a popular mandate and wide constitutional powers. Yet it was widely understood that the Communist Party's preferences on the presidential question reflected the fact that it had a popular and highly vis-

---

2. The two principal parties to the negotiations were the MSZMP and the Opposition Roundtable. The latter consisted of the MDF, the Szabad Demokraták Szövetsége (Alliance of Free Democrats), the Fiatal Demokraták Szövetsége (Alliance of Young Democrats), the Kereszténény Demokrata Néppárt (Christian Democratic People's Party), the Független Kisgazdapárt (Independent Smallholders' Party), the Magyar Demokrata Szocialista Párt (Hungarian Social Democratic Party), the Magyar Néppárt (Hungarian People's Party), the Democratic League of Independent Trade Unions, and the Bajcsy-Zsilinszky Friends' Society. The third side was composed of a group of mass-line organizations associated with the MSZMP, including the Patriotic People's Front, the National Council of Trade Unions, and the Communist Youth League.

ible candidate, Imre Pozsgay, who would almost certainly win an early election.

The Opposition Roundtable was split on this issue. Five of its members, including the MDF, yielded to the MSZMP's call for a presidential election in advance of parliamentary elections. The leaders of the other members of the Roundtable, eager to avoid the mistake made by Poland's Solidarity the previous year, resisted. They viewed the MSZMP's proposal as a political ploy aimed at restoring communist power. They insisted that parliamentary elections come first; a properly elected parliament would then elect a president. Refusing to sign the September 1989 protocol that formally ended the tripartite negotiations, the opposition parties called for a public referendum on the presidential question. Their position on the matter ultimately prevailed: following a furious public relations campaign spearheaded by the main liberal parties, the Szabad Demokraták Szövetsége (Alliance of Free Democrats, or SZDSZ) and the Fiatal Demokraták Szövetsége (Alliance of Young Democrats, or FIDESZ), the referendum narrowly won in November, clearing the way for parliamentary elections in spring 1990. The immediate consequence of the liberals' victory in the plebiscite was to thwart the Communists' strategy of salvaging their political position under the auspices of a Pozsgay presidency. Its long-term institutional significance was that it paved the way for the establishment of a parliamentary form of government dominated by a powerful prime minister.[3]

Decisions taken after Hungary's first multiparty elections heightened the centralization of power in the prime minister's office. The victor, the MDF, organized a coalition government controlling 59 percent of the seats in the National Assembly. While this constituted a substantial working majority, it created the specter of legislative impasse. Some of the new parliament's business would involve votes on constitutional issues, which under the terms of the new Hungarian Republic required a two-thirds majority. To avert a parliamentary stalemate that would imperil democratic consolidation, the MDF forged a compromise with the SZDSZ, the leading opposition party. The MDF agreed to the election of a prominent SZDSZ member, Arpád Göncz, as Hungarian president. In return, the SZDSZ agreed to reduce the number of constitutional laws subject to qualified majority voting. They also consented to the introduction of the procedure of constructive no confidence. This parliamentary device, modeled after the Federal Republic of Germany, allowed for the presentation

---

3. András Bozóki, "Political Transition and Constitutional Change in Hungary," in Bozóki, András Körösény, and George Schöpflin, eds., *Post-Communist Transition: Emerging Pluralism in Hungary* (New York: St. Martin's, 1992), 66–69; Bozóki, "Hungary's Road to Systemic Change," 293–95, 305–8.

of no-confidence motions against the prime minister but not against individual ministers. In essence, this meant that the opposition could only call an incumbent government to account simultaneously with the election of a new prime minister, thus increasing security of governmental tenure and reinforcing the prime minister's central position in the polity. The SZDSZ also agreed to a number of constitutional provisions that circumscribed the authority of the president of the republic to dissolve governments, convene the Parliament, make executive appointments, and control the armed forces. The main political instrument left to the Hungarian president was his capacity to refer acts of Parliament to the Constitutional Court—which President Göncz employed on several occasions during the MDF's four-year tenure in office.[4]

The upshot of these institutional choices was a democratic polity distinguished by an unusually high concentration of power in the prime minister's office. This institutional configuration carried several liabilities. A structure of power so dependent on a single person was vulnerable to breakdown if the personal authority of the prime minister faced a serious challenge—as it did midway through the MDF's term of office, when Prime Minister József Antall became terminally ill. Moreover, political inexperience and low levels of technical expertise within the prime minister's staff created a risk of incompetent governance. This problem was of special concern to a governing party like the MDF, which entered office with no policy-making experience. Finally, the centralization of executive authority created a tendency for decisions to be pushed upward when they could be made more appropriately at lower levels of the hierarchy. Bureaucrats in the government and state administration, operating under high uncertainty and unwilling to assume responsibility for passing judgment on policy issues, often referred these matters to higher-ranking officials. Senior ministerial officials, many of whom were political appointees of the prime minister, thus found themselves making decisions on issues for which they had little or no professional competence.[5]

---

4. András Bozóki, "All Things to Some Men: The Metamorphoses of the Hungarian Democratic Forum," *East European Reporter* 5, no. 2 (1992): 63–66; Gabriella Ilonszki, "Research Note: Tradition and Innovation in the Development of Parliamentary Government in Hungary," *Journal of Theoretical Politics* 5, no. 2 (April 1993): 261; Judith Patkai, "Hungary Makes Slow but Steady Progress," *Radio Free Europe/Radio Liberty Research Report* (hereafter cited as *RFE/RL Research Report*) (3 January 1992), 88; Péter Schmidt, "A Magyar Parlamentarizmus Közjogi Ellentmondásai" (The constitutional contradictions of Hungarian parliamentarism), in Sándor Kurtán et al., eds., *Magyarország Politikai Évkönyv 1991* (Hungarian political yearbook 1991) (Budapest: Demokrácia Kutatások Központi Alapívány, 1991), 47–57.

5. Mihály Bihari, "Rendszerváltás és Hatalomváltás Magyarországon, 1989–1990" (Change of regime and power in Hungary, 1989–90), in Kurtán et al., *Magyarország Politikai Évkönyv 1991,* 44–47.

But a strong prime ministerial government also possessed important advantages, especially for a fledgling democracy like Hungary undergoing wrenching economic change. The high stability, low governmental turnover, long tenure, and strong party discipline characteristic of this institutional setup insulated leaders from short-term political exigencies and facilitated the formulation of coherent policy programs whose benefits would take years to materialize. Clearly, the kind of prime ministerial government that emerged in Hungary after 1989 favored authoritative decision making at the expense of political accountability. But while accountability was less pronounced in this system than in presidential regimes and decentralized parliamentary systems, it was by no means absent in postcommunist Hungary. The president and parliamentary opposition enjoyed limited opportunities to challenge the MDF's tenure in office, but they did possess institutionalized means of holding the ruling coalition's policies and political behavior up for public scrutiny—factors that contributed to the MDF's defeat in the second national election in 1994. Thus, notwithstanding the anxiety of some Hungarian analysts over the MDF's "authoritarian" tendencies,[6] the institutional environment in which the MDF operated differed fundamentally from that of the Communist Party.

Political Parties and Rules of Electoral Competition

The formation of Hungary's multiparty system proceeded along three tracks. Several of the contestants in Hungary's new party system, notably the Independent Smallholders' Party and the Magyar Szocialista Demokrata Párt (Hungarian Social Democratic Party, or MSZDP), were organized out of the remnants of the pre-1948 system. The MDF, SZDSZ, and FIDESZ originated as proto-opposition movements during the late communist period. The principal left-wing parties emerged from the formal dissolution of the MSZMP in October 1989. The MSZP was organized out of the reformist faction of the old Communist Party; the conservative faction of Károly Grósz split off into a "revamped" MSZMP.

None of these parties possessed strong organizational bases by the time of the first parliamentary elections. The so-called nostalgia parties were led by septuagenarian veterans of the precommunist period. In addition to its aging leadership, the Smallholders' Party was hampered by a policy platform that appealed to a narrow rural constituency. The MSZDP had a broader potential constituent base but was wrought by fierce internecine conflicts.[7]

---

6. Bihari, "Rendszerváltás és Hatalomváltás Magyarországon," 44.7.
7. Barnabas Racz, "Political Pluralisation in Hungary: The 1990 Elections," *Soviet Studies* 43, no. 1 (January 1991): 112–17.

The MDF, SZDSZ, and FIDESZ enjoyed more vigorous leadership and more sophisticated policy programs but lacked strong grassroots links. The MDF began as an organization of populist writers and intellectuals critical of the Kádár regime's management of the economy and its hands-off approach to the mistreatment of the Hungarian minority in Romania. The MDF owed its existence in no small part to the tacit support of the reformist wing of the MSZMP, whose leader, Imre Pozsgay, attended the founding meeting of the MDF in Lakitelek in September 1987. As noted earlier, informal cooperation between the MDF and the Communist Party continued through the conclusion of the tripartite talks in September 1989—a factor that the liberal parties did not fail to exploit in the subsequent electoral campaign. The SZDSZ originated in 1987 as a collection of urban intellectuals, the Network of Free Initiatives, while the FIDESZ grew out of an organization of university students. These groups assumed a more openly confrontational stance toward the Communist Party than did the MDF. In June 1987, several members of the liberal opposition published "Társadalmi Szerződés" (Social contract) in the samizdat journal *Beszélő*. The document called for Kádár's removal, constitutional limits on the MSZMP's power, and a widening of the sphere of interest representation.[8]

But while the appearance of these organizations exemplified the growing discontent within Hungarian society over communist rule, in no sense were they mass-based movements. Their recognition as legal organizations and their eventual transition to party status resulted primarily from the progressive unraveling of the Communist Party's authority at the top, not mass mobilization from below. In January 1989, the Grósz regime, under pressure from the Pozsgay faction of the Central Committee as well as scores of "reform circles" within the local Party apparatus, agreed to enact the Law on Economic Association, permitting the establishment of civil organizations. The following month, Grósz, his hand further weakened by Pozsgay's success in reopening official debates over the 1956 revolution, conceded to the formation of a multiparty system. This in turn led to the creation of the Opposition Roundtable and the convening of the tripartite negotiations.[9]

In short, the progression of the liberal opposition groups from movement status to full-fledged political parties must be viewed in terms of the

---

8. Robert Jenkins, "Movements into Parties: The Historic Transformation of the Hungarian Opposition" (Department of Sociology, Yale University, 1992, mimeo), 22–40; Urban, "Hungary in Transition," 12–19.

9. Bruszt, "1989," 372–75; "'Text' of MSZMP Communique," *FBIS/EEU,* 13 February 1989, 31–32; "Pozsgay Reaffirms Stance on 'Popular Uprising,'" *FBIS/EEU,* 16 February 1989, 25–26.

deep fissures within the Communist Party. As we have seen, the SZDSZ and FIDESZ did succeed in mobilizing large numbers of voters in a short period of time for the November 1989 plebiscite on presidential elections. But their connections to Hungarian society remained shallow. By early 1992, the registered membership of SZDSZ numbered about 32,000, that of FIDESZ a mere 13,000. Altogether, only about 1 percent of Hungary's adult population were members of political parties.[10]

The successor parties of the old MSZMP faced a different set of problems. In contrast to the pre-1948 and liberal parties, Communist Party leaders began the negotiated transition with substantial organizational resources: factory-level cells, an armed Workers' Militia, and a sizable portfolio of physical and financial assets. As with the presidential question, the Opposition Roundtable was split on the issue of how to dispose of these resources, which would give the Communists a considerable advantage in the upcoming elections. The MDF and its allies signed the September protocol, which left these matters unresolved. The dissenting group led by SZDSZ and FIDESZ insisted that before legitimate elections could take place, the MSZMP had to disband its militia and its workplace committees and make a full public accounting of its assets. The liberal parties added these conditions to the November referendum. But intervening events basically resolved them by the time the plebiscite took place. In October 1989, the formal structure of the MSZMP was dissolved; shortly thereafter, the Parliament passed a law that met most of the liberals' demands.[11]

These developments left the MSZP and the rump MSZMP with two tasks: overcoming their intimate association with the discredited Communist Party and rebuilding their political organizations to meet the demands of multiparty contestation. The MSZMP would prove unable to meet these challenges, failing even to garner enough votes to enter the Parliament, while the MSZP would stage a dramatic comeback.[12]

The fragile constituent bases of the Hungarian parties magnified the importance of the rules governing the electoral system, variations in which would be decisive in an environment distinguished by exceptionally weak party loyalties and voter identities. Consequently, the framing of Hungary's new electoral law became one of the mostly hotly contested issues in the tripartite negotiations. The pre-1948 parties, surmising that their historical roles would confer comparatively strong collective identities,

---

10. Attila Ágh, "The Hungarian Party System and Party Theory in the Transition of Central Europe," *Journal of Theoretical Politics* 6, no. 2 (April 1994): 229.

11. Bozóki, "Hungary's Road to Systemic Change," 301, 303–6.

12. Barnabas Racz, "The Socialist-Left Opposition in Post-Communist Hungary," *Europe-Asia Studies* 45, no. 4 (1993): 647–70.

pushed for an electoral system based on party lists. Both the SZDSZ and the MSZMP preferred single-member districts, but for different reasons. The SZDSZ was little known as a party, but its membership included a number of individuals with high name recognition who would be competitive in elections in single-member districts. Conversely, MSZMP leaders reasoned that the Party's negative collective identity would hamper its ability to compete in a list-based system. The various negotiating positions taken by the parties on other electoral questions—the territorial bases of the elections, the method of screening of eligible parties, the level of the parliamentary threshold, the number of ballots in the election—similarly reflected their mutual determination to extract rules likely to advance their individual electoral prospects. But they also demonstrated interlocutors' sensitivity to the pervasive uncertainty in Hungary's new democracy, whose high electoral volatility induced negotiators to seek ways of hedging against potential losses.

This tension between institutional choice and political uncertainty resulted in a series of compromises that yielded one of the world's most complicated electoral laws. Some 46 percent of parliamentary seats would be filled through elections in single-member districts, with a second vote taken if no candidate received a majority in the first ballot. The remaining members of Parliament would be elected via a combination of countywide and national party lists, following the rules of proportional representation. To reduce party fragmentation, the negotiators agreed to establish a 4 percent parliamentary threshold as well as a complex nominating system aimed at winnowing the number of candidates running in single-member districts and the number of parties able to formulate lists for proportional representation (PR) districts.[13]

The effect of these electoral rules was to fortify the central position of Hungary's largest parties at the expense of marginal ones. Only six parties managed to qualify for admission to the Parliament. The mixed PR/majoritarian scheme allowed the MDF to transform its slender 24.7 plurality into a 42.5 percent share of seats in the new legislature. While this bias toward a handful of major parties weakened the representative dimension of the electoral system, it facilitated the formation of durable coalitions, which in turn promoted stability and effective governance. At

13. Bozóki, "Hungary's Road to Systemic Change," 298–300; Sharon Drumm and Samantha Durst, "Power to the Powerless or to the Powerful? The Political Consequences of Electoral Laws in Eastern Europe" (paper presented at the annual meeting of the Midwest Political Science Association, Chicago, Ill., 14–16 April 1994), 14–15; Ilonszki, "Research Note," 259–60; Wolfgang Merkel, "Problems of Democratic Consolidation in East Central Europe" (paper presented at the Ninth International Conference of Europeanists, Chicago, Ill., 31 March–2 April 1994), 13–14.

the same time, the screening procedures and the emphasis on closed lists reinforced the elitist bent of the big parties by placing candidate recruitment under the control of national-level organizations.

Decisions related to the legal codification and financing of political parties further augmented the centralizing tendencies within the Hungarian party system. Theoretically, the new parties could have been subsumed within the Law on Association, enacted in early 1989, which would have placed them on the same legal footing as trade unions and other interest associations. But the interlocutors chose to create a separate legal category covering parties. In October, the Parliament passed a law providing substantial financial assistance to all registered parties, with the amounts of state subsidies dependent on the size of their membership. The obvious effect of this measure was to give large organizations strong incentives to register as political parties rather than as interest associations, undercutting Hungary's already weak and heavily fragmented intermediary institutions.[14]

Intermediary Institutions in Hungary's New Democracy

Intermediary associations typically play a subordinate role in the early stages of democratic transitions. While interest organizations may be decisive in forcing authoritarian regimes from power, once the founding elections have been scheduled they are usually displaced by political parties, whose territorial constituencies are better suited for mobilizing broad-based support. The collective action problem further hampers functionally based associations in new democracies, particularly insofar as membership in them was compulsory under authoritarian rule. Free riding is likely to increase once the popular enthusiasm for mass mobilization attending the old regime's ouster has waned and local agents embrace the principle of voluntary participation in civil associations.[15]

These effects were especially pronounced in postcommunist Eastern Europe. While the state corporatist regimes of Southern Europe and Latin America imposed strict controls on trade unions and enterprise associations, those organizations maintained some separation from the political sphere. This enabled them to supply members with a minimal level of interest representation in the postauthoritarian period, even as the switch to voluntarism broadened incentives for free riding. With the notable exception of Poland, communist Eastern Europe had no semblance of an

14. Ágh, "The Hungarian Party System," 227; Bozóki, "Hungary's Road to Systemic Change," 296.

15. Philippe Schmitter, "The Consolidation of Democracy and Representation of Social Groups," *American Behavioral Scientist* 35, nos. 4–5 (March–June 1992): 430–33.

autonomous civil society. The civil associations of the region were not merely *regulated* but *subsumed* by the ruling party. Mass mobilization clearly played a key role in the abrupt demise of several East European communist regimes in 1989. But the complete interpenetration of polity and economy under communism deprived incipient interest groups of the institutional means to advance the claims of their members once the Communists were removed from power. At the same time, the legal successors of the old interest associations were hampered by their long affiliation with the Communist Party, now politically discredited and stripped of its organizational and financial assets.

As we saw in part 2, independent interest associations did not even exist in Hungary until the very end of the communist era. The intermediary interest representation that did occur took place through Party-controlled mass-line organizations like SZOT. SZOT's successor, the Magyar Szakszervezetek Országos Szövetsége (Hungarian National Federation of Trade Unions, or MSZOSZ), emerged as the largest trade union in the postcommunist period, representing some 45 percent of Hungarian workers. But its effectiveness as an independent workers' association was marred by the predecessor organization's historical connection with the MSZMP. Between 1990 and 1993, the MSZOSZ's membership plummeted from 3.5 million to 1 million. The remainder of organized labor was divided between six large confederations and a score of unaffiliated unions. In summer 1991, the Parliament passed a law requiring the division of SZOT's assets among the successor organizations, sparking public clashes between the unions that further undermined the labor movement's cohesion and political efficacy.[16]

The loose connections between the unions and the political parties underscored the subsidiary role of interest groups in postcommunist Hungary. By the time of the second national election in 1994, only one major party—the MSZP—had concocted a formal alliance with the MSZOSZ. But even in this case, party-union collaboration was limited. While signing its electoral agreement with the MSZOSZ, MSZP leaders emphasized their determination not to become "an operational arm of the unions."[17] In February 1994, the MSZP announced the selection of MSZOSZ chief

---

16. Interview, Central European University, 28 September 1993; Ken Kasriel, "Test of Strength: Will Hungary's Shop Councils Become Hotbeds of Union Militancy? Probably Not," *Business Central Europe* 1, no. 1 (May 1993): 22–23; Merkel, "Problems of Democratic Consolidation," 10; Joan Nelson, "Building Blocks or Stumbling Blocks? Labor and Business Roles in Dual Transitions" (Washington, D.C., Overseas Development Council, 1994, mimeo), 17; Judith Pataki, "Hungarian Government Signs Social Contract with Unions," *RFE/RL Research Report* 2, no. 5 (29 January 1993): 43–45.

17. Racz, "The Socialist-Left Opposition," 662.

Sándor Nagy as the second candidate on the Party's national list. However, like center-left parties in Spain and other transitional democracies, the MSZP generally sought to downplay its links to trade unions in order to broaden its electoral base—a strategy that was consistent with the electoral system's bias toward large parties organized for winning national elections, and which proved extremely successful for the MSZP in spring 1994.[18]

Employers' groups in postcommunist Hungary were even weaker and more fragmented than the trade unions.[19] Like the MSZOSZ, many were little more than spinoffs of the producer associations previously controlled by the Communist Party, and they therefore lacked legitimacy as independent interest-representation organizations. Equally important, the contraction of the state sector and the collapse of the cooperative system deprived large industrial enterprises and agricultural producers of the financial resources and economic leverage to wield much collective influence. At the same time, the more robust segments of the Hungarian economy, notably the private sector and small businesses, relied on individualistic economic strategies to achieve their goals.

Significantly, the one arena in which organized interest groups began to demonstrate an ability to influence economic policy was the budgetary sphere. In 1990, a tripartite bargaining institution, the Interest Representation Council (Érdekegyeztető Tanács) was formed. It was composed of representatives of the unions, employers' associations, and Ministry of Finance who met on a regular basis to discuss state budget policy. However, this organization was very much the exception to the rule, as the general weakness of Hungarian civil society impeded movements toward West European–style corporatism. And the political clout of the Council itself remained quite limited: while announcing that the Council had negotiated a pact concerning tax and welfare policies in fall 1993, the Minister of Finance emphasized that the agreement was in no way binding on the Parliament.[20]

This institutional combination of a highly centralized party system and weak intermediary organizations had the following consequences for

---

18. Nelson, "Building Blocks or Stumbling Blocks?" 30, 54–55; interview, Hungarian Parliament, 19 May 1993.

19. Attila Ágh, "A Polarizacio Éve" (The year of polarization), in Sándor Kurtán et al., *Magyarország Politikai Évkönyv 1993* (Hungarian political yearbook 1993) (Budapest: Demokrácia Kutatások Központi Alapívany, 1993), 40–57.

20. "Agreement Reached on Tax Policies," *Budapest Week*, 9–15 September 1993, 2; "There Is Life outside the Parliament: The Review's Roundtable Discussion," *Hungarian Economic Review* 7 (April 1992): 59–64; interview, SZDSZ National Party Office, 29 September 1993.

Hungary's fledgling democracy. First, it narrowed the sphere of representative politics to the parliamentary parties. With no strong mesolevel institutions available to mediate relations between Hungarian society and the national parties, political action was channeled into the Parliament, whose technical, organizational, and human resources quickly became overtaxed.[21] From the convening of the first legislature in May 1990 to the end of that year, the Parliament took over 2,200 votes, an average of 30 per day. During the same period, it enacted some 77 laws, many of which concerned vital constitutional questions, regulatory issues, and economic reform policy.[22] For a legislature facing such a heavy workload and lacking a large staff and well-developed committee system, the dangers of incompetent decision making were quite high.

Second, it broadened the already wide gap between the political parties and society at large. Lacking intermediary organizations through which they could transmit their concerns to the Parliament, growing numbers of Hungarian citizens lost a sense of efficacy in the political process. Their influence was concentrated in the national elections, which in contrast to the communist regime served as an effective check on political leaders, but which occurred infrequently owing to the constitutional setup and the rules of the electoral game. The chasm between the Hungarian parties and the rank and file was a major contributor to the alarming growth of voter apathy after 1990.[23]

But at the same time, the institutional structure of interest representation gave the new Hungarian government the governing *capacity*—a long time horizon, a stable governing coalition, high party discipline, and centralized executive power—to implement reforms imposing heavy distributional costs on large segments of society. In this respect, it enjoyed a comparative advantage over other postcommunist governments burdened by higher levels of institutional fragmentation.[24]

---

21. Attila Ágh, "A Strukurális Patthelyzet Éve" (The year of the structural stalemate), in Kurtán et al., *Magyarország Politikai Évkönyv 1991,* 26–33; Ágh, "The Hungarian Party System," 229–32.

22. Ilonszki, "Research Note," 262; Barnabas Racz, "The Hungarian Parliament's Rise and Challenges," *RFE/RL Research Report* (14 February 1992), 22–26.

23. Hungary's 1991 by-elections prompted single-digit voter turnout in some districts, which one Hungarian analyst has described as a "world record." Ágh, "A Strukurális Patthelyzet Éve," 23

24. For a comparative survey of the institutional structure in postcommunist Eastern Europe, see James McGregor, "Fragmentation and Capacity in Central and East European Parliaments" (paper presented at the annual meeting of the American Political Science Association, Washington, D.C., September 1993).

State Institutions and the Transition to Democracy

While the institutional configuration previously described enhanced governability, it also increased the risks of penetration of the Hungarian state by the governing parties. Throughout its four-year term, the Antall government came under fire for purging state officials associated with the previous regime, loading the bureaucracy with political sycophants, using privatization revenues for patronage, and meddling with the judiciary. The controversy over political manipulation of state institutions came to a head in early 1994, when the government sacked over a hundred employees of Hungarian Radio and Television for their alleged connections to the communist regime.[25]

But two factors blunted, if not entirely neutralized, the MDF's attempts to penetrate the state. First, the process of democratization erected barriers to deep and sustained penetration of the state. The advent of genuine competition in the electoral system, the appearance of opposition parties in the Parliament, and liberalization of the mass media gave the MDF's opponents ample opportunities to hold the government's conduct up for public scrutiny. This was demonstrated most vividly in fall 1991, when liberal intellectuals, alarmed by the rise of the nationalist right faction of the MDF, issued a "Democratic Charter" enunciating the conditions for liberal democracy. The Antall government soon faced attacks within its own ranks, as liberal members of the MDF's parliamentary group publicly indicted the leadership for the ruling coalition's drift to the right.[26] The MDF's attempts to appropriate privatization funds and other scandals similarly provoked extensive publicity, contributing to the precipitous decline in the Party's popularity after 1992 and its crushing defeat in the next parliamentary elections.[27]

Second, the specific circumstances of Hungary's negotiated transition gave contestants the incentives and opportunities to craft rules aimed at preventing each other from exploiting state resources for political pur-

---

25. László Lengyel, "Ezerkilencszázkilencvenegy" (Nineteen ninety-one), in Kurtán et al., *Magyarország Politikai Évkönyv 1991,* 43; Judith Pataki, "Controversy over Hungary's New Media Heads," *RFE/RL Research Report* 3, no. 31 (12 August 1994): 14–17; Miklós Sukosd, "The Media War," *East European Reporter,* March/April 1992, 69–71; "Broken Promises: Interview with Kata Beke," *East European Reporter* 4, no. 4 (spring/summer 1991): 22–24.

26. "The Coalition v. the Charter: Democracy in Hungary," *East European Reporter* 5, no. 1 (1992): 34–37; András Bozóki, "The Democratic Charter One Year On," *East European Reporter* 5, no. 6 (1992): 13–17.

27. The MDF garnered 10 percent of the 1994 vote, which yielded a meager 37 seats in the 386-member Parliament. János Dobszay, "Back to the Future: The 1994 Elections," *Hungarian Quarterly* 35 (summer 1994): 9–14.

poses. A case in point was the insistence of the liberal members of the Opposition Roundtable to disband the Hungarian Workers' Militia, terminate party control of the military, and place state security agencies under the Council of Ministers.[28] While the immediate objective of these measures was to defang the MSZMP, their long-term significance was to routinize civil-military relations and prevent the use of Hungary's armed forces and internal security apparatus for domestic political purposes.

Legal checks on political manipulation of the economic ministries of the Hungarian state proved more problematic. To a greater degree than the internal security agencies, those institutions created strong temptations for political leaders to divert financial resources to politically favored groups. This led to a number of abuses during the MDF's tenure in office. The Antall government began staffing the key economic agencies with state secretaries who acted less as professional civil servants than as political commissars for the prime minister's office.[29]

However, the very fact that the winner of the founding elections faced a credible reelectoral constraint, and hence a real possibility of losing the next round of competition, gave the leaders of the new government incentives to enact institutional reforms designed to insulate state institutions from political capture. In October 1991, the Hungarian Parliament passed a law codifying the authority of the National Bank. The final version of the law represented a compromise between the Antall government and the advocates of full central bank autonomy.[30] But notwithstanding the MDF's attempts to preserve prime ministerial oversight of monetary policy, the law created a significant measure of central bank autonomy. It made the Bank legally accountable to the Parliament rather than to the government, prescribed fixed terms for its president and vice presidents, established a legal limit on central bank financing of the state deficit, empowered the Bank to charge market interest rates on direct credits to the state, codified its authority to undertake open market operations, and formalized its preeminence in the foreign exchange sphere.[31]

These measures helped insulate the National Bank from political pressure to retreat from its dual strategy of tight money and real currency appreciation. In 1991, Bank officials rejected appeals by the Antall gov-

---

28. Bozóki, "Hungary's Road to Systemic Change," 303–4.

29. Interviews, UNIC Bank, 15 May 1991; International Training Center for Bankers, 20 May 1993.

30. Károly Okolicsányi, "New Hungarian Bank Laws Maintain Political Influence," *RFE/RL Research Report* (21 February 1992), 41–45.

31. "1991 Évi LX Törvény A Magyar Nemzeti Bankról" (Act LX of 1991 on the National Bank of Hungary), *Hatályos Magyar Jogszabályok* (Hungarian Rules of Law in Force), no. III/18, 15 September 1992, 1263–86.

ernment to set up special refinancing lines to support major loss-making enterprises—illustrating the degree to which the Bank's institutional authority had increased since the clash over monetary policy in the late 1980s.[32] Subsequently, they withstood lobbying by GE/Tungsram and other prominent exporters for large devaluation of the forint, whose real appreciation since 1989 had impaired the price competitiveness of Hungarian exports.[33] At the same time, the central banking law made the National Bank more publicly accountable for its policies. By obliging Bank leaders to report periodically to the Parliament, the law significantly reduced opportunities for incumbent governments to skew monetary and foreign exchange policy toward narrow political ends, as the communist regime did in the mid-1980s.

Institutional reforms undertaken after the founding elections also lessened the possibilities for political capture of fiscal policy. Prior to the central banking law, Finance Ministry officials could draw on their unlimited credit line with the National Bank to finance budget deficits. Now they faced a genuine budget constraint: new central bank credits carried the market rate of interest, and any deficit spending exceeding the legal threshold (3 percent of annual tax receipts) had to be financed through sales of treasury bills. The result was to create real crowding-out effects in the national budget. During the first year under the new deficit-financing procedures, the state's debt-service expenditures rose by HUF 30 billion, forcing the Finance Ministry to seek offsetting spending cuts.[34]

Reforms of the budgetary system accelerated the Finance Ministry's shift from a "spender" to a "saver" institution. Prior to the political transition, budget policy was the product of negotiations between bureaucrats in the National Planning Office and the Finance Ministry, following general guidelines set down by the MSZMP Central Committee. As shown in chapter 2, the separation of the national budget into current and capital expenditures created vast opportunities for financial legerdemain, while the absence of parliamentary oversight allowed state and Party officials to conceal the country's true financial status. In mid-1990, the National Planning Office was disbanded, leaving the Finance Ministry fully responsible for preparing budgetary projections for the Parliament. In the following year, the Ministry adopted Western-type reporting procedures aimed at rationalizing the budget process. It merged the current and capital

---

32. Interviews, National Bank of Hungary, 23 and 29 May 1991.

33. Interview, MIER, 18 May 1993; Ferenc Langmár, "Forint Overvalued?" *Hungarian Economic Review* 8 (June 1992): 3; Károly Okolicsányi, "Foreign Trade in Transition," *Bank & Tőzsde: Független Pénzügyi, Üzleti és Gazdasági Hetilap* 1, no. 30 (13 August 1993): 13–14.

34. Interview, Ministry of Finance, 30 May 1991.

accounts into a single consolidated budget and ended the longstanding practice of disguising enterprise subsidies under different budgetary categories. Meanwhile, the budget committees of the Hungarian Parliament— which under the terms of the MDF/SZDSZ postelection pact were dominated by the liberal parties—expanded their oversight activities, subjecting some of the Finance Ministry's reports to line-by-line scrutiny.[35] The parliamentary committees remained hampered by weak staffs and meager technical resources, allowing the Finance Ministry to dominate budget policy during the early postcommunist period. But the evolution of a credible legislative oversight capability, together with the rationalization of budgetary procedures, created barriers to politicization of fiscal policy that were wholly absent during the communist years.

Balance of Power within the State Administration

While the reforms of the monetary and fiscal spheres *enhanced* the state's capacity for global economic regulation, measures taken elsewhere *weakened* the agencies responsible for sector-level policy. The Ministries of Industry and Trade were merged into a single agency with significantly reduced authority.[36] Foreign trade was placed under the jurisdiction of the new Ministry of International Economic Relations (MIER). That agency quickly emerged as the chief advocate of export subsidies, regional developmental funds, and other measures aimed at supporting particular sectors of Hungarian industry. During the MDF's term in office, the leadership of the MIER engaged in an ongoing dispute with the National Bank and Ministry of Finance, claiming that the latter's stringent anti-inflation policies were preventing local producers from expanding their export markets. But the MIER lacked the institutional resources to prevail in this battle, allowing the Bank and Finance Ministry to continue their policies of real currency appreciation and tight macroeconomic control.[37] The one area where the MIER played a dominant role was import licensing. However, the main trajectory in that policy sphere was not dirigisme but deregulation—which meant that the primary force of the MIER's authority was applied in a direction that ultimately undercut its own regulatory capacity.[38] In 1994, the MIER itself was abolished.[39]

---

35. Interviews, Ministry of Finance, 30 May 1991 and 20 May 1993; Hungarian Parliament, 19 May 1993.

36. Interview, Ministry of Industry and Trade, 17 May 1991.

37. Interviews, MIER, 30 May 1991 and 18 May 1993.

38. László Csaba, "Macroeconomic Policy in Hungary: Poetry versus Reality," *Soviet Studies* 44, no. 6 (1992): 955.

39. Dobszay, "Back to the Future," 12.

The chief counterweight to the National Bank and Finance Ministry's domination of economic policy in the postcommunist period was the State Property Agency. The SPA was created in May 1990 to impose order on a privatization process that had become chaotic during the final years of communist rule, when state enterprise managers seized on the MSZMP's property reforms to arrange scores of "*nomenklatura* buyouts" and other questionable deals. The law establishing the SPA assigned primary oversight authority to the Hungarian Parliament.[40] But the MDF subsequently engineered several changes in the legal structure to exert greater governmental control of privatization policy. In late 1990, the Antall government amended the legal code in an attempt to enlarge the scope of political intervention in the issue area.[41] In 1991, it introduced a highly controversial law for reprivatization of land and church properties confiscated by the Communist Party after 1948.[42] In 1992, it created a new Ministry without Portfolio, headed by a close ally of Prime Minister Antall and given broad authority to oversee privatization policy. Later that year, it established a new agency, the State Asset Holding Company (SAHC), empowered to manage industrial enterprises and banks selected by the government to remain under permanent state ownership.[43]

These developments underscored one of the central ironies of the Hungarian transition. As I described in chapter 3, it was the Communist Party that initiated the transformation of ownership relations in Hungary. The property reforms undertaken by the MSZMP in the late 1980s spurred local agents to engage in abuses that undermined public confidence in the privatization process and prompted the democratically elected successor government to recentralize policy. The transition from communist rule to

---

40. "1990 Évi VII. Törvény as Allami Vagyonügynökségrol és a Hozzá Tartozó Vagyon Kezelésérol és Hasznosításáról" (Law No. VII of 1990 on the foundation of the State Property Agency with the purpose of the management and utilization of property pertaining to this), *Hatályos Magyar Jogszabályok* (Hungarian Rules of Law in Force), no. I/9, 15 May 1990, 485–500.

41. Tamás Sárközy, "Az Allami Szektor Muködtetesének és a Privatizacionak Törvény Rendezéserol" (On the statutory settlement of the operation and privatization of the state sector), in Kurtán et al., *Magyarorszag Politikai Évkönyv 1993,* 214–21; Sárközy, "A Legal Framework for the Hungarian Transition, 1989–91," in István Székely and David Newbery, eds., *Hungary: An Economy in Transition* (Cambridge: Cambridge University Press, 1993), 245–46.

42. David Bartlett, "The Political Economy of Privatization: Property Reform and Democracy in Hungary," *East European Politics and Societies* 6, no. 1 (winter 1992): 112–17.

43. "1992 Évi LIII. Törvény a Tartósan Allami Tulajdonban Maradó Vállalkozói Vagyon Kezelésérol és Hasznosításáról" (Act LIII of 1992 on the management and utilization of entrepreneurial assets permanently remaining in state ownership), *Hatályos Magyar Jogszabályok* (Hungarian Rules of Law in Force), no. III/20, 15 October 1992, 1389–1444.

democracy thus resulted in the *reinsertion* of the Hungarian state into the ownership sphere.

Beyond this, the institutional structure of privatization policy rendered the issue area more vulnerable to political capture than monetary and fiscal policy. The Antall government repeatedly intervened in the operations of the SPA, prevailing on that agency to give political supporters choice seats on the shareholding boards of newly privatized firms.[44] Its handling of the SAHC was even more heavy-handed. The SAHC leadership reported directly to the Minister without Portfolio, giving the prime minister's office considerable leverage over the organization's activities. Many of the 163 enterprises placed under SAHC management were chosen by the Antall government for purely political reasons.[45]

But these very attempts to politicize privatization policy ultimately proved heavy liabilities for the MDF. The MDF's meddling with the SPA and SAHC provoked widespread publicity and criticism, impairing its already dwindling reputation during the run-up to the second parliamentary elections in spring 1994. The lessons of the MDF's political fate were not lost on the winner of those elections. The new MSZP government soon announced plans to merge the SAHC and the SPA and bring privatization policy under closer parliamentary supervision.[46]

Consequences for Stabilization and Adjustment Policy

The upshot of these developments was to strengthen the *universalistic* dimension of the Hungarian state. The political transition left the key institutions of global economic regulation, the National Bank and the Ministry of Finance, in a stronger position than before, while weakening the agencies charged with overseeing particular sectors.

The reorientation of the Hungarian state from institutional particularism to universalism facilitated the use of market reforms for macroeconomic stabilization and structural adjustment. The central banking law gave the National Bank the political muscle to pursue a restrictive monetary policy during most of the postcommunist period, amid strong pressure to ease liquidity. The creation of legal limits on the Bank's deficit financing obligations ended the traditional practice of deficit monetization and hardened the budget constraints of the Ministry of Finance. This, combined with the rationalization of the Finance Ministry's budgeting procedures, laid the groundwork for a true separation of the monetary and fiscal spheres that enabled state authorities to execute an effective stabi-

44. Interview, Central European International Bank, 25 May 1993.
45. Interview, SPA, 21 September 1993.
46. Economist Intelligence Unit, *Country Report: Hungary,* 2d quarter 1994, 14–15.

lization program. At the same time, the advent of a legitimate oversight function in the Hungarian Parliament erected institutional safeguards against political plundering of the national treasury.

On the structural adjustment side, the elimination of the National Planning Office, the diminution of the power of the branch ministries, and the consolidation of the Finance Ministry's budgetary policy authority allowed the state to enact deep cuts in producer subsidies. By 1993, direct subsidies to the industrial sector were essentially ended.[47] Meanwhile, the Antall government enacted a series of laws that augmented the state's capacity to execute adjustment policy. In 1990, it established an office for economic competition empowered to regulate cartels, mergers, and unfair marketing practices.[48] In 1991, it passed a law prescribing procedures for bankruptcy and liquidation. In contrast to Hungary's 1985 bankruptcy law and those introduced in other postcommunist states, this legislation had real teeth. It included an automatic triggering mechanism that forced enterprises to declare bankruptcy if they had any debt payments that were 90 days overdue.[49] In 1992, it passed an accounting law aimed at bringing Hungarian financial reporting procedures up to international standards.[50] The introduction of double-entry bookkeeping, linear depreciation schedules, and other Western-type accounting practices allowed the SPA, the multilateral lending agencies, and private investors to assess the book value of state enterprises targeted for bankruptcy or divestiture.

These measures, combined with the collapse of the Eastern market and the rapid liberalization of Western imports, fundamentally transformed the environment in which Hungarian enterprises operated. The institutional links to the state that previously enabled local producers to soften the distributional effects of economic adjustment had been swept away, forcing them to confront hard budget constraints and genuine mar-

---

47. "State Subsidies Falling," *Hungarian Business Brief* 6 (24 March 1993): 3–4.

48. János Stadler, "Competition Policy in Transition," in Székely and Newbery, *Hungary,* 118–25.

49. "1991. Évi IL Törvény a Csodeljárásról, a Felszámolási Eljárásról és a Végelszámolásról" (Law IL of 1991 on bankruptcy procedures, liquidation procedures, and final settlement), *Hátalyos Magyar Jogszabályok* (Hungarian Rules of Law in Force), no. II/23, 1 December 1991, 1719–59. The 1991 legislation was so rigorous that it prompted a surge in bankruptcies and liquidations, overwhelming the Hungarian court system and forcing the MDF to amend the law in 1993. See Kálmán Mizsei, "Instituting Bankruptcy in the Post-Communist Economies of East Central Europe" (New York, Institute for Eastwest Studies, 1992, mimeo); Mizsei, "Bankruptcy and the Postcommunist Economies of East-Central Europe," *Russian and East European Finance and Trade,* March/April 1994, 53–58.

50. "Indokolás a Számvitelrol Szóló 1991. Évi XVIII Törvény" (Explanation to Law XVIII of 1991 on accounting), *Hátalyos Magyar Jogszabályok* (Hungarian Rules of Law in Force), no. III/1, 1 January 1992, 1–91.

ket competition. The result was the biggest contraction of GDP since the Great Depression. Between 1989 and 1992, industrial production in Hungary declined by one-third while unemployment rose from 1 percent to 14 percent.[51]

But while augmentation of the market-promoting features of the state did indeed accelerate the *contraction* of Hungarian industry, it did not hasten *restructuring* of the country's loss-making enterprises. As I show in chapter 6, state institutions were instrumental in downsizing loss makers, but not in restoring them to profitability. Achieving the latter required vast amounts of capital to upgrade plant, equipment, and local infrastructure. The funds needed to revitalize weak sectors were not forthcoming owing to (1) the unwillingness of Western investors to commit large amounts of capital to loss-making enterprises and (2) constraints on domestic capital formation emanating from the loan portfolio problems of the Hungarian commercial banks.

Conclusion: Parties, States, and Market Reforms

The central argument of this chapter is that Hungary's political transition accelerated economic reform by undercutting the institutional bases of opposition and strengthening the market-protecting elements of state agencies. On the one hand, democratization bolstered the policy-making capacity of the successor government by concentrating executive authority in the prime minister's office, placing a small number of parties in control of the electoral system, and hastening the fragmentation of intermediary interest associations. On the other hand, it instigated a reorientation of the Hungarian state from institutional particularism to universalism.

This latter shift was the result not of a necessary functional correspondence between democratization and universal law but of the dynamics of Hungary's negotiated transition. The combination of exceptionally high *uncertainty* and unusual latitude for institutional *innovation* stimulated Hungarian political elites to formulate rules designed to hinder each other from exploiting state institutions for partisan purposes. The first postcommunist government did indulge in a number of abuses of the state administration, a development that was hardly surprising in a country lacking a historical tradition of rule by law. But the MDF's penetration of the state was tempered by the presence of a robust parliamentary opposition, which lost little time in publicizing those activities. At the same time, the inevitability of another round of electoral competition induced the

51. "Hungarian Economic Monitor: Worsening Hard-Current Account Deficit Triggers Forint Devaluation and Brings Implementation of Measures to Slow Recovery," *PlanEcon Report* 10, nos. 25–27 (31 August 1994): 12, 20.

Antall government itself to embrace institutional reforms aimed at discouraging successor governments from manipulating state agencies to advance their own political ends.

Hungary's political transition thus illuminates the complex relationship between parties, state institutions, and market reforms: far from *impeding* marketization, pluralization of the party system *enhances* it by diverting distributional politics away from the state and creating mutual incentives for party leaders to erect barriers to partisan manipulation of state resources. Incentives to protect state institutions from political capture are especially pronounced in the fluid circumstances facing new democracies, where voter loyalties are weak, electoral volatility is high, and incumbent governments confront a strong probability of losing the next round of competition. But the choices made by leaders of fledgling democracies have long-term consequences that transcend short-term electoral incentives, creating institutional constraints that impinge on the political strategies of their successors.

CHAPTER 5

Stabilization Policy in the Postcommunist Period

The former communist countries of Eastern Europe pursued a variety of economic stabilization strategies.[1] In Germany, unification paved the way for the region's only true "big bang." By assuming the external debt of the GDR and absorbing its fiscal, monetary, and price systems, the Bonn government executed what amounted to an instantaneous stabilization. Poland's Balcerowicz Plan featured a radical price reform, a large currency devaluation, a harsh monetary squeeze, and strict wage controls. Subsequently, the Polish authorities negotiated a reduction of the country's hard currency debt. The Czech Republic, Bulgaria, and Romania implemented less draconian versions of "shock therapy."

Postcommunist Hungary represents a different pattern. The standard categorization of "gradualist" and "big bang" strategies of transition does not adequately capture its distinctive trajectory. In the sphere of foreign trade and exchange, Hungary moved along broadly similar lines as Poland and the Czech Republic, enacting sharp tariff cuts, liberalizing imports, and moving cautiously toward currency convertibility. And like those countries, Hungary sustained a policy of fiscal and monetary discipline during most of the post-1989 period. But in other respects it diverged from the rest of the region. Following the strategy of its predecessor, the Antall government combined import liberalization with real currency apprecia-

---

1. For surveys of the stabilization programs undertaken in postcommunist Eastern Europe, see Michael Bruno, "Stabilization and Reform in Eastern Europe: A Preliminary Assessment," *IMF Staff Papers* 39, no. 4 (December 1992): 745–53; Lászlo Csaba, "First Lessons in the Transformation of the Economic Systems in Central Europe," *Acta Oeconomica* 43, nos. 3–4 (1991): 231–50; Alan Gelb and Cheryl Gray, *The Transformation of Economies in Central and Eastern Europe: Issues, Progress, and Prospects* (Washington: World Bank, 1991), 12–17; András Köves, *Central and East European Economies in Transition* (Boulder: Westview, 1992), 17–36; Köves and Paul Marer, "Foreign Economic Liberalization in Eastern Europe and in Market Economies," in Köves and Marer, eds., *Foreign Economic Liberalization: Transformations in Socialist and Market Economies* (Boulder: Westview, 1991), 15–33; L. Halpern, "Hyperinflation, Credibility, and Expectations: Stabilization Theories and East European Stabilization Programs," *Acta Oeconomica* 43, no. 102 (1991): 103–8; "Developments in Selected Non-OECD Countries: Central and Eastern Europe and the Newly Independent States of the Former USSR," *OECD Economic Outlook,* December 1992, 123–29.

tion—a policy mix at odds with the orthodox stabilization remedy prescribed by the IMF and embraced by other East European countries. And it eschewed Polish-style debt relief, continuing the Communist Party's unblemished record of debt service.

Economists who have examined these cases focus on the theoretical foundations and programmatic elements of market reforms[2] or the debate concerning the proper pace and sequence of economic transition.[3] Other scholars emphasize the starting positions of the postcommunist countries.[4] What made Germany's big bang possible was a preexisting capitalist state capable of absorbing the GDR's socioeconomic and political systems and generating the massive financial flows needed to rebuild the East's industry and infrastructure. The Czech Republic's comparatively favorable macroeconomic situation made a "minibang" strategy feasible, while the hyperinflation besetting Poland at the time of the transition militated toward shock therapy. Similarly, Hungary's specific circumstances clearly influenced its economic policy course during the early postcommunist years. In particular, the reforms previously undertaken by the Communist Party alleviated price distortions and domestic shortages, obviating Polish-type stabilization.

But while the starting positions of the East European countries doubtlessly shaped their postcommunist trajectories, they do not fully explain the various patterns of economic transformation in the region. For example, it is not obvious that Hungary's economic circumstances preordained a moderate transition strategy. Indeed, its external debt situation was in some respects the most precarious in Eastern Europe. As table 5.1

2. Andrew Berg, "Does Macroeconomic Reform Cause Structural Adjustment? Lessons From Poland," *Journal of Comparative Economics* 18, no. 3 (June 1994): 376–409; Eduardo Borensztein, Dimitri Demekas, and Jonathan Ostry, "An Empirical Analysis of the Output Declines in Three Eastern European Countries," *IMF Staff Papers* 40, no. 1 (March 1993): 1–31; Guillermo Calvo and Fabrizio Coricelli, "Output Collapse in Eastern Europe: The Role of Credit," *IMF Staff Papers* 40, no. 1 (March 1993): 32–52.

3. I. Ábel and J. Bonin, "Two Approaches to the Transformation in Eastern Europe: The 'Big Bank' versus 'Slow but Steady,'" *Acta Oeconomica* 43, nos. 3–4 (1991): 213–29; Josef Brada, "The Transformation from Communism to Capitalism: How Far? How Fast?" *Post-Soviet Affairs* 9, no. 2 (1993): 87–110; David Lipton and Jeffrey Sachs, "Creating a Market Economy in Eastern Europe: The Case of Poland," *Brookings Papers on Economic Activity* 1 (1990): 75–145; Ronald McKinnon, *The Order of Economic Liberalization: Financial Control in the Transition to a Market Economy* (Baltimore: Johns Hopkins University Press, 1991); Peter Murrell, "What is Shock Therapy? What Did it Do to Poland and Russia?" *Post-Soviet Affairs* 9, no. 2 (1993): 111–40; Wing Thye Woo, "The Art of Reforming Centrally Planned Economies: Comparing China, Poland, and Russia," *Journal of Comparative Economics* 18, no. 3 (June 1994): 276–308.

4. Köves, *Central and East European Economies in Transition,* 31–33.

shows, by the time of the political transition Hungary was one of the world's most heavily indebted countries.

Disposition of the hard currency debt bequeathed by the MSZMP became a contentious issue in the campaign preceding the 1990 parliamentary elections. The leaders of the SZDSZ announced their intention to negotiate a reduction of the debt with Hungary's creditors. But the eventual winner, the MDF, opted to maintain Hungary's historical commitment to service all of its debts on schedule.[5] As I detail later in this chapter, that decision stemmed from the institutional structure of policy making in the postcommunist state, which induced the Antall government to defer to the Ministry of Finance and National Bank on international financial matters. Similarly, the government's pursuit of moderately restrictive fiscal and monetary policies was conditioned, but not wholly determined, by Hungary's relatively favorable macroeconomic situation. During the electoral campaign, the MDF proposed expansionary policies aimed at accelerating Hungary's recovery from the regional recession. Subsequently, progrowth factions within the governing coalition allied with the MIER to push for currency devaluation, tax credits, and budget subsidies to spur Hungarian exports.[6] Again, the "saver" agencies within the Hungarian state prevailed—underscoring the importance of *institutional* determinants of economic policy. In short, while economic circumstances delimited the range of alternatives available to the East European successor governments, policy outcomes were ultimately the result of deliberate *choices* made by political leaders operating under institutional constraints.

TABLE 5.1.   External Indebtedness of Selected Countries, 1989

Country	Gross Debt ($ million)	Debt Service ($ million)	Debt/GDP (%)	Debt Service/ Exports (%)	Debt/Per capita ($ million)
Brazil	114,731	15,691	23.8	40.5	644
Mexico	97,417	12,601	48.5	35.1	996
Argentina	59,890	10,882	92.5	92.8	1,443
Venezuela	32,931	4,487	75.1	28.3	1,298
Nigeria	31,951	2,909	109.0	27.8	221
Philippines	29,642	3,383	66.9	27.3	437
Hungary	20,391	3,455	71.3	40.6	1,939
Chile	18,863	2,811	74.7	29.2	1,117

Source: István Székely and David Newbery, *Hungary: An Economy in Transition* (Cambridge: Cambridge University Press, 1993), 220.

5. Interviews, UNIC Bank, 15 May 1991; National Bank of Hungary, 22 May 1991.
6. Interviews, MIER, 30 May 1991; Ministry of Finance, 23 May 1991.

In this chapter, I show how the institutional configuration outlined in chapter 4—a strong prime ministerial government, a state administration dominated by saver agencies, and a system of interest representation commanded by national political parties—shaped the course of Hungarian stabilization policy in the early postcommunist years. I begin by analyzing the institutional underpinnings of stabilization policy under the Antall government. I then examine four specific spheres of Hungary's stabilization program: debt management, exchange rate policy, monetary control, and fiscal policy.

I argue that democratization facilitated macroeconomic stabilization by concentrating policy-making authority in the state institutions responsible for global regulation and by weakening the capacity of local agents to engineer compensatory increases in domestic purchasing power. The political transition yielded a central banking law that simultaneously codified the National Bank's operational control of foreign exchange and established external checks on its international financial activities, the absence of which led to the rapid buildup of Hungary's hard currency debt under communist rule. The National Bank's institutional prerogatives in foreign exchange, technical and informational resources, and links to Western lending agencies enabled Hungary's central bankers to resist pressure by the liberal opposition parties to seek debt relief. They opted instead for a debt management strategy aimed at preserving Hungary's reputation as Eastern Europe's most creditworthy country in order to maintain favored access to international bond markets and sustain a net inflow of foreign capital. The institutional structure of the postcommunist state also allowed National Bank authorities to implement a politically unpopular exchange rate policy. Rejecting demands for currency devaluation by the MIER and major Hungarian exporters, the central bankers held to a strategy of combating inflation via real appreciation of the forint. Monetary policy similarly illustrated the dominant position of the saver institutions of the Hungarian state. The codification of National Bank independence, the diversification of that agency's policy instruments, and the reorientation of the Finance Ministry toward financial control laid the institutional groundwork for monetary discipline. At the same time, political and economic shifts after 1989 weakened the capacity of local agents to neutralize monetary contractions by bidding up wages and bank credit. Fiscal policy proved a partial exception to the general trend toward macroeconomic austerity in the postcommunist period. On the one hand, the Ministry of Finance engineered deep cuts in subsidies and implemented tax reforms that shifted the burden of taxation from the enterprise sector to Hungarian households. On the other hand, state authorities failed to lower social welfare expenditures, the main culprit behind Hungary's extraordinary level of budgetary centralization. Here, the distinctive structure of interest representation in Hungary's new democracy, namely the concentration of representative politics in the Parliament, dissuaded the Antall government from reducing the massive burden of social services inherited from the Communist Party. By the time of the second national election in 1994, contraction of the redistributive components of Hungary's fiscal system had emerged as the country's most vexing macroeconomic problem.

The Antall Government and the Politics of Stabilization

As I noted at the end of chapter 2, the lame-duck Németh administration negotiated a tough new stabilization agreement with the IMF in spring 1990. Before signing the accord, state officials obtained the tacit approval of the leaders of the major political parties, then immersed in the electoral campaign.[7] This did not prevent the MDF and its future coalition partners, the Independent Smallholders and the Christian Democrats, from including expansionary policies in their campaign platforms.[8] But the policy programs of the center-right parties were not well elaborated, reflecting the fact that the cream of Hungary's economic technocracy had gravitated toward the liberal and socialist parties. In an attempt to fill this expertise gap, Hungarian economists sympathetic with growth-oriented strategies created the so-called Bridge Group, which formulated detailed recommendations for the incoming government.[9] The liberal parties allied themselves with another expert advisory group, the Hungarian-International Blue Ribbon Commission, which endorsed a more thoroughgoing transformation of the economic system. The main liberal party, the SZDSZ, embraced the shock therapy proposals supported by János Kornai and other leading economists.[10]

The stabilization program the Antall government ultimately adopted assigned top priority to combating inflation through fiscal and monetary discipline while stopping short of the liberals' proposals for shock therapy. At the same time, the government explicitly rejected the SZDSZ's call for

---

7. Interview, National Bank of Hungary, 21 May 1991.

8. Interview, Kopint-Datorg, 28 September 1993.

9. The Bridge Group was headed by György Matolcsy and Béla Kádár, soon to emerge as the main advocates of progrowth policies, as the respective heads of the Economic Policy Secretariat of the prime minister's office and the MIER. Two-thirds of the members of the Bridge Group assumed positions in the Antall government. László Csaba, "Macroeconomic Policy in Hungary: Poetry versus Reality," *Soviet Studies* 44, no. 6 (1992): 951–52.

10. Gábor Oblath, "Macroeconomic Developments between 1990 and 1994," *Hungarian Quarterly* 35 (summer 1994): 18. On the eve of the political transition, Kornai laid out his proposals for a radical "surgery for stabilization" in *The Road to a Free Economy* (New York: W. W. Norton, 1990).

debt relief, insisting that the resultant loss of confidence of international financiers would imperil Hungary's economic transition.[11] The MDF's decision to abandon its campaign rhetoric about growth stemmed in part from adverse economic circumstances. By the time the new government assumed office in spring 1990, Hungary's hard currency reserves had fallen to about $300 million as a result of withdrawals of foreign deposits from the National Bank.[12] By the end of that year, the country's gross convertible currency debt exceeded $21 billion.[13] The erosion of Hungary's liquidity position forced the government to turn to Western governments and the multilateral lending agencies for financial assistance, ruling out any significant departure from the IMF standby. Meanwhile, developments in the East magnified Hungary's economic vulnerability. The collapse of the Soviet Union's payments system, the disruption of the East German market following reunification, and the recession in the other former communist countries caused a deep contraction of Hungary's ruble-denominated trade.[14]

However, the economic picture in 1991 was considerably brighter. That year, the economy registered a modest current account surplus, demonstrating the ability of Hungarian enterprises to weather the demise of their Eastern markets and reorient their exports toward the West.[15] A sharp increase in foreign direct investment markedly improved the country's reserve position, resulting in a reduction of the net hard currency debt to $13 billion, its lowest level since the early 1980s.[16] The economy's ostensible recovery appeared to give the Antall government justification to back off the austerity program, as the communist regime did in 1983–84. The fact that the successor government did not yield to the temptations of growth in the face of favorable economic news illustrated the institutional logic of stabilization policy in Hungary's new democracy.

First, the institutional safeguards against partisan manipulation of the budget and the money supply that were missing under communist rule

11. Government of the Republic of Hungary, *A Program of Conversion and Development for the Hungarian Economy: Stabilisation and Convertibility* (Budapest, March 1991), 25–28.

12. Csaba, "Macroeconomic Policy," 953; Oblath, "Macroeconomic Developments," 16.

13. National Bank of Hungary, *Monthly Report* 2–3 (1993): 45.

14. László Csaba, "Economic Consequences of Soviet Disintegration for Hungary," in István Székely and David Newbery, eds., *Hungary: An Economy in Transition* (Cambridge: Cambridge University Press, 1993), 30–31.

15. Csaba, "Economic Consequences of Soviet Disintegration," 32–34; Sándor Richter, "Hungary's Changed Patterns of Trade and Their Effects," *Soviet Studies* 44, no. 6 (1992): 972–79.

16. National Bank of Hungary, *Monthly Report* 2–3 (1993): 44.

were now in place as a result of the negotiated transition to democracy. The state institutions responsible for macroeconomic regulation possessed real, if limited, spheres of legal independence from the incumbent government. The evolution of a credible oversight capability within the Hungarian Parliament, whose key economic committees were controlled by the liberal opposition, erected additional barriers to exploitation of state resources.

Second, the electoral rules negotiated in 1989 insulated the Antall government itself from political pressures to ease the austerity program. With three years remaining before the second national election and scant prospects for a no-confidence vote in the Parliament, the prime minister had little incentive to enact economic stimulus measures that promised short-term gains at the expense of long-term recovery. At the same time, the constitutional setup of the Hungarian Republic concentrated political authority in the prime minister's office. This enhanced Antall's capacity to maintain discipline within the governing coalition, elements of which still favored expansionary programs. Antall allocated several ministerial portfolios—education, agriculture, labor, defense—to his coalition partners. But these were the weakest agencies in the state administration, whose institutional resources gave them little influence over stabilization policy. Antall meanwhile placed the key economic agencies, the National Bank and Ministry of Finance, in the hands of two officials, György Surányi and Mihály Kupa, whose political independence, technical expertise, and close ties to the Washington lending agencies allowed them to dominate economic policy making. Subsequently, Antall replaced both men with more politically reliable figures and reshuffled the state secretaries in the Finance Ministry.[17] But he left the subministerial ranks within those institutions largely intact, thereby imparting a high degree of continuity to monetary, fiscal, and foreign exchange policy. The shortage of economic expertise within the government and coalition parties reinforced the prime minister's reliance on the Hungarian state to carry out stabilization policy.

Finally, the weakness of intermediary associations in Hungary deprived workers and enterprise managers of the institutional means to pressure political leaders to relax stabilization policy. Owing to high organizational fragmentation and poor financing, organized resistance to economic austerity during the early postcommunist years was sporadic and ineffectual. The abrupt demise of the CMEA and the Soviet Union, the principal markets of Hungary's loss-making sectors, further undercut the mobilizational capacity of the economy's most vulnerable actors. Rising

---

17. László Lengyel, "What Derailed Mihály Kupa's Train?" *Hungarian Economic Review* 13 (April 1993): 2–5.

unemployment and declining output in these industries weakened the economic leverage of blue-collar workers and traditional enterprise managers, who lacked the skills to exit to thriving sectors and who became increasingly fearful that open mobilization placed them at higher risk of losing their jobs.[18] The most dramatic exhibition of collective political action in democratic Hungary involved not trade unions or enterprise associations but the taxi and truck drivers who staged a massive strike in October 1990 to protest fuel price increases. But while that brief crisis forced the Antall government to concoct a face-saving deal, it was not compelling evidence of a resurgent civil society. The efficacy of the strike stemmed from the literal ability of drivers to encircle Budapest and blockade most of the country's highways. In this respect it was a unique event, not to be repeated for the remainder of the MDF's term in office.[19]

Unable effectively to resist policies already enacted, the influence of societal actors over economic policy was concentrated at the initiation phase. But the ability of vulnerable agents to shape policy formation in the legislature and state administration was restricted owing to (1) the results of the founding elections, which left social democratic constituencies poorly represented in the Hungarian Parliament, and (2) the weak capacity of trade unions and enterprise associations to undertake institutionalized bargaining with state agencies. As I describe later in this chapter, budget policy proved an exception, as members of Parliament exhibited a keen sensitivity to the electoral repercussions of social welfare cuts.

But outside the social welfare sphere, the main effect of the institutional factors enumerated above was to endow the state administration with primary authority over stabilization policy while insulating state agencies from penetration by the governing parties and intermediary associations. At the same time, Hungary's negotiated transition prompted a shift in the balance of forces *within* the state, away from institutional particularism and toward universalistic market regulation.

The key contestants in the debate over stabilization policy were the National Bank, the Ministry of Finance, and the MIER. The policy program advanced by the former two agencies combined "orthodox" monetary and fiscal constraint with a "heterodox" strategy of real currency appreciation. The central objective of these measures was to contain inflation, which National Bank and Finance Ministry authorities regarded as the chief threat to Hungary's economic transformation. The leaders of the saver institutions meanwhile rejected any consideration of asking Hungary's creditors for debt relief or rescheduling of payments. Such measures

---

18. Interview, Hungarian Parliament, 19 May 1993.

19. Károly Okolicsányi, "Hungary: The Non-Existent Long-Term Economic Plan," *RFE/RL Research Report* (17 January 1992), 18.

would merely increase Hungary's interest payments over the long-term while impeding the flow of foreign direct investment essential for economic restructuring.[20]

The leadership of the MIER proposed an alternative strategy of economic transition. Hungary, like export-sensitive countries in the developing capitalist world, needed an aggressive industrial policy to stimulate supply-side responses, even at the risk of higher inflation: export credits, selective budget subsidies, preferential tax regulations, state investment in infrastructure and worker retraining, and currency depreciation. Absent these measures, the export boom would peter out and imperil the whole transition effort.[21]

But notwithstanding its close political connections to the prime minister's office, the sympathy of leaders of the coalition parties, and support by major Hungarian enterprises, the MIER ended up losing the battle over stabilization policy. What proved decisive were the institutional resources of the National Bank and Ministry of Finance: their spheres of legal jurisdiction over foreign exchange, monetary, and budget policies; their technical expertise and experience in financial regulation accumulated over decades of market socialism; and their authority and prestige in macroeconomic affairs deriving from extensive contacts with the international lending agencies.

The Debt Management Strategy of the National Bank

As shown in chapter 3, under the communist system Hungarian debt management policy was highly centralized but poorly institutionalized.[22] Key decisions concerning the external debt were the exclusive domain of János Fekete, the head of the National Bank's foreign exchange division, whose authority derived chiefly from his personal connections to the MSZMP leadership and not from the Bank's legal status in the communist state. The absence of effective institutional checks in this sphere caused the gross convertible currency debt to double between 1984 and 1986, when Fekete resumed aggressive borrowing in Western financial markets to support the Kádár regime's ill-fated economic stimulus program. During the same

---

20. Interviews, National Bank of Hungary, 23 May 1991 and 20 and 24 May 1993.

21. Interviews, MIER, 30 May 1991 and 18 May 1993; "Financial Discipline on the Supply Side: An Interview with Mr. Béla Kádár," *Hungarian Economic Review* 1 (April 1991): 8–10; "A Trend Reversed: Our Editor Talks with Béla Kádár, Minister of International Economic Relations," *Hungarian Economic Review* 10 (October 1992): 8–13.

22. The following discussion draws on David Bartlett, "Democracy, Institutional Change, and Stabilisation Policy in Hungary," *Europe-Asia Studies* 48, no. 1 (January 1996): 67–77.

period, the net debt nearly trebled—the result of Fekete's decision to borrow in yen and deutschmarks while placing the bulk of Hungary's hard currency assets in dollars, whose value plummeted after the Park Plaza Accord on currency realignment. The Németh government's subsequent revelation of the actual size of the debt further damaged the National Bank's reputation and underscored the lack of transparency in the foreign exchange arena.

The 1991 Law on Central Banking rectified this situation by codifying the National Bank's operational control of debt policy and establishing institutional checks on its foreign exchange activities. The law designated the Bank as the primary organization of foreign exchange, requiring commercial banks to obtain specific authorization to assume credits from abroad. At the same time, the law enhanced accountability by (1) obliging the National Bank president to report periodically to the Parliament; (2) prescribing procedures for the exchange of information between the Bank, the government, and other state institutions; and (3) creating a Central Banking Council, composed of the presidents and vice presidents of the Bank and several governmental appointees, to oversee overall banking policy.[23]

Against this legal framework, the new leadership of the National Bank formulated a strategy aimed at stabilizing Hungary's debt position and restoring international confidence in the state's financial probity. As I noted earlier, in relative terms Hungary's convertible currency debt was extremely large, prompting the leadership of the SZDSZ to call for a renegotiation. Western business leaders, including the head of the Hungarian-American Enterprise Fund, endorsed the liberal opposition's position on the debt question. Prominent Western economists concurred, citing successful cases of debt relief in the capitalist South.[24]

But National Bank leaders steadfastly resisted. They argued that what was decisive was not the literal size of Hungary's external debt but the country's ability to sustain a net inflow of capital to finance the transition to a market economy. While the high ratios of the debt to the country's GDP and population indicated in table 5.1 were hardly cause for celebration, they were somewhat misleading. What made Hungary's external position so precarious during the late 1980s was its burgeoning current account deficit. Unable to generate sufficient export revenues to service current debt payments, the country had to assume new credits and draw

---

23. "1991 Évi LX Törvény a Magyar Nemzeti Bankról" (Act LX of 1991 on the National Bank of Hungary), *Hatályos Magyar Jogszabályok* (Hungarian Rules of Law in Force), no. III/18, 15 September 1992, 1269–70, 1273–74, 1277.

24. "Official Says Rescheduling Debts Not Necessary," *FBIS/EEU*, 30 March 1992, 14; Richard Portes, "Discussion of Part Four," in Székely and Newbery, *Hungary*, 235.

down on hard currency reserves just to cover its outstanding debt obligations. The upshot of these developments was a net outflow of foreign capital, as the economy was trapped in a vicious circle of rising external debt and internal stagnation. Pressed to the limit by the deteriorating current account and dwindling reserves, the National Bank diverted the lion's share of fresh credits away from productive investments and toward payments on old loans.

National Bank authorities insisted that the key to reversing the capital flow was not negotiating a reduction of the *gross* size of the debt, but stabilizing the *net* debt, which measured the differential between the country's hard currency liabilities and assets. A high level of gross indebtedness was not in and of itself pernicious, so long as capital inflows were used for productive purposes and not for covering outstanding liabilities. By bolstering the asset side of the national ledger, the Bank could meet current payments while taking on new credits to promote economic development.[25]

The National Bank's strategy of stabilizing the net debt presupposed four things. First, the Bank had to improve the structure of the outstanding debt. This meant lengthening the maturity profile of the debt by shifting from short- to long-term financing and lowering interest payments by replacing bank loans with low-cost bonds. Hungary began issuing bonds in 1985, the first communist country to do so. By 1992, bond issues represented 38 percent of its total foreign borrowings, the result of a series of successful placements on the German, Austrian, and American markets.[26] Bond financing was substantially cheaper than commercial bank loans, whose interest charges included a variable base rate indexed to the London Interbank Overnight Rate as well as a margin.[27] But the lower interest costs of bonds came at the expense of diminished flexibility. Favored access to the international bond market demanded preservation of the debtor country's credit rating, which any request for debt relief would compromise. Furthermore, reliance on bond financing circumscribed opportunities for ex post debt rescheduling in the event the economy floundered. Unlike syndicated bank credits, which entailed groups of creditors who could negotiate reschedulings under the auspices of the London Club, bonds involved a multitude of private investors who lacked institutionalized means of renegotiating terms with the issuing state.

---

25. Interview, National Bank of Hungary, 24 May 1993.

26. National Bank of Hungary, *Monthly Report* 1 (1993): 30.

27. In the early 1990s, bank loans denominated in deutschmarks cost Hungary about 11 percent, compared with 6 to 8 percent for bonds. Interview, National Bank of Hungary, 22 May 1991; Hajna Istvanffy Lőrinc, "Foreign Debt, Debt Management Policy, and Implications for Hungary's Development," *Soviet Studies* 44, no. 6 (1992): 1009–13.

Second, the Bank's strategy demanded quick improvements in Hungarian exports to the convertible currency area. On this score, the economy's performance in the immediate postcommunist period was encouraging. Sharp increases in hard currency exports yielded current account surpluses in 1991 and 1992. As a result of the export surge, Hungary's hard currency reserves, which were nearly depleted when the Antall government took office in 1990, rose to $5.5 billion by the end of 1992. The debt-service ratio (annual debt payments relative to hard currency exports), which had peaked at 75 percent in 1986, fell to 30 percent. Most importantly, the net debt declined from its 1990 high of $16 billion to $13.1 billion in December 1992—a level that would enable the National Bank to service the outstanding debt on schedule while sustaining a positive net inflow of foreign capital into the local economy. The dramatic improvement in the country's liquidity position in the early 1990s prompted international financial experts to recommend reclassifying Hungarian debt to investment grade, which would strengthen the National Bank's capacity to refinance costly bank credits by tapping Western bond markets.[28]

Third, the National Bank and Ministry of Finance had to maintain tight reins on monetary growth and fiscal spending. Macroeconomic policy was linked to external debt management in two ways. On the one hand, sustaining a current account surplus demanded not only rising exports but restraints on import demand—which in turn necessitated contraction of domestic purchasing power through fiscal and monetary means. On the other hand, macroeconomic discipline was needed to keep the state budget deficit from expanding beyond the financing capability of the local population. If household savings proved inadequate to absorb issues of treasury bills, the National Bank would face great pressure to increase foreign borrowing to cover the remainder of the deficit. In short, Hungary's external debt was inextricably linked to its internal financial status.[29]

Finally, maintaining a net capital inflow required increases in foreign direct investment, which would bolster hard currency reserves and relieve the National Bank's dependence on external credits to cover the economy's financial needs. As with the current account, postcommunist Hungary's performance in the foreign investment sphere was surprisingly good, thanks in no small part to the legal and institutional groundwork established by the Communist Party. Between 1990 and 1994, total foreign

---

28. "Hungarian Monthly Economic Monitor," *PlanEcon Report* 9, nos. 11–12 (20 April 1993): 11, 17.

29. Gábor Oblath, "Hungary's Foreign Debt: Controversies and Macroeconomic Problems," in Székely and Newbery, *Hungary,* 212–17.

direct investment in Hungary approached $7 billion, more than the other East European countries combined excluding the former GDR.[30]

To sum up, the National Bank drew on its institutional prerogatives to formulate a debt management strategy designed to restore Hungary's reputation as Eastern Europe's most creditworthy country. By doing so, Bank officials sought to reduce the cost of debt service and maintain a net inflow of foreign capital into the economy. This strategy was truly unique in the region. Poland and Bulgaria negotiated reductions of their hard currency debts with the London and Paris Clubs. Nicolae Ceauşescu's austerity program had essentially wiped out Romania's debt before the 1989 revolution. The new government in Czechoslovakia inherited a comparatively small hard currency debt, the one positive legacy of its neo-Stalinist predecessor. And the Federal Republic of Germany simply assumed the debt of the GDR.

Hungary's debt strategy was highly risky: it could quickly unravel if the four preconditions previously noted shifted. By the time of the second national election in 1994, the first factor, the structure of the debt, was still moving in the desired direction, owing to the National Bank's ability to refinance bank credits with lower-cost bonds. Meanwhile, the remarkable influx of foreign direct investment continued. But the gap between Hungary and the other East-Central European countries had narrowed, generating concerns about the country's continued status as the most favored site of Western investors. Critics of the National Bank pointed to Hungary's relatively high labor costs, which had risen in dollar terms as a consequence of the Bank's overvaluation of the forint.[31] And the large increase in Western investment in Poland belied arguments of National Bank authorities that countries with subperfect credit records could not attract sufficient foreign direct investment to support economic modernization.[32] Other economic indices were less encouraging. As the MIER economists predicted, the export boom of 1991–92 ebbed, resulting in a shift of the current account from surplus to deficit in 1993. The deterioration of the external balance caused the net hard currency debt to return to its 1990 level of $16 billion. Meanwhile, the internal budget deficit

---

30. United Nations Secretariat of the Economic Commission for Europe, *Economic Survey of Europe in 1994–1995* (New York: United Nations, 1995), 151.

31. In 1993, the average gross monthly wage in Hungary was 46 percent higher than its dollar-equivalent in the Czech Republic, despite the fact that per capita income in the latter country was 25 percent higher. "Hungarian Economic Monitor," *PlanEcon Report* 10, nos. 25–27 (31 August 1994): 4.

32. For a cogent analysis of "the vice of being nice" in international debt management, see Jochen Lorentzen, *Opening Up Hungary to the World Market: External Constraints* (New York: St. Martin's, 1995), 49–62

approached 8 percent of GDP, breaching the limits specified in the IMF stabilization agreement.[33] As in the 1990 electoral campaign, these unfavorable economic developments prompted calls for a Polish-type debt relief. But owing to the institutional structure of the foreign exchange sphere, this required an explicit decision by the new socialist government to reverse the course set by the Hungarian National Bank, which brought its formidable array of technical and informational resources to bear to oppose such a policy shift.

Hungary's Heterodox Exchange Rate Policy

Postcommunist Hungary's exchange rate policy similarly reflected the strong imprint of the National Bank. The main lines of the Bank's strategy were clear by the time of the 1990 elections. Amid campaign rhetoric about economic growth and continuing uncertainty over the efficacy of monetary and fiscal policy as anti-inflation instruments, National Bank officials turned to exchange rate policy as their main tool. By anchoring the forint to a crawling peg based on a mixed basket of Western currencies and by allowing only incremental exchange rate adjustments, the central bankers sought to deliver an unambiguous signal of their determination to contain inflation.[34] This strategy caused the forint to appreciate sharply in real terms after 1989. As table 5.2 shows, exchange rate adjustments lagged far behind consumer price inflation between 1990 and 1994.

Hungary's policy of real currency appreciation reflected the view of National Bank leaders that inflation was the single biggest threat to stabilization and market reform. The inflationary bias of Hungary's transitional economy emanated from two sources. First, the combination of

TABLE 5.2. Inflation and Exchange Rate Adjustments in Hungary, 1990–94 (percentage)

	1990	1991	1992	1993	1994
Consumer price inflation	28.9	35.0	23.0	22.5	18.8
Change in nominal exchange rate[a]	6.9	18.2	5.8	16.5	14.3

Sources: Economist Intelligence Unit, *Country Report: Hungary* 2d quarter, 1994, *Központi Statisztikai Hivatal, Statisztikai Havi Közlemények* (*Monthly Bulletin of Statistics*), February 1995, 97; IMF, *Financial Statistics,* January 1996, 290.

[a]Calculated as the annual percentage increase over the previous year's average forint/dollar.

---

33. "Hungarian Economic Monitor," *PlanEcon Report* 10, nos. 25–27 (31 August 1994): 5, 7.

34. Interviews, UNIC Bank, 15 May 1991; National Bank of Hungary, 15 and 23 May 1991; Kopint-Datorg, 28 September 1993.

deep subsidy cuts, the contraction of supplies from the East, and the opening of the economy to world market prices generated strong "cost-push" pressures. Second, the sociopolitical disruptions of Hungary's dual transformation generated high inflationary expectations among the local population.[35]

From the standpoint of the National Bank, these circumstances ruled out the use of exchange rate policy for export promotion. For a country like Hungary undergoing systemic transformation, the line between moderate inflation and hyperinflation was a very fine one. The 30 percent annual inflation prevailing in the early postcommunist period could easily skyrocket to 50 or 100 percent if the saver institutions relaxed their vigilant anti-inflation stance. Hungary was not yet a full-fledged market economy, and state enterprises were still exhibiting some of their old behavioral traits. The favorable export performance of 1991 was a result not of exchange rate policy but of the forced reorientation of trade toward the West following the collapse of the Eastern market. The small devaluations enacted by the National Bank in 1989–90 had not induced local producers to expand export production. Instead, they seized on the consequent rise in domestic prices to ratchet up the prices of their own goods. This quasi-automatic adjustment of domestic prices in response to exchange rate shifts made currency devaluation a very risky proposition. And in any event, the performance of Hungarian exporters depended on a wide array of factors outside of relative prices: quality, reliability, packaging, servicing, distribution, and reduction of Western trade barriers. Devaluation was no substitute for the broader economic restructuring needed to bring Hungarian industry up to world standards. It was precisely the economy's least efficient sectors (e.g., steel) whose competitive position was undermined by high export prices. Sustaining real currency appreciation would force those enterprises to cut costs and raise productivity.[36]

Senior officials in the MIER countered that the National Bank's obsession with fighting inflation betrayed an ignorance of the "real processes" driving Hungary's economic transition. While the export surge of 1991 was heartening, Hungarian enterprises remained woefully unprepared to compete in the world economy. While upwards of 90 percent of imports had been liberalized, no more than 40 percent of Hungarian exports were truly competitive in Western markets. Far from increasing financial discipline, the Bank's currency overvaluation and macroeconomic squeeze were aggravating the underlying structural weaknesses of local producers. While devaluation was of limited use to advanced open-

---

35. "Look at the Trend—Not the Figure! The Review's Roundtable," *Hungarian Economic Review* 6 (February 1992): 13–52.

36. Interview, National Bank of Hungary, 12 May 1993.

market economies like Switzerland, whose exports were mainly high-end products, it was an effective instrument for countries like Hungary. The competitive position of Hungary's key export industries—agriculture, tourism, semimanufactured goods—was highly dependent on relative prices. The experiences of Poland, Bulgaria, and Romania had clearly demonstrated the efficacy of devaluation in transitional economies. Hungary's high inflation rate and mounting budget deficits made it quite unlikely that the National Bank could indefinitely sustain its strategy of real currency appreciation. The risk was that delaying devaluation would leave Hungary with a seriously overvalued forint, killing off exports and forcing the National Bank to make a huge ex post adjustment—which really would create a serious danger of hyperinflation.[37]

The MIER found enthusiastic support from prominent Hungarian exporters. For instance, the head of GE/Tungsram blamed the rising forint for the company's sizable losses in 1990–91. Despite increases in labor productivity and an upgraded product line, the enterprise had failed to turn a profit—the result of the National Bank's policy of overvaluation. The managing director of another major Hungarian-American venture, Schwinn-Csepel Bicycle Manufacturer, inveighed, "There is no other country that gives so little support to exports as Hungary."[38]

But these efforts to reverse exchange rate policy were unavailing. While enterprises like GE/Tungsram enjoyed high visibility in the Hungarian press, they lacked the institutional means to lobby the state for a change in strategy. Enterprise associations remained underfinanced and organizationally fragmented. Moreover, the political transition had foreclosed most opportunities for individualized bargaining with state authorities. The agency chiefly responsible for exchange rate policy, the National Bank, had severed its direct connections with the enterprise sector. And the agency most sympathetic with the standpoint of Hungarian exporters, the MIER, had little legal jurisdiction in the issue area.

In addition to limited points of access to key decision makers in the state administration, the crosscutting effects of exchange rate adjustments prevented a coordinated response by Hungarian enterprises. Exchange rate policy created cleavages within the enterprise sector. Export-dependent companies like Tungsram and local enterprises threatened by low-cost imports clearly favored devaluation. But for exporters whose products had high import content, currency devaluation was a double-

37. Interviews, MIER, 30 May 1991 and 18 May 1993; interview, Kopint-Datorg, 28 September 1993; Kopint-Datorg, *Economic Trends in Eastern Europe* 1, no. 3 (1992): 160–61.

38. Ferenc Langmár, "Forint Overvalued?" *Hungarian Economic Review* 8 (June 1992): 3.

edged sword, as increased input costs would neutralize declines in final export prices. For instance, General Motors Hungary and Magyar Suzuki endorsed the Bank's strategy of currency appreciation, which helped to contain their heavy import bills.[39]

Equally important as weak resistance from below was the structure of the postcommunist state, which concentrated authority over exchange rate policy in the National Bank of Hungary. The central banking law authorized the Bank to make exchange rate adjustments freely within a 5 percent band. Adjustments outside that band required the assent of the cabinet, which was composed of representatives from the prime minister's office and the key economic ministries.[40] This institutional arrangement facilitated the National Bank's strategy of incremental forint devaluations based on a crawling peg. The legal code allowed the Bank to enact small, periodic adjustments on its own initiative and without advance public notice, which served to hedge against currency speculation. And in the event a deteriorating current account generated political pressure for a big devaluation, the MIER would have to assemble a majority of votes within the economic cabinet—an improbable scenario due to the fact that the cabinet was chaired by the Minister of Finance, who shared the National Bank's aversion to inflation and who consistently supported the Bank's position on exchange rate policy.[41] The National Bank president, while not a voting member of the cabinet, was invited to attend meetings, enabling him to draw on the Bank's store of information and expertise to argue the case against large devaluations.

The National Bank's exchange rate-based stabilization strategy policy succeeded in reducing inflation in the early postcommunist years. As indicated in table 5.2, consumer price inflation peaked at 35 percent in 1991, then subsided to the low 20 percent range in 1992–93. But during the same period, the current account deteriorated, underscoring the tension between the goals of controlling inflation and spurring exports. However, senior officials in the National Bank and Finance Ministry insisted that the erosion of Hungary's balance of payments was due chiefly to the continuing crisis in the agricultural sector and to protectionist policies in the West.

---

39. Károly Okolicsányi, "Foreign Trade in Transition," *Bank & Tőzsde: Fuggelten Pénzügyi, Üzleti és Gazdasági Hétilap* 1, no. 30 (13 August 1993): 13–14; interview, MIER, 18 May 1993.

40. "A Magyar Nemzeti Bank Jogállása és Alapveto Feladata" (Legal status and function of the National Bank of Hungary), *Hatályos Magyar Jogszabályok* (Hungarian Rules of Law in Force), no. III/18, 15 September 1992, 1265; interview, National Bank of Hungary, 12 May 1993.

41. "Szabó Rejects Substantial Devaluation of Forint," *Hungarian Times,* 24 May 1993, 1.

A big currency devaluation would do little to ameliorate these problems while increasing the danger of reigniting inflation.[42]

In early 1995, National Bank President György Surányi, recently restored to his post by the new socialist government of Gyula Horn, initiated a more aggressive exchange rate policy. The Bank devalued the forint by 9 percent before placing the currency on a monthly schedule of incremental, preannounced adjustments. The result was an aggregate devaluation that year of 27 percent, Hungary's largest exchange rate shift in the postcommunist period. But this represented less than half of what was needed to correct fully the forint's cumulative real appreciation over the previous five years. Moreover, the inflation rate in 1995 itself virtually matched the nominal currency depreciation, neutralizing short-term effects on relative prices.[43]

Of course, Hungary was not the only East European country to exhibit real currency appreciation in the early 1990s, a common malady in high-inflation economies undergoing exchange rate-based stabilization. But what distinguished Hungary from other former communist states was the National Bank's institutional capacity to resist use of the exchange rate as a balance-of-payments tool in the face of serious current account problems. By contrast, Poland enacted a very large (250 percent) zloty devaluation at the launching of the Balcerowicz Plan in 1990, then followed with a second big devaluation in spring 1991 to compensate for inflation. The Polish authorities later shifted to a crawling-peg regime, devaluing the zloty by 74 percent between 1992 and 1994 in an attempt to keep exports price-competitive in Western markets.[44] Even Czechoslovakia, long noted for its monetary conservatism, devalued the koruna by 175 percent as part of its 1991 "minibang" stabilization program before fixing the currency at a unified commercial/official rate. Subsequently, the Czech Republic's

---

42. "Forint Comes to Fore in Inflation Fight," *Budapest Sun,* 16–22 September 1993, 5–6.

43. Organization for Economic Cooperation and Development, Center for Cooperation with the Economies in Transition, *Hungarian Economic Assessment* (Paris, January 1996); "Country Overviews: Hungary," *Central European Report,* February 1996.

44. Eduardo Borensztein and Paul Masson, "Exchange Arrangements of Previously Centrally Planned Economies," in *Financial Sector Reforms and Exchange Arrangements in Eastern Europe,* IMF Occasional Paper 102 (Washington, D.C.: IMF, 1993), 47–49; Branko Milanovic, "Poland's Quest for Economic Stabilisation, 1988–91: Interaction of Political Economy and Economics," *Soviet Studies* 44, no. 3 (1992): 521–27; Ben Slay, "Poland: The Rise and Fall of the Balcerowicz Plan," *RFE/RL Research Report* (31 January 1992), 41–42, Jan Winiecki, "The Polish Transition Program: Stabilisation Under Threat," *Communist Economies and Economic Transformation* 4, no. 2 (1992): 206–7; Központi Statisztikai Hivatal, *Statistical Bulletin* 4 (1994): 16.

favorable external balance and low inflation rate allowed the Klaus government to avert further exchange rate corrections.[45] Hungary's exchange rate strategy also differed from those of many developing capitalist countries. South Korea and other East Asian newly industrialized countries employed currency devaluations both to spur exports and to soften the impact of import liberalization on domestic industry.[46] Hungary combined radical import liberalization with real currency appreciation, confronting import-sensitive producers with a double whammy of increased foreign competition *and* lower import prices. And unlike the sub-Saharan countries, which revalued their currencies to maintain low consumer prices for politically vital urban constituencies,[47] Hungary's policy of currency appreciation demonstrated not the government's sensitivity to societal pressures but rather the domination of exchange rate policy by a powerful central bank.

State Institutions and Monetary Policy

The second prong of the National Bank's anti-inflation strategy was monetary policy. This was not as potent an instrument as exchange rate policy, since a variety of factors outside the Bank's direct control (inflows of foreign capital, interenterprise credits, repatriation of earnings by Hungarians living abroad) affected growth of the economy's total liquidity stock. But as table 5.3 shows, the Bank managed to implement a moderately restrictive monetary policy, whose distributional effects amplified the exogenous shocks stemming from the demise of the CMEA and Soviet Union.

In chapter 2, I identified three institutional features of Hungary's communist system that restricted the efficacy of monetary policy. The first was the political weakness of the National Bank, exemplified by its subordinate position within the state administration and its vulnerability to selective intervention by Communist Party elites. The second was the Bank's limited repertoire of global regulatory instruments. The monetary

45. Borensztein and Masson, "Exchange Arrangements," 49–52; Joshua Charap, Karel Dyba, and Martin Kupka, "The Reform Process in Czechoslovakia: An Assessment of Recent Developments and Prospects for the Future," *Communist Economies and Economic Transformation* 4, no. 1 (1992), 5–9; Központi Statisztikai Hivatal, *Statistical Bulletin* 4 (1994): 7, 16.

46. Stephan Haggard, Richard Cooper, and Chung-in Moon, "Policy Reform in Korea," in Robert Bates and Anne Krueger, eds., *Political and Economic Interactions in Economic Reform Policy: Evidence from Eight Countries* (Cambridge: Basil Blackwell, 1993), 325.

47. Robert Bates, *Markets and States in Tropical Africa: The Political Bases of Agricultural Policies* (Berkeley: University of California Press, 1981), 35–38.

TABLE 5.3.   Macroeconomic Indices in Hungary, 1990–94 (percent change or as indicated)

	1990	1991	1992	1993	1994
Real GDP	–3.5	–11.9	–4.5	–1.0	2.9
Consumer prices	28.9	35.0	23.0	22.5	18.8
Unemployment (rate)	1.7	7.7	12.3	13.3	11.4
Gross investment	–7.9	–17.0	–24.7	na	na
Broad money supply	29.2	29.4	27.3	16.8	13.5
Domestic credit	11.1	7.2	11.1	18.4	16.8
Budget deficit (% of GDP)	0.8	4.9	7.4	7.1	8.0

Sources: Gábor Bakos, "Hungarian Transition after Three Years," *Europe-Asia Studies* 46, no. 7 (1994): 1207; Guillermo Calvo and Manmohan Kumar, "Money Demand, Bank Credit, and Economic Performance in Former Socialist Economies," *IMF Staff Papers* 41, no. 2 (June 1994): 318–19; "Hungarian Economic Monitor," *PlanEcon Report* 10, no. 25–27 (31 August 1994): 32; Economist Intelligence Unit, *Country Report: Hungary,* 2d quarter 1994, 3; IMF, *International Financial Statistics,* January 1996, 290; "Hungarian Economics," *Central European Report,* February 1996.

officials depended on quantitative devices, which increased their susceptibility to particularistic bargaining and regulatory exceptionalism. The
third was the capacity of local agents to neutralize monetary contractions.
Hungarian workers utilized Party-controlled trade unions to secure compensatory wage increases; enterprise directors employed the plan bargaining system to negotiate individual exceptions to financial controls; commercial bank managers used their operational control under joint stock
ownership to divert funds to illiquid clients. In the following discussion, I
show how Hungary's political transition transformed all three factors in a
manner that enhanced the National Bank's capacity to contract domestic
purchasing power via monetary means.

The Political Power of the National Bank
in Hungary's Democracy

As we have seen, monetary policy in communist Hungary was little more
than a residual of the central planning process. Even after the transition to
the two-tiered system in 1987, National Bank authorities continued to
approach monetary policy as an income-balancing exercise, basing their
decisions on net income targets issued by the National Planning Office and
Ministry of Finance. The logic of Hungary's version of "flow equilibrium"
led to heavy levels of deficit monetization in the late 1980s, as the Bank
lacked the political muscle to engineer cuts in enterprise credit to offset the
burgeoning liabilities of the state, household, and foreign sectors.

    The political transition altered the institutional foundations of mone-
tary policy. The remnants of the central planning system dissolved as a

result of the elimination of the National Planning Office, the diminution of the power of the branch ministries, and the reorientation of the Finance Ministry toward macroeconomic control. Subsequently, the Law on Central Banking codified the National Bank's power to control the money supply and established limits on its obligation to finance budget deficits. These developments allowed Bank officials to shift to a "stock equilibrium" approach to monetary control that emphasized aggregate liquidity targets. Whereas monetary authorities previously operated under net income goals determined by other agencies, now they started with estimates of overall money demand, which in turn yielded annual targets for total domestic credit expansion.[48]

To be sure, the National Bank's capacity to regulate monetary aggregates did not match that of strong central banks in the West. While Germany's Bundesbank and the United States' Federal Reserve base their decisions on a priori monetary targets devised by internal staff, Hungary's central bankers negotiated domestic credit goals with the prime minister's office and the Ministry of Finance. This led National Bank officials to make periodic concessions on monetary policy. For instance, in 1991 they grudgingly agreed to set up a special refinancing line to support agriculture cooperatives withering under a severe draught. But such episodes were very much the exception to the rule in the postcommunist period. The Bank's negotiating position was much stronger than before, owing to its ability to resist pressure from commercial banks, enterprises, and budgetary officials to expand credit lines.[49]

The macroeconomic indicators displayed in table 5.3 demonstrate the National Bank's increased control of monetary aggregates. Growth of the broad money supply roughly matched the consumer price index in 1990 and fell below it in 1991. Monetary policy in 1992 was mildly expansionary. But this was due not to external pressure to loosen the money supply but rather to an internal decision by National Bank leaders to ease domestic liquidity and nudge down commercial lending rates, whose high levels were causing a severe credit crunch in the enterprise sector. The following year, Bank officials retightened monetary policy.[50]

In addition to bolstering the National Bank's standing within the state, Hungary's transition to democracy created institutional safeguards against arbitrary political interference in monetary policy. The central banking law vested supreme authority over monetary affairs in a Central Banking Council, composed of the president and the five vice presidents of

---

48. Interview, National Bank of Hungary, 23 May 1991.

49. Interview, National Bank of Hungary, 21 May 1991.

50. Interviews, National Bank of Hungary, 24 May 1993; Central European International Bank, 25 May 1993.

the National Bank and of additional members (whose number agreed with the number of vice presidents) appointed by the prime minister. A representative of the government attended the meetings of the Council, but in a nonvoting capacity. While the composition of the Council provided external checks on central banking operations, its voting procedures ensured that National Bank leaders would prevail in policy disputes. A simple majority was required to pass resolutions, with the chairman of the Council—the National Bank president—casting the deciding vote in the case of a tie. Meanwhile, the Bank's superior information, technical resources, and links to the multilateral lending agencies gave central bank executives considerable advantages over the external members of the Council.[51]

This institutional configuration left power of appointment of National Bank leaders as the prime minister's main instrument in the monetary sphere. The appointment procedures specified in the central banking law followed the lines of most Western countries. The president of the Bank was appointed for a six-year term, the vice presidents for staggered three-year terms. Early in the MDF's term, Prime Minister Jozsef Antall wielded his appointment power in an attempt to rein in the National Bank. Upon assuming office in spring 1990, Antall promised the incoming National Bank president, György Surányi, that the government would behave as if the draft law on central banking prepared by the Németh administration were already enacted. This gave the National Bank a free hand to sustain its monetary squeeze through 1990 and the first part of 1991. The prime minister submitted the law to the Parliament in June 1991. But before the legislature could act, Antall, under pressure from conservative elements of the governing coalition disenchanted with the National Bank's independent policies, changed his mind and introduced several amendments aimed at watering down the law. While the amended law retained the original draft's provision making the National Bank legally responsible to the Parliament, the coalition inserted a clause obliging the Bank to "support" the government's economic program.[52] The liberal opposition responded to Antall's rightward shift by issuing the "Democratic Charter," which took the government to task for its etatist approach to economic reform. Surányi's decision to sign the Charter provided Antall with a pretext to dismiss him in fall 1991, just before the new central banking law went into effect. Antall appointed as the new National Bank chief Péter Akos Bod, who was personally associated with the prime

51. "1991 Évi LX Törvény a Magyar Nemzeti Bankról," 1277.
52. "1991 Évi LX Törvény a Magyar Nemzeti Bankról," 1263.

minister and was therefore regarded as more politically reliable than Surányi.[53]

But notwithstanding its efforts to politicize the appointments process, Antall was unable to alter the basic trajectory of monetary policy. The subpresidential ranks of the Bank remained essentially intact after the Surányi affair, and Bod himself followed the main policy lines set down by his predecessor. Nor did the government's amendments of the central banking law change the substance of monetary policy, whose formulation followed the dictates of the Central Banking Council and not those of the government.

Policy Instruments of the National Bank

The National Bank's growing repertoire of policy instruments and increasing sophistication with Western-type monetary regulation augmented its institutional position in Hungary's new democracy. The clash over refinancing policy in 1987–88 had demonstrated that the Bank's reliance on credit quotas and other quantitative techniques increased its vulnerability to particularistic bargaining. That experience prompted Bank officials to shift toward price-based techniques, which were more conducive to universalistic regulation. By 1991, they had virtually eliminated refinancing quotas, relying instead on interest rate policy, rediscounting of commercial bills, and open market operations.

Previously, the Bank's base rates on refinancing loans were set well below inflation, fueling credit demand in the enterprise sector. In 1989, the Bank indexed the refinancing rate to its own cost of money, which it calculated in terms of the value of its hard currency assets and the real exchange rate of the forint.[54] The result was to drive commercial lending rates above the inflation rate. In 1991, Hungary's peak inflation year, commercial banks were charging as high as 50 percent on short-term credits. The advent of positive real interest rates bit so deeply into enterprise credit demand that National Bank officials decided to ease liquidity in 1992.[55]

During the early phase of the banking reform, National Bank officials used rediscounting of bills of exchange as a coercive tool, requiring the commercial banks to rediscount a specified amount of bills as condition for access to its refinancing facilities. Subsequently, the Bank adopted a

---

53. Interviews, National Bank of Hungary, 21 May 1991; International Training Center for Bankers, 20 May 1993; Central European Investment Bank, 25 May 1993.

54. National Bank of Hungary, *Annual Report,* 1989, 72.

55. National Bank of Hungary, *Monthly Report* 2–3 (1993): 64.

more discriminating approach to rediscounting policy. It applied differential rates to a broader variety of bills, in a manner similar to rediscounting methods used by Western central banks. It designated certain types of bills as eligible for rediscounting at the base rate without restrictions, with lower-quality commercial paper subject to higher rates. The expanded role of bills of exchange in Hungary's banking system advanced two objectives: raising allocative efficiency and strengthening control of monetary aggregates. Since the rediscount rate (and collaterally the discount rate paid by commercial banks on bills presented to them by Hungarian enterprises) were based on qualitative criteria, the most efficient producers were the ones most encouraged to use those criteria. This in turn enabled the National Bank to implement a general monetary contraction without damaging the economy's best performers, which could adjust to the credit squeeze by issuing readily discountable commercial paper. Weaker enterprises would be unable to tap the commercial bill market, as banks and other producers would be unwilling to accept low-quality paper. The monetary restriction would thus force loss-making enterprises to streamline production, cut the payroll, and enact other internal measures that they might otherwise forgo if credit were cheap and plentiful.[56]

Finally, Bank officials turned increasingly to open market operations as a regulatory mechanism. The 1991 central banking law played a decisive role in this development. The law not only established a legal cap on central bank financing of budget deficits but abolished direct National Bank credits to the state. This meant that central bank financing of the budget deficit took place entirely through National Bank purchases of treasury bills and government bonds. The securitization of deficit financing enlarged the National Bank's portfolio of marketable securities, broadening its capacity to regulate aggregate liquidity through open market operations.[57]

The diversification of the National Bank's regulatory instruments had a dramatic impact on monetary policy procedures in Hungary. At the time of the creation of the two-tiered banking system, refinancing credits represented the overwhelmingly largest source of funding for the new commercial banks. It was precisely the dominant role of those credits in the regu-

56. Interviews, National Bank of Hungary, 28 April, 13 June, and 22 July 1988; "Budapest Paper Chase: Hungarian Companies Bypass Banks," *International Herald Tribune,* 21 May 1993, 13. For a trenchant analysis of the role of bills of exchange in transitional economies, see McKinnon, *The Order of Economic Liberalization,* 7–8, 143–44.

57. Interviews, National Bank of Hungary, 30 May 1991; Central European International Bank, 25 May 1993; Saul Estrin, Paul Hare, and Marta Surányi, "Banking in Transition: Development and Current Problems in Hungary," *Soviet Studies* 44, no. 5 (1992): 794–95.

latory system that compelled the National Bank to concentrate the entire burden of monetary austerity on its refinancing facility, provoking strong resistance by banks, enterprises, and farm cooperatives and triggering intervention by Communist Party elites. By the early 1990s, refinancing credits represented less than 10 percent of commercial bank liabilities. This illustrated the National Bank's shift from quota-based procedures to global monetary regulations, which were impervious to particularistic bargaining.[58]

Responses of Local Agents

The success of the monetary squeeze presupposed the inability of workers, enterprise directors, and commercial bank managers to offset stabilization policy by boosting domestic purchasing power. In this regard, the transition to democracy reinforced the effects already described: while the institutional standing of the National Bank and Finance Ministry rose, the capacity of local agents to oppose the policies of those agencies declined.

Organized Labor
As described in chapter 2, in 1988–89 Hungarian workers seized on wage liberalization to secure income hikes that neutralized the Communist Party's attempts to implement an IMF stabilization program. The efficacy of labor mobilization in the late communist period emanated from (1) the spearheading of the labor movement by the ruling party's own trade union organization and (2) the convergent interests of workers and enterprise managers to bid up wages, which reflected the skewed incentive structure of Hungary's socialist halfway house.

The Antall government continued the MSZMP's policy of devolving wage bargaining to the factory level. But because the political transition reduced workers' capacity to extract compensatory income hikes, wage liberalization did not produce the same sort of push-pull dynamic that so beset the Communist Party. The collective bargaining power of labor in the late 1980s derived from the peculiar structure of Hungary's communist system, which deprived workers of independent representation while channeling their grievances into the Party-controlled trade union. The demise of that system disrupted the institutional bases of collective bargaining. On the one hand, Hungarian workers emerged from the transition without a strong, fully independent trade union comparable to Poland's Solidarity. The independent union organizations that formed in the early 1990s were small, fragmented, and poorly financed. On the other hand, the largest

---

58. Interview, National Bank of Hungary, 24 May 1993.

labor organization, the MSZOSZ, lacked popular legitimacy owing to its association with the discredited communist regime.

Labor representatives did partake in tripartite bargaining with state authorities and enterprise managers under the auspices of the Interest Representation Council. But that organization proved too ineffectual to advance the interests of Hungarian workers. In November 1992, Finance Minister Mihály Kupa signed an agreement with the other members of the Council on incomes policy. Kupa made some minor concessions to the unions, agreeing to reduce the value-added tax from 8 to 6 percent. He also assented to a 14 percent cost-of-living increase for pensioners in 1993, above the originally planned 12.3 percent. But this was still far below the inflation rate, which meant that real household income continued to erode in line with the state's austerity program. The Finance Minister meanwhile reduced the eligibility period for unemployment compensation from 18 to 12 months and rejected the unions' demands to exempt food items from the value-added tax.[59]

The weakness of intermediary associations left workers heavily dependent on the Parliament to advance their interests. But two factors limited the effectiveness of legislative strategies. First, the very wage liberalization that the Communists initiated in the late 1980s, and which workers exploited to secure compensatory income hikes, essentially removed wage policy from the Parliament's legislative agenda. Primary responsibility for incomes policy fell to the Ministry of Finance, which employed tax penalties to enforce wage discipline. Second, the specific results of the first national election compounded the political weakness of labor's intermediary associations. The left-wing vote was split between the rump MSZMP, the MSZDP, the Agrarian Alliance, and the MSZP. Only the latter garnered enough votes to qualify for admission to the Parliament. The combined vote of the leftist parties in 1990, 25 percent, indicated a large reservoir of potential support for an alternative to the center-right and liberal parties that now dominated the political landscape.[60] But this was of little use to workers in the immediate postcommunist years, as the rules of Hungary's electoral system virtually ensured that the next parliamentary election would not occur until 1994.

The weakness of intermediary institutions and labor's exclusion from the legislature left Hungarian workers to their own devices: How success-

---

59. Judith Patkai, "Hungarian Government Signs Social Contract with Unions," *RFE/RL Research Report* 2, no. 5 (29 January 1993): 42–43.

60. Tamás Kolosi, Iván Szelényi, and Bruce Western, "The Making of Political Fields in Post-Communist Transition: Dynamics of Party and Class in Hungarian Politics, 1989–90," *Working Papers on Transitions from State Socialism,* Cornell University, #90.7, August 1990; Barnabas Racz, "Political Pluralization in Hungary: The 1990 Elections," *Soviet Studies* 43, no. 1 (January 1991): 124–33.

fully they defended themselves against the distributional effects of stabilization policy depended on their ability to negotiate favorable contracts with enterprise managers, who had served as their de facto allies in the wage battles of the late 1980s. But the ensuing changes in the politico-economic environment transformed the bargaining strategy of Hungarian managers. As a result of the collapse of the Eastern market, radical import liberalization, deep subsidy cuts, and stringent bankruptcy laws, state enterprises faced much harder budget constraints and hence stronger incentives to contain wage costs. Consequently, trade unions could no longer count on management's compliance when the time came to negotiate new contracts. Dramatic shifts in the Hungarian labor market further undercut workers' collective bargaining power. Unemployment, which as late as 1989 was virtually nonexistent, quickly escalated into double digits. The rapid contraction of output in steel, mining, and other loss-making sectors cowed many workers into submission. Blue-collar workers, lacking the skills to exit to the expanding private sector, avoided open confrontations with management for fear of losing their jobs.[61]

The political and economic liabilities of organized labor in postcommunist Hungary enabled the Ministry of Finance to execute an incomes policy that relied on modestly punitive enterprise taxes to discourage producers from excessive wage payments.[62] The aim of this regulatory scheme was to keep growth of Hungary's aggregate wage bill within the inflation rate and thereby prevent domestic purchasing power from expanding and neutralizing the National Bank's monetary program. The Finance Ministry generally succeeded in this goal: real industrial wages did not increase until the second half of 1993, by which time the economy was showing the first signs of recovery from the postcommunist recession.[63]

Hungary's incomes policies differed in important ways from other East European countries. In Poland, the Mazowiecki government adopted far more draconian tax penalties to subdue wage-push inflation.[64] In Yugoslavia, where workers exercised even greater bargaining power than

---

61. Interview, Hungarian Parliament, 19 May 1993; interview, Central European University, 28 September 1993; Ken Kasriel, "Test of Strength: Will Hungary's Shop Councils Become Hotbeds of Union Militancy? Probably Not," *Business Central Europe* 1, no. 1 (May 1993): 22–23.

62. Interview, Ministry of Finance, 30 May 1991.

63. "Hungarian Economic Monitor," *PlanEcon Report* 10, nos. 25–27 (31 August 1994): 29.

64. Guillermo Calvo and Fabrizio Coricelli, "Stagflationary Effects of Stabilization Programs in Reforming Socialist Countries: Enterprise-Side and Household-Side Effects," *World Bank Economic Review* 6, no. 1 (1992): 73–78; Fabrizio Coricelli and Ana Revenga, "Wages and Unemployment in Poland: Recent Developments and Policy Issues," *Policy Research Working Papers: Macroeconomic Adjustment and Growth,* Country Economics Department of the World Bank, WPS 821, January 1992, 1–7, 19–28.

their Polish counterparts, the Marković government resorted to an out-right wage freeze as part of its 1990 stabilization program.[65] Incomes policy in Czechoslovakia took a different course. In one of the regions' first true demonstrations of corporatist bargaining, Czechoslovak workers negotiated an agreement with enterprise managers and government officials in 1991 to reduce real wages.[66] By contrast, the ability of Hungarian state authorities to contain wage growth through a moderately restrictive incomes policy while eschewing formal wage bargaining with the trade unions underscored the exceptionally weak position of organized labor in the postcommunist period.[67]

Enterprise Managers

As I already noted, Hungarian plant directors faced dramatically different circumstances after 1989. Externally, the collapse of their previously secure markets in the East and the opening of the economy to Western imports created a genuine competitive constraint. Internally, the fiscal safety devices that long shielded state enterprises from the consequences of their own inefficiencies unraveled as a result of the termination of producer subsidies and the reorientation of the Finance Ministry toward financial control.

One defense mechanism that plant directors frequently used during the communist period did survive the political transition to help producers soften monetary austerity: interenterprise credits. The National Bank's monetary program resulted in a steep decline in commercial bank lending to the enterprise sector. Enterprise credits fell from 79 percent of bank assets in 1987, the first year of the two-tiered system, to 58 percent in 1991.[68] Enterprises responded to the liquidity squeeze by expanding their use of nonbank instruments, notably interenterprise credits. A sizable portion of the interfirm arrears accumulated between 1989 and 1991 assumed

---

65. The Marković Program collapsed by the time of the outbreak of the Yugoslav civil war. András Köves, *Central and East European Economies in Transition: The International Dimension* (Boulder: Westview, 1992), 26–27.

66. Simon Commander, "Inflation and the Transition to a Market Economy: An Overview," *World Bank Economic Review* 6, no. 1 (1992): 10–11; interview, SZDSZ, 29 September 1993.

67. In spring 1994, a prominent Hungarian economist proposed a voluntary wage constraint agreement to arrest an inflationary "wage-price spiral." "Kornai Calls for Wage Restraint Deal," *Budapest Sun*, 5–11 May 1994, 5–6. However, time-series data indicated that Hungarian inflation stemmed primarily from cost-push factors, not wage-price pressures. Ábel and Bonin, "Two Approaches to the Transformation in Eastern Europe," 219–20; "Look at the Trend—Not the Figure!" 14.

68. István Ábel and Pierre Siklos, "Constraints on Enterprise Liquidity and Its Impact on the Monetary Sector in Formally Centrally Planned Economies," *Comparative Economic Studies* 36, no. 1 (spring 1994): 23.

the form of involuntary trade credits issued to illiquid firms. As before, the large financial imbalances within the enterprise sector frustrated efforts by National Bank authorities to contract purchasing power through monetary means.[69]

But two factors restricted the utility of interenterprise credit as an alternative liquidity source for producers. First, the changes the National Bank instituted in its rediscounting procedures, described earlier, created safeguards against monetization of the enterprise sector's arrears. Previously, the Bank operated under a de facto obligation to monetize interfirm credits. It now employed differential discount rates to discourage suppliers from accepting bills of exchange from illiquid enterprises. Producers left holding low-quality commercial paper at the end of the transaction chain could not easily liquidate it, as the National Bank's new rules made certain kinds of enterprise credits ineligible for rediscounting. Second, the 1992 bankruptcy law significantly raised the costs of credit arrears by forcing enterprises to declare themselves bankrupt if they had any debt payments overdue by 90 days. The law's automatic triggering mechanism produced the desired effect on Hungarian managers, who moved quickly to retire their outstanding supplier credits in order to avert bankruptcy proceedings that would imperil their jobs. After reaching their peak in March 1992, interenterprise arrears fell sharply as the bankruptcy law took hold.[70]

In short, the continuation of market reforms after 1989 enlarged the range of nonbank instruments available to Hungarian enterprises. But whereas under communist rule such mechanisms served to prop up illiquid enterprises, the institutional changes enacted in the early 1990s placed loss makers under genuine financial constraints that limited their capacity to neutralize monetary policy by creating alternative liquidity supplies.

Commercial Banks
As described in chapter 3, the Hungarian commercial banks responded to the National Bank's 1987–88 monetary squeeze by diverting credit from strong to weak clients. This strategy exemplified the distortions besetting Hungary's financial sector. Heavy state subsidies and lax accounting practices transformed illiquid enterprises into creditworthy customers for the new banks. The loan portfolio problem created further inducements for irrational lending policies. Loan officers sustained credit lines to loss-making enterprises, enabling those clients to maintain a trickle of payments and allowing the banks to report old debts as performing assets.

---

69. Interview, National Bank of Hungary, 15 May 1991.
70. Ábel and Siklos, "Constraints on Enterprise Liquidity," 23–25.

The structure of joint stock ownership produced additional complications, simultaneously broadening the operational control of bank managers and sharpening the contradictions of the communist state as equity owner.

As I discuss in detail in chapter 6, the loan portfolio problem continued to plague Hungary's banking system sector, inhibiting the use of commercial credit as a structural adjustment tool. But the commercial banks' response to the National Bank's post-1989 monetary program contrasted markedly with their earlier strategy. Rather than channeling credit to their weakest clients, the banks beat a retreat from the enterprise sector altogether. Between January 1991 and July 1993, enterprise credits as a share of total commercial bank lending declined from 73.8 to 51.9 percent. During the same period, credits to government agencies rose from 7.2 to 29.1 percent of lending, demonstrating the banks' greatly increased activity in the treasury bill market.[71]

The dramatic shift in the composition of the banks' portfolios was a consequence of changes on both the demand and supply sides of the credit market. As noted earlier, the National Bank's decision to raise its base refinancing rate resulted in a steep increase in commercial lending rates. The banks, faced with more rigorous loan classification and capital adequacy regulations, pushed interest rates even higher in order to build up their loss reserves. The arrival of strongly positive real interest rates cut deeply into credit demand by Hungarian enterprises, whose liquidity position was already weakened by the contraction of output and the elimination of producer subsidies. On the supply side, new bankruptcy and financial accounting laws forced the banks to become extremely cautious in their enterprise lending. They turned increasingly to treasury bills, which offered lower yields than enterprise credits but also far less risk.[72] The consequent contraction of enterprise credit reinforced the National Bank's policy of squeezing domestic liquidity via monetary means.

Thus, whereas the institutional setting of market socialism prompted the Hungarian banks to *divert* credit to loss-making producers, the post-communist environment induced them to *reduce* their exposure to the enterprise sector as a whole. The combination of external shocks and internal changes significantly raised the risks of commercial lending to illiquid firms, which previously drew on their particularistic links to the communist state to secure fiscal compensation for monetary austerity.

---

71. Guillermo Calvo and Manmohan Kumar, "Money Demand, Bank Credit, and Economic Performance in Former Socialist Economies," *IMF Staff Papers* 41, no. 2 (June 1994): 335.

72. In January, the average annual yield on 90-day treasury bills was 31.6 percent, compared with 36 percent on short-term enterprise credits. Consumer price inflation for that year was 23 percent. National Bank of Hungary, *Monthly Report* 2–3 (1993): 60, 64.

Fiscal Austerity in Hungary's Democracy

Hungary's political transition yielded three important changes in the institutional underpinnings of fiscal policy. First, it transformed the Ministry of Finance, previously the bastion of the central planning system, into an agency geared toward financial control. As a consequence of the elimination of the National Planning Office and diminution of the branch ministries, budgetary authority was concentrated in the Finance Ministry. The shortage of technical expertise within the prime minister's office and the coalition parties augmented the Ministry's preeminence in budgetary matters. Meanwhile, the enactment of Western-style accounting laws improved the quality of the information reaching the Ministry, while the merger of the current and capital accounts into a single consolidated budget rationalized the agency's internal procedures and reduced opportunities for partisan exploitation of the treasury.

Second, the appearance of democratic institutions heightened public accountability in the fiscal realm. Whereas previously the Hungarian Parliament operated as a rubber stamp for the Communist Party, it now possessed a credible oversight capability that insulated the budgetary process from partisan manipulation. Control of the Parliament's budget committee by the opposition SZDSZ and liberalization of the print media further enhanced transparency in the fiscal sphere during the postcommunist period.

Finally, the political transition altered the relationship between the Ministry of Finance and the National Bank of Hungary. Under communist rule, fiscal policy overwhelmed monetary policy. The National Bank supplied the Finance Ministry with an unlimited credit line, resulting in deficit monetization and increased inflationary pressures. Meanwhile, the emission of massive producer subsidies through the state's budgetary system nullified whatever monetary contractions the Bank managed to engineer. Developments in the post-1989 period changed this state of affairs. The central banking law established a cap, equivalent to 3 percent of annual tax receipts, on National Bank financing of the budget deficit. It also laid the groundwork for the securitization of deficit financing by enabling the Bank to switch from direct state credits to purchases of government bonds. As noted earlier, this enlarged the Bank's inventory of marketable securities and strengthened its capacity to undertake open market operations.

These shifts in the institutional landscape of fiscal policy had important consequences for Hungarian stabilization policy. As we saw in chapter 2, the separation of the national budget and the absence of effective legislative oversight permitted the Communist Party to conceal huge capital expenditures on the Gabcikovo-Nagymaros dam and other ill-conceived projects. The reforms of the budgetary system compelled the Ministry of Finance to report the true size of the national budget. Capital spending, heretofore funded by the State Development Institute by way of a special refinancing line from the National Bank, was added to the consolidated budget as a direct expenditure. Increased transparency and expanded oversight authority allowed members of Parliament to target specific capital projects for reductions. Expenditures on Hungary's atomic energy program and the CMEA gas pipeline were reduced, while funding of the Danubian dam project was terminated altogether.[73]

The changes in deficit financing procedures also enhanced fiscal probity in the postcommunist state. The cap on central bank financing of the deficit forced the Ministry of Finance to fill the gap through public auctions of treasury bills, which carried market interest rates. The result was a dramatic increase in the state's debt-service burden. In 1992, payments of principal and interest amounted to HUF 190 billion, a 78 percent increase from the previous year. This represented over 19 percent of total state expenditures for that year.[74] Meanwhile, the securitization of deficit financing eased pressure on the central bank to cover revenue shortfalls by printing money. Unlike direct central bank credits to the state, public sales of government bonds involved actual withdrawals of money from circulation. Increases in the budget deficit thus ceased to lead automatically to expansion of the money supply. The consolidation of the current and capital accounts, the rising costs of deficit financing, and increased parliamentary scrutiny created genuine crowding-out effects that induced Finance Ministry officials to enact deep reductions in state expenditures.

In the early 1990s, the main burden of the spending cuts fell on producer subsidies. Table 5.4 shows developments in Hungary's subsidy program between 1989 and 1993. The data indicate that consumer price subsidies were halved while budgetary grants to Hungarian industry were completely eliminated. The only sector spared from budget cuts in the post-1989 period was agriculture, laboring under a severe draught and beset by rising trade barriers in the European Union. The contraction of producer subsidies facilitated macroeconomic stabilization by preventing enterprise managers from offsetting credit restrictions through budgetary concessions. It also narrowed the scope for selective export promotion programs endorsed by the MIER. In short, fiscal policy no longer neutralized monetary policy and indeed began to move with it.

---

73. Interview, Ministry of Finance, 30 May 1991.
74. National Bank of Hungary, *Monthly Report* 1 (1993): 25.

TABLE 5.4.   State Subsidies in Hungary, 1989–93 (billions of forints)

	1989	1990	1991	1992	1993
Household subsidies	na	120	113	89	82
Consumer goods	na	37	40	19	20
Housing	na	83	73	70	62
Producer subsidies	na	67	59	60	54
Industry	66	57	27	0	0
Agriculture	na	10	32	60	54
Total subsidies	201	187	172	149	136
Subsidies as % of GDP	11.8	9.0	7.5	5.4	4.1

Sources: "State Subsidies Falling," *Hungarian Business Brief: Business and Economic Review* 6 (24 March 1993): 3–4; National Bank of Hungary, *Monthly Report* 1 (1993): 17.

But while the National Bank and Ministry of Finance demonstrated a growing capacity to coordinate the fiscal and monetary components of stabilization policy, the institutional changes I have described had no perceptible effect on the total size of the state budget relative to national income. In 1992, total tax revenues amounted to 60.1 percent of GDP, expenditures 62.3 percent. This represented almost exactly the same level of budgetary redistribution of national income as obtained during the final decade of communist rule in Hungary.[75]

Equally troubling was the growing gap between revenues and expenditures. By 1993, the state budget deficit approached 8 percent of GDP, surpassing the target set in Hungary's stabilization agreement with the IMF. The rising budget deficit resulted from a combination of soft revenues and hard expenditures. On the revenue side, budgetary authorities grappled with declining receipts amid the East European recession and rising tax evasion by Hungary's burgeoning population of small-scale enterprises and private entrepreneurs. On the spending side, they struggled to contain Hungary's mounting social welfare expenditures. While subsidy cuts provoked little opposition by trade unions and enterprise associations, the Antall government balked at welfare reform, underscoring its sensitivity to the electoral consequences of antagonizing a population long inured to social services.

---

75. János Kornai, "The Postsocialist Transition and the State: Reflections in the Light of Hungarian Fiscal Problems," *American Economic Review* 82, no. 2 (May 1992): 5

Revenue Collection by the Postcommunist State

The Communist Party introduced a major reform of Hungary's tax system in 1988. The goals of the reform were twofold. First, it sought to lighten the heavy burden of enterprise profits taxation by creating a valued-added tax and personal income tax as supplementary revenue sources. By shifting the tax burden away from enterprise profits and toward the household sector, the designers of the reform sought to advance both the microeconomic objective of raising allocative efficiency and the macroeconomic goal of contracting domestic consumption. Second, the reform aimed to enhance uniformity in the taxation system. Previously, the Hungarian tax code was riddled with scores of different enterprise taxes and a vast array of loopholes, encouraging individualized bargaining between plant managers and state officials.

The tax policies of the Antall government followed the main lines of the MSZMP's reform blueprint. In 1992, the new government introduced a uniform corporate income tax designed to reduce regulatory exceptionalism and eliminate discrimination against private enterprises. As a result, the average effective rate of enterprise profits taxation, which approached 90 percent in the late communist period, fell to about 35 percent. In the same year, the authorities enacted changes in the personal income tax system in order to broaden the tax base and simplify revenue collection. They reduced the number of income brackets from 11 to 4 and lowered the top marginal rate from 60 to 40 percent. The government retained the three-tiered value-added tax scheme established in 1988 but subsequently removed utilities from the list of exempted consumer items.[76]

These measures had a profound impact on the distribution of the tax burden in Hungary. In 1987, the last year before the tax reform, direct taxes paid by enterprises represented 70.6 percent of total tax revenue, those by individuals 6.5 percent. Adding import duties and turnover taxes, the share of enterprise contributions exceeded 80 percent of total receipts.[77] But by 1993, enterprise taxes accounted for barely 22 percent of budgetary revenue. Over two-thirds of revenue now came from consumption and income taxes levied against Hungarian citizens.[78] The ability of a democratically elected government to execute a tax reform generating such heavy distributional effects testified to the consequences of institutional

---

76. Jenő Koltay, "Tax Reform in Hungary," in Székely and Newbery, *Hungary,* 253–56, 260–61.

77. See table 2.3.

78. National Bank of Hungary, *Monthly Report* 1 (1993): 78–79; "Hungarian Economic Monitor," *PlanEcon Report* 10, nos. 25–27 (31 August 1994): 30.

change in Hungary, which insulated state and government agencies from societal demands.

But the tax reform also contributed to Hungary's mounting budget deficits. From a near balance in the Antall government's first year in power, the treasury posted large deficits in 1991, 1992, and 1993. The growth of deficit spending in the early postcommunist years stemmed from an array of factors. The collapse of the Eastern market deepened the contraction of industrial production and domestic consumption, reducing receipts from the corporate income tax and the value-added tax. The demise of the CMEA also deprived the state of tax revenue from the windfall profits earned by Hungarian exporters, which charged world market prices in intraregional trade while paying artificially low import prices. The addition of the capital account to the consolidated budget and a sharp increase in debt-servicing costs created additional pressure on the budget. Finally, the new revenue system expanded opportunities for tax evasion. With the formal state sector eroding and small-scale private ventures expanding, a sizable portion of personal income went unreported and untaxed. While this phenomenon was encouraging from the standpoint that it indicated rising entrepreneurial activity, it also added to the treasury's growing revenue gap. Meanwhile, enterprises explored ways of evading the corporate income tax.[79]

Shortfalls of the personal income tax and corporate tax forced the authorities to compensate with higher consumption taxes. In summer 1993, the Parliament approved a budget amendment increasing the second tier of the value-added tax to 10 percent and removing electricity, natural gas, and water from the 0 percent category. Subsequent budgetary decisions further squeezed Hungarian households. In fall 1993, the Parliament increased the top rate of the personal income tax and lowered the threshold for the 0 percent bracket.[80] These measures represented a clear setback for the Interest Representation Council, which had previously obtained the Finance Ministry's agreement to hold the value-added tax to 6 percent and maintain exemptions for household utilities. But while state and gov-

79. Interviews, Ministry of Finance, 30 May 1991 and 20 May 1993; interview, Kopint-Datorg, 28 September 1993; István Hetényi, "A Budget of Survival," *Hungarian Economic Review* 11 (December 1992): 6–7; Melinda Kamasz, "Revenues and Expenditures," *Hungarian Economic Review* 11 (December 1992): 2–3; Kornai, "The Postsocialist Transition," 12–13.

80. Economist Intelligence Unit, *Country Report: Hungary,* 1st quarter 1994, 11; "VAT Will Be Increased Under Government Plan," *Budapest Sun,* 20–26 May 1993, 1, 3; "Supplementary Budget and VAT Bill Passed," *Bank & Tőzsde: Fuggelten Pénzügyi, Üzleti és Gazdasági Hétilap* 1, no. 27 (23 July 1993): 15; "Milestones of Transition," *Transition: The Newsletter about Reforming Economies* (Policy Research Department of the World Bank) 4, no. 5 (June 1993): 14.

ernment officials encountered weak opposition to tax reform, they proved unable to contract social welfare expenditures, the main source of Hungary's high level of budgetary centralization.

The Dilemmas of Social Welfare Reform

Like other East European countries, Hungary was an "early born welfare state."[81] The communist parties of the region delivered an array of social services incommensurate with the level of development of the local economies. The fiscal burden of social welfare was especially heavy in Hungary, where the Kádár regime expanded benefits to secure the population's acquiescence in the aftermath of the 1956 Revolution. Between 1981 and 1987, social expenditures grew by 29 percent against a GDP growth of only 3 percent. By the end of the communist period, total social expenditures exceeded 25 percent of GDP, comparable to levels in the OECD countries.[82] Developments after 1989 deepened the social welfare problem. The postcommunist recession simultaneously increased the number of people eligible for unemployment benefits and reduced payroll contributions to the social security fund. Meanwhile, low retirement ages and adverse demographic trends heightened the welfare system's dependency rate. By 1992, 4.2 million Hungarian workers were supporting 2.7 million pensioners.[83] Mounting costs and declining revenues forced the Antall government to raise payroll taxes. As a result, social security contributions increased to 65 percent of gross salary, the highest in the industrialized world. The exorbitant withholding rates combined with low-quality welfare services increased incentives for tax evasion, generating additional stress on the social security fund. By the end of 1992, the Social Security Administration was running a deficit of HUF 40 billion. Enterprise arrears to the fund amounted to HUF 100 billion.[84]

Officials in the Ministry of Finance and the liberal opposition parties offered a number of proposals aimed at resolving the social welfare crisis: raising the retirement age from 60 to 63, introducing fees for certain kinds of services, and reducing transfer payments to nonpoor groups. But the Antall government, fearful of the electoral consequences of social welfare

81. László Csaba, "After the Shock: Some Lessons from Transition Policies in Eastern Europe," *Kopint-Datorg Discussion Papers* 8 (October 1992): 16.

82. Kornai, "The Postsocialist Transition," 15; Károly Okolicsányi, "The Social Safety Net: Misused and Expensive," *Bank & Tőzsde: Fuggelten Pénzügyi, Üzleti és Gazdasági Hétilap* 1, no. 26 (16 July 1993): 13.

83. Okolicsányi, "The Social Safety Net," 13.

84. Csaba, "After the Shock," 17; Delia Meth-Cohn and Ken Kasriel, "Holes in the Net," *Business Central Europe* 1, no. 3 (July–August 1993): 30–31.

cuts, shunned these measures. The main beneficiaries of the welfare system were not poor people but citizens in the middle strata of Hungarian society—pensioners, manual workers, civil servants, rural laborers—who not only represented the core constituencies of the governing parties but comprised the largest and most politically active bloc of voters in the electoral system. MDF leaders concluded that deep reductions of benefits to these groups would mean political suicide in the next parliamentary election.[85]

The Antall government's irresolution demonstrated the institutional ratchet effects of the social welfare policies of the Hungarian Communist Party. Decades of goulash communism had inculcated in the population high expectations of the state's capacity to deliver a full range of social services: free education and health care, extended maternity and sick leaves, housing subsidies, early retirement, even coverage of funeral costs. These programs, once established, could not be scaled back without provoking broad-based resistance.[86] The institutional structure of interest representation in postcommunist Hungary heightened the political risks of social welfare reform. Lacking strong intermediary associations that would allow them to forge compromises on welfare issues, vulnerable groups were left to express their preferences at the ballot box. As we have seen, Hungary's intermediary institutions proved ineffectual in tax policy as well. But the nature of that issue area left disaffected agents with alternative ways of softening the distributional effects of reform policy. Whereas elderly pensioners and unemployed workers possessed few economic means of compensating cuts in welfare benefits, households and enterprises could pursue individualistic strategies (e.g., shifting from state to private sector activities, where nominal rates were lower and opportunities for evasion greater) to lighten their tax liabilities. The losers of welfare reform were far more dependent on the electoral system. While the high costs of electoral mobilization in the postcommunist period mitigated popular resistance to other elements of reform policy, the prospects of alienating such a large stratum of voters in the second national election sufficed to deter the MDF from acting on the welfare problem.

The most important development in social welfare policy after 1989 was the government's decision to transfer responsibility for Hungary's health and pension funds from the Social Security Administration to two executive boards composed of representatives of labor and management. The boards were given ownership rights over the assets of the funds as well as the authority to advise the Parliament on social security issues. In May

---

85. Interviews, Hungarian Parliament, 19 May 1993; Kopint-Datorg, 28 September 1993; SZDSZ, 29 September 1993.
86. Kornai, "The Postsocialist Transition," 16.

1993, national elections were held to determine the composition of the trade unions' delegations on the new boards. The legal successor of the old communist-controlled union, the MSZOSZ, won those elections.[87]

But while these measures reshuffled administrative control of the welfare system, they did not address the underlying problem: the inability of the Hungarian economy to support Scandinavian-level social services. Meanwhile, the Hungarian state retained ultimate responsibility for the deficits of the social security funds. Adding the shortfalls of the social security funds to the consolidated central budget, the total budget deficit for 1994 reached HUF 350 billion, or 11.5 percent of GDP—double the level set in Hungary's standby agreement with the IMF.[88]

Conclusion: Economic Stabilization and Hungarian Democracy

In part 2, I showed how the institutional setting of Hungarian communism undermined stabilization policy. The Communist Party's experiment with market socialism generated a push-pull dynamic that defeated IMF-sponsored stabilization programs. Far from raising allocative efficiency, the devolution of decision-making power to the factory level induced local agents to bid up wages, investment, and bank credits. The structure of the communist state prevented the National Bank and Ministry of Finance from applying countercyclical brakes on the expansion of purchasing power. The failure of market-type instruments to stabilize the economy left Party leaders with the alternative of reimposing central controls. But owing to the authority already relinquished to the local level, full restoration of the status quo ante was no longer possible. The permeability of state institutions and the nature of Communist Party power magnified the tension between market reforms and macroeconomic stabilization. Enterprise directors drew on their particularistic links to the state administration to negotiate exceptions to wage regulations. Commercial bank managers thwarted the National Bank's monetary squeeze by diverting credit from their strongest clients and provoking Communist Party leaders to intervene on their behalf. And Hungarian workers utilized the Party-controlled trade union to secure wage increases that compensated for the distributional effects of austerity.

The shift from communism to democracy facilitated macroeconomic stabilization in several ways. It resulted in a constitutional structure that

---

87. Judith Patkai, "A New Era in Hungary's Social Security Administration," *RFE/RL Research Report* 2, no. 27 (2 July 1993): 57–60.

88. Károly Okolicsányi, "Hungary's Budget Deficit Worsens," *RFE/RL Research Report* 3, no. 2 (14 January 1994): 38; interview, Kopint-Datorg, 28 September 1993.

concentrated political power in the prime minister's office and it established an electoral system skewed toward a small number of parliamentary parties. This institutional setup gave the new government the autonomy and tenure in office to resist pressure to back off the stabilization program and initiate growth-oriented policies. The particular circumstances of Hungary's negotiated transition allowed political elites to establish checks on partisan exploitation of state resources, the absence of which had permitted Communist Party leaders to manipulate the country's fiscal, monetary, and foreign exchange systems. The transition further promoted stabilization policy by weakening the branch ministries and increasing the government's dependence on the National Bank and Ministry of Finance, the key agencies of macroeconomic regulation. Their technical and informational resources, connections to the multilateral lending agencies, and legally prescribed jurisdictional spheres allowed those institutions to dominate stabilization policy. At the same time, the establishment of a multiparty system relieved the Bank and Finance Ministry of the burden of particularistic bargaining, by channeling distributional conflicts into the electoral arena, where the losers of economic austerity operated at a distinct disadvantage in the early postcommunist years. The lack of robust intermediary associations placed additional constraints on organized resistance to macroeconomic stabilization.

The trajectory of Hungarian stabilization policy in the post-1989 period clearly demonstrated the effects of these institutional changes. In the foreign exchange arena, National Bank authorities rejected calls for debt relief and withstood pressure for forint devaluation, opting instead for a strategy aimed at improving Hungary's international credit rating and squelching inflation via real currency appreciation. In the monetary sphere, the central bankers pursued a policy of moderate macroeconomic discipline, briefly easing off the liquidity squeeze when commercial lending rates rose to prohibitive levels. In contrast to the communist period, when local agents neutralized the National Bank's efforts to contract the liquidity supply, enterprise directors, bank directors, and workers now lacked the institutional means to counter monetary austerity. And notwithstanding attempts by the governing coalition to politicize the appointment process, the institutional structure of Hungary's new democracy discouraged partisan intervention in macroeconomic policy. The saver agencies enjoyed broad operational control of foreign exchange and monetary policy, while their superior technical resources induced the Antall government to defer to them on most key policy questions.

The fact that fiscal policy emerged as the main exception to this general trajectory reflected the distinctive structure of interest representation in postcommunist Hungary. Finance Ministry officials met with little organized opposition to subsidy cuts and tax reforms, illustrating (1) the weakness of intermediary associations of labor and business and (2) the ability of enterprises and households to offset those measures through tax evasion, exit to the private sector, and other individualistic economic strategies. A different political dynamic obtained in social welfare policy. The principal beneficiaries of Hungary's extensive welfare system lacked both institutionalized access to state agencies and private economic means of compensating for cuts in social services. This left the Parliament as the main mechanism for registering their grievances. While the electoral rules negotiated in 1989 weakened popular resistance to other elements of Hungarian stabilization policy, the electoral connection proved quite effective in the social welfare sphere. The reluctance of members of Parliament to reduce benefits underscored the politically sensitive nature of the social welfare problem, resolution of which risked alienating a citizenry long accustomed to cradle-to-grave services.

CHAPTER 6

Structural Adjustment in Hungary's
New Democracy

As shown in chapter 3, the contradictions of market socialism thwarted the Hungarian Communist Party's structural adjustment program in the 1980s. Market reforms broadened the decision-making power of local agents while inducing those actors to behave in ways contrary to adjustment policy. For instance, the introduction of joint stock ownership into Hungary's financial sector simultaneously enlarged the operational autonomy of bank managers and created incentives for credit officers to channel funds to illiquid enterprises. As the new banks declined to use commercial credit as an adjustment tool, Party officials turned to administrative methods, creating several new state and governmental agencies empowered to oversee industrial restructuring. But far from spurring structural adjustment, these institutional innovations expanded access points for particularistic bargaining and pulled MSZMP leaders into conflicts over the pace and extent of economic adjustment.

International and domestic developments after 1989 radically altered the complexion of Hungarian adjustment policy. Externally, the abrupt disintegration of the CMEA and Soviet Union confronted local producers with an ipso facto adjustment. State enterprises, heretofore geared toward ruble-based trade with the socialist countries, suddenly had to reorient production for the far more demanding Western markets. Internally, the political transition dissolved the institutional channels that previously allowed local agents to extract compensation for the distributional fallout of adjustment. The skewing of the electoral system toward a few parliamentary parties, the concentration of executive authority in the prime minister's office, the ascent of saver agencies within the state administration, and the fragmentation of intermediary interest associations enabled the successor government to enact a succession of measures aimed at disciplining producers: deep subsidy cuts, rigorous bankruptcy and accounting laws, antitrust legislation, and rapid import liberalization.

But while the external shocks and internal political shifts profoundly changed the competitive environment of local producers, they left a number of obstacles to structural adjustment. These developments resulted in a substantial *downsizing,* but not a significant *restructuring,* of Hungarian industry. Industrial output declined sharply as a consequence of the loss of the traditional Eastern markets, the elimination of producer subsidies, and the bankruptcy law. However, restoring weak enterprises to profitability required not merely elimination of loss-making production lines and reduction of the workforce but also massive infusions of capital to upgrade plant and equipment. The fixed capital investment needed to modernize Hungary's industrial base was not available owing to constraints on domestic capital formation and the unwillingness of Western investors to commit funds to loss-making sectors. As a result, the dominant trend in Hungarian adjustment policy after 1989 was inertia: total industrial production contracted, but what remained of the state sector stagnated because of the acute shortage of investment capital.

This chapter examines adjustment policy in postcommunist Hungary, focusing on financial sector reform, industrial restructuring, and privatization. The transformation of the politico-economic environment prompted Hungarian commercial banks to reduce lending to the enterprise sector as a whole. Insofar as allocative efficiency was concerned, this represented an advance over the pre-1989 period, when the perverse incentive structure of market socialism induced banks to divert credit to illiquid clients. Loan officers now exhibited a keen sensitivity to credit risk, rate of return, and other business criteria conspicuously lacking in their earlier lending decisions. But their retreat from the enterprise sector frustrated adjustment policy, impeding the mobilization of domestic capital for industrial restructuring. Continuing problems with the loan portfolios of the banks and delays in bank privatization further hindered the deployment of commercial credit for adjustment purposes.

The banks' withdrawal from enterprise lending aggravated the problems of Hungarian industry, already reeling under the impact of shifts in the international and domestic environments. Externally, the collapse of the CMEA and Soviet Union deprived local producers of their once secure Eastern markets. Internally, the termination of industrial subsidies and other measures enacted by the successor government severed the institutional links that previously shielded enterprises from market forces. The postcommunist state's one attempt at a selective industrial policy—a "crisis management" program targeting thirteen firms for special restructuring programs—had virtually no effect, owing to a severe shortage of funds needed to reorganize the companies. Enterprise managers, lacking political means of defending their positions via particularistic bargaining and intermediary representation, turned to individualistic economic strategies. Some producers managed to resume commercial relations with the Soviet successor states; others succeeded in reorienting their production lines for exports to the West. But most Hungarian enterprises simply drifted, running down their capital stocks to generate enough revenue to stay afloat and buy time until privatization.

The commercial banks' disengagement and the Hungarian state's inability to enact proactive industrial policies heightened the importance of privatization as an adjustment instrument. In theory, Hungary's privatization strategy, which relied on direct sales of enterprises to Western investors, was better suited to promoting industrial recapitalization than were mass voucher schemes and other approaches that emphasized transfers of state property to local agents. But while Hungary's favorable investment climate attracted impressive amounts of foreign direct investment in the postcommunist period, the bulk of it went toward greenfield investments, joint ventures, and equity stakes in the country's strongest enterprises. Western investors largely bypassed loss-making industries, coincidentally the ones most in need of recapitalization. Privatization officials thus confronted a catch-22: foreign investors declined to move into weak sectors until the Hungarian state restructured them; but restructuring loss makers in preparation for privatization demanded large infusions of foreign capital.

Financial Liberalization in Hungary's Transitional Economy

Ronald McKinnon cogently describes the hazards of premature financial liberalization in transitional economies. In his optimal "order of economic liberalization," macroeconomic stabilization precedes financial decentralization. Governments that pursue banking reform before establishing fiscal and monetary control encourage credit expansion in the economy's weakest sectors. Deregulation of interest rates in the face of high inflation increases the dangers of adverse selection. Newly liberalized banks respond to mounting inflation by raising commercial lending rates to exorbitant levels, which are most likely to be accepted by their riskiest and least creditworthy clients. Meanwhile, the banks exhibit a growing tendency toward moral hazard in lending activities, as state ownership of their equity shares creates an implicit guarantee of governmental coverage of loan losses. Credit allocation consequently spirals out of control and imperils the whole transition effort.[1]

As we saw in chapter 3, perverse incentives in commercial lending

---

1. McKinnon, *The Order of Economic Liberalization: Financial Control in the Transition to a Market Economy* (Baltimore: Johns Hopkins University Press, 1991), 4–10, 39–42, 51–54, 84–91, 138–44.

beset the Hungarian banking system in the late 1980s. High rates of enterprise profits taxation and antiquated accounting procedures prevented the new banks from discriminating between applicants, while the unremitting flow of subsidies to loss-making sectors brought the economy's weakest performers to the fore of the credit queue. Majority state ownership of commercial bank shares created expectations of an eventual governmental bailout of portfolio losses, encouraging credit officers to refinance bad loans inherited from the prereform period and keep them on the books as performing assets. By 1990, commercial loans officially classified as doubtful amounted to HUF 46 billion, nearly 50 percent of the total registered capital of Hungary's banks. The distribution of these assets was equally ominous: Over 84 percent of the bad debts were carried by the country's five largest commercial banks.[2]

The loan portfolio problem worsened dramatically after the political transition. By the end of 1992, the stock of classified bank loans totaled HUF 262 billion. Bad loans inherited from the monobanking system represented only about HUF 20 billion of this amount, demonstrating that most of the portfolio deterioration occurred *after* 1987. In spring 1993, a confidential World Bank report declared the two largest Hungarian banks, Magyar Hitel Bank and Kereskedelmi & Hitel Bank, technically insolvent.[3]

But in contrast to the 1987–89 period, when the banks issued large amounts of fresh credit to unprofitable enterprises, the main problem in the postcommunist years was not expansion of new enterprise loans. Indeed, as table 6.1 shows, total commercial lending to the enterprise sector dropped sharply after 1989. Moreover, the main burden of the credit squeeze fell on Hungary's loss-making sectors. The mining and metallurgical industries, which had received generous credit allotments in the late 1980s amid the skewed incentive structure of reform communism, saw their credit lines virtually disappear in the early 1990s.

The data indicate that the two primary goals of the Communist Party's banking reform—contraction of the *total* emission of bank credit to state enterprises and reallocation of the flow of credit *within* the enterprise sector—actually came to fruition in the early postcommunist period.

---

2. Z. Spéder and E. Várhegyi, "On the Eve of the Second Banking Reform," *Acta Oeconomica* 44, nos. 1–2 (1992): 55, 66.

3. "Two State Banks Declared Insolvent," *Budapest Sun,* 27 May–2 June 1993, 5; "Classified Loans Increase," *Bank & Tőzsde: Független Pénzügyi, Üzleti és Gazdasági Hetilap* 1, no. 36 (24 September 1993): 18. In 1990, the Hungarian state offered the banks a one-shot opportunity to write off 50 percent of outstanding loans issued in the prereform period. This, together with provisioning of nonperforming assets after 1987, significantly reduced the stock of "inherited" bad loans. Interviews, Credit Lyonnais Bank, 17 May 1993; Ministry of Finance, 26 May 1993; Magyar Befektetési és Fejlesztési Bank, 23 September 1993.

TABLE 6.1. Composition of Loan Portfolios of Hungarian Commercial Banks, 1992–93 (percentage of total bank lending)

Allocation of Credit by Enterprise Sector	January 1992	July 1993
Enterprises	73.8	51.9
Government	7.2	29.1
Households	9.9	12.0
Nonresidents	9.1	7.0

Allocation of Credit by Enterprise Sector	January 1992		March 1993	
	Short-Term	Long-Term	Short-Term	Long-Term
Agriculture	7.4	8.4	6.2	6.5
Mining	2.1	1.1	1.1	0.8
Metallurgy	1.7	0.5	1.4	0.1
Food processing	15.1	9.6	13.9	8.9
Chemicals	6.1	21.1	6.3	19.9
Engineering	9.5	6.0	10.0	4.7
Light industry	9.6	6.1	8.1	4.8
Waste recycling	1.8	4.3	0.8	3.5
Utilities	1.8	1.4	1.2	1.6
Construction	4.5	0.5	4.6	0.4
Domestic trade and repair services	23.2	4.4	21.4	4.1
Hotels and restaurants	0.8	5.2	1.1	4.7
Transport and communications	3.0	9.7	4.2	14.8
Financial intermediation	5.6	3.4	8.1	3.0
Small enterpreneurs	3.5	8.4	4.0	9.2
Other	4.4	9.8	7.6	12.9

Sources: National Bank of Hungary, *Monthly Report* 2–3 (1993): 61–62; Guillermo Calvo and Manmohan Kumar, "Money Demand, Bank Credit, and Economic Performance in Former Socialist Countries," *IMF Staff Papers* 41, no. 2 (June 1994): 335.

The Hungarian banks retreated from enterprise lending and moved aggressively into the bond market, where rates of return were nearly as high and risks markedly lower.

In short, the central dilemma of financial liberalization in postcommunist Hungary was not adverse selection and moral hazard, as the commercial banks were now displaying an exemplary degree of prudence in their lending decisions. The continued deterioration of the banks' loan portfolios emanated from two other sources. First, transformation of the legal and economic environment of Hungarian enterprises, detailed later in this chapter, forced many producers into bankruptcy and intensified pressure on commercial bank portfolios. Second, augmentation of the regulatory capacity of the Hungarian state, described in the following section, compelled the banks themselves to reclassify a large number of loans as nonperforming assets.

State Institutions and Financial Regulation

Prior to the political transition, the Hungarian state lacked effective institutional mechanisms to regulate the financial sector. In 1987, the Communist Party established an Office of Banking Supervision to oversee the operations of the new commercial banks. However, its activities during the early phase of the banking reform were negligible. The first chief of that office, János Radnótzi, enjoyed considerable personal authority as a result of his instrumental role in designing the two-tiered system. But the agency itself possessed a tiny staff and limited legal standing, preventing it from performing a credible oversight function.[4]

The regulatory capacity of the state grew substantially after 1989. In 1991, the Antall government enacted a law on financial institutions codifying the Office of Banking Supervision's supervisory powers. The office, previously attached to the Ministry of Finance, was granted exclusive authority to enforce financial regulations. Like the leaders of the National Bank, the president and deputy presidents of the office were given fixed six-year terms to discourage governmental meddling in the banking sector. Meanwhile, the staff of the office was enlarged, providing the agency with the personnel and technical resources to carry out its regulatory duties.[5]

Two of the Office of Banking Supervision's regulatory tools proved especially important in shaping the operations of the Hungarian banks in the postcommunist period. First, the Act on Financial Institutions created a four-tiered loan classification scheme. Loans qualified as "good" required no reserve assets to cover potential losses. In the case of loans rated as "substandard," banks were obliged to generate risk reserves equivalent to 20 percent of the assets. "Doubtful" assets required 50 percent backing, "bad" debts 100 percent. These requirements not only forced the banks to downgrade a number of loans previously classified as performing assets. They compelled bank managers to widen the spread between lending and deposit rates in order to raise profits and augment their loss reserves, magnifying the National Bank's interest rate hikes and further suppressing credit demand in the enterprise sector. Second, the Act required the banks to raise their capital adequacy ratios (capital assets available for covering losses as a percentage of risk-weighted loans) to 8 percent, the standard level prescribed by the Bank for International Settlements. This provision generated additional pressure on the banks to follow cautious lending policies. With the new classification rules forcing them to

---

4. Interview, National Bank of Hungary, 13 May 1988.

5. "1991. Évi LXIX Törvény a Pénzintézetekrol és a Pénzintézeti Tevékenységrol" (Act LXIX of 1991 on financial institutions and financial institutional activities), *Hatályos Magyar Jogszabályok* (Hungarian Rules of Law in Force), no. II/24, 15 December 1991, 1812–14.

downgrade growing numbers of outstanding debts, the only way the banks could meet the capital adequacy requirement was to restrict the issuance of fresh loans to local producers while enlarging their registered capital.[6]

These changes in Hungary's regulatory system, together with the recession in the enterprise sector, caused a dramatic erosion of the commercial banks' financial position. As noted earlier, the aggregate stock of risk-qualified commercial bank loans increased nearly six-fold between 1990 and 1992. But while the expansion of classified loans demonstrated the Hungarian state's newfound capabilities in universalistic market regulation, it also aggravated greatly the banking sector's loan portfolio problem and impeded the deployment of commercial credit for structural adjustment policy.

The Loan Portfolio Problem

The rapid deterioration of the banks' balance sheets compelled state authorities and the Hungarian Banking Association hastily to assemble a loan consolidation plan in December 1992. The design of the Hungarian plan illuminated the dilemmas of resolving bad debts in transitional economies.[7] Under the program, the Ministry of Finance would exchange classified enterprise loans for 20-year variable yield bonds. Banks could convert loans issued before 31 December 1991 at 50 percent of book value, loans issued after that date at 80 percent. The loans of a select group of major state enterprises were convertible at 100 percent of book value. The Finance Ministry would then transfer the loans to a new state-owned investment bank, the Magyar Befektetési és Fejlesztési Bank. The banks presented a total of HUF 153 billion for conversion, which under the terms of the program yielded HUF 117 in state bonds. Finance Ministry officials, facing a mounting budget deficit, added a participation fee, equal

---

6. "1991. Évi LXIX Törvény a Pénzintézetekrol és a Pénzintézeti Tevékenységrol," 1797–99; László Antal, "Banks Undergoing Therapy," *Hungarian Economic Review* 13 (April 1993): 7; Saul Estrin, Paul Hare, and Marta Surányi, "Banking in Transition: Development and Current Problems in Hungary," *Soviet Studies* 44, no. 5 (1992): 805.

7. All of the postcommunist countries grappled with large stocks of bad bank debts. "Banking and Investment Survey: No Half Measures," *Business Central Europe* 1, no. 2 (June 1993): 35–40; Guillermo Calvo and Manmohan Kumar, "Financial Markets and Intermediation," in *Financial Sector Reforms and Exchange Arrangements in Eastern Europe,* Occasional Paper No. 102 (Washington: IMF, 1993), 13–16; Calvo and Kumar, "Money Demand, Bank Credit, and Economic Performance in Former Socialist Countries," *IMF Staff Papers* 41, no. 2 (June 1994): 337–44; Gerard Caprio and Ross Levine, "Reforming Finance in Transitional Socialist Economies," *World Bank Research Observer* 9, no. 1 (January 1994): 15–19; Daniel Hardy and Ashok Kumar Lahiri, "Bank Insolvency and Stabilization in Eastern Europe," *IMF Staff Papers* 39, no. 4 (December 1992): 778–800.

to 50 percent of the interest the banks would earn on the bonds, to reduce the costs of the program.[8]

The plan quickly provoked widespread criticism. Commercial bank managers complained that the long maturity of the bonds and the high participation fee hardly made it worthwhile to take part in the program. Indeed, the bonds were more like liabilities than assets.[9] The president of the Budapest Bank, who had already diverted large amounts of retained earnings for loan provisioning, claimed that the program set a bad precedent for the banking system. It would reward less foresighted banks by allowing them to draw down on treasury funds to purge their portfolios of bad assets.[10] The program also left unsettled the final disposition of the loans removed from the banks' portfolios. The new holder of those assets, the Magyar Befektetési és Fejlesztési Bank, was organized for the express purpose of restructuring loss-making enterprises. But like the big commercial banks, it was a state-owned financial institution. By transferring the loans from the former to the latter, the authorities were merely shifting bad assets from one part of the state sector to another.[11] Finally, World Bank authorities argued that the scheme would temporarily clean the banks' portfolios while leaving them severely undercapitalized. Recapitalization of the banking sector was the key to resolving the loan portfolio problem. Absent a massive injection of capital into the banks, the Hungarian state would be compelled to undertake repeated rescue operations. Undercapitalization was particularly acute in the two largest banks, the Magyar Hitel Bank and the Kereskedelmi & Hitel Bank, whose capital

---

8. "Credit Consolidation Agreement," *Hungarian Business Brief: Business and Economic Review* 2 (25 January 1993): 1–2; "Credit Consolidation—Further Conditions," *Bank & Tőzsde: Független Pénzügyi, Üzleti és Gazdasági Hetilap* 1, no. 4 (12 February 1993): 12; "Credit Consolidation, Reorganization, Privatization," *Privinfo: Privatization in Hungary* 2, no. 7 (April 1993): 16–17; interview, Ministry of Finance, 26 May 1993.

9. Interview, Central European International Bank, 25 May 1993; "Loan Consolidation Changes Forcing Banks Out of Plan," *Budapest Business Journal* 1, no. 13 (15 February 1993): 1, 9.

10. The Budapest Bank earmarked *all* of its 1991 profits for loan provisioning, a strategy that significantly strengthened the Bank's portfolio but that provoked the enmity of tax collectors in the Ministry of Finance, who looked to the banking sector as a key source of revenue. Interview, Budapest Bank, 30 September 1993.

11. This circularity problem forced the Ministry of Finance to devise accounting schemes that artificially lowered the burden of keeping nonperforming assets within the state sector. The Magyar Befektetési és Fejlesztési Bank was a state-owned company whose portfolio consisted almost entirely of bad loans excised from the commercial banks. To enable that bank to accept the assets and at the same time fulfill the legal requirements of the Act on Financial Institutions, the Finance Ministry transferred the loans at a 100,000:1 discount. Thus, a loan with a book value of HUF 100,000 was recorded on the bank's balance sheet as HUF 1—sufficiently low for the bank's auditors to declare it a performing asset. Interview, Magyar Befektetési és Fejlesztési Bank, 23 September 1993.

adequacy ratios were actually negative according to World Bank estimates.[12]

The deficiencies of the 1992 loan consolidation scheme prompted state authorities to formulate a new plan that placed greater emphasis on bank recapitalization. To help finance the revised program, they began negotiations with the World Bank for a $300 million structural adjustment loan. But this sum fell far short of the capital needed to salvage the commercial banking sector. Finance Ministry specialists estimated that bringing the country's major banks up to the capital adequacy standard of the Bank for International Settlements demanded an injection of $4 billion.[13]

The high costs of bank recapitalization placed Hungarian policymakers in a severe quandary. Assistance from the multilateral lending agencies represented only a small fraction of the required funds, while the soaring budget deficit restricted the state's capacity to finance bank bailouts. Private domestic capital was an unlikely source of money in light of the low levels of accumulation during the communist years and the immature state of development of Hungary's financial intermediation system. This left private Western capital as the primary means of recapitalizing the commercial banks. But to attract significant quantities of foreign direct investment in the banking sector, Hungarian authorities had to surmount a paradox: the vulnerable portfolios of the banks greatly reduced their attractiveness as privatization targets for Western investors, but resolving the loan portfolio was not possible without large injections of private foreign capital.

Obstacles to Bank Privatization

The Act on Financial Institutions stipulated that the Hungarian state reduce its ownership share of the commercial banks to 25 percent by 1997.[14] By the end of 1991, state ownership of the major banks averaged 42 percent of outstanding equity, a sizable drop from the level obtaining at the start-up of the two-tiered system in 1987. However, the state's shift

---

12. Interview, National Bank of Hungary, 20 May 1993; interview, World Bank, 3 September 1993; István Ábel and John Bonin, "Bank Recapitalization: Hungary's Second Attempt at Resolving Its Credit Market Crisis" (Budapest University of Economics and Department of Economics, Wesleyan University, Middletown, Conn., July 1993, mimeo); "Agencies to Play Big Part in Credit Consolidation Plan," *Budapest Business Journal* 1, no. 15 (1 March 1993): 1, 14.

13. From *The Budapest Sun:* "World Bank Sees Change in Bank Plan," 11–17 November 1993; "Szabó: Bank Plan Essential to Stability," 16–22 December 1993; "World Bank Pushes for Lending Reforms," 31 March–6 April 1994, 5.

14. "1991. Évi LXIX Törvény a Pénzintézetekrol és a Pénzintézeti Tevékenységrol," 1794.

from "majority" to "minority" shareholder exaggerated the real magnitude of the change in the banking sector's ownership structure. The decline in the state's percentile share resulted mainly from expansion of the banks' total equity capital via sales to nonofficial investors, not from divestiture of state shares. Furthermore, the provision of the Act on Financial Institutions applied only to *direct* ownership by Hungarian state institutions. Adding shares held by state enterprises and local governments, the overwhelming majority of commercial bank equity remained in "nonprivate" hands.[15] A genuine transformation of the banking system's ownership structure required the sale of a majority of outstanding shares to full-fledged *private* investors.

By 1994, only two of the original Hungarian banks, the Budapest Bank and the Magyar Külkereskedelmi Bank, appeared credible prospects for privatization. The former institution, which possessed the banking sector's weakest portfolio at the time of the political transition, was ready for divestiture thanks to the management's aggressive loan-provisioning program in 1991–92. Budapest Bank was ultimately sold to a group of foreign investors that included General Electric Capital and the European Bank for Reconstruction and Development, with the Hungarian state retaining a minority share.[16] The Magyar Külkereskedelmi Bank had started with a comparatively clean portfolio and extensive Western contacts as Hungary's chief foreign trade bank, assets that made it a ripe candidate for privatization.[17] Foreign investors meanwhile established a score of new banks, insurance companies, auditing firms, and investment funds, some wholly owned and others under mixed ownership.

But while these greenfield and joint venture investments altered the competitive environment of Hungary's financial system, their impact on the economy's aggregate credit flows was limited. Some 80 percent of total

---

15. "Green Light for Change in Ownership in Banks," *Privinfo: Privatization in Hungary* 2, no. 4 (February 1993): 3; David Bartlett, "Banking and Financial Reform in a Mixed Economy: The Case of Hungary," in Perry Patterson, ed., *Capitalist Goals, Socialist Past: The Rise of the Private Sector in Command Economies* (Boulder: Westview, 1993), 188; Estrin, Hare, and Surányi, "Banking in Transition," 801; Emilia Papp, "A New Bank Ownership Structure," *The Hungarian Economy: A Quarterly Economic and Business Review* 20, no. 2 (1992): 19.

16. "Banking Industry Report," *Central European Report,* 2 February 1996.

17. Interviews, Magyar Külkereskedelmi Bank, 22 May 1991 and 22 September 1993; Budapest Bank, 30 September 1993. In spring 1993, the Magyar Külkereskedelmi Bank became the first East European financial institution to place a bond issue in the West without a sovereign guarantee—a move aimed at distinguishing it from the other Hungarian banks and increasing its attractiveness to foreign investors. Ryan Tutak, "On its Own," *Business Central Europe* 1, no. 2 (June 1993): 51–54.

credit still came from the original Hungarian-owned banks.[18] Outside the Budapest Bank and Magyar Külkereskedelmi Bank, the prospects for privatizing the banking sector were dismal. Hungarian negotiators could scarcely persuade foreign investors to buy equity shares in the Magyar Hitel Bank and other big banks whose portfolios remained burdened with nonperforming assets. At the same time, policymakers had no hope of restoring those banks to solvency without heavy injections of capital.

This paradox illuminated the tension between bank privatization and financial restructuring in postcommunist Hungary. Severe restrictions of the supply of domestic capital forced policymakers to look to Western investors to privatize the banks. But coaxing foreign investors to participate in the privatization effort required Hungarian officials to restructure the banks' portfolios, which in turn necessitated large infusions of cash from the West. This was a different kind of paradox than the one that confronted Communist Party leaders in the late 1980s. During that period, the main barrier to financial reform was the contradictory position of the communist state as "equity owner": the perverse incentives and institutional setting of market socialism enabled bank managers to play off the state's conflicting interests as shareholder and executor of adjustment policy. The successor government faced a different sort of problem. Owing to the transformation of enterprises' competitive environment and the bolstering of the state's financial regulations, the incentive structure and institutional framework for a capitalist-type banking system were in place in Hungary. What was missing was the capital.

Consequences for Adjustment Policy

The problems of Hungary's banking sector had major repercussions for structural adjustment policy. Like other postcommunist countries, Hungary lacked a well-developed capital market to facilitate its economic transition. The Budapest Stock Exchange, launched in the late communist years, had yet to emerge as an effective medium of capital formation. By 1994, only a handful of companies were listed on the exchange, and turnover of shares remained minuscule. The local bond market was more substantial, but its usefulness for corporate financing was limited owing to the glut of treasury bills issued by the Hungarian state to cover mounting budget deficits. As noted in chapter 5, a commercial paper market also emerged in the early 1990s. But its purpose was to provide enterprises with working capital funds to cover current transactions, not to finance fixed capital investment.

---

18. Bartlett, "Banking and Financial Reform," 189.

The thinness of the capital market underscored the importance of the commercial banks as suppliers of credit and intermediary services for Hungarian enterprises undergoing the wrenching transition to a market economy. But the barriers to financial sector reform, already described, prevented the banks from performing this role. Continued portfolio deterioration compelled bank managers to reduce their exposure to the enterprise sector and shift to the far safer bond market. Austerity measures taken by Hungarian state agencies hastened the banks' retreat from enterprise lending. The National Bank's monetary squeeze sharply increased the real cost of money, forcing the banks to raise interest rates to levels that were prohibitive for many borrowers. The Finance Ministry terminated industrial subsidies, preventing illiquid producers from concealing losses from credit officers. It also enforced a strict bankruptcy law that pushed many enterprises into insolvency and exacerbated the banks' own liquidity problems. Finally, the Office of Banking Supervision imposed rigorous loan classification and capital adequacy requirements that obliged the banks to widen their lending margins to build up loss reserves.

In short, both Hungarian state institutions and commercial banks began to exhibit many of the behavioral traits of agents in full-fledged market economies: The former were implementing universalistic financial regulations; the later were hedging against further losses by contracting enterprise credits. But the result was to *diminish* the utility of commercial credit as an adjustment tool in the enterprise sphere. With the commercial banks in retreat and the local capital market unequipped to supply investment finance, the funds needed to restructure Hungarian industry could only come from the West.

Industrial Restructuring in the Postcommunist Period

Hungary's long history of market reforms left local producers better positioned than other East European enterprises to cope with the upheavals of 1989–91. Decentralization of central planning gave them experience with autonomous decision making; liberalization of foreign trade allowed them to forge contacts with Western partners; price reform softened their exposure to world market forces. But despite these advantages, the abrupt transformation of the politico-economic environment generated a tremendous shock for Hungarian industry. Table 6.2 shows the decline of output in Hungary's major industries.

Economic performance within these sectors exhibited considerable variation. For example, pharmaceutical and petroleum processing companies weathered the collapse of the Eastern market by expanding sales to the West. Other firms managed to resume exports to the East by cultivating informal barter arrangements with the Soviet successor states. But for the bulk of Hungarian industry, the early postcommunist years proved very traumatic. Mining, textile, machine tool, construction, rubber, fertilizer, consumer electronics, and precision engineering companies suffered precipitous losses. Iron and steel producers, which had actually expanded output during the final years of communist rule, virtually disappeared from the scene after 1989.[19]

And notwithstanding the cushioning effects of Hungary's large second economy,[20] the socioeconomic fallout of industrial decline was substantial. Table 6.3 shows reduction of employment in key industries between 1987 and 1991.

By August 1992, officially registered unemployed persons numbered 600,000. Adding unregistered workers who had given up finding new jobs, the total number of unemployed exceeded 800,000, close to 15 percent of the labor force. This was an *eight-fold* increase from the level obtaining just two years before. Among the West European countries, only Spain and Ireland displayed comparable rates of unemployment, the social effects of which were partially compensated by their membership in the

TABLE 6.2. **Indices of Volume of Output in Hungarian Industry, 1988–91 (1987 = 100)**

Sector	1988	1989	1990	1991
Mining	96.3	94.8	88.2	89.1
Electric energy	100.1	100.2	100.2	92.0
Metallurgy	104.3	104.4	81.0	67.3
Engineering	100.0	100.2	83.8	65.1
Building material	101.6	98.4	95.0	67.0
Chemicals	101.3	96.1	94.6	81.5
Light industry	100.2	95.2	88.3	75.1
Food industry	97.5	101.0	99.1	90.3
Industry total	100.0	99.0	90.8	78.5

Source: Josef Brada, Inderjit Singh, and Ádám Török, "Firms Afloat and Firms Adrift: Hungarian Industry and the Economic Transition," *Eastern European Economics,* January-February 1994, 39.

19. Josef Brada, Inderjit Singh, and Ádám Török, "Firms Afloat and Firms Adrift: Hungarian Industry and the Economic Transition," *Eastern European Economics,* January–February 1994, 38–64; Ádám Török, "On the Edge of Deindustrialization? Trends and Patterns in Enterprise Behavior," part 1, *Bank & Tőzsde: Független Pénzügyi, Üzleti és Gazdasági Hetilap* 1, no. 23 (25 June 1993): 13.

20. László Csaba notes that the officially reported drop in national income after 1989 overstates the decline in living standards. About one-third of Hungarian households derived income from the entrepreneurial sector, whose contribution to GDP was not fully captured by state statistical services. "Macroeconomic Policy in Hungary: Poetry versus Reality," *Soviet Studies* 44, no. 6 (1992): 949.

TABLE 6.3.   Employment in Hungarian Industry, 1987–91 (thousands)

Sector	1987	1988	1989	1990	1991
Mining	112	103	93	78	65
Electric energy	42	43	42	44	41
Metallurgy	83	79	72	64	51
Engineering	469	460	442	422	318
Building material	65	62	61	59	50
Chemicals	110	108	110	110	95
Light industry	331	318	303	283	232
Food industry	207	203	204	199	181
Miscellaneous	36	32	29	24	17
Industry total	1,455	1,408	1,356	1,283	1,050

Source: Josef Brada, Inderjit Singh, and Ádám Török, "Firms Afloat and Firms Adrift: Hungarian Industry and the Economic Transition," *Eastern European Economics,* January-February 1994, 43.

European Union. The distinctive character of Hungary's unemployment problem magnified its socioeconomic repercussions. Despite periodic recessions, the aggregate number of jobs in the OECD countries increased in the 1970s and 1980s. By contrast, postcommunist Hungary suffered an absolute reduction in available jobs, the result of the huge drop in industrial output and overall labor demand. This meant that a sizable portion of the workforce faced the prospect of semipermanent joblessness. The surge of claims for long-term unemployment compensation placed enormous pressure on a state budget already beset by declining revenues and rising expenditures. The uneven geographical distribution of Hungarian unemployment further complicated the problem. Unemployment rates exceeded 40 percent in some rural areas, with the high of costs of public transport inhibiting mobility to Budapest and other urban districts where jobs were more plentiful.[21]

The decline of Hungarian industry resulted from a confluence of foreign and domestic factors. Externally, the disintegration of the Soviet Union prompted a deep contraction of Hungary's single biggest export market. Sales to the USSR as a share of total Hungarian exports dropped from 33 percent in 1987 to 12 percent in 1991. On the import side, the switch to dollar accounting caused a steep increase in the cost of oil, gas, and raw materials purchased from the Soviet successor states, whose prices were previously subsidized via an artificial forint/transferable ruble

21. Kopint-Datorg, *Economic Trends in Eastern Europe* 1, no. 3 (1992): 185–192; András Toth, "The Social Impact of Restructuring in Rural Areas of Hungary: Disruption of Security or the End of the Rural Socialist Middle Class Society?" *Soviet Studies* 44, no. 6 (1992): 1039–43.

exchange rate. Meanwhile, Hungarian trade with the other East European countries plummeted in the aftermath of German unification and the demise of the CMEA. Exports to the former GDR declined by one-third in 1990, as revaluation of the East German mark priced most Hungarian products out of the local market. Sales to the remaining members of the now-defunct CMEA, which like Hungary were mired in a deep depression, shrank by about 50 percent.[22]

Internally, measures enacted by the Antall government amplified the effects of the sudden loss of Hungary's Eastern markets. The termination of industrial subsidies removed the fiscal safety net that had previously shielded inefficient enterprises from market forces. Radical import liberalization, deep tariff reductions, and real currency appreciation increased local producers' vulnerability to competition by high-quality, low-cost imports from the West and the East Asian newly industrialized countries.[23] The introduction of Western-type accounting procedures foreclosed opportunities for concealing losses through financial sleight of hand, while the passage of strict bankruptcy legislation forced insolvent enterprises to confront the genuine possibility of liquidation. Finally, changes in the institutional structure of industrial policy closed off channels through which plant directors lobbied the state for particularistic benefits. The Office of Price and Materials, through which enterprise managers negotiated exceptions to market pricing rules, was abolished. A successor organization, the Hungarian Competition Office, was established to regulate mergers, cartels, unfair business practices, and consumer protection laws.[24] The chief advocates of the enterprise sector, the Ministry of Industry and Trade and the MIER, lacked the budgetary funds and political muscle to undertake export promotion and other selective policies. Primary responsibility for overseeing Hungarian industry fell to the State Property Agency (SPA), whose central mission was to sell local enterprises to private investors.

---

22. László Csaba, "Válság Vagy Visszaesés?" (Crisis or recession?), *Közgazdasági Szemle* 39, no. 2 (1992): 93–108; Csaba, "Economic Consequences of Soviet Disintegration," in István Székely and David Newbery, eds., *Hungary: An Economy in Transition* (Cambridge: Cambridge University Press, 1993), 30–34; András Köves, *Central and East European Economies: The International Dimension* (Boulder: Westview, 1992), 27–30, 84–90.

23. Import liberalization proved a nearly fatal blow to Hungarian companies that heretofore enjoyed quasi-monopoly status in the local market (e.g., Taurus Rubber) and to major consumer electronics firms (Orion, Videoton, Radion) unable to withstand competition from West European and East Asian suppliers. Brada, Singh, and Török, "Firms Afloat and Firms Adrift," 41, 87–88; Gábor Hoványi, "Radion Radio and Electrical Works: 'The Whiz Kid Grown Old?'" *Eastern European Economics* 31, no. 6 (winter 1993–94): 101–13.

24. János Stadler, "Competition Policy in Transition," in Székely and Newbery, *Hungary,* 118–25.

But while the external economic shocks and internal political changes fundamentally transformed the competitive environment of Hungarian producers, they did not lead to a full-fledged restructuring of local industry. Contraction of output and downsizing of the labor force in loss-making sectors constituted only a part of the broader task of structural adjustment. Making Hungarian industry truly competitive in world markets demanded huge infusions of capital to upgrade plant and equipment, much of which was hopelessly antiquated. As we have seen, Hungary's own financial sector could not supply the funds needed to modernize the country's industrial base. The capital market was too poorly developed to generate sufficient levels of bond and equity financing, while the loan portfolio problem compelled commercial banks to withdraw from enterprise lending. Constraints on domestic capital formation caused gross fixed investment, which represented 29 percent of GDP in 1980, to diminish to less than 18 percent in 1990.[25]

These circumstances left foreign capital as Hungary's only credible source of industrial finance. The country's favorable foreign investment environment placed it in a strong position to bid for Western capital. Indeed, in the early 1990s Hungary attracted more foreign direct investment than any other East European country except the former GDR. However, the largest share of foreign investment went toward joint ventures and greenfield investments. While these sorts of investments were important insofar as they enlarged the aggregate share of private ownership and promoted the diffusion of Western technology and managerial expertise, they did not advance the goal of recapitalizing extant state enterprises, where most of Hungary's industrial capacity remained. Foreign direct investment that did flow into preexisting enterprises favored the economy's strongest performers, exemplifying the reluctance of Western investors to commit funds to loss-making companies prior to restructuring. Thus, the tension between privatization and restructuring that impeded recapitalization of the financial sector proved even more acute in the industrial sphere.

In the following discussion, I explore the dilemmas of industrial restructuring in postcommunist Hungary. I begin by assessing the responses of enterprise managers and workers to the economic disturbances of the early 1990s. I then examine the political dynamics of industrial policy under the Antall government. I argue that the demise of the communist state deprived factory-level agents of the institutional means to secure compensation for the distributional fallout of industrial decline, forcing them to rely on individualistic economic strategies. While many

25. Economist Intelligence Unit, *Country Report: Hungary,* 1st quarter 1994, 17.

actors managed to exit to Hungary' growing private sector, the transition left a sizable number of workers and enterprise managers tied down to moribund parts of the state sector. The locus of power within the Hungarian state shifted toward financial control agencies, reinforcing the liabilities of those agents. But while that shift enhanced the state's capacity for universalistic market regulation, it prevented the Antall government from implementing selective industrial policies to revitalize loss-making enterprises. This, together with the acute shortage of investment capital, left major portions of Hungarian industry to stagnate with few prospects for recovery.

Hungarian Enterprises and Structural Adjustment

Hungarian enterprises were less vulnerable to the contraction of the Eastern market than their counterparts in other former communist countries. At the time of the political transition, sales to the CMEA represented 40 percent of Hungary's total exports, compared to 44 percent of Poland's, 47 percent of Czechoslovakia's, and 61 percent of Bulgaria's.[26] But combined with the recession in the domestic economy, the sudden demise of the socialist trading system severely weakened Hungarian enterprises, which had previously looked to the East as a receptacle of goods unmarketable in the convertible currency area. At the same time, the Antall government's acceleration of import liberalization under real forint appreciation placed local producers under mounting pressure from goods manufactured in the West and in East Asia. By 1992, 90 percent of imports no longer required licenses to enter the Hungarian market, exposing more than 70 percent of domestic industry to direct foreign competition.[27] The government meanwhile reduced tariffs to an average of 13 percent—higher than most OECD countries, but lower than nations in the capitalist South at comparable levels of development.[28]

The collapse of the communist regime left Hungarian enterprises with few institutional means of defending themselves against world market forces. In contrast to Latin America, where organizations of local enterprise managers, civil servants, and urban workers formed the social base

---

26. David Tarr, "Problems in the Transition from the CMEA: Implications for Eastern Europe," *Communist Economies and Economic Transformation* 4, no. 1 (1992): 27.

27. MIER, *Newsletter* 4, no. 1 (February 1992): 2.

28. Bart Édes, "Import Liberalization and Industry Protection: International Precedents and Possible Options for Hungary," *Russian and East European Finance and Trade,* winter 1992–93, 37–38; Gábor Oblath, "A Magyarországi Importliberalizalas Korláti, Sikerei és Kérdojelei" (Limitations, successes, and question marks of import liberalization in Hungary), *Külgazdaság* 35, no. 5 (1991): 4–13.

of import substitution industrialization,[29] no such coalition existed in communist Hungary. Plant directors relied on their particularistic links to Party and state agencies to obtain price supports, subsidies, and regulatory exemptions that mitigated the impact of market competition. As described in chapter 3, de jure import liberalization actually began in the late 1980s at the MSZMP's initiative. But the institutional structure of the communist state obviated organized resistance by import-sensitive producers, which could secure protection via individualized bargaining.

The transition to democracy left these agents in the lurch. The demise of the communist state dissolved the institutional channels that enabled plant directors to negotiate exceptions to market rules, while the lack of a preexisting framework for organized interest representation circumscribed their opportunities for collective political action. Several intermediary associations—for example, the National Federation of Hungarian Industrialists, the Hungarian Association of International Companies, and the Hungarian Iron and Steel Industrial Association—did emerge in the early 1990s to represent industrial interests, but they lacked the organizational resources to effectively lobby the new government for changes in economic policy. The equivocal preferences of Hungarian producers over foreign trade further hindered coordinated responses to trade liberalization. While import liberalization subjected enterprises to increased foreign competition, it also enlarged access to the advanced capital goods needed to modernize their production lines while holding down prices in local supplier markets.

The absence of strong resistance from below enabled the Antall government to proceed with import liberalization and to sever the flow of subsidies that previously kept illiquid enterprises afloat. What concessions Antall made to industrial groups in the early postcommunist years were periodic and limited. For example, in March 1992 the government agreed to impose quotas on iron and steel imports, whose penetration of the Hungarian market weakened an already beleaguered metallurgical sector. In November of the same year, it raised the tariff on cement imports. But in both cases, the protectionist measures were targeted at goods imported from the former CMEA countries, not from the West. Hungary's Association Agreement with the European Union proscribed the use of most kinds of tariffs and nontariff barriers to protect local industry. The pull of politico-economic integration with the West induced Hungarian authori-

---

29. Stephan Haggard, *Pathways from the Periphery: The Politics of Growth in the Newly Industrialized Countries* (Ithaca: Cornell University Press, 1990), 37–40, 165–78; John Waterbury, *Exposed to Innumerable Delusions: Public Enterprise and State Power in Egypt, India, Mexico, and Turkey* (Cambridge: Cambridge University Press, 1993), 21–23, 190–211.

ties to converge toward the European Union's liberal standards, discouraging use of protectionist measures in precisely the trading area where local enterprises were least competitive. And in any event, the government's repertoire of selective protectionist instruments was limited owing to budgetary constraints and the meager institutional capacity of the MIER and the Ministry of Industry and Trade, industry's foremost advocates within the state administration.[30]

These circumstances left local producers to their own devices, compelling them to devise individualistic economic strategies to cope with the new competitive environment. The collapse of the Soviet payments system, the attempted coup in Moscow in August 1991, and the dissolution of the USSR in December of that year disrupted Hungary's commercial relations with its principal trading partner. Some Hungarian enterprises managed to soften the blow through informal barter arrangements with the Soviet successor states, whose shortage of foreign reserves limited their ability to execute cash transactions. For instance, Müszertechnika shipped personal computers to the Commonwealth of Independent States (CIS) in exchange for steel, which it then resold to Western Europe for hard currency.[31] Others formed joint ventures with Russian partners to resume shipments to the East. The oil and gas equipment manufacturer Dunántúli Kőolajipari Gépgyár signed an agreement with a Russian producer to form a new company called DKG-East. The Hungarian partner parlayed its control of high-demand capital inputs to secure majority ownership in the venture and guaranteed access to Russia's large petroleum industry.[32] Still others used Western intermediaries to restore commercial relations with the former Soviet republics. By 1993, 30 to 40 percent of Hungary's trade with the CIS took place through German, Swiss, and Austrian intermediaries. The enterprise sector's increased reliance on Western financial intermediation reflected the inability of Hungarian commercial banks and state agencies to supply local producers with export financing credits, without which expansion of hard currency trade with the cash-starved CIS was impossible.[33]

---

30. Édes, "Import Liberalization," 35–48; Károly Okolicsányi, "Foreign Trade in Transition," *Bank & Tőzsde: Független Pénzügyi, Üzleti és Gazdasági Hetilap* 1, no. 30 (13 August 1993): 13–14.

31. Brada, Singh, and Török, "Firms Afloat and Firms Adrift," 69–72.

32. Ádám Török, "Trends and Motives of Organizational Change in Hungarian Industry—a Synchronic View," *Journal of Comparative Economics* 17, no. 2 (June 1993): 375–76; Judit Zsarnay, "Industry Case Study: Dunántúli Kőolajipari Gépgyár," *Eastern European Economics* 31, no. 6 (1993/94): 93–100.

33. A Hungarian exporter might engineer a sale to an Austrian trading company but then deliver the actual goods to Ukraine—with the transaction officially registered as a bilateral deal between Hungary and Austria. The process also worked in reverse, with Hungarian

However, these cases were very much the exception to the rule in the early 1990s, when the contraction of the Eastern market inflicted heavy losses on many of Hungary's largest enterprises. For instance, the demise of the Soviet Union had a devastating impact on Ikarus Karosszéria és Jármőgyar, the giant bus manufacturer whose production line was specifically designed to supply vehicles for the USSR's dilapidated road system. Ikarus had about 150,000 buses in operation in the Soviet Union, along with an extensive network of service stations and spare parts facilities. Undeterred by the freeze on ruble-based exports in January 1990 and the growing concerns over the USSR's solvency, Ikarus continued production to fulfill its outstanding contracts with the Soviet government. In summer 1991, the Soviets acquired 30 percent of the company's equity, promising to buy 6,000 buses per year to replace obsolete vehicles. They ended up purchasing only one-third of this total, leaving Ikarus with thousands of unmarketable buses in its inventory. By 1992, mounting losses forced Hungarian state authorities to place the enterprise under receivership. The repercussions of the Ikarus crisis were collateralized to Rába, Taurus Rubber, Csepel Autogyár, and other heavy manufacturers whose domestic sales depended on delivery of components to the bus company. Shipbuilding and agricultural machinery companies, whose production was similarly tailored for exports to the socialist countries, also incurred huge losses as the CMEA and USSR unraveled.[34]

Under communist rule, enterprises could run such losses with high confidence that Party officials would ultimately prevail on state agencies to supply them with subsidies and bridging credits. As late as spring 1990, the managing director of Ikarus was still operating under the expectation of an eventual bailout for whatever losses resulted from execution of the

importers purchasing Russian products through West European intermediaries, in some cases paying lower prices than if they had bought them directly. The disarray attending the collapse of the USSR and CMEA created opportunities for Hungarian enterprises to employ other imaginative—but legally dubious—trading strategies. Notwithstanding the official conversion to dollar-denominated trade in January 1991, local producers continued to export goods to the Soviets in exchange for rubles, which they then presented to the National Bank of Hungary for conversion into forints. By summer of that year, the Soviet Union was effectively insolvent, leaving the National Bank with hundreds of millions of essentially worthless rubles. The Soviet authorities had previously agreed to convert Hungary's ruble surplus into dollars, with repayment spread over five years. But the disintegration of the USSR rendered that agreement moot, leaving Hungary with $1.6 billion in uncollectible payment arrears from the now-defunct Soviet Union. Interview, National Bank of Hungary, 29 May 1991; interview, MIER, 27 May 1993; "The HER Roundtable: The CIS Connection," *Hungarian Economic Review* 13 (April 1993): 61–64.

34. Judit Ványai and Erzsébet Viszt, "Foreign-Trade Reorientation and the Freeze on Ruble-Based Exports: The Lessons of a Machine-Industry Survey," *Russian and East European Finance and Trade*, fall 1992, 77–82; interview, MIER, 27 May 1993.

company's production contract with the Soviet Union.[35] However, it soon became apparent that little or no financial assistance to Hungarian industry was forthcoming. The Antall government signaled its unwillingness to support floundering companies by terminating industrial subsidies, while the commercial banks withheld export credits for fear of aggravating their loan portfolio problems. Facing a rapidly shrinking Eastern market and an acute shortage of export financing, Hungarian enterprises turned to the West. As table 6.4 demonstrates, their efforts resulted in a substantial reorientation of trade.

The data show that imports from the CIS remained at nearly the same level as before the USSR's collapse, illustrating Hungary's continued dependence on the Russian Federation and other successor states for energy and raw materials. Otherwise, the magnitude of the trade shift was truly impressive. By 1993, two-thirds of Hungary's trade turnover was conducted with the advanced industrialized countries. A surge in exports to the West produced balance-of-trade surpluses in 1990, 1991, and the first three quarters of 1992. But the export boom then petered out, returning the balance of trade in hard currency to a deficit.[36]

TABLE 6.4.   Regional Composition of Hungarian Trade, 1989 and 1993 (percent of total)

	1989	1993
Exports		
Advanced industrialized countries	43.1	67.7
Developing countries	14.2	5.4
Soviet Union/CIS	25.1	15.2
Eastern Europe[a]	15.8	11.1
Other	1.8	0.6
Imports		
Advanced industrialized countries	49.3	65.3
Developing countries	9.9	4.4
Soviet Union/CIS	22.1	21.8
Eastern Europe[a]	17.1	7.8
Other	1.6	0.7

Sources: Economist Intelligence Unit, *Country Report: Hungary,* 2d quarter 1994, 23–24; András Köves, *Central and East European Economies in Transition: The International Dimension* (Boulder, Colo.: Westview Press, 1992), 87–88.

[a]Bulgaria, Czechoslovakia, East Germany, Poland, Romania.

35. Ványai and Viszt, "Foreign-Trade Reorientation," 81.

36. *PlanEcon Report* 9, nos. 11–12 (20 April 1993): 9–11; Economist Intelligence Unit, *Country Report: Hungary,* 2d quarter 1994, 3. Under the CMEA, intraregional trade was settled in transferable rubles, whose dollar exchange rate was artificially inflated by local authorities. Therefore, the data in table 6.4 (while as reliable as any currently available) may

Officials at the MIER pointed to the appreciating forint as the main cause of Hungary's deteriorating trade balance. However, the country's underlying trade patterns suggested that the problem went well beyond exchange rate effects. While local producers responded admirably to the forced reorientation of commercial relations, the commodity composition of Hungarian trade indicated that major structural difficulties continued to plague the enterprise sector.

On the export side of table 6.5, agriculture's share of sales remained at virtually the same level as before. The farming sector's stagnation resulted from an array of factors—draught, credit crunch, disruptions from the MDF's reprivatization program, and barriers to entry to the West European market—in addition to real appreciation of the forint. The share of consumer goods, another commodity group that was presumably highly sensitive to relative price shifts, increased by nearly 10 percent between 1989 and 1993. But the share of machinery and equipment, a vital source of high value-added exports, declined by roughly the same amount—illustrating both the impact of the CMEA collapse on heavy industry and the low competitiveness of Hungarian capital goods in Western markets. On the import side, the shares of both consumer and capital products increased, clearly demonstrating the effects of import liberalization. In 1993, imports of machinery and equipment rose by over 45 percent from the previous year.[37]

The influx of Western capital goods was a welcome development insofar as it promoted modernization of Hungary's industrial base and enlarged overall production capacity. Yet sustaining imports of high-cost capital products without increasing the country's already onerous hard currency debt presupposed the ability of Hungarian enterprises to generate compensatory export revenues. Here, the general trend in the early postcommunist period was not encouraging. The export sector staged a modest comeback in 1994. But the biggest gains came from fuels and electricity (which occupied a marginal position among the principal commodity groups) and agriculture (which had nowhere to go but up following its disastrous performance in 1990–92). Export sales of Hungary's largest industrial sectors (raw materials and semifinished goods, machinery and

---

exaggerate the dollar value of intraregional trade before 1989 and hence the degree of geographical reorientation of Hungarian trade after 1989. But while the peculiarities of the socialist trading system make it difficult to calculate precisely the magnitude of the postcommunist trade shift, there is little debate among specialists in Hungary that the collapse of the Eastern markets created a tremendous shock for local producers and that the reorientation of trade toward the West in the early 1990s was quite substantial.

37. Economist Intelligence Unit, *Country Report: Hungary,* 2d quarter 1994, 22.

equipment) stagnated. Even the consumer goods sector, whose exports exhibited robust growth in the early part of the decade, encountered increasing difficulties penetrating Western markets.[38]

In short, while some Hungarian enterprises succeeded in rejuvenating commercial relations with the former communist countries and/or redirecting exports toward the West, most simply struggled to survive in the harsh new competitive environment. About 60 percent of local producers adopted a strategy of "drifting."[39] Here, plant directors focused on day-to-day subsistence, keeping afloat long enough to attract investors willing to privatize their enterprises. The position of these companies differed from both traditional socialist enterprises and full-fledged capitalist firms. Unlike enterprises in the communist system, drifting enterprises faced "hard" budget constraints: they could no longer count on state subsidies or bank credits to save them from insolvency. But in contrast to privatized companies, whose owners could force managers to augment the value of capital assets, the ownership structure of drifters was ambiguous. The Hungarian state possessed formal ownership rights, but the responsible

TABLE 6.5. Commodity Composition of Hungarian Trade, 1989 and 1993 (percent of total)

	1989	1993
Exports		
Semifinished goods	36.3	36.2
Consumer goods	15.6	25.3
Agricultural products	21.6	21.2
Machinery and equipment	24.0	14.0
Fuels and electricity	2.7	3.3
Imports		
Semifinished goods	51.6	33.6
Consumer goods	12.4	21.2
Agricultural products	7.1	5.9
Machinery and equipment	16.9	26.5
Fuels and electricity	12.0	12.7

Sources: Economist Intelligence Unit, *Country Report: Hungary* 1 (1991): 15; *Country Report: Hungary,* 2d quarter 1994, 22.

38. "Hungarian Economic Monitor," *PlanEcon Report* 10, nos. 25–27 (31 August 1994): 6.

39. This term was coined by Ádám Török, "On the Edge of Deindustrialization? Trends and Patterns in Enterprise Behavior," part 2, *Bank & Tőzsde: Független Pénzügyi, Üzleti és Gazdasági Hetilap* 1, no. 24 (2 July 1993): 17.

agencies, the SPA and SAHC, lacked the technical resources to supervise effectively the managerial activities in the multitude of firms in their port-folios. This allowed local managers to stay afloat by consuming the company's fixed assets, running down plant and equipment to generate just enough revenue to avert bankruptcy.[40]

The upshot of the drifting phenomenon was increased support for privatization among state enterprise managers. Indeed, the central goal of the strategy was to buy time until private investors came along to resuscitate the enterprises and salvage managers' jobs. Plant directors looked eagerly to foreign capital to spur privatization, as the domestic credit crunch deprived them of the funds needed to finance managerial buyouts. But the drifting strategy led to the progressive erosion of the capital stock of these very same enterprises, reducing their attractiveness as privatization candidates. The result was to trap major segments of Hungarian industry in a vicious cycle of stagnation and undercapitalization.

Responses of Hungarian Workers

As described in part 2, the institutional structure of reform communism enabled Hungarian workers to circumvent the MSZMP's efforts to restructure local industry in the 1980s. Pressures to meet the ruling party's production goals induced enterprise managers to hoard labor for deployment during rush periods, which kept total labor demand high even in loss-making sectors targeted for downsizing. This, combined with high degrees of income leveling, discouraged labor mobility and weakened incentives for workers to raise productivity. Toward the end of its tenure, the Communist Party introduced wage reforms aimed at increasing income differentiation and heightening labor productivity. But Hungarian workers responded to wage liberalization by utilizing the Party's own trade union to secure across-the-board income hikes in order to neutralize consumer price inflation.

The economic shocks of the post-1989 period dramatically transformed labor's position. For the first time since the communist takeover in 1948, Hungarian workers faced the prospect of open unemployment. Some Western scholars have argued that the sudden advent of mass unemployment in Eastern Europe, where decades of central planning inured workers to the full employment guarantee, significantly raised the dangers of a political backlash against market reforms. For instance, Adam Przeworski offers the following observation about the Polish case.

---

40. Török, "Trends and Motives of Organizational Change," 377–78, 382–83.

While Poles support promarket reforms and the institutions that forge them when incomes decline and prices mount, they are not willing to continue reforms and withdraw confidence from democratic institutions in the face of mounting unemployment. And, in the end, fear of unemployment overwhelms everything else.

Przeworski cites public opinion polls showing that growing anxiety over unemployment was the key factor undercutting popular support for Poland's crash marketization program. By April 1990, four months into the program, the proportion of respondents deeming unemployment "despicable" had risen to 85 percent. "And those threatened with unemployment were willing to resist it: 65 percent of them said . . . that they were willing to strike in defense of their jobs." The failure of Polish political leaders to address the socioeconomic repercussions of marketization typifies top-down reform programs like the Balcerowicz Plan, which seek to impose technocratic blueprints without consulting the societal agents who are most affected.[41]

Hungary, whose unemployment rates in the early 1990s nearly matched Poland's[42] and whose policy-making process was even less inclusive of societal actors, exhibited an altogether different dynamic: far from *intensifying* political opposition to economic transition, rising unemployment *diminished* it.

The passivity of Hungarian labor in the postcommunist period was partly attributable to the country's extensive system of unemployment compensation. Unemployment benefits were introduced in Hungary in 1989 by the last communist government of Miklós Németh. In 1991, the Antall government created a Solidarity Fund—financed by state budgetary transfers and compulsory payroll contributions—which expanded the range of benefits for jobless people. Like Hungary's pension system, the unemployment fund was quite generous in international comparative

---

41. Przeworski, "Economic Reforms, Public Opinion, and Political Institutions: Poland in the Eastern European Perspective," in Luiz Carlos Bresser Pereira, José María Maravall, and Przeworski, *Economic Reforms in New Democracies: A Social-Democratic Approach* (Cambridge: Cambridge University Press, 1993), 180–81.

42. While the initial shock of the Antall government's "gradualist" strategy was less severe than the Balcerowicz Plan, by 1992 Hungary's unemployment level reached 12.3 percent, compared with Poland's 14 percent. But an estimated one-third of officially unemployed workers in Poland actually had jobs—demonstrating that Poland's informal private sector, like Hungary's, played an important role in mitigating the socioeconomic effects of market reform. Calvo and Kumar, "Money Demand, Bank Credit, and Economic Performance," 318; Wing Thye Woo, "The Art of Reforming Centrally Planned Economies: Comparing China, Poland, and Russia," *Journal of Comparative Economics* 18, no. 3 (June 1994): 294–95.

terms. It paid 70 percent of previous earnings in the first year of unemployment, compared with 60 percent or less in most OECD countries. Rising long-term unemployment generated mounting pressure on the state budget. By 1993, beneficiaries were registered for an average of 269 days, compared to 118 two years earlier. For nonmanual unskilled workers, the average duration of joblessness had risen to 508 days, a clear indication of the magnitude of Hungary's long-term unemployment problem. But while unemployment benefits were substantial, the Hungarian state lacked the resources to implement proactive measures designed to retool displaced workers for reentry into the labor force. The government did set up an Employment Fund for worker retraining. However, budgetary constraints and the rising number of people on the unemployment rolls limited the fund's effectiveness. Between 1990 and 1993, retraining funds available per unemployed worker declined from HUF 96,000 to 15,500. During this period, only a small number of jobless people actually enrolled in retraining courses, and even fewer stayed in them until completion. Prolonged joblessness lowered the chances of eventual reemployment, as labor skills eroded and social networks contracted. The upshot was an economically immobile and politically inert population of hard-core unemployed workers who were far more inclined to stay on the public dole than to undertake active opposition to market reforms.[43]

For workers who remained employed but were situated in vulnerable sectors of industry, the politico-economic environment of the postcommunist period erected major obstacles to mobilization against reforms. First, the absence of a preexisting independent trade union left Hungarian workers without effective intermediary institutions to represent their interests once the communist regime collapsed. As we have seen, the legal successors to the communist-controlled trade union were hampered by declining membership, high fragmentation, and disputes over the allocation of the predecessor organization's assets. And Hungary's inchoate system of tripartite bargaining did not afford workers much influence over employment policy. In 1991, the Antall government created a Labor Market Committee and National Training Board, which supervised the disbursal of Employment Fund monies under the auspices of the Interest Representation Council.[44] But as I already noted, the budgetary resources of the fund were insufficient to keep pace with the rapid changes in labor market conditions.

43. Kopint-Datorg, *Economic Trends in Eastern Europe* 1, no. 3 (1992): 192–98; Toth, "The Social Impact of Restructuring," 1043; Erzsébet Viszt and Judit Ványai, "Employment and the Labor Market in Hungary," *Eastern European Economics,* July–August 1994, 34–39, 45–46

44. Viszt and Ványai, "Employment and the Labor Market in Hungary," 34–35.

Second, slack labor demand sharply diminished the efficacy of production strikes. What was significant about Hungary's labor market was not merely rising unemployment but declining overall labor demand. Between 1989 and 1992, the total number of jobs in local industry dropped by 35 percent. The contraction of the supply of available jobs was particularly severe in heavy industry: 51 percent in mining, 45 percent in engineering, 43 percent in metallurgy.[45] Postcommunist Hungary's labor crisis thus differed from the experiences of new Western democracies like Spain, where high unemployment rates coexisted with strong aggregate labor demand. The problem confronting the latter was *structural* unemployment, whereby joblessness resulted primarily from a mismatch between the skills of unemployed workers and the demands of the labor market. By contrast, Hungary faced not merely the challenge of upgrading the skills of hard-core unemployed workers under severe budgetary constraints, but also of stemming the erosion of the total supply of jobs resulting from the regional recession and the systemic transition from central planning to market economy.[46]

For industrial workers who still held jobs, organizing strikes under these circumstances was hardly a feasible strategy. If "fear of unemployment" provoked active resistance to market reforms in Poland, it cowed workers into submission in Hungary. With their weak trade union organizations inhibiting intraindustry mobilization, and with sluggish labor demand narrowing their prospects of finding new jobs at comparable pay, most Hungarian workers abstained from open confrontation with management. In short, rather than enhancing workers' leverage over employment policy, production strikes merely increased the risk of losing their jobs.[47]

These barriers to organized resistance left Hungarian workers to their own devices. For workers possessing fungible assets, the expansion of the small-scale business sector in the early 1990s broadened exit opportunities. Between 1989 and 1991, the share of the labor force employed in firms with fewer than 50 workers increased from 2 percent to 7.2 percent, while the share of firms with 50 to 300 employees rose from 11.8 to 19.2 percent. During the same period, there was a marked growth in private entrepreneurship. By June 1993, officially registered individual entrepreneurs numbered over 500,000.[48] But while these developments signaled that a process of decentralization was underway in Hungary's highly concentrated indus-

45. Viszt and Ványai, "Employment and the Labor Market in Hungary," 24.

46. Kopint-Datorg, *Economic Trends in Eastern Europe* 1, no. 3 (1992): 193.

47. Interview, Central European University, 28 September 1993.

48. Hungarian Ministry of Finance, *Economic Processes of 1993* (Budapest, August 1993), 21; Viszt and Ványai, "Employment and the Labor Market in Hungary," 45.

try, most workers remained tied down to large-scale enterprises—precisely the sector where their political and economic leverage was weakest. Nearly three-fourths of Hungarian workers were still employed in firms with over 300 employees, nearly half in companies with over 1,000 employees. And notwithstanding the changing structure of local industry, the absorptive capacity of small and medium-sized businesses was limited. In 1992, those sectors produced only 2.6 percent new jobs, most of which went to high-skilled workers and recent entrants holding university degrees.[49] For industrial workers lacking transferable assets or advanced degrees, these circumstances dictated a highly defensive posture: in a labor market that provided few means of exit from large-scale industry, these agents could best protect their positions by laying low and holding on to their current jobs.

Industrial Restructuring and the Hungarian State

The Antall government's policies toward Hungarian industry reinforced the liabilities of enterprise managers and workers, already described. Progrowth factions of the governing coalition pushed for export subsidies, tax credits, regional development funds, and other measures aimed at spurring recovery in Hungary's crisis sectors. But the responsible state organizations, the Ministry of Industry and Trade and the MIER, lacked the institutional assets to undertake selective industrial policies. The former agency, which was the product of the merger of the Ministries of Industry and Domestic Trade, emerged from the political transition with limited legal jurisdiction and meager budgetary resources. Its primary function in the postcommunist period was to analyze microeconomic data and submit policy recommendations to the SPA and SAHC, which now held ownership rights to state enterprises.[50] The head of the MIER, Béla Kádár, enjoyed high personal visibility and close links to the prime minister's office. But the MIER itself lacked the means to carry out interventionist measures. The agency's political power derived from its administration of Hungary's import licensing system and its authority to conduct international trade negotiations. As we have seen, the main trend in those spheres was not dirigisme but liberalization: by overseeing the dismantling of import controls and negotiating free trade agreements with the European Union, the MIER operated in a fashion that progressively undercut its own regulatory capacity.

---

49. National Bank of Hungary, *Monthly Report* 1 (1993): 15.
50. Interview, Ministry of Industry and Trade, 17 May 1991.

The one exception to the dearth of selective industrial policies in post-communist Hungary was a crisis management program supervised by the Ministry of Industry and Trade. The program encompassed thirteen large state enterprises that faced severe liquidity problems but that ministerial officials regarded as salvageable.[51] The Industry Ministry was charged with formulating recovery plans for each of the targeted firms, subject to ratification by the Economic Cabinet, the prime minister's office, and the Parliament. Bureaucratic red tape delayed implementation of the program: by summer 1993, only one plan had received final governmental approval. But even when the Ministry received formal ratification by the political leadership, it remained unclear how the program would be financed. The big commercial banks, which held the bulk of the enterprises' debt, declined to become involved for fear of worsening their loan portfolio problems. The Corvinbank, a small bank that was not heavily exposed to the enterprise sector, offered to manage bond issues in order to recapitalize the thirteen firms. But it would do so only if the Hungarian state underwrote the issues, and only after the liquidity position of the firms was stabilized—underscoring again the tension between structural adjustment and recapitalization in loss-making sectors. The program remained at an impasse by the time of the 1994 national elections.[52]

Measures state officials pursued in the area of bankruptcy law, which were emphatically *not* selective in nature, proved far more significant to Hungarian industry than the "crisis management" program. As shown in chapter 3, the legal instruments for bankruptcy did exist in communist Hungary. In an attempt to tighten discipline in the enterprise sector, the MSZMP introduced a bankruptcy law in 1985. But the institutional logic of market socialism discouraged creditors from using the law against insolvent enterprises. Suppliers declined to pursue legal sanctions against other producers, confident that the communist state would ultimately supply debtors with the funds to cover interenterprise arrears. Nor did the new commercial banks utilize the bankruptcy law. Between the inauguration of the two-tiered banking system in 1987 and the dissolution of the Communist Party in 1989, there was only *one* major bank-initiated bank-

---

51. Included on the list were such major companies as Raba, Ikarus Karosszéria és Jármőgyar, Taurus Gumiipari Vállalat, Borsodi Vegyi Kombinát, and Peti Nitrogen Müvek. The debts of the thirteen firms totaled HUF 45 billion. "Wiping Slate of Thirteen Companies," *Bank & Tőzsde: Független Pénzügyi, Üzleti és Gazdasági Hetilap* 1, no. 32 (27 August 1993): 12.

52. "Reorganization Bonds Proposed," *Bank & Tőzsde: Független Pénzügyi, Uzleti és Gazdasági Hetilap* 1, no. 22 (18 June 1993): 14; interviews, Ministry of Finance, 20 May and 20 September 1993; interview, MIER, 18 May 1993; interview, Kopint-Datorg, 28 September 1993.

ruptcy case. And while the economic shocks of the 1989–91 period caused a sharp increase in company liquidations, creditors still proved reluctant to initiate legal proceedings against debtor enterprises. Of the 1,268 liquidations in 1991, only 182 were initiated by major institutional investors, of which merely 9 were started by commercial banks.[53]

The bankruptcy law enacted by the Antall government in 1992 fundamentally transformed the legal environment of Hungarian enterprises.[54] To overcome the reluctance of creditors to initiate bankruptcy procedures, designers of the new law inserted an automatic triggering mechanism. Enterprises over 90 days in arrears on any financial obligation had to declare bankruptcy. Bankrupt firms were granted a three-month moratorium on payments to creditors, during which time they were obliged to formulate restructuring programs. Unanimous consent by all of the enterprises' creditors was required for approval of the recovery plans. Failing this, the firms would be liquidated.[55]

The law precipitated a flood of bankruptcies and liquidations. During the first month in which the law was in effect, over 2,200 Hungarian enterprises were declared bankrupt, while liquidation procedures were initiated against nearly 1,300 firms. By the end of 1992, the number of bankruptcies exceeded 4,200, while liquidations totaled 10,700. These numbers overwhelmed the Hungarian court system, which was not equipped to enforce Western-type bankruptcy laws. The Budapest Court, which was responsible for 30 to 40 percent of the cases, had only eight judges qualified to adjudicate bankruptcy cases. The logjam in the court system compelled the government to introduce amendments that softened the law's trigger-

---

53. "Bankruptcy Law Came into Force," *Hungarian Business Brief: Business and Economic Review* 9 (13 May 1992): 2.

54. Despite its wide socioeconomic implications, the 1992 bankruptcy law provoked little controversy within the Antall government. The law was drafted by the Ministry of Justice in consultation with the key economic ministries and was approved *unanimously* by the Hungarian Parliament—illustrating both the government's heavy reliance on the state administration in economic reform policy and the shortage of technical expertise within the prime minister's office and the Parliament. Interviews, Hungarian Parliament, 19 May 1993; Ministry of Finance, 25 May 1993.

55. The automatic triggering feature of Hungary's bankruptcy law distinguished Hungary from other former communist countries. The Czech Republic's legal code was designed to delay bankruptcy until after privatization, giving partial exemptions to Czech firms targeted for inclusion in the Klaus government's mass voucher program. Poland's bankruptcy law was designed to spur bank-initiated enterprise reorganizations. The Polish government allowed commercial banks holding 30 percent or more of an enterprise's debt to convert it into equity, thereby encouraging bank participation in industrial restructuring. Delia Meth-Cohn and Pat Koza, "The Heat is On," *Business Central Europe* 1, no. 2 (June 1993): 7–9; Kálmán Mizsei, "Bankruptcy and the Postcommunist Economies of East-Central Europe," *Russian and East European Finance and Trade,* March–April 1994, 45–46.

ing mechanism. Under the revised legislation, creditors were required to take a preliminary, confidential vote before the formal announcement of a bankruptcy. The debtor enterprise would only be declared bankrupt if at least 51 percent of the creditors approved beforehand. To accelerate the legal process, the amended law abolished the unanimity rule governing enterprise restructuring programs. Approval of recovery plans now required the consent of only a majority of creditors.[56] But notwithstanding these changes, the law greatly increased pressure on Hungarian enterprise managers. Confronted for the first time with a serious threat of creditor-initiated bankruptcy, plant directors faced strong inducements to restore loss-making firms to profitability in order to avoid public disclosure of their professional shortcomings.

However, the bankruptcy law's impact on broader structural adjustment policy was mixed. On the one hand, the law strengthened incentives for managers to formulate recovery programs acceptable to their creditors, because the next step in the legal process—liquidation—meant probable loss of their jobs. On the other hand, the very fact that liquidations substantially outnumbered bankruptcies suggested that managers and creditors often failed to reach agreements on reorganizing insolvent firms. As I already noted, by the end of 1992 more than twice as many liquidations were underway than bankruptcies. A study of cases adjudicated by the Budapest Court indicated that a very high percentage of bankruptcies eventually turned into liquidations.[57] Liquidation was of course a perfectly legitimate method of structural adjustment, since it provided a means of redeploying the fixed capital assets of failed enterprises. The problem was that Hungary's low level of domestic capital accumulation and the high cost of bank credit discouraged local entrepreneurs from bidding for the assets of liquidated firms. Foreign investors, who unlike local agents enjoyed ample financial resources, showed little interest in buying used plant and equipment, especially insofar as liquidators typically charged unrealistically high prices.[58] Consequently, while liquidation served to accelerate the *downsizing* of weak segments of Hungarian industry, it did not promote the *redeployment* of productive assets in a manner aimed at restoring lost capacity.

Equally important, the pattern of creditor-initiated bankruptcies in

56. Mizsei, "Bankruptcy and the Postcommunist Economies," 55–56; "Amendments to the Bankruptcy Law," *Hungarian Business Brief: Business and Economic Review* 7 (8 April 1993): 1–2; interview, Ministry of Finance, 25 May 1993.

57. "Bankruptcies and Liquidations," *Hungarian Business Brief: Business and Economic Review* 17–18 (10 September 1992): 2–3.

58. "Liquidation Is Not Squandering of Property," *Privinfo: Privatization in Hungary* 2, no. 17 (September 1993): 7.

the early 1990s suggested that the Hungarian commercial banks remained disengaged from the restructuring process. Suppliers proved far more eager to initiate bankruptcies, as repayment of interfirm arrears allowed them to strengthen their own liquidity positions and preempt claims by other creditors in the transaction chain. The big commercial banks operated under different constraints. The sheer size of the enterprise debts in their portfolios increased the risks of initiating bankruptcies, which would set off a costly and time-consuming scramble for debtors' assets.[59] Moreover, the legal code did not permit bankruptcy proceedings against the banks themselves. Bank liquidation was legally possible, but only at the behest of the Office of Banking Supervision—a quite improbable occurrence given the high concentration of the country's financial assets in the major banks. The continued disengagement of the Hungarian banks, which unlike suppliers possessed the credit facilities crucial to enterprise reorganizations, demonstrated the limits of bankruptcy as an adjustment instrument in the postcommunist period.

Privatization and Structural Adjustment

The problems of financial sector reform and industrial restructuring amplified the importance of privatization in structural adjustment processes. As the commercial banks withdrew from enterprise lending and as financially strapped state agencies struggled vainly to implement a crisis management program, privatization emerged as the principal means of channeling capital into local industry. To this end, the Antall government eschewed mass distribution, a privatization strategy employed by other former communist countries; it instead concentrated on direct sales of state enterprises to Western investors. The liabilities of Hungarian workers and enterprise managers, described earlier in this chapter, made this strategy *politically* feasible. Lacking strong intermediary institutions to influence the formation of privatization policy, factory-level agents put up little resistance to a divestiture strategy that largely excluded them from the decision-making process. What made the direct sale approach *economically* advantageous was its capacity to attract "real" capital into the state sector. By negotiating sales with Western buyers, privatization authorities could surmount the barriers to domestic capital formation that were hindering reorganization of stagnant industries.

   In this section, I show the results of this strategy. Hungary's favorable foreign investment climate produced heavy inflows of Western capital in the early 1990s, but only a minority share of foreign direct investment

---

59. Mizsei, "Bankruptcy and the Postcommunist Economies," 57–58.

entered the country by way of privatization of extant state-owned enterprises. The preference of foreign capital for greenfield and joint ventures reflected the determination of Western investors that inefficient sectors of Hungary industry were not worth salvaging. As a result, loss-making enterprises fell deeper into the vicious cycle of stagnation and undercapitalization, further diminishing their attractiveness as privatization targets. After an initial flurry of sales of Hungary's blue-chip companies, large-scale privatization ebbed. Under pressure from the liberal opposition to "privatize the privatization," the Antall government implemented a succession of measures (manager-initiated transformations, employee share-ownership programs, compensation vouchers) aimed at decentralizing the divestiture process and stimulating local participation. But continuing limitations on domestic capital formation thwarted these initiatives. By the end of the MDF's term, local agents had purchased only a small portion of state property, leaving most large state-owned enterprises in the hands of state privatization agencies. Thus, Hungary's privatization strategy, rather than spurring industrial restructuring, ended up reinforcing the general inertia of structural adjustment policy in the postcommunist period.

Key Features of Hungarian Privatization Strategy

As discussed in chapter 3, the MSZMP's property reforms had a substantial impact on ownership relations in Hungary. During the 1980s, the Communist Party legalized most second economy activities, initiated a securities market, liberalized foreign investment, and established a legal framework for the formation of new private companies and the divestiture of existing state-owned enterprises. These measures placed the Antall government at a comparative advantage vis-à-vis Eastern Europe's other new democracies. By 1994, foreign direct investment in Hungary reached $6.9 billion, more than the other East European countries combined.[60] The influx of Western investment reflected both the country's unusually attractive foreign investment laws and high investor confidence in local managers, widely regarded as the best in the region.[61] The growth of entrepreneurial skills under reform communism also facilitated the successor government's small-scale privatization program. By 1994, private

---

60. By contrast, cumulative foreign direct investments reached $3.3 billion in the Czech Republic, $1.6 billion in Poland, $0.5 billion in Romania, $0.4 billion in Slovakia, $0.37 billion in Slovenia, and $0.2 billion in Bulgaria. United Nations Secretariat of the Economic Commission for Europe, *Economic Survey of Europe in 1994–1995* (New York: United Nations, 1995), 151.

61. Roman Frydman and Andrzej Rapaczynski, *Privatization in Eastern Europe: Is The State Withering Away?* (London: Central European University Press, 1994), 113.

investors had purchased about 90 percent of Hungary's 10,000 state-owned retail stores, restaurants, and service shops. Meanwhile, scores of new private ventures appeared. By the end of the MDF's term, the total number of private entrepreneurs approached 500,000. While the relative size of the Hungarian private sector remained small (25 to 30 percent of total assets), it produced a disproportionate share (40 to 50 percent) of GDP.[62]

Transformation of the ownership structure of large-scale industry proved far more difficult. Hungary's large-scale privatization strategy, which relied on direct sales of state enterprises to Western investors, differed in important ways from the approaches of other former communist states. The mass voucher programs introduced in the Czech Republic, Romania, and Russia enjoyed the benefits of speed and social equity: by transferring shares of local industry to the population, the governments of those countries could quickly divest state enterprises while promoting an Eastern variant of "peoples' capitalism." However, mass voucher schemes did little to recapitalize state enterprises, as domestic households possessed limited investable funds. Mass distribution of state property also hindered corporate governance, as wide dispersion of shares of state-owned enterprises among unaffiliated citizen-owners weakened discipline on enterprise managers. Low capitalization and corporate control problems also beset Poland, whose privatization strategy featured an eclectic mix of public stock issues, managerial buyouts, sales of shares to employees, leasing, and indirect mass distribution.[63]

Since it relied on case-by-case deals, the Hungarian program was necessarily slower than Czech-style mass distribution. And because it systematically excluded workers from the decision-making process, the program was less socially equitable than Poland's.[64] But insofar as corporate gover-

---

62. Károly Okolicsányi, "The Hungarian State Sector's Dismal Performance," *RFE/RL Research Report* 3, no. 15 (15 April 1994): 22; Tamás Szabó, "The Past Three Years and the Preliminaries of Privatization in Hungary," *Privinfo: Privatization in Hungary* 2, no. 16 (August 1993): 3.

63. Frydman and Rapaczynski, *Privatization in Eastern Europe,* 113–16, 156–63.

64. Poland's Law on Privatization, enacted in summer 1990, gave worker councils veto power over corporatization decisions and specified that 20 percent of the shares of state enterprises be sold to employees at deeply discounted prices. By contrast, Hungarian law required only that the SPA *inform* factory-level associations and trade unions about privatization decisions; the SPA could proceed with sales without labor's assent. The legal code also left it to the SPA to determine on a case-by-case basis whether, and on what terms, Hungarian workers would be given opportunities to purchase blocks of shares. David Bartlett, "The Political Economy of Privatization: Property Reform and Democracy in Hungary," *East European Politics and Societies* 6, no. 1 (winter 1992): 109–10; András Gidai and László Gyetvai, "Evaluation of the Most Frequent Criticisms of Privatization Policy," *Privinfo: Privatization*

nance and recapitalization were concerned, Hungary's privatization strategy had major theoretical advantages. By selling state enterprises directly to private investors, state authorities could narrow separation of ownership and control and bring local managers under closer supervision by new owners. And because it emphasized sales to foreign buyers, Hungary's program was better suited to refurbishing the capital stock of domestic industry. Unlike households, workers' councils, and local managers, Western investors possessed the financial wherewithal to replenish plant and equipment. Extensive links to Western distribution networks, which were crucial for expansion of Hungarian exports, gave foreign capital an additional edge over local buyers.

But Hungary's strategy also had an obvious liability: Its success hinged almost entirely on the willingness of foreign investors to support the privatization process. I show in the following discussion that while Hungary attracted more foreign direct investment than any other East European country, only a small portion of it went toward the sectors of local industry most in need of recapitalization. As direct sales to Western investors abated, state authorities diversified their repertoire of policy instruments in an attempt to stimulate spontaneous privatizations at the local level. But while those measures accelerated the transformation of state enterprises into corporate forms, the shortage of domestic capital inhibited actual transfers of state property into private hands. The lion's share of large-scale industry thus remained under de facto state ownership. Slow progress in large-scale privatization left Hungarian policymakers with the responsibility of managing the assets of the scores of major companies remaining in the state's portfolio—a task for which postcommunist state institutions were technically and financially ill equipped.

Foreign Capital and Large-Scale Privatization

Privatization of large-scale industry involved two main components. The first was the transformation of state enterprises into shareholding companies. Here, the legal structure left by the Hungarian Communist Party played a critical role. In 1989, the MSZMP enacted the Law on Transformation, prescribing the legal mechanisms for the corporatization of state enterprises: registration of the companies as joint stock, limited liability, or other corporate forms; appraisal of their assets; and appointment of boards of directors. The second dimension of privatization was the actual transfer of corporate shares from the Hungarian state to private investors.

---

in Hungary 2, no. 13, (July 1993): 19–20; Frydman and Rapaczynski, *Privatization in Eastern Europe,* 23, 26, 108–9.

As table 6.6 shows, postcommunist Hungary made far more progress in the first dimension of privatization than in the second.

The data show that the Antall government transformed 17.5 percent of Hungary's 2,200 large state enterprises into corporate forms, a significant achievement given the legal complexities of corporatizing an industrial sector that was almost completely socialized after 1948. But only a very small percentage of the equity shares of Hungary's 386 transformed companies were actually sold to private buyers. The bulk of the shares—72 percent—remained with the SPA. Two percent were transferred to local governmental councils. Loan assumptions, representing 23 percent of share capital, mostly entailed debt-equity swaps with the big Hungarian commercial banks, which themselves remained under majority ownership by state and quasi-state actors. The two categories involving direct sales of state property to full-fledged *private* buyers—(1) foreign capital and (2) local investors subsumed under the heading "Other"—together constituted less than *3 percent* of the equity shares of transformed firms. Of those groups, foreign capital played the overwhelmingly dominant role. While Western investors participated in only a small proportion (52 of 386) of company transformations, those transformations represented *96 percent* of private capitalization between 1990 and 1992—illustrating Hungary's extraordinarily high dependence on foreign capital in the privatization process.

But while foreign investors dominated Hungary's privatization program, they were not primarily interested in buying preexisting state enter-

TABLE 6.6. Privatization of State-Owned Enterprises in Hungary, 1990–92

	1990	1991	1992	Total
Number of transformed state-owned enterprises[a]	36	197	153	386
Number of transformations with foreign participation	16	33	3	52
Ownership structure of transformed state-owned enterprises (% of Share Capital)				
SPA	65.5	88.1	65.6	72.2
Local governments	3.4	2.9	1.4	2.0
Foreign investors	12.3	8.01	0.09	2.9
Loan assumption[b]	14.1	0.6	33.2	22.6
Other[c]	4.7	0.4	0.04	0.3

Source: Privinfo: Privatization in Hungary 2, no. 6 (March 1993): 20–23.

[a]State-owned enterprises formally transformed into shareholding companies. At the beginning of 1990, the number of state-owned enterprises in Hungary was approximately 2,200.

[b]Ownership shares acquired through debt-equity swaps.

[c]Shares acquired through managerial buyouts, employee ownership programs, and public stock issues.

prises. Table 6.7 shows the patterns of foreign direct investment in Hungary through 1993.

While the absolute number of privatizations (27) represented over half of Hungary's biggest foreign investments, new companies created through joint ventures and greenfield investments constituted the largest share (46.7 percent) of committed funds. Moreover, the bulk of the foreign capital that entered Hungary via privatization moved into sectors not geared for hard currency exports. The largest share, 40 percent, went toward producers of low-export foods (soft drinks, confectionery, sugar, cigarettes, and liquor), whose quasi-monopolies in the local market made them attractive privatization targets.[65] A significant portion, 34 percent, did go toward manufacturing industries with high convertible currency export content (electronics, motor vehicles, pharmaceuticals, and consumer goods). But foreign direct investment in these sectors was concentrated in a very small number of companies possessing strong technological bases and internationally competitive product lines (e.g., Tungsram, Ganz-Ansaldo, Chinoin). Indeed, one of those investments—General Electric's $550 million purchase of the lightbulb company Tungsram—alone consumed over 60 percent of the group's total. A sizable amount of foreign capital also went to Hungary's service sectors; notably, Marriot purchased the Duna Intercontinental Hotel, Accor acquired the Pannonia hotel chain, and Alitalia acquired a minority share of the national airline Malév. These latter investments helped to revitalize Hungary's tourist industry, which was a major contributor to foreign exchange. But they did not augment export capacity, the critical factor determining the country's debt-servicing capability.

The profile of nonprivatization foreign direct investment was somewhat more favorable to Hungary's industrial base. The largest portion, more than $1.1 billion, went toward investments in four new automobile plants: Audi Hungária Motor, General Motors Hungary, Magyar Suzuki, and Ford Hungária. Each of these ventures was aimed at establishing low-cost production sites for exports of components and assembled cars to Western Europe as well as for sales to the local market.[66] Five hundred and eighty million dollars was dedicated to Hungary's telecommunications system, modernization of which was vital to long-term industrial development.[67]

---

65. András Gidai, "Effects of Hungarian Privatization: A Survey of Company Balance Sheets," *Russian and East European Finance and Trade,* winter 1993–94, 75–76, 87–88.

66. Károly Okolicsányi, "Hungary: A Car Industry is Born," *RFE/RL Research Report* 1, no. 19 (8 May 1992): 39–42.

67. The flow of foreign direct investment into the telecommunications sector peaked in early 1994, when a German/American consortium purchased a 30 percent share of the state

TABLE 6.7. Foreign Direct Investment in Hungary by Sector and Type, 1993 (cumulative, millions of dollars)

Sector	Privatization	Joint Venture	Greenfield	Other[a]	Total
Manufacturing					2,020
Consumer goods	65				65
Electronics	680				680
Motor vehicles	50	550	520		1,120
Pharmaceuticals	100				100
Chemicals		55			55
Food Industry					1,037
Food and detergents	160				160
Soft drinks	215				215
Confectionery	174				174
Sugar	140				140
Cigarettes	188				188
Distilling	60				60
Coffee	100				100
Raw Materials					505
Aluminum		165			165
Paper		160			160
Glass		110			110
Steel	70				70
Infrastructure					989
Telecommunications	94	580		55	729
Motorway construction				200	200
Waste management	60				60
Energy					242
Industrial gases	120				120
Gas distribution			122		122
Services					900
Airline travel	100				100
Insurance		220			220
Banking		87			87
Hotels	129		95		224
Retail	109			54	163
Office development			56		56
Packaging			50		50
Miscellaneous				240	240
Total	2,614	1,927	843	549	5,933
Share of Total ($%)	44.0	32.5	14.2	9.3	100.0

Source: Economist Intelligence Unit, *Country Report: Hungary,* 2d quarter 1994, 33–34.

[a]Share placements, foreign concessions, and investments of the European Bank for Reconstruction and Development.

But foreign capital shied away from Hungary's loss-making industries, coincidentally the ones most in need of fixed investment. Only two privatizations with foreign participation involved enterprises situated in crisis sectors: Voest-Alpine's purchase of the steel company Dunai Vasmü and the Russian Federation's equity stake in Ikarus. The former company was a special case in that it was the only Hungarian steel manufacturer operating in the black. Western investors declined to commit funds to the industry's loss makers.[68] And as we have seen, Russia failed to meet its commitments to Ikarus, leaving the Hungarian company with a huge inventory of unmarketable buses. What interest foreign buyers exhibited in local industry focused almost entirely on the economy's strongest performers. In 1990–91, the SPA managed to find buyers for a handful of comparatively robust enterprises. However, it could not coax foreign capital to enter weak sectors. As table 6.6 shows, foreign participation in acquisitions of state-owned enterprises plummeted once Hungary's "crown jewels" were snapped up. In 1992, Western investors participated in a mere *three* company transformations.

In short, while the aggregate flow of foreign capital was remarkable for an economy Hungary's size, the general pattern of foreign direct investment in the postcommunist period did not accelerate adjustment processes in core manufacturing industries, whose capacity to generate high value-added exports was crucial to the country's international solvency. The strong preference of Western investors for new ventures left the overwhelming majority of Hungary's large state enterprises severely undercapitalized, reinforcing the "drifting" phenomenon described earlier in this chapter.

State Institutions and Privatization Policy

The foregoing analysis shows that while Hungary's privatization strategy generated a substantial amount of new private capital formation, it yielded meager results within the state sector itself. By 1993, the SPA had divested

---

telephone company Matav, a transaction not included in table 6.7's data set. At $875 million, the Matav sale was the third largest foreign investment in postcommunist Eastern Europe, surpassed only by Volkswagen's purchase of the Czech car manufacturer Skoda and by Chevron's investment in Kazakhstan's petroleum industry. Károly Okolicsányi, "Hungarian Telephone Company's Landmark Privatization Deal," *RFE/RL Research Report* 3, no. 6 (11 February 1994): 41–43.

68. As described in chapter 3, in 1989 the German firms Korf AG and Metallgesellschaft AG initiated an equity investment in the Özd ironworks, Hungarian steel's biggest loss maker. But by fall 1991, both of the German partners had withdrawn, leaving it to the SPA to find another buyer. Economist Intelligence Unit, *Country Report: Hungary,* no. 3, 1991, 26.

only about $4 billion of state property out of $150 billion total national assets. Lagging privatization revenues and rising operational losses by the companies remaining in the SPA's portfolio pushed the agency's balance sheet into the red.[69]

Under fire from the liberal opposition for the slow pace of the program, the Antall government recast the institutional structure of privatization policy. The SPA, which had heretofore focused on case-by-case deals negotiated directly with foreign buyers, engaged a number of consulting firms to manage divestitures and initiated a "self-privatization" program aimed at stimulating spontaneous transformations at the factory level. The government introduced an employee share-ownership program to spur worker participation.[70] The National Bank created a special facility, the Existence Credit, to finance employee share purchases and managerial buyouts. Finally, the Parliament created the SAHC, a new agency designed to free the SPA of the burden of asset management and to allow the SPA's overburdened staff to concentrate on privatization. But while these measures served to decentralize the privatization process, they did not overcome the foremost obstacle to transformation of Hungarian industry: the dearth of buyers possessing *real* capital.

The SPA's self-privatization program, launched in October 1991, involved some 687 small and medium-sized state enterprises authorized to initiate their own divestitures. By summer 1993, 398 of these companies, nearly 60 percent of the total, had transformed themselves into corporate forms. Over half of the transformed firms found buyers, the majority of whom were local rather than foreign investors—suggesting that the government's efforts to stimulate domestic capital formation were beginning

---

69. Okolicsányi, "The Hungarian State Sector's Dismal Performance," 22; "Privatization Revenues and Expenses," *Privinfo: Privatization in Hungary* 2, no. 17 (September 1993): 34.

70. "1992 Évi XLIV. Törvény a Munkavállalói Résztulajdonosi Programról" (Act XLIV of 1992 on the Employees' Part-Ownership Programme), *Hatályos Magyar Jogszabályok* (Hungarian Rules of Law in Force), no. III/20, 15 October 1992, 1375–88. Hungary's law on employee share-ownership programs was substantially less generous than worker ownership legislation in other former communist countries, underscoring the political weakness of organized labor in the post-1989 period. The law provided no preferential allocations to Hungarian workers, stipulated that transactions be cash-based, and required the assent of 40 percent of the workforce to form employee share-ownership programs. By contrast, Poland allowed workers to buy up to 20 percent of state-owned enterprises' equity share at deeply discounted prices. The Czech Republic's mass privatization program allowed workers to purchase vouchers at nominal prices. And Russia's mass voucher scheme involved free distribution of 25 percent of share capital to workers, with options to buy an additional 10 percent at a 30 percent discount. Victor Supyan, "Privatization in Russia: First Results and Future Development" (Institute for the study of the USA and Canada of the Russian Academy of Sciences, 1994, mimeo).

to bear fruit. But transfers to private buyers represented only about 25 percent of the book value of the participating companies, with the remainder of equity shares remaining with the SPA, local governmental councils, and the state-owned commercial banks.[71] The so-called Existence Credit, launched in April 1991, was designed to promote spontaneous privatizations by giving domestic investors access to low-cost loans with generous repayment and collateral requirements. But the funds National Bank authorities were willing to make available for the facility were too meager to make a significant impact on the privatization process. By mid-1993, sales of state property via Existence Credits amounted to less than HUF 20 billion, a tiny fraction of the outstanding assets of transformed enterprises. Moreover, nearly 40 percent of the 7,000 participants in the program used the credits to buy small businesses with fewer than ten employees—which indicated that domestic buyers had little more interest in large-scale state-owned enterprises than did foreign investors. Compensation vouchers, issued by the Antall government to claimants of properties confiscated by the communist regime after 1948, similarly played a marginal role. Of the HUF 40 billion vouchers in circulation by 1993, only HUF 3 billion were used to purchase shares of state enterprises.[72] In short, notwithstanding the SPA's attempts to "privatize the privatization," the limited supply of domestic capital severely restricted the ability of local buyers to participate in the process.

The most important institutional change in Hungarian privatization policy in the early 1990s was the establishment of the SAHC. Some 163 large industrial firms, utility companies, and banks, representing 40 to 50 percent of GDP, were transferred from the SPA to the new institution. The rationale behind the formation of the SAHC was twofold. First, simultaneous responsibility for privatization and asset management had seriously overburdened the SPA, the majority of whose 350-person staff lacked professional skills in corporate governance. Company registration, financial auditing, and other tasks were draining manpower and limiting the agency's ability to divest state property. Shifting asset management to the SAHC would free up the SPA's resources and allow the latter agency to accelerate privatization. Second, by specifying the firms to remain perma-

---

71. "Results of the First and Second Phases of Self-Privatization for the First Six Months of 1993," *Privinfo: Privatization in Hungary* 2, no. 16 (August 1993): 12–36.

72. Éva Hegedus, "E-Credit and Payment-in-Installment Allowance Employed in Privatization," *Privinfo: Privatization in Hungary* 2, no. 9 (May 1993): 2–3; Melinda Kamasz, "Money You Can Use," *Hungarian Economic Review* 14 (June 1993): 51; "Facts About Privatization," *Privinfo: Privatization in Hungary* 2, no. 17 (September 1993): 35; "Utilization of Compensation Vouchers as of July 31, 1993," *Privinfo: Privatization in Hungary* 2, no. 17 (September 1993): 41.

nently under full or partial state ownership and placing them under the SAHC's jurisdiction, governmental authorities sought to clarify the Hungarian state's ownership role. The SPA was a budgetary organization enjoying full rights of divestiture: until the Parliament issued a decree limiting or excluding privatization of the firms remaining in the agency's portfolio, the SPA board could sell any or all of its assets. By contrast, the head of the SAHC reported directly to the Minister of Privatization and was responsible for overseeing firms earmarked by the prime minister's office as politically, economically, or strategically vital.[73]

But the creation of a division of labor between the SPA and SAHC did not resolve the central dilemmas of Hungarian privatization: the unwillingness of foreign capital to invest in existing state-owned enterprises, the acute shortage of domestic buyers, and the lack of budgetary funds needed to support a selective industrial policy for rejuvenating stagnant sectors. While the SAHC's portfolio was numerically smaller than the SPA's, it contained a disproportionate share of Hungary's industrial and financial assets, including the economy's biggest loss makers. Portfolio losses pushed the new agency into the red in its very first year in operation, with a large portion of the deficit emanating from the thirteen "crisis firms" and the big commercial banks.[74] Lacking the financial and technical resources to restore these companies to profitability, the SAHC could not attract the private buyers needed to reduce state equity shares to the levels targeted by the Antall government (51 percent for most industrial firms, 25 percent for the banks). Thus the same tension between structural adjustment and privatization that beset the SPA plagued the SAHC: restructuring loss makers required huge infusions of private capital, but those very same enterprises were also Hungary's least attractive privatization candidates. In 1995, the new MSZP government abandoned the experiment with a dual institutional structure and merged the two privatization agencies.

Conclusion: Structural Adjustment and Democratic Institutions

Structural adjustment policy in transitional economies involves three basic objectives: diversion of productive resources into new private ventures, elimination of redundant capacity and noncompetitive production in existing enterprises, and rejuvenation of surviving parts of local industry.

---

73. Interview, SPA, 21 September 1993; "The State Holding Company Introduces Itself," *Privinfo: Privatization in Hungary* 2, no. 9 (May 1993): 38; "Facts About Hungarian Privatization, 1990 to 1992," *Privinfo: Privatization in Hungary* 2, no. 12 (June 1993): 16–20.

74. Okolicsányi, "The Hungarian State Sector's Dismal Performance," 24.

The primary finding of this chapter is that postcommunist Hungary made rapid movement in the first and second dimensions of adjustment but achieved little progress in the third. The country's new private sector displayed impressive growth in the post-1989 period. Small-scale entrepreneurship flourished, while Western capital financed a number of major joint ventures and greenfield investments. However, recapitalization of large-scale industry languished. Hungarian state-owned enterprises underwent a deep contraction of output as their traditional Eastern markets folded, Western import competition mounted, and state subsidies disappeared. But owing to low levels of accumulation under decades of communism and a poorly developed capital market, domestic investors were unable to supply the funds needed to revive state industry. The state administration, financially strapped and dominated by saver agencies, lacked the resources to enact selective industrial policies. And Western investors, on whom Hungarian authorities relied to drive the privatization process, proved unwilling to inject capital in those sectors of industry that most needed it. As a result, the majority of Hungary's large state-owned enterprises were left in a state of drifting, lacking the funds needed to refurbish their fixed capital and facing few credible prospects of attracting buyers. The progressive erosion of the capital stock of these enterprises raised the specter of incipient deindustrialization.

Policy trajectories in the three issue areas addressed in this chapter illuminate the effects of institutional change on adjustment processes. As discussed in part 2, the Hungarian Communist Party initiated a major reform of the financial system in the late 1980s. But far from using the credit instrument to promote economic adjustment, the new commercial banks diverted funds to their weakest clients—exemplifying the perverse incentive structure of Hungary's socialist halfway house. The transformation of the institutional environment after 1989—notably the ascent of the National Bank and the increased regulatory capacity of the Ministry of Finance and the Office of Banking Supervision—yielded marked changes in the banks' behavior. But while the reorientation of the Hungarian banks toward risk-averse lending policies signaled an advance over the pre-1989 period, it did not foster the broad goals of structural adjustment. The banks not only ceased extending credits to loss-making enterprises but effected a retreat from enterprise lending altogether—aggravating the already acute liquidity shortage within local industry and diminishing fixed capital investment. In short, the political transition heightened the commercial banks' sensitivity to market forces, but that very same "market" behavior of the banks exacerbated the problem of undercapitalization in the enterprise sector.

Industrial restructuring policy similarly demonstrated the impact of institutional change. The institutional structure of the Marxist-Leninist system defeated the MSZMP's restructuring program in the 1980s, as enterprise managers and workers utilized their particularistic links to communist state agencies to secure exemptions from market rules. The failure of market reforms to spur adjustment processes forced the ruling party to resort to administrative techniques, whose use merely broadened opportunities for individualized bargaining. Postcommunist institutions afforded local agents few means of evading the distributional effects of economic adjustment. The successor government severed the fiscal safety net that had previously kept illiquid enterprises afloat, eliminated most import barriers, slashed tariffs, and enacted Eastern Europe's toughest bankruptcy law. Aside from an ineffectual "crisis management" program, no selective industrial policy emerged in postcommunist Hungary—exemplifying the severe shortage of budgetary funds as well as the shift in the balance of power within the state administration toward agencies of global economic regulation. Factory-level agents, lacking both particularistic ties to the state and effective intermediary institutions, turned to individualistic economic strategies. While actors with fungible assets managed to exit to the emergent private sector, most workers and enterprise managers remained tied down to stagnant parts of the state sector, where their economic leverage was weakest.

Privatization policy exhibited a different dynamic across the two time periods. The Hungarian Communist Party initiated a privatization program in the late 1980s but lacked the institutional resources to regulate the process competently. The result was a rash of *nomenklatura* buyouts and other rent-seeking activities that compelled the successor MDF government to recentralize privatization policy. The concentration of divestiture authority in the SPA did serve to impose order on a privatization process that had become chaotic in the late communist period. Yet the agency's deliberate, case-by-case approach soon provoked criticism by the liberal opposition, prompting the Antall government to decentralize privatization policy in 1991. But while revamping the institutional framework hastened spontaneous transformations of state enterprises into corporate forms, it did not overcome the foremost obstacle to large-scale privatization: the paucity of buyers.

Thus, the central lesson of Hungarian adjustment policy in the early 1990s is this: while the shift from the institutional particularism of communism to the universalistic bias of democracy generated the market forces needed to spur adjustment processes, market-type institutions did not ensure that the funds needed to recapitalize large-scale industry would be forthcoming. Indeed, the dominant "market" response of both foreign and domestic agents in the postcommunist period was to avoid that part of the Hungarian economy. In short, postcommunist Hungary established most of the institutional underpinnings of a market economy. But with such a large portion of national assets tied down in sectors unable to attract private investment, the prospects for its transition to full-fledged capitalism appeared doubtful.

Part 4
Conclusions

CHAPTER 7

Implications and Comparative Perspectives

In this final chapter of the book, I use the institutional theory developed in chapter 1 to generalize from the case study. I begin by discussing the implications of Hungary's experience for the relationship between democracy and market in Eastern Europe, arguing that the clash between political and economic liberalization in the region is less acute than commonly supposed. I continue by assessing the normative consequences of Hungary's dual transformation: while the political transition enhanced the accountability dimension of Hungarian democracy, the representative element was lacking owing to the institutional weakness of postcommunist civil society. I then address the electoral triumph of the MSZP in Hungary's second national election. I claim that the tension between choice and uncertainty animating Hungary's negotiated transition yielded effective institutional constraints on incumbent power—belying fears of Western analysts that the political resurgence of former Communists imperiled democratic consolidation. I conclude by placing Hungary in a comparative perspective, contrasting its politico-economic trajectory with those of other East European countries and of the East Asian newly industrialized countries. Institutional theory advances on both the "big bang/gradualism" and "dirigisme/neoliberalism" debates by showing the specific ways in which party and state organizations mold transition strategies. But my comparative survey also underscores the limitations of institutional approaches: shortages of private investment capital, a factor not captured by institutional analysis, make it highly unlikely that Hungary and other transitional socialist economies will follow the route of the East Asian developmental states.

Democracy and Market in Eastern Europe

As noted in the introduction and chapter 1, in the early 1990s a number of Western scholars voiced skepticism about the ability of Eastern Europe's new democracies to weather the hazards of simultaneous economic and political transformation. The experiences of postcommunist Hungary confounded these expectations, adding to the growing body of empirical evidence demonstrating the compatibility of democracy and market in the region.[1]

Standard explanations of how dual transformations occur do not shed much light on the Hungarian case. Hungary's successor government did not enjoy a honeymoon, an interlude of "extraordinary politics" during which postcommunist euphoria boosted public receptivity to bold economic measures.[2] In fact, the most dramatic exhibition of popular resistance to market reforms, the taxi strike of fall 1990, took place very early in the MDF's term. Organized opposition thereafter declined. Nor did the government simply defuse opposition by enacting a "gradualist" strategy that lowered the costs of adjustment to a socially tolerable level.[3] While the distributional fallout of that program was less severe than the "shock therapies" undertaken elsewhere in Eastern Europe, the socioeconomic conditions for a backlash against reform clearly existed in Hungary. GDP and household income suffered their biggest declines since the Great Depression. Unemployment, virtually nonexistent in 1989, reached 13 percent in 1993, approaching Poland's jobless rate and well surpassing the Czech Republic's. Moreover, key elements of Hungary's strategy (monetary contraction, subsidy cuts, import liberalization) followed the basic lines of the shock therapy programs, while others (renunciation of debt relief, real currency appreciation, rigorous bankruptcy legislation) produced unusually sharp distributional effects. Nor did Hungarian policymakers mollify popular resistance by widening inclusion of workers and enterprise managers. Consultation with societal groups was limited to the deliberations of the Interest Representation Council, whose capacity to shape reform policy fell well short of neocorporatist institutions in other East Central European countries.

The central argument of this book is that what enabled Hungary to pursue simultaneous economic and political liberalization in the 1990s was the transformation of party and state institutions attending the collapse of communism. The institutional logic of reform communism defeated the

---

1. Leslie Armijo, Thomas Biersteker, and Abraham Lowenthal write: "One of the great surprises of the last few years has been the coexistence, the apparent compatibility, and even the complementarity of democratization and market-oriented reform. In spite of dire predictions about the future of efforts at dual transition, most states have continued to pursue both processes." "The Problems of Simultaneous Transitions," *Journal of Democracy* 5, no. 4 (October 1994): 174.

2. Leszek Balcerowicz, "Understanding Postcommunist Transitions," *Journal of Democracy* 5, no. 4 (October 1994): 84–87.

3. Adam Przeworski, "Economic Reforms, Public Opinion, and Political Institutions: Poland in the Eastern European Perspective," in Luiz Carlos Bresser Pereira, José María Maravall, and Przeworski, eds., *Economic Reforms in New Democracies: A Social Democratic Approach* (Cambridge: Cambridge University Press, 1993), 146–47, 150–51.

predecessor regime's attempts to use market mechanisms as stabilization and adjustment devices. While that system circumscribed possibilities for collective action outside the Communist Party, it expanded opportunities for local agents to secure individual exceptions to market rules. The exigencies of austerity strengthened the pull of particularistic bargaining, inducing workers and enterprise managers to lobby Party and state organizations for protection from the distributional effects of adjustment. The resultant increase in domestic purchasing power compromised macroeconomic equilibrium, generating pressure on political officials to intervene and restore central controls. But owing to the decision-making authority already relinquished to factory-level agents, full restoration of the status quo ante was impossible. Hungarian Communist Party leaders thus faced a quandary: market reforms impelled local agents to behave in ways contrary to adjustment policy while weakening the Party's capacity to correct those distortions via recentralization. This distinctive push-pull dynamic undercut both Hungary's economic performance and the ruling party's political authority, factors that played a decisive role in the negotiated transition to democracy in the late 1980s.

Democratization fundamentally altered the institutional setting of Hungary's market reforms. The advent of multiparty contestation greatly enlarged possibilities for citizens to articulate their preferences through the electoral arena. But the political transition narrowed opportunities for interest representation via nonelectoral means. The demise of the Communist Party, whose penetration of the state administration formed the basis of the "plan bargaining" system, removed the institutional channels through which local agents extracted compensation for economic adjustment. Intermediary interest representation was similarly ineffectual during the postcommunist period. The successors of the communist-controlled associations were hampered by their long affiliation with the ancien régime and by internecine conflicts over the disposition of assets, while new organizations of labor and business were hindered by low financing and high fragmentation. The weakness of Hungary's intermediary institutions funneled interest representation into the Parliament. But the national legislature also proved of little use to the losers of market reform. The elitist bent of Hungary's parliamentary parties widened the gap between members of Parliament and local constituencies, while the concentration of executive authority in the prime minister's office allowed the Antall government to resist pressure from progrowth elements of the coalition to back off the austerity program. Meanwhile, democratization bolstered the capacity of the Hungarian state to execute reform policy by shifting the locus of power toward the agencies responsible for universalistic market regulation and by erecting institutional barriers—codified spheres of jurisdiction, a vigorous parliamentary opposition, and a liberalized print media—to partisan exploitation of state resources.

In short, far from *unleashing* popular resistance to market reforms, Hungary's democratic transition *subdued* it. Local agents, lacking particularistic links to the state, strong intermediary institutions, and close ties to the major political parties, turned to individualistic economic strategies. For actors possessing fungible assets, this meant exit to the country's burgeoning entrepreneurial sector. For plant directors in the majority of large state enterprises, it involved day-to-day subsistence to avert liquidation and buy time until privatization. For low-skilled workers situated in those same companies, it entailed abstention from open mobilization to minimize the risk of losing their jobs. Thus, the societal actors *most* vulnerable to economic reform were also the ones *least* well positioned to defend themselves against market forces.

The Hungarian case thus defies arguments positing an intrinsic clash between democratization and marketization in Eastern Europe. The course of the region's dual transformations depends on where and how distributional conflicts arising from economic transformation are mediated—which can only be explained by analyzing the institutional configurations subsumed within the regime type of "democracy."

Institutions and the Quality of Democracy

Institutional analysis also illuminates the normative dimensions of Eastern Europe's transition to democracy. While postcommunist institutions bolstered the ability of policymakers to enact market reforms, their exclusionary character raised serious questions about the "quality" of Hungary's new democracy. Of what value was democratization when it diminished the mobilizational capacity of citizens most vulnerable to market forces?

Hungary's political transition clearly enhanced the accountability dimension of democracy. This was the critical element missing under reform communism: while the Communist Party devolved economic control to the factory level and enlarged the sphere of policy debates within the Marxist-Leninist system, the absence of a legal opposition and the lack of constitutional checks on Party power relieved the MSZMP of public accountability for its actions. The creation of a liberal constitution, the advent of competitive elections, the appearance of a robust parliamentary opposition possessing credible oversight capabilities, and the liberalization of the media profoundly changed Hungary's political landscape. The country's negotiated transition produced a political system that skewed power toward elite-dominated parties, created long intervals between elections, and concentrated executive authority in the prime minister's office. But as the MDF government discovered in the second election, the transition also yielded a genuine electoral constraint. To be sure, the exigencies of democratic contestation raised temptations for successor governments to appropriate state resources for partisan ends. But in contrast to the Communist Party, whose penetration of the Hungarian state allowed it to plunder national resources with impunity over several decades, postcommunist governments that misused state agencies faced a virtual certainty of disclosure of those activities by the parliamentary opposition and the press.[4]

But this high degree of accountability was not matched by a comparable level of representativeness. The weak representative dimension of Hungarian democracy was attributable to two factors. First, the poorly developed grassroots organizations of the major parties widened the gap between national party offices and rank-and-file members and deepened popular perceptions that Hungary's political elites were out of touch with the concerns of ordinary citizens. Second, communist rule vanquished independent, horizontally organized intermediary associations—the mesolevel institutions that in Western civil societies perform the vital functions of buffering social demands, promoting trust between local agents, supplying collective goods, and inculcating a sense of political efficacy among the mass citizenry.[5] The low "social capital" of postcommunist intermediary organizations concentrated the burden of representation onto the Hungarian Parliament, whose institutional structure afforded societal groups few access points and whose members faced the electorate only infrequently.

Both of these hindrances to representation were likely to diminish over time as the parties expanded their local networks and as new civil organizations arose to challenge the communist-affiliated associations of workers and enterprise managers. However, the degree to which Hungary evolved along the lines of Western civil society was not apt to favor the segments of the populace most vulnerable to market reforms. Rather, the probable trajectory would favor entrepreneurial agents enjoying privileged access to the organizational resources, social networks, and private

---

4. The electronic media remained an exception: even after the 1994 election, the parliamentary parties continued to grapple over control of Hungarian Radio and Television. But Hungary's print media matched the Western press in its diversity of standpoints and irreverent style, ensuring immediate and extensive publicity of the machinations of the political parties. Judith Patkai, "Controversy over Hungary's New Media Heads," *RFE/RL Research Report* 3, no. 31 (12 August 1994): 14–17.

5. Robert Putnam, *Making Democracy Work: Civic Traditions in Modern Italy* (Princeton: Princeton University Press, 1993), 163–85.

capital needed to build strong interest associations.[6] Low-skill actors tied down to stagnant sectors of local industry would continue to rely on the legal successors of the communist-controlled organizations, like the MSZOSZ, whose economic leverage was waning and whose policy preferences even a putatively sympathetic socialist government could not easily accommodate. Thus, the members of society most likely to benefit from augmentation of the representative element of democratic institutions were not the ones whose socioeconomic circumstances created the greatest demand for political representation—suggesting that Hungarian democracy would become somewhat more "inclusive" but not more socially "equitable."

Democratic Consolidation and the Return of Former Communists

Scholars of the "third wave" of democratization note that outright reversals of democratic transitions (as occurred in Peru, Burma, and Haiti) have proven infrequent.[7] The main threat to postauthoritarian countries is "democratic backsliding," whereby rising cynicism, declining participation, and continuing economic stagnation instigate a progressive erosion of constitutional norms and public institutions. Declining confidence in the ability of democratic governments to manage the economy gives rise to quasi-authoritarian parties offering populist solutions to the crisis.[8] The electoral triumphs of former Communists in Lithuania, Poland, Bulgaria, and Hungary prompted Western journalists to voice similar anxieties about the future of democracy in Eastern Europe.[9]

In my view, while the Balkan countries and Soviet successor states justify such concerns, the East Central European nations do not. The Czech Republic, Poland, and Hungary have crossed the Rubicon to "con-

---

6. An example of such an organization was the National Association of Entrepreneurs, a small but increasingly visible organization of local capitalists that was headed by János Palotás, the flamboyant Hungarian millionaire who played a central role in mediating a resolution of the 1990 taxi drivers' strike. Károly Okolicsányi, "Hungary: Modest Growth of Private Companies," *RFE/RL Research Report* (10 January 1992), 30–32; National Association of Entrepreneurs, *NAE-News,* May 1991, 2–4.

7. Philippe Schmitter, "Dangers and Dilemmas of Democracy," *Journal of Democracy* 5, no. 2 (April 1994): 59.

8. Stephan Haggard and Robert Kaufman, "Economic Adjustment and the Prospects for Democracy," in Haggard and Kaufman, eds., *The Politics of Economic Adjustment* (Princeton: Princeton University Press, 1992), 348–350; Stephan Haggard and Robert Kaufman, "The Challenges of Consolidation," *Journal of Democracy* 5, no. 4 (1994): 6–7.

9. A. M. Rosenthal, "The Ghost People," *New York Times,* 9 August 1994, sec. A, p. 23.

solidated democracies," in which a critical mass of the populace has ceased to view restoration of authoritarianism as a credible option and has accepted the electoral system as fair and legitimate—even when the results of elections displease large numbers of citizens.[10] While the victories of socialist parties in the latter two countries clearly revealed widespread discontent with incumbent governments that implemented unpopular economic policies, they hardly constituted rejection of democracy itself.[11] Indeed, the fact that former Communists could win multiparty elections— and, more importantly, gain broad *recognition* as the legitimate winners— showed that democratic norms had taken hold in the region.

External factors clearly contributed to democratic consolidation in East Central Europe: The pull of integration into the European Union locked regional governments onto a trajectory of unilateral convergence toward Western-style legal and political systems. As Common Market membership facilitated democratization in Spain, Portugal, and Greece in the 1980s, the "road to Brussels" represented the surest route to stable democracy for the Czech Republic, Poland, and Hungary in the 1990s. The socialist governments that took power in the latter two countries gave no indication of abandoning their predecessors' efforts to gain full admission to the European Union.[12]

The institutional approach of this book offers a different explanation of the acceptance of democratic norms by former Communists. In chapters 1 and 4, I argued that Eastern Europe's negotiated transitions differed from those of the capitalist South in two important ways. First, the abrupt demise of communism created unprecedented opportunities for institutional innovation that gave negotiators wide latitude to formulate rules aimed at advancing their own partisan interests. Second, inchoate party

---

10. This conception of democratic consolidation draws on Adam Przeworski's notion of "organized uncertainty." Here, a democracy becomes self-enforcing, and therefore stable, when a preponderance of actors accepts the political order as legitimate in advance of knowledge of the outcomes of democratic contestation, the winners of those contests refrain from harassing the losers, and the losers desist from overturning the results and bide their time for the next round of competition. Successful completion of the second postauthoritarian election is therefore a critical indicator of consolidation. Przeworski, *Democracy and the Market: Political and Economic Reforms in Eastern Europe and Latin America* (Cambridge: Cambridge University Press, 1991), 11–50.

11. Philippe Schmitter observes that voters in new democratic countries undergoing economic adjustment typically direct their ire at governments rather than democracy as a system. "Dangers and Dilemmas of Democracy," 72.

12. For an analysis of the dynamics of "anticipatory adaptation" in the East, see Stephan Haggard, Marc Levy, Andrew Moravcsik, and Kalypso Nicolaïdis, "Integrating the Two Halves of Europe: Theories of Interests, Bargaining, and Institutions," in Robert Keohane, Joseph Nye, and Stanley Hoffmann, eds., *After the Cold War: International Institutions and State Strategies in Europe, 1989–1991* (Cambridge: Harvard University Press, 1993), 182.

organizations, fragile constituent bases, and high electoral volatility produced great uncertainty that compelled interlocutors to devise mechanisms for hedging against potential losses. The outcomes of 1989's negotiated transitions mirrored this tension between choice and uncertainty. While political agents naturally sought institutional arrangements that maximized their immediate electoral prospects, they also looked for ways of minimizing the consequences of losing elections. Under conditions of high uncertainty, strategies of "self-binding" are *rational* to the degree that voluntary acceptance of constraints on the power of the winners of democratic contestation reduces the political dangers facing the losers.

In the following discussion, I show how the logic of self-binding shaped the political conduct of the Hungarian Socialists. In 1989, representatives of the outgoing MSZP conceded to the establishment of institutional checks on the power of incumbent governments—notably a Constitutional Court possessing broad authority to annul acts of Parliament—which subsequently shielded Party members from attempts by the MDF government to prosecute former Communists. Those very same mechanisms remained in place in 1994, when the Socialists parlayed widespread voter discontent into an electoral landslide. By creating effective institutional constraints on the behavior of successor governments, Hungary's negotiated transition reduced the risk that the electoral triumph of former Communists would endanger democratic consolidation.

Resurgence of the Hungarian Socialists

The same six parties that crossed the legislative threshold in 1990 won parliamentary seats in Hungary's spring 1994 elections. The MDF suffered a crushing defeat. From its 164-seat plurality in 1990, the MDF garnered a paltry 38 seats. Several factors contributed to the MDF's downfall. The prolonged illness and eventual death of József Antall created a leadership vacuum that hampered the Party during the run-up to the national elections. Low levels of expertise within the prime minister's office and the MDF's parliamentary faction reinforced the Party's reputation for stodginess—a liability that the more technically competent socialist and liberal parties exploited in their appeals for greater professionalism in governance. Widely publicized scandals and clashes between the centrist and right-wing elements of the governing coalition further damaged the MDF's position. Finally, the MDF was held accountable for the state of the Hungarian economy, which had only barely emerged from the postcommunist recession by the time of the elections. To a considerable degree, the expulsion of the MDF was a case of shooting the messenger. Much of the contraction of output and living standards after 1990 stemmed from the exogenous shock of the collapse of Eastern markets rather than deliberate policy decisions of the Antall government. But the resultant economic dislocations created a large number of disillusioned voters strongly disposed to punish the incumbent government at the polls.[13]

The comeback of the MSZP, the legal successor of the old MSZMP, was truly stunning. From 33 seats in 1990, the MSZP won 209 of 386 parliamentary seats in 1994. But despite their capture of an absolute majority in the Parliament, the Socialists formed a coalition with the SZDSZ, the leading liberal party. This power-sharing arrangement had a clear political logic: an alliance with the SZDSZ would allow MSZP leaders to reposition themselves closer to the center of the political spectrum and thereby allay domestic and international concerns over socialist control of Hungary's powerful prime ministerial government. And since it was apparent that the state of the economy necessitated continuation of the austerity program initiated by the MDF, the Socialists looked to a governing partner to share the blame for the socioeconomic fallout of adjustment policy. The coalition controlled a remarkable 72 percent of the seats in Parliament, sufficient to pass any major legislation as well as constitutional amendments.[14]

Despite their overwhelming majority in the Parliament, the leaders of the new government moved quickly to increase discipline within the coalition parties. Deputies were forbidden to propose amendments to bills or to summon cabinet ministers for testimony without the written consent of their caucus leaders. The speaker of the Parliament was authorized to ban deputies from the legislature for up to 30 days if they engaged in conduct deemed "unacceptable" by party leaders. These rules heightened concentration of power in an already highly centralized parliamentary system. The government also undertook reforms of the state administration. It abolished the MIER, thereby eliminating industry's foremost proponent of growth-oriented policies. It also merged the SPA and SAHC, expanded

---

13. Károly Okolicsányi, "Macroeconomic Changes in Hungary, 1990–1994," *RFE/RL Research Report* 3, no. 24 (17 June 1994): 21–26. Poland, whose economy was actually growing at the time of the Democratic Left Alliance's victory in September 1993, similarly demonstrated how the social uneasiness attending postcommunist transformations induced voters to penalize governments that implemented market reforms. The high rate of defeat of incumbent governments in Eastern Europe contrasts with the experiences of developing capitalist countries in the 1980s, when a number of governments that initiated sweeping austerity programs won reelection. Joan Nelson, "Poverty, Equity, and the Politics of Adjustment," in Haggard and Kaufman, *The Politics of Economic Adjustment,* 253–58.

14. János Dobszay, "Back to the Future: The 1994 Elections," *Hungarian Quarterly* 35 (summer 1994): 14; Edith Oltay, "Hungary's Socialist-Liberal Government Takes Office," *RFE/RL Research Report* 3, no. 33 (26 August 1994): 6–7.

parliamentary oversight of the consolidated agency, and enacted new legislation aimed at increasing transparency in the privatization sphere. The government meanwhile appointed two of Hungary's leading reform economists, György Surányi and Lajos Bokros, to head the National Bank and Ministry of Finance.[15] These measures reinforced the institutional trajectory set in 1989, insulating the governing parties from particularistic pressures and bolstering the state's capacity to execute stabilization and adjustment policy.

But while the Hungarian Socialists sought ways of strengthening executive power in the aftermath of the 1994 elections, they yielded to institutional checks on incumbent governments established in the earlier phase of Hungary's political transition. For example, the MSZP followed the procedures initiated in 1990 to discourage partisan exploitation of budgetary funds. At that time, the MDF government ceded control of the Parliament's budget committee to the SZDSZ, ensuring the liberal opposition's ability to conduct oversight of fiscal policy. In 1994, the MSZP government placed the budget committee under the chairmanship of Béla Kádár, the former head of the disbanded MIER who was now a member of the MDF's parliamentary faction—permitting the *conservative* opposition to check the budgetary maneuvers of the new socialist-liberal majority.[16]

The government's willingness to relinquish chairmanship of such a vital parliamentary committee illustrated the institutional logic of self-binding in negotiated transitions: notwithstanding the MSZP's landslide victory in 1994, the high electoral volatility of the postcommunist period gave the Socialists little confidence of winning the next round of competition. Hungary's fluid politico-economic circumstances induced MSZP leaders to hedge against potential future losses. By continuing the practice of allocating prime committee chairmanships to minority parties, the Socialists preserved a norm of mutual reciprocity—lowering the risks that succeeding governments would manipulate state resources for partisan purposes.

Equally important, the Socialists complied with the rulings of the Hungarian Constitutional Court, whose power of judicial review circumscribed the government's ability to implement legislature. The decision to

---

15. Károly Okolicsányi, "New Hungarian Government's Economic Plan," *RFE/RL Research Report* 3, no. 30 (29 July 1994): 31–34; Judith Patkai, "Hungary's New Parliament Inaugurated," *RFE/RL Research Report* 3, no. 29 (22 July 1994): 10–11; "Finance Minister and NBH Head Nominated," *Bank & Tőzsde: Fuggetlen Pénzügyi, Üzleti és Gazdasági Hétilap* 3, no. 5 (17 February 1995): 11.

16. Patkai, "Hungary's New Parliament Inaugurated," 9.

endow the Court with unusually broad authority to void acts of Parliament was taken before the founding elections in 1990, illustrating the strong incentives of political agents to establish mutual institutional checks prior to the first round of democratic contestation. Hungary's Constitutional Court has been characterized, with only slight hyperbole, as "the most powerful constitutional court in the world."[17] The two most noteworthy cases adjudicated by the Court between 1990 and 1994 involved legislation sponsored by the MDF government and opposed by the key opposition parties: a law on compensation covering properties confiscated by the Communists after 1948 and a bill calling for the suspension of the statute of limitations for murder and treason. The main intent of the latter measure was to permit the prosecution of former Communists for their role in crushing the 1956 uprising. This was an issue of no small concern to the SZDSZ and MSZP, many of whose members were once active in the old Communist Party and one of whose leaders (Gyula Horn, the future prime minister) was personally implicated in the suppression of the Revolution. The Court ruled both pieces of legislation unconstitutional.[18]

Yet the same power of judicial review that protected the Hungarian Socialists as minority party after the first democratic election constrained their actions as majority party after the second one. Facing bulging deficits in the balance of payments and state budget, the Horn government announced a harsh new austerity program in March 1995. The package, assembled by Finance Minister Bokros, featured cuts in public sector wages, an import surcharge, and tuition fees for university students. For the first time, the Hungarian authorities moved aggressively on welfare reform, proposing deep reductions in state expenditures on hospitals and means testing of maternity and child care benefits. The Bokros Program incited fierce public opposition: university students staged demonstrations to protest the tuition fees; importers' associations issued statements denouncing the border tax; welfare recipients complained bitterly that the Socialists had abandoned their core constituency. But the popular outcry over the austerity package was of little practical consequence, as the coalition's huge parliamentary gave it ample means of enacting controversial legislation. In May 1995, the Horn government secured the legislature's

---

17. Jon Elster, "On Majoritarian Rights," *East European Constitutional Review* 1, no. 3 (fall 1991): 22–23.

18. Barnabas Racz, "The Hungarian Parliament's Rise and Challenges," *RFE/RL Research Report* (14 February 1992): 23; Judith Patkai, "Dealing with Hungarian Communists' Crimes," *RFE/RL Research Report* (28 February 1992), 21–24.

approval of the Bokros Program, with only six defections from the socialist/liberal bloc.[19]

As it turned out, the main impediment to the Socialists' austerity plan was not social opposition but the Constitutional Court. A month after the parliamentary vote, the Court voided several components of the Bokros Program: it struck down proposed reductions in state compensation to sick workers, nullified the government's plan to introduce social security taxes on honoraria and royalties, and delayed cuts in child care and maternity benefits. The Court ruled that the program violated constitutional protection of families with children, giving parents inadequate time to adjust to reductions in benefits. The decision underscored the extreme political sensitivity of the social welfare crisis in postcommunist Hungary. It also revealed the breadth of the Court's conception of "judicial review": what would be regarded in most Western countries as distributional issues were treated in Hungary as constitutional questions.[20]

At the same time, the Constitutional Court's ruling illustrated the unanticipated consequences of institutional constraints voluntarily accepted by political agents in the initial phase of Hungary's democratic transition. The decision to create a powerful judiciary protected the Socialists from retaliation when they occupied a minority position in the Parliament; that very same decision limited the Socialists' range of maneuver when they reacquired power as leaders of a majority government in 1994. Like the MDF government, the MSZP government reaped the fruits of the 1989 negotiations, whose institutional results—centralized prime ministerial power, high party discipline, stable parliamentary majorities, strong macroeconomic regulatory agencies—enhanced the capacity of postcommunist governments to pursue unpopular economic policies.[21] But those negotiations also yielded credible legal constraints on incumbent

---

19. "Tightening the Belt," *Bank & Tőzsde: Fuggetlen Pénzügyi, Üzleti és Gazdasági Hétilap* 3, no. 11 (31 March 1995): 11; "Fuzzy Growth," *Business Central Europe* 3, no. 20 (April 1995): 13–14; "Igen a Bokros-Csomagra" (Yes to the Bokros Package), *Magyar Hírlap,* 31 May 1995, 1; "Coalition Stands Together as Austerity Package Wins OK," *Budapest Sun,* 1–7 June 1995, p. 1.

20. Rick Bruner, "Court Attacks Economic Reforms, Budget Savings in Doubt," *Hungary Report* 1, no. 14 (3 July 1995); Tibor Vidos, "Constitutional Court Vetoes Certain Paragraphs of the Bokros Package," *Hungary Report* 1, no. 15 (9 July 1995).

21. Despite the Constitutional Court's efforts to water down the Bokros Program, the MSZP government's austerity measures cut deeply into local purchasing power. Nominal wages fell by 10 percent and domestic consumption by 3 percent in 1995. GDP growth, which staged a modest recovery in 1994 following the postcommunist recession, dropped to 0.2 percent. "Hungarian Economics," *Central European Report,* February 1996; "Bokros in London: Structural Reforms Must Not Fall Victim to Political Temptations," *Central European Report,* 13 February 1996.

power, impinging on successor governments in ways unforeseen at the time the institutional choices were made. In sum, the tension between choice and uncertainty animating Hungary's negotiated transition produced an institutional configuration that reduced the danger of postcommunist governments abandoning the road to consolidated democracy—even when former Communists themselves mounted a political resurgence and won the second round of democratic contestation.

Hungary in Comparative Perspective

Hungary's politico-economic trajectory was in many respects unique. Unlike other East European countries, Hungary's postcommunist government inherited a legacy of market reforms stretching back to the 1960s. And in contrast to the East Asian countries, most of which remained under quasi-authoritarian rule in the early 1990s, Hungary pursued economic liberalization amid full multiparty contestation. In this concluding section of the book, I situate Hungary within a broad comparative context. What insights can one draw by comparing its strategy of economic transition with those of other former communist countries and the East Asian newly industrialized countries?

I argue the following. It has become customary among Western scholars to evaluate East European reform policy in terms of the relative virtues of "big bang" and "gradualist" strategies of transition. I maintain that this scholarly exchange largely misses the essential lessons of the East European experience. A true big bang occurred in only one country, the former GDR, whose circumstances were not replicable anywhere else in the region. The shock therapy programs undertaken in Poland and other countries did achieve rapid liberalization of prices and foreign trade. But while those measures were significant, they constituted only a small part of the wider transition effort. Other elements of market reform—Western-style central banks, effective revenue collection mechanisms, bankruptcy and accounting laws, systems of financial intermediation—required arduous, time-consuming institution building. The most important difference between Hungary and other East European countries related not to variations in program design stemming from the choice of gradualist or big bang strategies but to the institutional remnants of twenty years of reforms preceding democratization. Yet despite these factors that gave Hungary a comparative advantage in the institutional dimension of marketization, its economic transition, like those of other East European countries, ran up against a severe shortage of investment capital. The scarcity of private capital in all countries outside of East Germany placed unavoidable constraints on restructuring of state enterprises.

The literature on East Asian political economy focuses on (1) the presumed connection between political authoritarianism and economic development in the region and (2) the merits of dirigiste strategies of marketization. East Asia's spectacular growth record has prompted some Western scholars to urge the East European countries to emulate the strategies of the "developmental states." But I claim that the East Asian model is not suitable for former communist countries. First, the experiences of Hungary and other East European countries dispel the notion of an affinity between authoritarianism and marketization. The East Asian countries maintained authoritarian political structures *despite,* not because of, market reforms. Second, the key factors underpinning East Asian export-led development—state institutions equipped for selective promotion of export industries and large supplies of investment capital—are missing in Eastern Europe.

Modes of Transition in Eastern Europe: Big Bang or Gradualism?

The big bang/gradualism debate has dominated scholarly analysis of East European reform policy.[22] But the empirical record reveals a more complex picture of transition processes in the East. If the "big bang" refers to a comprehensive strategy aimed at achieving a swift transition to a market economy, the only East European country that truly underwent one was the GDR. The Federal Republic's absorption of the East's fiscal, monetary, and price systems made possible an instantaneous macroeconomic stabilization. On the structural adjustment side, the Treuhandanstalt mobilized the vast stock of West German capital to engineer history's most sweeping privatization campaign. The unique circumstances of German unification distinguished the GDR from the rest of Eastern Europe, including Poland and other countries that implemented radical stabilization programs.

Specific features of Hungary's "gradualist" strategy did differ from the programs undertaken elsewhere in the region. Reforms enacted by the Communist Party before 1989 obviated radical price liberalization. Hungary's choice of an exchange rate regime (real appreciation of the forint, based on a crawling peg anchored to a mixed basket of Western currencies) contrasted with those of Poland and the Czech Republic, which enacted

---

22. The basic lines of this debate are brought in sharp relief in the exchange between two leading economists in *Post-Soviet Affairs* 9, no. 2 (1993): 87–140: Josef Brada, "The Transformation from Communism to Capitalism: How Far? How Fast?"; Peter Murrell, "What is Shock Therapy? What Did It Do in Poland and Russia?."

large currency devaluations in the early phases of their stabilization programs. The Hungarian authorities meanwhile rejected mass privatization schemes, choosing instead a strategy emphasizing direct sales of state enterprises to Western investors. But other components of Hungarian reform policy did not differ markedly from the strategy of shock therapists. Like Poland and the Czech Republic, Hungary sharply reduced tariffs and import quotas. And like those countries, it pursued a strategy of cautious liberalization of foreign exchange: full external currency convertibility, internal convertibility for current account transactions, and maintenance of central controls on the capital account.

Not only does the big bang/gradualism typology unduly simplify East European transition strategies. Policy outcomes in the post-1989 period do not justify firm conclusions about *which* strategy is superior. Poland's Balcerowicz Plan succeeded in halting hyperinflation and eliminating domestic shortages. Moreover, devaluation of the zloty and liberalization of foreign trade produced an unexpectedly large surplus in the first year of the program. By 1993, Poland and other countries that implemented radical reforms were registering strong growth rates. Meanwhile, the country widely regarded as the archetype of gradualism, Hungary, continued to stagnate, prompting some Western economists to declare the victory of big bang approaches.[23]

But a closer analysis casts doubt on the achievements of Polish-type strategies. The shock therapy programs restored macroeconomic equilibria, an impressive feat given the magnitude of the price distortions prevailing in Eastern Europe. Moreover, small-scale private enterprises grew rapidly in some countries. But the speed and magnitude of the output decline in large-scale industry well surpassed the expectations of the multilateral lending agencies.[24] On the surface, the collapse of production in the state sector could be interpreted as demonstration that the structural adjustment components of the programs were taking effect.[25] But empiri-

---

23. For example, Anders Åslund writes: "Once considered the success story of gradualism, Hungary has now faded. In addition to Poland, the Czech Republic, Estonia, and Latvia have all pursued radical economic policies; their respective track records too may serve as evidence that sweeping systemic change leads to the earliest upturn in GDP. Indeed, those countries are set to compete for the title of Europe's fastest-growing economy in 1994. To judge from the record to date, a fast and comprehensive transition leads to the smallest decline in GDP, the fastest return to growth, and probably the highest level of growth as well." "The Case for Radical Reform," *Journal of Democracy* 5, no. 4 (October 1994): 70.

24. Michael Bruno, "Stabilization and Reform in Eastern Europe: A Preliminary Evaluation," *IMF Staff Papers* 39, no. 4 (December 1992): 744–45, 761–64.

25. For instance, Andrew Berg argues that the Balcerowicz Plan yielded significant gains in allocative efficiency in Poland despite the slow pace of privatization and financial sector reform. He cites data showing diversion of resources from the state sector to private

cal evidence suggested that little adjustment occurred in East European industry during the early 1990s. One group of IMF economists set up regression analyses to assess the relative importance of national and sector-level variables in the contraction of production. They determined that macroeconomic supply-and-demand shocks accounted for nearly all of the variation in output in the region since 1989. Moreover, intrasectoral patterns of resource allocation gave little indication that key industries had reoriented production in directions consistent with their comparative advantages.[26]

Long adjustment lags were of course not unique to Eastern Europe. Industrial restructuring in postwar Western Europe took years to complete, even with substantial external support via Marshall Plan aid. The abrupt collapse of the CMEA and Soviet Union, which represented the principal market for most East European enterprises, deepened the disruption of local industry. The demise of the traditional Eastern markets had a devastating effect on Finland, whose well-developed but highly trade-dependent economy could not elude a sizable drop in GDP similar to that suffered by the former CMEA countries.[27]

But certain institutional factors distinctive to transitional socialist economies impeded factory-level responses to the external shocks and internal stabilization efforts. In particular, the rigidities of the East European financial systems prolonged the recession in state industry. The problem went beyond the thin capital markets characteristic of many developing capitalist economies. In the East, the longstanding separation of the household and enterprise monetary "circuits" hindered the channeling of personal savings into the productive sphere, raising the cost of credit and squeezing an already tight liquidity supply. Further, the large stock of interfirm debt inherited from the communist period penalized strong enterprises by collateralizing the recessionary effects of credit squeezes

---

industry, reorientation of trade from East to West, increased supply of final and intermediate goods, and reduced investment in inventory. However, he concedes that evidence indicating structural adjustment *within* state-owned enterprises is largely "anecdotal." "Does Macroeconomic Reform Cause Structural Adjustment? Lessons From Poland," *Journal of Comparative Economics* 18, no. 3 (June 1994): 376–409.

26. Eduardo Borensztein, Dimitri Demekas, and Jonathan Ostry, "An Empirical Analysis of the Output Declines in Three Eastern European Countries," *IMF Staff Papers* 40, no. 1 (March 1993): 18–22.

27. Bruno, "Stabilization and Reform," 753. World Bank specialists estimated that the CMEA trade shock accounted for about 60 percent of the contraction of output in Poland and Hungary in the early postcommunist period. Simon Commander and Fabrizio Coricelli, "Output Decline in Hungary and Poland in 1990–91: Structural Change and Aggregate Shocks," *Policy Research Working Papers Transition and Macro-Adjustment,* Country Economics Department of the World Bank, WPS 1036, November 1992, 17.

across the entire state sector. Efficient producers, burdened by the weight of credits involuntarily issued to illiquid firms over previous years, and unable to tap nonbank credit sources, were forced to delay their own supply-side responses. Economists estimated that 20 percent of the output decline in Poland during the first phase of the Balcerowicz Plan stemmed from the initial credit contraction.[28]

Owing to its long history of reforms, Hungary enjoyed an advantage in the institutional aspects of stabilization and adjustment policy. Its central bank had acquired considerable experience in Western-type monetary regulation, while its comparatively advanced legal and financial systems facilitated industrial restructuring. As noted in chapter 6, Hungary's bankruptcy laws placed local producers under even more severe competitive constraints than those faced by enterprises in countries that had supposedly eschewed gradualist strategies. But like the other East European countries, the paucity of buyers possessing "real" capital inhibited rehabilitation of Hungarian industry. Structural adjustment involved more than downsizing capacity and sloughing off excess labor: it required heavy infusions of fixed capital investment to modernize plant, equipment, and local infrastructure.

Foreign Investment, Privatization, and Adjustment Strategies in the East

Like small, resource-poor countries in Western Europe, the international competitiveness of the East Central European economies hinged on capital-intensive investment—particularly insofar as current trends in the global economy lowered the relative importance of labor costs and heightened the significance of research and development, advanced technology, and sophisticated quality-control systems.[29] But unlike comparably endowed, wealthy capitalist countries in the West (e.g., Austria, Switzerland, Denmark), the former communist states possessed meager stocks of domestic capital for investment in local industry. Roman Frydman and Andrzej Rapaczynski estimate that even if Polish citizens had committed

---

28. Guillermo Calvo and Fabrizio Coricelli, "Stagflationary Effects of Stabilization Programs in Reforming Socialist Countries: Enterprise-Side and Household-Side Factors," *World Bank Economic Review* 6, no. 1 (1992): 72–85; Calvo and Coricelli, "Output Collapse in Eastern Europe: The Role of Credit," *IMF Staff Papers* 40, no. 1 (March 1993): 33–44; Daniel Hardy and Ashok Kumar Lahiri, "Bank Insolvency and Stabilization in Eastern Europe," *IMF Staff Papers* 39, no. 4 (December 1992): 778–81, 798–99.

29. Jochen Lorentzen, *Opening Up Hungary to the World Market: External Constraints and Opportunities* (New York: St. Martin's, 1995), 130–32; John Stopford and Susan Strange, *Rival States, Rival Firms: Competition for World Market Shares* (Cambridge: Cambridge University Press, 1991), 4–5.

20 to 30 percent of their savings to purchases of equity in state-owned enterprises in the early 1990s (an improbable scenario owing to the Balcerowicz Plan impact on real household income), the funds available for privatization would have represented less than 4 percent of the book value of state enterprises.[30] Private savings in Hungary amounted to less than 10 percent of the value of state assets at the beginning of the post-communist period.[31] Even Czechoslovakia, blessed with the region's highest per capita income, possessed total private savings equivalent to just 16 percent of the book value of state-owned enterprises slated for privatization.[32]

The exceptionally poor physical state of East European industry, the result of decades of intensive use and inefficient investment flows, compounded the problems created by the shortage of domestic capital. Whereas about 40 percent of the fixed capital of West European industry was less than five years old in the late 1980s, the age structure of Eastern industry deteriorated markedly during the final decade of communist rule: Between 1980 and 1988, the share of capital assets under five years old dropped from 41 to 29 percent in Hungary, from 32 to 23 percent in Czechoslovakia, and from 35 to 19 percent in Poland.[33] Estimates of the total investment required to bring East European industry up to Western standards by the turn of the century ranged between $2.5 and 4.2 trillion.[34]

The low domestic accumulation and high capital needs of the transitional socialist economies magnified the importance of Western investment in the postcommunist transition. However, the overall pattern of international capital flows during the early 1990s was not propitious for Eastern Europe. Between 1990 and 1994, long-term financial commitments (both official and private) to the developing world (including the transitional socialist economies) totaled $822 billion. Of this, Eastern Europe captured $66 billion, a mere 8 percent.[35] Moreover, the composition of financial flows to the region was not conducive to recapitalization of preexisting state enterprises, where the overwhelming majority of industrial assets resided. Table 7.1 shows the allocation of external finance to Eastern Europe by source.

30. *Privatization in Eastern Europe: Is the State Withering Away?* (London: Central European Press, 1994), 22.

31. Lorentzen, *Opening Up Hungary to the World Market,* 166.

32. Nemat Shafik, "Making a Market: Mass Privatization in the Czech and Slovak Republics," *World Development* 23, no. 7 (1995): 1155.

33. Paul Welfens and Piotr Jasinski, *Privatization and Foreign Direct Investment in Transforming Economies* (Aldershot, England: Dartmouth, 1994), 23–24.

34. Lorentzen, *Opening Up Hungary to the World Market,* 153.

35. United Nations Secretariat of the Economic Commission for Europe, *Economic Survey of Europe in 1994–95* (New York: United Nations, 1995), 147.

TABLE 7.1.   External Financial Flows to Eastern Europe by Source, 1990–94 (billions of dollars)

	1990	1991	1992	1993	1994
Official sources					
IMF	0.7	3.7	1.3	0.3	1.9
Multilaterial development agencies[a]	0.8	1.9	2.1	1.2	2.2
Bilateral credits	0.1	0.6	0.8	0.4	0.4
Grants	1.2	1.7	1.2	0.5	0.5
Private sources					
Capital markets[b]	1.4	1.7	1.5	6.3	3.6
Commercial credits[c]	3.0	1.7	1.5	3.7	4.4
Portfolio investment	—	—	—	0.4	0.5
Foreign direct investment	0.6	2.3	3.1	4.0	3.0
Special finance[d]	10.4	9.6	7.4	5.9	4.0
Total external financial flows	18.2	23.2	18.9	22.7	20.5

Source: United Nations Secretariat of the Economic Commission for Europe, *Economic Survey of Europe in 1994–95* (New York and Geneva: United Nations, 1995), 148.

Note: "Eastern Europe" encompasses Bulgaria, the Czech Republic, Hungary, Poland, Romania, Slovakia, and Slovenia.

[a]World Bank, International Finance Corporation, European Bank for Reconstruction and Development, and European Investment Bank.

[b]External bond issues and medium- and long-term commercial bank loans.

[c]Other commercial bank loans, supplier credits, and bank credits guaranteed by export credit agencies.

[d]Arrears and debt deferrals.

Among official sources of finance, credits from the IMF and multilateral development agencies represented the single largest share. But only a small percentage of these loans were dedicated to extant state enterprises. The IMF's standby credits were used primarily for balance of payments purposes rather than fixed capital investment. The World Bank undertook a number of structural adjustment and sectoral adjustment programs in the former communist countries. However, the loans from these programs emphasized modernization of regional agriculture, finance, and infrastructure—which no doubt generated indirect benefits for local manufacturers but which left unresolved the task of replenishing the plant and equipment of state-owned enterprises. The other development institutions (the European Bank for Reconstruction and Development, the International Finance Corporation, and the European Investment Bank) did allocate financial resources to East European manufacturing industries. But the sum committed by those agencies to manufacturing sectors—$1.5 billion between 1989 and 1994—fell well short of regional needs.[36] The remaining

36. United Nations, *Economic Survey of Europe in 1994–95,* 157.

categories of official finance, bilateral credits and grants, consisted mainly of government-to-government loans and concessions aimed at enlarging the Eastern sales of West European exporters. European Union governments used these instruments as a supplement to multilateral lending, which was not directly tied to bilateral trade opportunities.[37]

The modest level of official financial flows to Eastern Europe demonstrated that a second Marshall Plan was not in the offing, underscoring the pivotal role of private Western investment in the postcommunist transition. Table 7.1 shows that aggregate private investment in the region indeed surpassed official funding. However, the proprietary interests of Western investors dissuaded them from dedicating funds to the sectors that most needed it. The largest share of private finance came by way of capital market investments. However, this exaggerated the importance of Eastern Europe's capital markets as an investment medium. One country, Hungary, accounted for the majority of bonds and long-term credit financing. And as we saw in chapter 5, Hungary's activities in international capital markets were more closely tied to the National Bank's debt management strategy than to structural adjustment policy. Commercial bank credits represented the second largest share. But like IMF standby loans, these were used chiefly to cover short-term current account needs, not industrial restructuring. The high cost of commercial credits and the heavy debts already accumulated by several East European countries (e.g., Hungary, Poland) further limited their importance as a long-term financing vehicle. Meanwhile, portfolio investment made only a marginal contribution to private capital formation in Eastern Europe, reflecting the inchoate state of the region's stock exchanges.[38]

Clearly, the most important long-term source of capital for Eastern Europe was foreign direct investment. As we have seen, Hungary was by far the most successful of the former communist countries attracting foreign investment, breaking into the top ten recipients among developing countries in the early 1990s.[39] However, the largest share of foreign invest-

---

37. Stephan Haggard and Andrew Moravcsik, "The Political Economy of Financial Assistance to Eastern Europe, 1989–1991," in Keohane, Nye, and Hoffmann, *After the Cold War,* 252–58, 279–85.

38. The Warsaw Stock Exchange was reopened in 1991. Two years later, a mere 20 corporate stocks, worth roughly $1.5 billion, were being traded on the exchange. The Budapest Stock Exchange, the most advanced in Eastern Europe, had 25 listed shares by the mid-1990s, only a handful of which were actively traded. Zdeněk Drábek, "Non-Banking Financial Sector and the Link to Foreign Investment," in Stephany Griffith-Jones and Zdeněk Drábek, eds., *Financial Reform in Central and Eastern Europe* (New York: St. Martin's, 1995), 24.

39. The others, in descending order of magnitude, were China, Malaysia, Mexico, Thailand, Portugal, Argentina, and Brazil. Lorenzten, *Opening Up Hungary to the World Market,* 153, 188.

ment in Hungary between 1990 and 1993 was dedicated to joint ventures and greenfield investments, not preexisting state enterprises. Moreover, most of the Western investment that entered Hungary via acquisitions of state-owned enterprises was concentrated in a handful of "blue-chip" companies, leaving the vast majority of state firms undercapitalized and ill prepared to entice private buyers. The pace of large-scale privatization picked up after the second postcommunist election. In 1995, the new MSZP government sold $3.5 billion of state assets, placing Hungarian policymakers in an unaccustomed position of battling over the distribution of surplus privatization proceeds.[40] But as before, most of these revenues emanated from a very small number of highly publicized divestitures, notably the sales of Hungary's telecommunications, oil, gas, and electricity companies whose monopolies or quasi-monopolies in the local market offered strong inducements to Western investors.[41]

The other East European countries saw few benefits from the global expansion of foreign direct investment. Between 1990 and 1992, foreign direct investment worldwide totaled $478 billion. Of this, over 75 percent went toward the advanced industrialized countries, with the United States and the European Union capturing the lion's share. External capital flows to developing countries grew rapidly in the early 1990s, with the East Asian newly industrialized countries and the large Latin American states posting the biggest gains. But foreign investment in Eastern Europe and the Russian Federation combined amounted to less than 7 percent of total foreign direct investment in developing economies during the first half of the decade. While the number of foreign affiliate registrations in the region increased sharply after the collapse of communism, the aggregate value of external commitments fell far short of what was needed to recapitalize East European industry.[42]

Some postcommunist governments sought to leapfrog the constraints on domestic capital formation through mass privatization programs, of which the most ambitious was the Czech voucher campaign. Such schemes promised speedier results than Hungary's case-by-case approach. By mov-

40. "Extra Privatization Revenues Will Be Used to Decrease the National Debt," *Central European Report,* 19 January 1996.

41. Articles by Zsofia Szilagyi in *Open Media Research Institute Daily Digest II:* "Hungary Begins Privatizing Electric Energy Sector," 17 October 1995; "Eastern Europe's First Gas Supplier Sale," 4 December 1995; "Hungary Signs Electricity, Gas Privatization Contracts," 11 December 1995; "Hungary's Opposition Is Against Energy Privatization," 12 December 1996; and "Hungary Privatizes Oil, Telecommunications Companies," 14 December 1995.

42. United Nations, *Economic Survey of Europe in 1994–95,* 147–48; United Nations Conference on Trade and Development, Program on Transnational Corporations, *World Investment Report 1993: Transnational Corporations and Integrated International Production* (New York: United Nations, 1993), 16, 45, 56–57, 243.

ing quickly to distribute shares of state-owned enterprises to local citizens, the Czech authorities sought to avoid costly restructuring of state enterprises and lengthy negotiations with individual buyers. Mass privatization also offered greater distributive justice than Hungarian-style direct sales. While the latter method placed Western investors in a favored position in the bidding for national assets, the Czech program permitted all adult citizens to participate for a nominal fee.[43] In December 1994, the Klaus government announced that the second and final phase of the voucher campaign would raise the share of private ownership to 80 percent of national assets.[44] The European Bank for Reconstruction and Development, charged with tracking private sector development in the region, offered a similarly favorable appraisal, giving the Czech Republic a score of 4 (on a scale of 1 to 4) in large-scale privatization—the only former communist country so ranked.[45]

Yet these figures greatly exaggerated the extent to which "real" privatization—in the sense of transfers of state property to private agents possessing an unambiguous interest in augmenting the capital stock of divested firms—was achieved in the Czech Republic. While the mass voucher campaign shifted formal title of many state-owned enterprises to Czech citizens, it did not create an ownership structure capable of promoting industrial restructuring. Nearly three-quarters of the citizen-owners ended up placing their vouchers with investment privatization funds licensed to manage the assets of privatized state-owned enterprises. In theory, such financial intermediaries alleviate the agency problems common to mass distribution schemes. But the result of the Czech program was to concentrate ownership in a few large funds, whose oversight capacity was compromised by their fiduciary ties to commercial banks burdened by bad loans issued to divested firms. While the investment privatization funds were operationally independent of the founding banks, the Czech legal code provided no American-style "Chinese walls" separating commercial and investment banking—permitting the banks to dominate the strategies of their affiliated funds. Like commercial banks throughout Eastern Europe, the Czech banks' portfolio problems generated strong incentives for credit officers to roll over dubious loans rather

43. Hilary Appel, "Justice and the Reformulation of Property Rights in the Czech Republic," *East European Politics and Societies* 9, no. 1 (winter 1995): 30–32; Josef Brada, "The Mechanics of the Czech Mass Voucher Plan in Czechoslovakia," *RFE/RL Research Report* 1, no. 17 (24 April 1992): 42–45.

44. Nicholas Denton, "Czech Sell-Off Broader than It Is Deep," *Financial Times,* 19 December 1994, 3.

45. European Bank for Reconstruction and Development, *Transition Report,* October 1994.

than prevail on enterprise managers to undertake costly restructuring programs that might lead to bankruptcy.[46] The fact that the Czech state—whose leaders were not anxious to instigate a spate of bankruptcies and liquidations in local industry—retained a substantial equity stake in the financial sector further undermined the banks' corporate governance role.

Some Western economists claim that the East Central European countries made substantial progress in structural adjustment despite the limited supply of private investment capital. For instance, Saul Estrin, Alan Gelb, and Inderjit Singh analyzed the responses of 43 Czech, Polish, and Hungarian state enterprises between 1990 and 1992. They reported a strong correlation between privatization and adjustment: nearly all of the firms under partial or full private ownership had formulated long-term restructuring plans. Polish enterprises displayed the weakest responses, reflecting the muddled state of privatization policy in that country. Czech enterprise managers reacted more vigorously, devising adjustment strategies in the aftermath of the first phase of voucher privatization. But Estrin, Gelb, and Singh admit that while the Czech firms had offered restructuring proposals, they had not begun to implement them. The authors also concede that Czech managers were already searching for ways to entrench themselves against their new owners, illustrating the corporate governance problems attendant to mass privatization.[47] Equally important, Estrin, Gelb, and Singh provide no evidence at all that the "privatized" Czech firms were surmounting the recapitalization problem, a critical factor in an economy endowed with a skilled labor force but burdened by an outdated capital stock. Intersectoral patterns in the early 1990s cast further doubt on the willingness of Czech enterprise managers to reorient production in a direction consistent with the economy's presumed comparative advantages. Marie Bohata found that the main "winners" of the postcommunist transition—measured in terms of export sales and productivity growth—were not high-technology, skilled-labor sectors (e.g., electronics, precision engineering) but energy-intensive, low value-added, environmentally unfriendly bastions of old socialist industry (iron and steel, rubber, paper, chemicals).[48] In sum, empirical evidence on the progress of structural adjustment in the Czech Republic, widely seen as the most successful of the

---

46. Jim Adox et al., "TATRA a.s., Kopřivnice" (William Davidson Institute of Operational Analysis, University of Michigan School of Business Administration, 17 December 1994, mimeo), 20–21; Delia Meth-Cohn, "Directors in Waiting," *Business Central Europe* 1, no. 1 (May 1993): 58–59.

47. "Shocks and Adjustment by Firms in Transition: A Comparative Study," *Journal of Comparative Economics* 21, no. 2 (October 1995): 143–49.

48. "Performance of the Manufacturing Industry during Transformation," *Eastern European Economics,* January–February 1995, 76–95.

East European countries that embraced mass privatization, is ambiguous at best.

Estrin, Gelb, and Singh found the most robust firm-level responses in Hungary, coincidentally the one East European country outside of the former GDR to pursue a cash-based privatization strategy. While fewer state-owned enterprises were privatized in Hungary than in the Czech Republic, those in Hungary exhibited more sophisticated corporate governance, greater implementation of long-term restructuring plans, and higher investment in new technology—a consequence of the fact that, unlike Polish and Czech enterprises, most of the Hungarian firms in the sample enjoyed large infusions of fresh capital by Western partners. But while the Hungarian case demonstrates how foreign direct investment reduces corporate governance and recapitalization problems, the findings of Estrin, Gelb, and Singh hardly give grounds to expect that large numbers of state-owned enterprises will duplicate that outcome. The authors concede a sample bias: most of the Hungarian firms in their investigation were financially viable, comparatively robust enterprises capable of attracting Western buyers.[49] For the rest of the Hungarian state sector, the costs of modernizing plant and equipment were sufficiently high to deter foreign investors, leaving the majority of state-owned enterprises in a vicious cycle of stagnation and undercapitalization.

In short, building capitalism in the East demanded massive amounts of capital. Short of absorption into a wealthy state à la East Germany (an impossibility, given that country's unique historical circumstances) or much larger commitments of Western capital in the style of a Marshall Plan (an improbability, given political and economic conditions in the West), transformation of state industry in Hungary and the rest of Eastern Europe was bound to take a long time—irrespective of policymakers' choice of a big bang or gradualist strategy.

Export-Led Development in East Asia: The Virtues of Dirigisme?

East Asia's politico-economic trajectory differed markedly from Eastern Europe's. South Korea, Taiwan, Hong Kong, and Singapore moved from import substitution industrialization to export-led development while maintaining authoritarian political structures. Some analysts view the economic successes of the East Asian "tigers" as demonstration of the virtues of postponing democratization in developing economies. Whereas authoritarianism in communist Eastern Europe was an end in itself, East Asia's

---

49. "Shocks and Adjustment by Firms in Transition," 147–48.

"soft authoritarianism" was purely instrumental, designed to give state technocrats the political space needed to engineer the shift to export-led development.[50]

The institutional analysis of this book demonstrates that the presumption of an instrumental connection between economic transformation and political authoritarianism is theoretically and empirically unfounded. Market economies have proven compatible with a wide array of regime types, from the liberal democracies of the West to the bureaucratic authoritarian regimes of Latin America to the transitional democracies of Southern and Eastern Europe.[51] The evidence demonstrating a causal link between authoritarianism and export-led development in East Asia is tenuous. The main explanation of East Asia's "democratic lag" is not the exigencies of economic development but a nexus of external conditions (U.S. support of authoritarian regimes during the Cold War, Japan's passivity in promoting regional democracy) and internal factors (e.g., collective memories of failed experiments with democracy in the early post–World War II period).[52] If the sheer magnitude of the social costs of marketization determined prospects for political liberalization, then Eastern Europe would be *less* fertile territory for democratization than East Asia, whose high growth rates better enabled political leaders to compensate local agents.

Other scholars, while rejecting East Asia's political model, contend that its economic strategy of state-led export growth constitutes a useful guide for Eastern Europe. Like the East Asian newly industrialized countries, the former communist countries possess strong human capital and egalitarian income distributions. But the successor governments squandered those advantages. Local authorities, imbued with hostility toward the state accumulated during the communist years, and goaded by likeminded technocrats in the Washington lending agencies, embraced neoliberal adjustment strategies incommensurate with the needs of backward

50. Chalmers Johnson, "The Nonsocialist NICs: East Asia," in Ellen Comisso and Laura Tyson, eds., *Power, Purpose, and Collective Choice: Economic Strategies in Socialist States* (Ithaca: Cornell University Press, 1986), 388. South Korean President Park Chung Hee put the case for authoritarianism even more bluntly: "In order to ensure efforts to improve the living conditions of the people in Asia, even undemocratic emergency measures may be necessary. . . . The Asian peoples want to obtain economic equality first and build a more equitable political machinery afterward." Quoted in Stephan Haggard, *Pathways from the Periphery: The Politics of Growth in the Newly Industrializing Countries* (Ithaca: Cornell University Press, 1990), 62.

51. Dietrich Rueschemeyer, Evelyne Huber Stephens, and John Stephens, *Capitalist Development and Democracy* (Chicago: University of Chicago Press, 1992).

52. Minxin Pei, "The Puzzle of East Asian Exceptionalism," *Journal of Democracy* 5, no. 4 (October 1994): 93–94.

economies. Market forces alone cannot accomplish the task of structural adjustment. Bringing East European industry up to world standards demands aggressive state intervention à la East Asia.[53]

But two factors distinguish the East Asian experience from that of Eastern Europe. First, postwar East Asia never underwent a systemic transformation comparable to Eastern Europe's. In the late 1980s, South Korea, Taiwan, and Hong Kong began limited political liberalization. But in each case, the political opening was initiated and controlled by incumbent regimes that retained most of their preexisting state institutions. East Asia's high level of institutional continuity allowed local authorities to effect the transition to export-led development by retooling the dirigiste state agencies built during the period of import substitution industrialization. The military regime that assumed power in Korea in 1961 inherited a state bureaucracy that boasted a long tradition of economic intervention but that had degenerated into rent-seeking and corruption under the civilian government of Syngman Rhee. The Park regime enacted a series of administrative reforms designed to advance the alternative model of export-led development: concentration of policy-making authority in the executive to weaken the clientelistic networks that had penetrated the legislature, creation of an Economic Planning Board granted broad power to dispose of the claims of branch ministries, and introduction of meritocratic recruiting procedures to upgrade the bureaucracy's technical capacity. Even as the Korean government loosened import controls and cut tariffs to conform to the standards of the General Agreement on Tariffs and Trade in the 1980s, it retained the Ministry of Trade and Industry's flexible tariff-adjustment and import-surveillance systems to target specific sectors for protection. And even as they liberalized Korea's financial system, state authorities maintained tight reins on interest rates and repeatedly prevailed on commercial banks to reschedule debts and issue new loans to loss-making firms.[54]

---

53. Alice Amsden, Jacek Kochanowicz, and Lance Taylor, *The Market Meets Its Match: Restructuring the Economies of Eastern Europe* (Harvard: Harvard University Press, 1994), 14–16, 30–31, 40–49, 70–78, 96–111, 120–28, 161–70.

54. Byung-Sun Choi, "Financial Policy and Big Business in Korea: The Perils of Financial Regulation," in Stephan Haggard, Chung Lee, and Sylvia Maxfield, eds., *The Politics of Finance in Developing Countries* (Ithaca: Cornell University Press, 1993), 40–53; Peter Evans, "The State as Problem and Solution: Predation, Embedded Autonomy, and Structural Change," in Haggard and Kaufman, *The Politics of Economic Adjustment,* 154–58; Stephan Haggard, Richard Cooper, and Chung-In Moon, "Policy Reform in Korea," in Robert Bates and Anne Krueger, eds., *Political and Economic Interactions in Economic Reform Policy: Evidence from Eight Countries* (Cambridge: Basil Blackwell, 1993), 296–97, 305–10; Soo-gil Young, "Import Liberalization and Industrial Adjustment," in Vittorio Corbo and Sang-mok Suh, eds., *Structural Adjustment in a Newly Industrialized Country: The Korean Experience* (Baltimore: Johns Hopkins University Press, 1992), 177–83.

As we have seen, the East European communist states also exhibited a strong particularistic bias. But whereas institutional particularism in East Asia was geared toward the development of world-competitive export industries, its purpose in Eastern Europe was to help state enterprises fulfill physical production goals to supply the domestic and CMEA markets—which operated under wholly different competitive rules than the world economy. And while the East Asian countries engineered the shift from import substitution industrialization to export-led development by reorienting state agencies that had already developed a strong capacity for selective intervention, the East European states underwent a tumultuous systemic transformation. The events of 1989 disrupted Eastern Europe's peculiar variant of institutional particularism. The demise of the Communist Party unhinged the particularistic ties between enterprises and state institutions that formed the cornerstone of central economic planning. Even Hungarian state agencies, whose administrative structures remained basically intact amid the political upheavals, found themselves in a markedly different politico-economic environment after 1989. Hungary's negotiated transition erected institutional barriers to discretionary use of state resources by successor governments, while the macroeconomic shocks of the early 1990s—which *far* exceeded those facing East Asia in the 1970s and early 1980s—deprived state authorities of the financial means to undertake selective industrial policies. Like their counterparts in East Asia, postcommunist state institutions sought to develop export industries capable of competing in demanding Western markets. But to accomplish that goal, they had to draw on a much narrower range of policy instruments.

The second factor distinguishing East Asia from Eastern Europe was the former's ability to mobilize large amounts of investment capital for local industrial development. Like the transitional socialist countries in the 1990s, the East Asian states began the postwar period with modest levels of domestic savings, rendering them heavily dependent on external finance to promote industrialization. But they enjoyed several critical advantages in the bidding for foreign capital. During the 1950s, geopolitical factors prompted the United States to commit very large amounts of official aid to the region. Between 1953 and 1962, American concessionary assistance comprised 80 percent of fixed capital formation in South Korea and nearly 40 percent in Taiwan. Foreign direct investment in East Asia did not reach significant levels until the 1960s, by which time high rates of economic growth and consolidation of state institutions permitted regional authorities to negotiate favorable terms regarding sectoral allocation, local equity participation, and domestic content requirements. Subsequently, the expansion of commercial bank lending lowered the region's dependence on foreign direct investment by providing an alternative source of capital. South Korea was especially active in Western credit markets during the 1970s and 1980s, as its export-led development successes allowed state officials to undertake heavy borrowing while keeping the country's debt-service ratio within tolerable limits. Sharp increases in local accumulation further augmented the bargaining power of the East Asian states. In 1960, domestic savings represented merely 1 percent of Korean GDP. By 1982, the ratio had increased to 24 percent, surpassing the average of the advanced industrialized countries and far exceeding savings levels in the postcommunist countries in the early 1990s. Of the four Asian tigers, only Singapore remained highly dependent on foreign direct investment (measured in terms of shares of export earnings and domestic capital formation emanating from foreign investment) by the late 1980s. Indeed, by that time both Taiwan and Korea had become net capital exporters.[55]

As we have seen, in the 1980s East Asia's dirigiste states began to liberalize their financial systems, including regulations of foreign direct investment, as part of a general convergence toward Western norms. But the region's unique position in the world economy conferred powerful advantages over other developing areas in the bidding for foreign capital. In addition to robust levels of local accumulation, the East Asian countries benefited from the thriving export markets of the Pacific Basin as well as from foreign direct investment by Japanese multinationals and the ethnic Chinese business community. The 50 million Chinese residing outside of China controlled between $1.5 and 2.0 *trillion* dollars in liquid assets, creating a massive pool of transnational capital to fuel regional development.[56] Even as foreign direct investment in Latin America and other "emerging economies" grew rapidly in the 1990s, the Asian countries continued to snare over half of private capital inflows to developing regions.[57]

Eastern Europe's successor states operated from a much weaker bargaining position. With the Cold War over, local authorities could scarcely parlay geopolitical concerns into large commitments of foreign aid from

---

55. Richard Barrett and Soomi Chin, "Export-Oriented Industrializing States in the Capitalist World System: Similarities and Differences," in Frederic Deyo, ed., *The Political Economy of the New Asian Industrialism* (Ithaca: Cornell University Press, 1987), 36–41; Stephan Haggard and Tun-jen Cheng, "State and Foreign Capital in the East Asian NICs," in Deyo, *The Political Economy of the New Asian Industrialism,* 86–103, 113–17; Barbara Stallings, "The Role of Foreign Capital in Economic Development," in Gary Gereffi and Donald Wyman, eds., *Manufacturing Miracles: Paths of Industrialization in Latin America and East Asia* (Princeton: Princeton University Press, 1990), 59–66, 70–84.

56. Pei, "The Puzzle of East Asian Exceptionalism," 95–96.

57. United Nations, *World Investment Report 1993,* 43–46.

Western governments in the fashion of Korea and Taiwan during the 1950s. As table 7.1 shows, not only did official capital flows to the former communist countries fall short of regional demands. Only a small share of the total went directly toward recapitalizing extant state-owned enterprises. Nor could postcommunist governments tap private commercial banks for the funds needed to rejuvenate local industry. In contrast to heavily indebted East Asian states like Korea, which entered Western credit markets in the midst of the "deepening" phase of export-led development, the communist regimes diverted bank loans for immediate balance-of-payments purposes and/or squandered them on ill-considered fixed investment projects that did little or nothing to augment export capacity—leaving successor governments ill disposed to take on substantial new debts. Finally, Eastern Europe's new democracies were poorly situated to lure foreign direct investment on terms favorable to local industry. Whereas East Asia began attracting large amounts of foreign direct investment in the 1960s, Western investors exhibited little interest in Eastern Europe until the 1990s—by which time the foreign investment market was much more competitive and the ability of capital importing countries to negotiate the terms of entry far more limited.

As shown in chapter 6, Hungary's favorable investment climate enabled successor governments to attract impressive amounts of foreign capital in the early postcommunist period. However, only a small portion of Western investment went toward preexisting state industry, the sector of the economy most in need of recapitalization. By the mid-1990s, Hungary had established most of the institutional groundwork for a market economy—technically competent regulatory agencies, Western-type bankruptcy and accounting laws, a relatively well developed system of financial intermediation—which hardened the budget constraints of local enterprises. But while state agencies enjoyed the institutional means to accelerate the downsizing of inefficient producers, they did not possess the financial wherewithal to restore those firms to profitability. Facing meager levels of local capital accumulation, and lacking the bargaining leverage to entice Western investors to enter loss-making sectors, Hungarian policymakers could not mount the selective industrial policies needed to spur East Asian–style export growth.

Conclusion: Political Institutions and Economic Transition

The foregoing comparative survey demonstrates both the utility and limitations of new institutionalist theory for studies of Eastern Europe's dual transformation. On the one hand, institutional analysis transcends the big bang/gradualism and dirigisme/neoliberalism debates by showing how party and state organizations shape economic transition strategies. On the other hand, institutional theory cannot account for the ways in which structural factors, notably ownership relations, delimit possibilities for economic development. While postcommunist institutions fostered impersonal market forces in Eastern Europe, they could not overcome the shortage of private capital hindering the region's transition to full-fledged capitalism. This suggested the following, long-term trajectory for Eastern Europe: progressive erosion of capital-starved state industry combined with gradual expansion of new private firms, with local entrepreneurs driving small business development and Western multinationals playing an increasingly visible role in large-scale joint ventures and greenfield investments.[58]

In sum, Eastern Europe's transition to market capitalism demands both institution building and heavy infusions of capital. Hungary and other countries have made considerable progress in the institutional aspects of marketization—underscoring the ways in which democratization enhances the market-promoting elements of the state's role in transitional socialist economies. But in the sphere of capital formation, they lag seriously behind the East Asian newly industrialized countries. Neither local ownership structure nor Eastern Europe's position in the global economy give much reason to expect that the former communist countries will soon overcome the recapitalization problem.

---

58. Michael Landesmann and István Székely aptly dub these the "destructive" and "constructive" dimensions of structural adjustment in Eastern Europe. Introduction to Landesmann and Székely, eds., *Industrial Restructuring and Trade Reorientation in Eastern Europe* (Cambridge: Cambridge University Press, 1995), 4–5.

Appendix

The empirical evidence for the book is based on (1) a wide array of primary and secondary source materials, both in English and Hungarian, all of which are cited in the footnotes; (2) relevant statistical data from the pre- and post-1989 periods, which were obtained from Hungarian sources (the Central Statistical Office, the National Bank, the Ministry of Finance, the Ministry of Industry and Trade, the MIER, the SPA, and Kopint-Datorg) and Western sources (PlanEcon, the IMF, the United Nations, and the Economist Intelligence Unit); and (3) 120 interviews conducted in Hungary in 1986, 1988, 1991, 1993, and 1995. The interview subjects included (a) senior officials in the Central Committee of the Hungarian Communist Party and successor parties, National Bank of Hungary, National Planning Office, Ministry of Finance, SPA, Ministry of Industry and Trade, MIER, Chamber of Commerce, Hungarian Parliament, Council of Ministers, and office of the prime minister; (b) executives in all of the major Hungarian commercial banks and selected accounting and financial consulting firms; and (c) economists, sociologists, and political scientists at Budapest University of Economics (formerly Karl Marx University), Central European University, the Law Faculty of Budapest University, Budapest School of Politics, and the Hungarian Academy of Sciences. I supplemented the Hungarian research with a smaller number of interviews of officials at the World Bank in Washington.

My technique was to ask very specific questions aimed at illuminating the particular aspect of economic reform policy and Hungarian politics that interested me. Whenever possible, I "triangulated," posing the same question to several subjects in order to achieve a balanced assessment of what had actually occurred. In some cases, I conducted multiple interviews of the same person.

Needless to say, I am fully responsible for the book's interpretation of the information gleaned from the interviews. To preserve confidentiality, I have left out the names of individual interview subjects from the footnotes. Their identities and institutional affiliations are provided in the following list.

István Ábel	Budapest Bank
Lajos András	MDF
László Antal	Financial Research Institute, Ministry of Finance
	Hungarian Council of Ministers
László Arva	MDF
Tamás Bácskai	Karl Marx University of Economics
	International Training Center for Bankers Ltd.
László Ballai	MSZMP Central Committee
Miklós Bányai	Ministry of Industry
Katalin Baratossy	National Savings Bank
János Bartha	Credit Suisse First Boston Ltd.
Tamás Bauer	Institute of Economics, Hungarian Academy of Sciences
	SZDSZ
Chris Bennett	Price Waterhouse Budapest
Mihály Bihari	University of Budapest, Faculty of Law
Lajos Bokros	National Bank of Hungary
	Ministry of Finance
Imre Boros	National Bank of Hungary
Zoltán Bősze	Ministry of Finance
Mária Brüll	Karl Marx University of Economics
László Bruszt	Central European University
László Csaba	Kopint-Datorg
Péter Csilik	Hungarian Credit Bank
Sándor Czirják	National Bank of Hungary
Margaret Dezse	Price Waterhouse Budapest
István Farkas	National Bank of Hungary
János Fekete	National Bank of Hungary
Péter Felcsuti	National Bank of Hungary
	UNIC Bank
Ida Földesi	National Bank of Hungary
Tamás Földi	Ministry of Finance
	Hungarian Banking Association
Gerhard Fürnrohr	Central European International Bank Ltd.
Péter Gedeon	Budapest University of Economics
András Giday	Ministry of Finance
Cheryl Gray	World Bank
Katalin Gyurák	Ministry of Finance
Jenő Hámori	MIER
Gabor Hamza	University of Budapest, Faculty of Law
Péter Hardi	Institute of International Affairs, Hungarian Academy of Sciences

Ágnes Hargita	Ministry of International Economic Relations
Frigyes Hárshegyi	National Bank of Hungary
András Horvai	World Bank
Zsigmond Jarai	Budapest Bank
Gábor Jurányi	Citibank Budapest
Győző Kenéz	Magyar Befektetési és Fejlesztési Bank
Martha Kismarti	Budapest Bank
László Kovács	MSZMP Central Committee
Mihály Laki	Institute of Economics, Hungarian Academy of Sciences
Sándor Ledniczky	Magyar Külkereskedelmi Bank
János Lendvai	Ministry of Industry and Trade
Sándor Ligeti	Karl Marx University
Péter Lőrincz	National Bank of Hungary
Péter Lőrincze	Hungarian Chamber of Commerce
Thomas Lynch	American Embassy, Budapest
Gábor Markovits	National Bank of Hungary
György Mohai	National Planning Office
László Mohai	MSZMP Central Committee
Wayne Neil	American Embassy, Budapest
Antal Nicodémus	Ministry of Finance
Rezsö Nyers Jr.	Magyar Hitelbank
Ágota Odry	Magyar Hitelbank
László Orbán	Budapest Bank
Sándor Patyi	Magyar Külkereskedelmi Bank
László Redei	Ministry of Finance
István Rév	Karl Marx University of Economics
András Réz	Ministry of Finance
György Rosta	Credit Lyonnais Bank
Lajos Roth	Országos Kereskedelmi és Hitelbank
Béla Sándor	National Bank of Hungary
Andres Solimano	World Bank
Károly Soós	Institute of Economics, Hungarian Academy of Sciences
	Hungarian Parliament
István Stumpf	Budapest School of Politics
György Surányi	Ministry of Finance
	World Bank
	Hungarian Council of Ministers
	National Bank of Hungary
	Central European International Bank Ltd.
István Szalkai	Hungarian Council of Ministers

János Szaz	Karl Marx University
György Szelényi	National Bank of Hungary
Imre Tarafás	National Planning Office
	National Bank of Hungary
Márton Tardos	Institute of Economics, Hungarian Academy of Sciences
	Hungarian Parliament
Elemér Terták	Magyar Hitelbank
László Timár	MIER
Zoltan Tindler	Magyar Külkereskedelmi Bank
Veronika Tomori	National Savings Bank
István Tömpe	Daiwa-Magyar Külkereskedelmi Bank Investment and Securities Co. Ltd.
Béla Török	Office of the prime minister
Charles Twyman	SPA
György Varga	Figeylő
Éva Várhegyi	Financial Research Institute, Ministry of Finance
Áttila Végh	Hungarian Credit Bank
Robin Winchester	Citibank Budapest

Index